puṣpikā

A puṣpikā ('little flower') is the scribes' way of marking the end of the main text and the beginning of the colophon. The present logo is an artistic impression by Shubhani Sarkar based on such a scribal flourish seen on a Nepalese manuscript.

Puṣpikā

Tracing Ancient India, through Texts and Traditions

Contributions to Current Research in Indology

Volume 4

Proceedings of the Seventh International Indology Graduate Research Symposium (Leiden, 2015)

Edited by

Lucas den Boer
Daniele Cuneo

OXBOW | books
Oxford & Philadelphia

Published in the United Kingdom in 2017 by
OXBOW BOOKS
The Old Music Hall, 106–108 Cowley Road, Oxford OX4 1JE

and in the United States by
OXBOW BOOKS
1950 Lawrence Road, Havertown, PA 19083

Paperback Edition: ISBN 978-1-78570-756-8
Digital Edition: ISBN 978-1-78570-757-5 (epub)

A CIP record for this book is available from the British Library

For a complete list of Oxbow titles, please contact:

UNITED KINGDOM
Oxbow Books
Tel (01865) 241249, Fax (01865) 794449
Email: oxbow@oxbowbooks.com
www.oxbowbooks.com

UNITED STATES OF AMERICA
Oxbow Books
Tel (800) 791-9354, Fax (610) 853-9146
Email: queries@casemateacademic.com
www.casemateacademic.com/oxbow

Oxbow Books is part of the Casemate Group

Contents

Preface

Lucas den Boer & Daniele Cuneo

We are delighted to present the fourth volume in the Indological series *Puṣpikā: Tracing Ancient India Through Text and Traditions*. This book contains the proceedings of the seventh International Indology Graduate Research Symposium (IIGRS 7), which was held at the Leiden University Institute for Area Studies (LIAS), 15 to 18 October, 2015. The purpose of the conference series is to bring together graduate students and early career researchers working with primary sources in Indology and South Asian studies so that they can build contacts and present, discuss and publish their research. Since such opportunities are largely lacking for fledgling students of Indology, the first symposium was inspired by a wish to provide a public platform for graduate and post-graduate students to share their work in a sympathetic, cooperative and encouraging atmosphere.

Thanks to the success of the first conference, which took place at the University of Oxford in 2009, IIGRS has become an annual event. The following instalments were held at different universities across Europe: the University of Cambridge (2010), Université Sorbonne Nouvelle-Paris 3 (2011), University of Edinburgh (2012), Ruhr-Universität Bochum (2013) and Universität Hamburg (2014). The Leiden symposium followed in 2015, while the latest IIGRS conference has recently been held at the Ludwig-Maximilians-Universität München in October 2016.

Leiden was chosen as the venue for the seventh IIGRS in celebration of 150 years of Sanskrit studies in the Netherlands and its history of scholarly excellence stretching all the way back to the establishment of the chair of Sanskrit for Hendrik Kern in 1865. For this occasion, a special exhibition of Sanskrit manuscripts and books was held at the University Library for both the participants of the symposium and the wider audience. Among the numerous treasures preserved within the university collections, it was a pleasure to display the renowned Cōḻa copper plates, which record eleventh-century royal grants made to ensure the upkeep of Buddhist monasteries; two eleventh-century Nepalese manuscripts of the renowned and devoutly revered *Prajñāpāramitā*; and numerous illuminated Devanāgarī manuscripts from North India, as well as selected Sanskrit manuscripts in Grantha script from the yet understudied collection of Johan van Manen.

The conference was launched with Prof. Peter Bisschop's keynote lecture on the history of Sanskrit studies in the Netherlands, which focused on the importance of the international network that Sanskrit scholars have created since the very beginning of the discipline, but also looked at the different roles of Sanskrit studies within Dutch academia at large—with an eye to the hopefully bright future of a field whose richness of possibilities remains to be fully tapped. The event continued with 24 papers by scholars from across the globe, which covered a rich variety of topics related to the intellectual traditions of South Asia such as grammar, poetry and philosophy, examined from a plurality of disciplinary perspectives, with a particular emphasis on philology, history and sociology.

In the attempt to respect the wide variety of topics and approaches found in the different contributions, the articles of the present volume have been grouped into four main sections.

The first four articles of the volume focus on the Sanskrit language, from the strictly linguistic and historical perspective to the wider political issue of its uses and abuses.

In the first contribution, Dániel Balogh discusses some metrical anomalies with regard to the caesura (*yati*) in selected samples of Sanskrit poetry, and argues for the existence of patterns and rules behind the seemingly abnormal variations usually branded as poetic licence. Taking inspiration from the field of generative metrics, Balogh goes beyond the usual disciplinary field of South Asian studies in order to build his argument that the ratio behind these unusual caesurae is concealed in a set of abstract metrical schemata that underlie the fixed quantitative metres of classical Sanskrit verse.

Through a case study of the adposition *prati*, the second contribution, by Małgorzata Sulich-Cowley, tackles the complex issue of the semantics of Sanskrit particles from the emic perspectives of the linguistic traditions of ancient South Asia (*nirukta* and *vyākaraṇa*). The historical focus on the different views on the meaningfulness or meaninglessness of particles held by authors such as Yāska, Pāṇini and Bhartṛhari is counterbalanced by a close linguistic analysis that attempts to identify the core sense of the particle *prati* common to the staggering variety of its actual uses.

Martina Palladino's insightful contribution is a linguistic and cultural study of the several Iranian loanwords present in sections from various Sanskrit *Purāṇa*s that deal with the Maga Brāhmaṇas. Beside the thorough etymological analysis, the paper draws attention to how this group of Indo-Scythian priests, accepted in India as Brahmins and thus 'Hinduized', contributed to the development of the sun cult and became a living and integral force within the religious milieu of the South Asian subcontinent.

By intertwining a plurality of disciplinary perspectives such as anthropology, linguistics and political studies, Patrick McCartney offers a sociolinguistic and sociocultural analysis of Sanskrit as a living language in selected 'Sanskrit-speaking' villages within the Hindi-speaking belt of North India. The symbolic capital that the culturally prestigious Sanskrit language can offer to rural villagers who attempt to learn it today is here dissected into its political and cultural components, ranging from its agenda-driven appropriation by the Hindu right to the utopian aspiration to create a morally bettered community by the mere use of the 'eternal', sacred language of the gods.

The second section of the volume deals with issues in poetry, aesthetics and performative arts, ranging from classical Sanskrit *mahākāvya*s to contemporary Kathak dance.

The article by Judith Unterdörfler focuses on the description of nature in Sanskrit poetry by offering the first-ever survey of a yet unpublished work from sixteenth-century Gujarat, the *Śrīgovindavilāsamahākāvya*, a poem on the amorous exploits of Kṛṣṇa and the *gopī*s. The intrinsic, mirroring correlation between the description of nature and the inner emotions of the depicted characters is highlighted by a thorough analysis of numerous verses from the first canto, in constant comparison with the works of illustrious predecessors in the history of *kāvya*—renowned figures such as Hāla, Kālidāsa and Māgha.

In her contribution, Lidia Szczepanik-Wojtczak attempts to triangulate the cultural positioning of the *Bhaṭṭikāvya* (sixth/seventh century) within the three fields of *kāvya* 'poetry', *vyākaraṇa* 'grammar' and *alaṃkāraśāstra* 'poetics' and thus identify its peculiar status and purpose as an educational tool. Through a case study of the fourteenth canto of the poem and a wider set of reflections on educational resources and their limits in classical South Asia, the author proposes an interpretation of the *Bhaṭṭikāvya* as no mere grammar book, but as a veritable textbook of poetry itself, which budding poets would have treasured as the perfect repository of concrete examples, ready-made forms and conceptual categories for the composition of their own poems.

In his contribution, Prakash Venkatesan offers an in-depth analysis of the theoretical concept of *vaṇṇams*, musical formulae that are claimed to have been followed by Tamil bards in the earliest, unattested period of Tamil literary history. In particular, the author argues that the *vaṇṇam*s were adapted and incorporated into Tamil poetic conventions by the author of the *Tolkāppiyam*, the oldest extant Tamil grammar (possibly from the early centuries CE). In the true spirit of scholarship, Venkatesan's contribution raises more questions than it offers answers and is thus destined to stimulate further research in such an understudied field.

Employing historical, textual and anthropological approaches, the article by Katarzyna Skiba is a scrupulous attempt at understanding the recent history of Kathak as a case of the 'invention of tradition', in which the pursuit of the cultural and religious prestige granted by a Sanskritic pedigree determined the recent creation of a fair degree of shared dance vocabulary and a partial homogenization of practice. However, the reality on the ground is still that of a plurality of dance practices connected to different gurus and their lineages. Hence, the connection to Sanskrit treatises is argued to have more of a symbolic role than being an actual factor of transformation.

The next section of the volume is focused on the philosophical traditions of South Asia (and beyond), with an eye to both a strictly historical approach and a more argumentative and evaluative one.

Through a comparative analysis of several commentaries on the *Sāṃkhyakārikās*, the seminal text of the Sāṃkhya school of philosophy, Jooyoung Lim's article deals with the understudied history of the varying lists of superhuman powers (*aiśvaryas*). The ambitious aim of this paper is to provide an insight into the historical relations among the various commentaries, whose mutual connections and relative chronology are far from settled. This approach proves to be extremely fruitful in providing chronological clues that are doomed to be missed by solely investigating philosophical developments within the system.

The article by Lucas den Boer provides an argumentative analysis of a debate on the existence of the soul that appears in the *Tarkarahasyadīpikā*, a fifteenth-century commentary by Guṇaratna Sūri on Haribhadra Sūri's *Ṣaḍdarśanasamuccaya* (eighth century). Instead of focusing on the question of whether we can attribute the Cārvāka arguments to a real historical movement, the article analyses the conceptual structure of the debate to discern the argumentative function of the Cārvāka position in the text itself. From this perspective, it is argued that the refutation of the sceptical Cārvāka arguments works as a rhetoric device that is of crucial help in establishing the position of the author.

Material culture and its relations to both the historical and the ideological are the themes treated in the last section of the volume.

Johannes (Danny) Eijsermans explores several ancient Khmer reliefs and inscriptions related to the figure of Viṣṇu and his myths. The article proposes to interpret the mythical stories depicted in Angkorean temple art as visual counterparts of their occurrence in the inscriptional discourse of *praśastis*. These praises present the king as equal to Viṣṇu, or even surpassing him, by placing thematic emphasis on specific royal virtues, such as military prowess, righteousness or benevolence. The figurative representations assume the same ideological role visually expressed, while also highlighting the various aspects of a 'good kingship' by minor differences in the modes of depiction.

Arguing that the scholarly emphasis on elite dispensations has often marginalized the contributions of local political actors and communities in the creation of temple complexes, Elizabeth Cecil reintegrates the 'local' within discussions of religious giving through an analysis of some inscriptions of the North Konkan Śilāhāras between the ninth and twelfth century CE. Her focus on the ways in which religious institutions fostered collaboration between individuals from various social strata contributes a more nuanced understanding of the North Konkan's religious and social history, and the practice of temple patronage more broadly.

We would like to express our sincerest thanks to the International Institute for Asian Studies (IIAS), the Leiden University Institute for Area Studies (LIAS), the Society of Friends of the Kern Institute (VVIK), the De Cock Fund and the Gonda Fund, which provided generous financial contributions to support the symposium and the publication of the present volume. We are particularly grateful to Peter Bisschop for his help and support at different stages of the organization and realization of the event. We are pleased to thank the senior panel of the conference, i.e., three organizers of previous IIGRS conferences, Nina Mirnig, Giovanni Ciotti and Robert Leach, who agreed to come to Leiden and to attend the conference in order to give their valuable scholarly input during the Q&A sessions, and thus greatly contributed to the creation of a friendly environment as well as the maintenance of academic continuity with earlier instalments of the IIGRS. A special thanks goes to Kristen de Joseph, who proofread the whole volume and gave numerous helpful suggestions that greatly improved the final result you are now holding in your hands. Our gratitude also goes to Oxbow publications, especially in the person of its editor in chief, Clare Litt, who provided us with her constant and speedy support. We would like to conclude this short preface with a sincere expression of gratitude to the many anonymous reviewers who contributed immensely to the scholarly level of the volume, with its improved quality as their sole, selfless reward.

150 Years of Sanskrit Studies in the Netherlands: The *Karṇapurāṇa*

Keynote Lecture[1] at the Seventh International Indology Graduate Research Symposium (IIGRS), Leiden University, 15–17 October, 2015

Peter C. Bisschop

150 years ago, on 18 October 1865, Hendrik Kern delivered his inaugural lecture upon taking up the then newly established chair of Sanskrit and Comparative Linguistics at Leiden University. The title of his lecture, *Het Aandeel van Indië in de Geschiedenis der Beschaving en de Invloed der Studie van het Sanskrit op de Taalwetenschap* [The Contribution of India to the History of Civilisation and the Influence of the Study of Sanskrit on Linguistics], speaks of the need to convince his audience of the relevance of studying Sanskrit and premodern India.

Only three years before, in 1862, a leading Dutch periodical, *De Nederlandsche Spectator*, had published a letter to the editor, addressing the subject of the proposed chair of Sanskrit, in no ambiguous terms:

> We are [...], dear Sir, sons of a commercial race; we have no need of all this expensive science.[2]

Although 150 years may seem like a long time, the Netherlands was in fact quite late in establishing the academic study of Sanskrit. The first European chair of Sanskrit was established at the Collège de France in Paris in 1815 (Antoine-Léonard de Chézy),[3] followed by Berlin in 1821 (Franz Bopp) and the Boden chair at Oxford in 1832 (Horace Hayman Wilson). My predecessor, Henk Bodewitz, has addressed the background of this late interest in Sanskrit in his farewell

1 The text of the original lecture has been slightly modified to make it fit the present volume, but it retains the characteristics of the oral presentation.

2 Cited from 'T HART 1989: 132.

3 I thank Isabelle Ratié for pointing out to me that de Chézy, and not Burnouf, was the first occupant of the chair at the Collège de France. Eugene Burnouf took over in 1832.

lecture, *De Late 'Ontdekking' van het Sanskrit en de Oudindische Cultuur in Europa* [The Late 'Discovery' of Sanskrit and Ancient Indian Culture in Europe] (Bodewitz 2002).

I am very pleased that we can celebrate this 150 years of the academic study of Sanskrit in the Netherlands not with a nostalgic look back into the past, but with a promising look at the present and near future, with the Seventh International Indology Graduate Research Symposium. The future lies ahead of us. Nevertheless, it is an appropriate moment to stand back and reflect on how we have gotten here in Leiden in the first place. With this in mind I would like to take you, in giant steps, through 150 years of Sanskrit studies in the Netherlands. Following the model of the texts that are at the heart of my own research, the Sanskrit Purāṇas, I will present to you the *Karṇapurāṇa* [The Ancient Tale of Karṇa/Kern], divided into four parts:

1. *Ādikhaṇḍa* [Book of the Beginning];
2. *Karṇakhaṇḍa* [Book of Kern] or *Karṇamāhātmya* [Greatness of Kern];
3. *Karṇaśiṣyapraśiṣyakhaṇḍa* [Book of Kern's Pupils and Their Pupils];
4. *Bhavadbhaviṣyatkhaṇḍa* [Book of the Present and Future].

1 *Ādikhaṇḍa* [Book of the Beginning]

What did the state of Sanskrit studies look like before Kern appeared on the scene? Raising this question brings to mind the notion of *The Stillness of the World Before Bach*, the title of a collection of poems by Lars Gustafsson (1988), or, closer to home, Hanneke 't Hart's biographic article 'Imagine Leiden Without Kern' (1989). However, there were some predecessors. To properly appreciate the enormous impact of Kern's teaching and scholarship on Sanskrit and Indology in the Netherlands, a look at the state of Sanskrit studies in the years before Kern is revealing.

There can be no doubt that Dutch authors, Protestant missionaries to be more precise, played a huge role in opening up India's culture to the intellectual elite of Europe. One author in particular stands out: Abraham Rogerius (1609–1649), a protestant missionary to the Dutch trade centre Paliacatta (now Pulicat) on the Coromandel Coast. His wonderfully titled *Open-deure tot het Verborgen Heydendom* [Open Door to Hitherto Concealed Heathenism] (1651) is one of the key texts in the history of Oriental scholarship. In his recent review of the history of Orientalism, *The Birth of Orientalism*, Urs App (2010) breaks down much of the model put forward in Edward Said's influential *Orientalism* (1978). Stressing the key role of religious notions in shaping Europeans' ideas about the East, App writes:

> ... the role of colonialism (and generally of economic and political interests) dwindles to insignificance compared to the role of religion. (2010: x)

Abraham Rogerius is an excellent example. Aside from authoring the *Open-deure*, Rogerius is credited with one of the first ever printed translations of Sanskrit poetry in a European language, Bhartṛhari's *Śatakatraya*. Translations into Dutch of two of the three *śataka*s, the ones on *vairāgya* 'indifference' and *nīti* 'conduct', were published as an appendix to the *Open-deure*, entitled 'Hondert Spreucken van den Heydenschen Barthrouherri, Onder de Bramines op de Cust Chormandel Befaemt, Handelende van den Wegh na den Hemel' [Hundred Aphorisms on the Path to Heaven by the Heathen Bhartṛhari, Famous Amongst the Brahmans on the Coromandel Coast] and 'Hondert Spreucken van den Heydenschen Barthrouherri, Handelende van den Redelijcken Ommegangh Onder de Menschen' [Hundred Aphorisms on Reasonable Social Conduct Amongst Men by the Heathen Bhartṛhari] (ROGERIUS 1651). The translation was not his own, but a Dutch rendering of a translation provided by a Brahman informant of his.[4] Nevertheless, it was a wonderful start, although we had to wait another 200 years before the actual establishment of a chair in Sanskrit studies in the Netherlands.

A second author who could lay a claim on having had a rudimentary knowledge of Sanskrit, although this may have been limited to a bit of vocabulary, is the eighteenth-century travel writer Jacob Haafner (1754–1809). The stories about his travels to India and Sri Lanka, published in the early nineteenth century, were very popular and widely read. One of his best known travel stories is *Reize in eenen Palanquin* [Travels in a Palanquin] (1808), which tells of his travels along the Coromandel Coast in 1781 and how he falls in love with an Indian dancing girl, Mamia. It has recently been rendered into contemporary Dutch by the literary writer Thomas ROSENBOOM, published under the alluring title *Exotische Liefde* [Exotic Love] (2011). The reason for mentioning Haafner here, however, is different. In 1823 his son, C.M. Haafner, brought out his father's translations of part of the *Rāmāyaṇa* under the title *Proeve van Indische Dichtkunde, Volgens den Ramayon* [Sample of Indian Poetry on the Basis of the Ramayana]. To what extent did Haafner actually know Sanskrit? Although his son claims that his father translated directly from the Sanskrit original, this is in fact highly doubtful. Paul van der Velde concludes:

> Haafner's rendering of the Ramayana offers a correct excerpt of the Ramayana which he must have based on oral sources and on Tamil, Hindi, and Bengal versions of the Ramayana.[5]

4 Rogerius mentions in the preface to the poems that this Brahman informant, named Padmanaba, 'for some reason' did not want to translate the part on *śṛṅgāra* 'amorous passion': 'Yeder Boeck is af-gedeelt in thien Capittelen: ende yeder Capittel begrijpt thien Spreucken; doch in twee Capitelen sult ghy bevinden, dat de thiende Spreuck ontbreeckt, mits dat se oock in den Originelen niet en was, waer uyt dese Spreucken my den Bramine Padmanaba heeft vertaelt, uyt-gheseyt de Amoureuse die hy om eenighe reden, soo het scheen, my niet en wilde verduytschen' (ROGERIUS 1651: 217).

5 VAN DER VELDE n.d.; see also DE MOOR & VAN DER VELDE 1991.

Nevertheless, his was the first rendering of the Rāma epic into Dutch and as such Haafner deserves his place in the history of Dutch Indology.

One of the first Dutch academics to have known some Sanskrit was the Leiden professor of Oriental languages (especially Arabic) Hendrik Hamaker (1789–1835). Two of his publications on Sanskrit, listed on the treasure trove *Dutch Studies on South Asia, Tibet and Classical Southeast Asia*, the bibliographical website set up and maintained by Dory Heilijgers,[6] may be mentioned here:

1. *Over de Sakontala van den Indischen dichter Calidas* [On the Sakuntala of the Indian Poet Kalidasa] (Hamaker 1823);
2. *Akademische Voorlezingen over het Nut en de Belangrijkheid der Grammatische Vergelijking van het Grieksch, het Latijn en de Germaansche Tongvallen met het Sanskrit* [Academic Lectures about the Use and Importance of the Grammatical Comparison of the Greek, Latin and German Accents with the Sanskrit]. (Hamaker 1835)

The first, published in 1823, indicates that Hamaker had no real knowledge of Sanskrit, for he excuses himself to his audience for rendering the *Śākuntalā* into Dutch on the basis of William Jones's English translation and not from the original Sanskrit.[7] His 1835 series of lectures is rather an exercise in comparative linguistics. Hamaker boldly claims here to be the first and only person in the Netherlands to have seriously studied Sanskrit. Addressing his learned audience, he says:

> ... as far as known, he who speaks to you at present, is the first and only one [among his countrymen] who has seriously and with great success studied the ancient Sanskrit, without whose knowledge it is impossible to bring order and regulation and scientific precision in the subject of word formation.[8]

On the other hand, we do not find much evidence from Hamaker's publications that he actually read Sanskrit texts.[9] The subject of the *Academic Lectures* remains

6 Heilijgers n.d. This website has been my main source of reference for biographies and bibliographies of the scholars discussed in this paper.

7 'Voor als nog onbekend zijnde met de talen van Hindostan, heb ik mijne vertaling moeten inrigten naar de Engelsche van Sir William Jones; de eenige bron waaruit wij tot nog toe de Sakontala kennen, en tevens een der meesterstukken van dien smaakvollen en onvergelijkelijken geleerde' (Hamaker 1823: 237).

8 '... [N]aar het geen bekend en openbaar is te oordeelen, is hij, die thans tot u spreekt, de eerste en eenigste, die zich met ernst en belangrijk gevolg heeft toegelegd op de aloude Sanskrita, zonder wier kennis het onmogelijk is orde en regelmaat en wetenschappelijke nauwkeurigheid in de leer der woordvorming te brengen' (Hamaker 1835: vii).

9 Cf. also Bodewitz (2012: 13): 'De eerste Nederlandse geleerde die misschien een beetje Sanskrit gekend heeft was de Leidse hoogleraar Oosterse Talen Hamaker (1789–1835), al blijkt uit zijn publicaties meer interesse dan praktische beoefening.'

limited to noticing some linguistic parallels in word formation across a few Indo-European languages.

Before we move on to Kern himself we must mention the Leiden professor of Hebrew, Antonie Rutgers (1805–1884). Rutgers studied theology with Hamaker and thus must have acquired his knowledge of Sanskrit from him. It was Rutgers who taught Kern the beginnings of Sanskrit and Kern indeed regarded him as the founder of Indian studies in the Netherlands. Kern's first book published in Dutch, a translation of the *Śākuntalā* (1861), is dedicated to him. One of the few publications on Sanskrit by Rutgers is a booklet on Sanskrit typography: *De Sanskrit-drukletters: Typographisch Gerangschikt en met eene proeve van Sanskrit-tekst Voorzien* [The Sanskrit Printing Types: Typographically Arranged and Provided with a Piece of Sanskrit Text], published by Brill in 1851. This little booklet (16 pages in total) deserves a place in the history of printing of *Devanāgarī* script in Europe, an interesting topic in its own right. The fonts used in this early Brill publication go back to the original *Nāgarī* font commissioned by August Wilhelm von Schlegel, which was further developed by Franz Bopp in Berlin and has been very much in use (cf. Stiehl 2005).

2 *Karṇakhaṇḍa* [Book of Kern] or *Karṇamāhātmya* [Greatness of Kern]

Now starts the *Karṇapurāṇa* proper, with the *Karṇakhaṇḍa* or *Karṇamāhātmya.* It is impossible to do justice to the life and works of Kern in the context of this limited paper. Kern is not for nothing one of the very few Sanskritists to bear the distinction of having a street named after him (the Kernstraat in the Professorenwijk in Leiden). Compared to his predecessors Hamaker and Rutgers, Kern took the study of Sanskrit to unprecedented heights and he easily fits into the description in the FAQ on the IIGRS website ('FAQ | IIGRS', 2015):

> Am I an Indologist?
>
> You are if you study any topic concerning Indian civilization such as its literature, rituals, religion, philosophy, grammar, science and social history or archaeology and art history on the basis of texts in the original language. If you are still uncertain that your contribution would be suitable, please don't hesitate to contact us at iigrsuk(at)googlemail(dot)com.

Kern did all of this, and he would certainly not have felt the need to contact the googlemail address provided. However, like his fellow nineteenth-century academics, Kern did much more. He was a true polymath. Aside from his many great contributions to classical Indological subjects such as Sanskrit, Pali and Buddhism, one should mention for example his work on German and Dutch philology. Closer to the field of Indology, and in a way at the heart of it, are his founding contributions to the study of Austronesian linguistics and Old Javanese philology, including translations of *kakawins* and editions of texts and inscriptions. Just to mention one example, attesting to his great and lasting scholarship in this field: his *editio princeps* of the Old Javanese *Rāmāyaṇa* was republished only this year in Romanized form by Willem van der Molen, along with a modern English translation by Stuart Robson, in the newly established series *Javanese Studies* from Tokyo University. Kern was a native to Java: he was born in Central Java (Purworejo) in 1833, the son of a captain, later major, in the Royal Netherlands Army ('T HART 1989: 23). And like his countrymen at the time, he not only published in English, German, French and Latin,[10] but also in his native language, Dutch. In fact most of his publications are in Dutch, including some of his major works, like his monumental *Geschiedenis van het Buddhisme in Indië* [History of Buddhism in India], published in two volumes in Haarlem in 1882 and 1884.[11]

Kern took up the chair of Sanskrit in 1865, after Matthias de Vries, Professor of Dutch, and Rutgers had lobbied for his position for many years ('T HART 1989: 129). Before that Kern had spent several years outside Leiden, having first studied for two years with Franz Bopp and Albrecht Weber in Berlin; the latter became his major teacher in Sanskrit. It was Weber who directed him to the study of Jyotiḥśāstra. Two of Kern's still highly regarded works in this field are his edition and translation of the *Bṛhatsaṃhitā* of Varāhamihira and an edition of the *Āryabhaṭīya* (1865 and 1874). It should come as no surprise that Kern was directed towards astronomy, for—as you will recall from your *Mahābhārata* readings, or from seeing Peter Brook's version of the epic—Karṇa was actually a son of Sūrya, the Sun. I fancy that this parental affiliation with the Sun can also explain the following words from a letter (quoted from 'T HART 1989: 23) Kern wrote to Matthias de Vries on 28 February 1862, from Maastricht, where he had settled as a teacher at the Athenaeum after his return from Germany:

> The sun has seldom shone on the path of my life during the last ten years and I believe that this explains my longing for the sun of Hindustan.

In 1864 Kern set sail for India to teach Sanskrit at Brahmana's and Queen's College in Benares, taking over from Georg Bühler.

A year later Kern took up the chair of Sanskrit in Leiden. Kern fulfilled the position with great success, energy and ambition, teaching students who would

10 KERN's PhD thesis (1855), on Greek and Old Persian, was in Latin: *Specimen historicum exhibens Scriptores Graecos de rebus Persicis Achaemenidarum monumentos collatos.*

11 For Kern's contributions to Buddhist studies, see SILK 2012: 125–154.

become influential Indologists in their own right, the subject of the next *khaṇḍa*. One significant outcome that should be mentioned before we close the present *khaṇḍa*, and which speaks of Kern's influence as well as his training in Dutch philology, was the inclusion of a rule in the Higher Education Act of 1876 that Sanskrit was to be a compulsory course in the curriculum of Dutch studies (Heilijgers n.d.):

> This requirement made the teaching of Sanskrit necessary at the universities of Utrecht, Amsterdam and Groningen, where chairs for Sanskrit were founded in 1906, 1919 and 1962, respectively.

It also explains why theses dealing with purely Indological subjects that were done between 1876 and 1921 carry the somewhat curious line on the title page that they form a 'Thesis for the Degree of Doctor in Dutch Philology'.[12]

3 *Karṇaśiṣyapraśiṣyakhaṇḍa* [Book of Kern's Pupils and Their Pupils]

This section could be easily called 'A Who's Who of Dutch Indology' as well, since practically all lines in Sanskrit studies and Indology in the Netherlands lead back, in one way or another, to the founding father Kern. For example, my own *paramparā* is as follows: Hendrik Kern (Leiden) → Willem Caland (Leiden, Utrecht) → Jan Gonda (Utrecht) → Jacob Ensink (Utrecht, Groningen) → Hans Bakker (Groningen) → Peter Bisschop (Groningen, Oxford, Edinburgh, Leiden). In my case we start in Groningen and end in Leiden, which has much to do with the current situation of Indological studies in the Netherlands, a topic reserved for the last part of this paper. Let us first have a look at some of the direct pupils of Kern. This involves a bit of Dutch topography, since they took up different positions in Leiden, Utrecht, Amsterdam and Groningen, and established their own schools there. I single out 'the big three' (place names in order of their biographies): Jacob Speijer (Leiden, Amsterdam, Groningen, Leiden), Christian Cornelis Uhlenbeck (Leiden, Amsterdam, Leiden), Willem Caland (Leiden, Utrecht).

The first student to be mentioned is Jacob Speijer (1849–1913). He started his PhD under the supervision of Kern in Leiden in 1872 and subsequently became, among other things, lector in Sanskrit in Groningen (1877–1888), extraordinary professor in Amsterdam (1888–1889), full professor in Groningen (1889–1903) and finally full professor in Leiden (1903–1913). Personally I hold him in the highest regard, if only because he inaugurated the teaching of Sanskrit—although his

12 'Proefschrift ter verkrijging van de graad van doctor in de Nederlandse letteren' (Heesterman 1989: 118).

main position was in Latin—at the place where I was taught, the University of Groningen. However, I am pretty sure that many of you have been taught by him as well, through his eternally reprinted *Sanskrit Syntax* (1886). Incredible as this may seem, it remains to this day *the* study of Sanskrit syntax. Speijer also made great contributions to Buddhist studies (e.g. a translation of the *Jātakamālā*, 1895, and an edition of the *Avadānaśataka*, 1906–1909). His most influential student was undoubtedly Johan Huizinga, the great Dutch historian, famous outside the field of Indology for his *Herfsttij der Middeleeuwen* [The Waning of the Middle Ages] (1919). Huizinga did his PhD with Speijer in Groningen on *De Vidūṣaka in het Indisch Toneel* [The Vidūṣaka in Indian Theatre] (1897), which may explain his lifelong interest in the role of play, culminating in his influential *Homo Ludens* (1938) on the seriousness of play in culture.

Christian Cornelis Uhlenbeck (1866–1951), the second main student of Kern, was a comparative philologist who, after doing his PhD at Leiden, became extraordinary professor at the University of Amsterdam (1892–1899) and subsequently full professor in Leiden (1899–1926) in Gothic, Anglo-Saxon, Middle High German and (Indo-)Germanic Languages. Arlo GRIFFITHS (2008–2009: 73) writes the following in an article devoted to Uhlenbeck's role in the history of Dutch Indology:

> Uhlenbeck's significance in the history of Dutch Indology does not lie in his publications in the field. To Uhlenbeck falls the exceptional honour of having trained two successive and internationally most successful occupants of the chair of Sanskrit in the Netherlands, J.Ph. Vogel and F.B.J. Kuijper.

This takes us to two greats indeed. Jean Philippe Vogel (1871–1958) was that rare combination of Sanskritist and archaeologist; it is in the field of Indian archaeology that he made his major and lasting contributions, even serving for a decade as officiating general of the ASI (Archaeological Survey of India, 1910–1920). Aside from his very many academic achievements, which includes the delightful *The Goose in Indian Literature and Art* (1962)—not a bad topic for somebody whose surname means 'Bird'—he was also the founder of the Kern Institute at Leiden University (1925), named after our central character, Hendrik Kern. This institute would play a leading role in Dutch Indology for the rest of the century and build great collections of books, manuscripts, rubbings, photographs etc., now held at the University Library and which we benefit from to the present day. Uhlenbeck's other student, F. B. J. Kuiper (1907–2003), studied not only with Uhlenbeck, but also with Vogel and Caland; his research was truly unique and far-reaching. In the words of Michael WITZEL (2004: 191), who referred to him in his obituary as 'my last Guru':

> Kuiper's oeuvre represents some of the most innovative and lasting research done in our field during the past century.

Kuiper was also, together with Jan Willem de Jong, the founder of the *Indo-Iranian Journal*, which I am at present co-editing with my Leiden colleague Jonathan Silk.

One more of the three great students of Kern remains: Willem Caland (1859–1932). How to do justice to him in a few words? In the study of Vedic ritual his work is unsurpassed. He read and opened up a huge amount of Vedic ritual literature, from the *Pitṛmedhasūtra*s to the *Kauśikasūtra*, from the *Baudhāyanaśrautasūtra* to the *Āpastambaśrautasūtra*, and from the *Vaitānasūtra* to the *Jaiminīyasaṃhitā*. Every student of Vedic ritual ends up reading Caland. Quite telling in this connection is that David Knipe, in the acknowledgments to his book *Vedic Voices*, which came out this year, should thank him, 86 years after his death, for 'making editions and minutiae of Āpastamba texts accessible and sensible' (Knipe 2015: xx). Caland became full professor of Sanskrit, comparative linguistics and Indo-Persian at the University of Utrecht (1917–1929), and in that capacity taught, among others, F.B.J. Kuijper and the towering figure of Jan Gonda.

If one *praśiṣya* of Kern deserves more than a mere mention of his name in this necessarily limited survey of Dutch Indology, it should be Jan Gonda (1905–1991). His sheerly endless list of publications, which form a treasure trove for almost any conceivable Indological subject—if you are considering the study of a Sanskrit or Old Javanese word or phrase, first of all make sure to check whether Gonda has not already collected the references—speaks for itself. Confronted with Gonda's phenomenal academic output, one can only stand back in amazement and wonder how it is possible for a human being to publish so much in one lifetime. Henk Bodewitz made the following calculation:

> In 60 years he published approximately one book and five articles per year, about rather diverse subjects.[13]

Aside from this, however, Gonda built up a flourishing Institute for Eastern Languages (Instituut voor Oosterse Talen)—some would say a little empire—at the University of Utrecht, which he ruled like a veritable emperor.[14] Again, just a telling number: he guided a staggering 61 PhD students to promotion, including the likes of Andries Teeuw, Johanna van Lohuizen-de Leeuw (one of the very few women in this heavily male-dominated history of Dutch Indology), Jacob Ensink, Johannes van Buitenen, Jan Heesterman, Henk Bodewitz and Gerrit Jan Meulenbeld. As editor Gonda oversaw the voluminous *A History of Indian Literature*, whose volumes all of us continue to use on a regular basis. Last but not least, he left behind a bequest

13 'In 60 jaar publiceerde hij gemiddeld per jaar ongeveer 1 boek en 5 artikelen, over nogal uiteenlopende onderwerpen' (Bodewitz 1992: 13).

14 A personal impression of life and study at this institute may be found in Van der Velde 2014: 33–47.

to the Royal Netherlands Academy of Arts and Sciences (KNAW) with which the J. Gonda Foundation was set up (1992). This fund has provided and continues to provide fellowships in Indology, funded several Indological book publications and series (including the *Gonda Indological Studies* [GIS]) and organizes the annual Gonda Lecture in Amsterdam.

I have to round off this account of Kern's thriving lineage of *śiṣyapraśiṣya*s in some way or another in order to reserve some time for the final part of this presentation. The pupils of Kern's pupils taught their own pupils in turn, resulting in a true blossoming of the great tree of Kern's lineage, dividing into various branches. This subject will have to be reserved for some other occasion, perhaps the next anniversary. We can conclude that the twentieth century was a period of great growth for Indology in the Netherlands, with thriving centers in Leiden, Utrecht, Amsterdam and Groningen, each with their own subject specializations. This situation was not meant to last, however. Without going into detail, let me simply end this *khaṇḍa* with a quote from the *Dutch Studies* website, which sums up the outcome in a nutshell:

> In the late 1980's, the Dutch universities were confronted with serious cuts in their budgets. The Indological department at the University of Amsterdam was closed down in 1988, while the Groningen department was transferred to the Faculty of Theology and reduced in size. A few years later the Indological departments of Leiden and Utrecht were merged together and located in Leiden. (HEILIJGERS n.d.)

4 *Bhavadbhaviṣyatkhaṇḍa* [Book of the Present and Future]

So this is where we are now: back in Leiden, where it all started. Groningen managed to keep up the tradition of Sanskrit studies for another 25 years, but only because of the personal leadership of Hans Bakker. With his retirement in 2013, the teaching of Sanskrit and classical Indology was sadly terminated in Groningen as well. His retirement from the University of Groningen has not, however, led to a retirement from academic life, for he is currently working as a project curator at the British Museum in London, in the ERC Synergy project 'Asia Beyond Boundaries: Religion, Region, Language and the State', in which I myself am involved as well.

The Asia Beyond Boundaries project is a good starting point for addressing the present and future. First of all, this project, which investigates the Gupta kingdom and its networks across Asia, in a way explains the presence of us all here. For the two organizers of this symposium, Daniele Cuneo and Lucas den

Boer, are both based in Leiden because of the project: Daniele Cuneo to take over my teaching during my research leave, and Lucas den Boer to do PhD research on the development of Jaina epistemology in the Gupta age. Externally funded projects such as this have increasingly come to define our field and form a new reality in institute building. The kind of strict *śiṣyapraśiṣyaparamparā* that I have outlined in this paper is already becoming something of a relic of the past, and is gradually being replaced by a dynamic setup in which the community of students and academics is no longer defined on a national but on an international level, with scholars studying and working jointly across the globe. The project of the critical edition of the *Skandapurāṇa* in which I am currently engaged with Yuko Yokochi (Kyoto), Diwakar Acharya (Oxford) and Judit Törzsök (Lille), meeting twice a year in Leiden and Kyoto, is another good example of this. And looking at the various Dutch Indologists of the present, they are in fact spread across Europe, with, e.g., Johannes Bronkhorst in Lausanne, Arlo Griffiths in Lyon, Jan Houben in Paris, and Harunaga Isaacson in Hamburg.

But we can also see this in an event like the IIGRS, which will forge new friendships and, I am sure, collaborative international projects for the future.

śubham astu!

References

App, U. (2010). *The birth of Orientalism.* Philadelphia: University of Pennsylvania Press.

Bodewitz, H. W. (1992). Levensbericht J. Gonda. In H.W. Bodewitz (Ed.), *Levensberichten en herdenkingen* (pp. 7–16). Amsterdam: Koninklijke Nederlandse Akademie van Wetenschappen.

—. (2002). De late 'ontdekking' van het Sanskrit en de Oudindische cultuur in Europa. Rede uitgesproken door H.W. Bodewitz bij zijn afscheid als hoogleraar Sanskrit aan de Universiteit Leiden op 1 november 2002. Retrieved from https://openaccess.leidenuniv.nl/bitstream/handle/1887/5267/OR033.pdf.

De Moor, J. C. L. & Van der Velde, P. (1991). De 'heilige taal des lands': Jacob Haafner als voorloper van de studie van het Sanskrit in Nederland. In van den Muyzenberg, H. & de Bruijn, T. (Eds.), *Waarom Sanskrit? Honderdvijfentwintig jaar Sanskrit in Nederland* (pp. 86–94). Leiden: Kern Institute.

Gonda, J. (Ed.). (1973–1984). *A history of Indian literature* (vols. 1–10). Wiesbaden: Harrassowitz.

Griffiths, A. (2008–2009). C. C. Uhlenbeck's work on Sanskrit and his role in the history of Dutch Indology. *Canadian Journal of Netherlandic Studies, 29.2/30.1,* 71–77.

Gustafsson, L. (1988). *The stillness of the world before Bach.* New York, NY: New Directions.

HAAFNER, J. (1808). *Reize in eenen palanquin.* Amsterdam: Allart.

—. (1823). *Proeve van Indische dichtkunde, volgens den Ramayon.* Amsterdam: Van der Hey en Zoon.

HAMAKER, H. A. (1823). Over de Sakontala van den Indischen dichter Calidas, eene voorlezing. *Mnemosyne, 12*(2): 213–255.

—. (1835). *Akademische voorlezingen over het nut en de belangrijkheid der grammatische vergelijking van het Grieksch, het Latijn en de Germaansche tongvallen met het Sanskrit.* Leiden: Hoek.

HEESTERMAN, J. C. (1989). Sanskrit and Indian studies. In Otterspeer, W. (Ed.), *Leiden Oriental connections: 1850–1940* (pp. 118). Leiden: Brill.

HEILIJGERS, D. (n.d.). *Dutch studies on South Asia, Tibet and classical Southeast Asia.* Retrieved from http://dutchstudies-satsea.nl/home-dutch-studies.html.

HUIZINGA, J. (1897). *De vidūṣaka in het Indisch toneel.* Groningen: Noordhoff.

—. (1919). *Herfsttij der Middeleeuwen.* Haarlem: Willink.

—. (1938). *Homo ludens.* Haarlem: Willink.

KERN, J. H. C. (1855). *Specimen historicum exhibens scriptores graecos de rebus Persicis Achaemenidarum monumentis collatos.* Leiden: Hazenberg.

—. (1861). *Çakuntalâ.* Amsterdam: Funke.

—. (1882–1884). *Geschiedenis van het Buddhisme in Indië.* Haarlem: Willink.

—. (1865). *The Bṛhat Sañhitá of Varáha-mihira.* Calcutta: Baptist Mission Press.

—. (1874). *The Āryabhaṭīya.* Leiden: Brill.

— and VAN DER MOLEN, W. (2015). *Rāmāyaṇa: The Story of Rāma and Sītā in Old Javanese.* Tokyo: Research Institute for Languages and Cultures of Asia and Africa, Tokyo University of Foreign Studies.

KNIPE, D. (2015). *Vedic voices. Intimate narratives of a living Andhra tradition.* New York: Oxford University Press.

ROBSON, S. (2015). *The Old Javanese Rāmāyaṇa: A new English translation with an introduction and notes.* Tokyo: Research Institute for Languages and Cultures of Asia and Africa, Tokyo University of Foreign Studies.

ROGERIUS, A. (1651). *De open-deure tot het verborgen heydendom.* Leiden: Hackius.

ROSENBOOM, T. (2011). *Exotische liefde.* Amsterdam: Athenaeum-Polak & Van Gennep.

RUTGERS, Antonie. (1851). *De Sanskrit-drukletters typographisch gerangschikt en met eene proeve van Sanskrit-tekst voorzien.* Leiden: Brill.

SAID, E. (1978). *Orientalism.* New York: Pantheon Books.

SILK, J. A. (2012). Kern and the study of Indian Buddhism. With a speculative note on the Ceylonese dhammarucikas. *Journal of the Pali Text Society, 31*: 125–154.

SPEIJER, J. S. (1886). *Sanskrit syntax.* Leiden: Brill.

—. (1895). *Jâtakamâlâ, Garland of birth-stories.* London: Frowde.

—. (1906–1909). *Avadānaçataka: A century of edifying tales belonging to the Hīnayāna.* St. Petersburg: Commissionnaires de l'Académie Impériale des Sciences.

STIEHL, U. (2005). Fonts for Itranslator 99. Retrieved from www.sanskritweb.net/itrans/s99fonts.pdf.

't Hart, H. (1989). Imagine Leiden without Kern. In Otterspeer, W. (Ed.), *Leiden Oriental connections: 1850–1940* (pp. 126–140). Leiden: Brill.

Van der Velde, P. J. C. L. (2014). *Tatoeage van de ziel. Persoonlijke beschouwingen over Aziatische religies.* Budel: Damon.

Van der Velde, P. G. E. I. J. (n.d.). Jacob Haafner (1754–1809). Retrieved from www.paulvandervelde.nl/haafner/biography.html.

Vogel, J. Ph. (1962). *The goose in Indian literature and art.* Leiden: Brill.

Witzel, M. (2004). F. B. J. Kuiper (1907–2003). *Indo-Iranian Journal, 47*(3/4), 173–191.

FAQ | IIGRS. n.d. Retrieved from http://iigrs.byethost17.com/faq/.

The Abominable *Yati*

Or, An Intriguing Relic of the Prehistory of Sanskrit Verse

Dániel Balogh

Classical Sanskrit metrical verse patterns prescribe obligatory positions for caesurae (*yati*). The testimony of preserved texts shows that poets painstakingly observed these restrictions most of the time, yet in a number of instances the rules seem to have been interpreted with some laxity. This paper demonstrates, through a study of the use of *yati* in some samples of Sanskrit poetry from dramas and epigraphic texts, that a large proportion of these 'abominable *yati*s' actually follow rules of their own. Namely, a caesura masked by vowel *sandhi* is neither an error (*yatibhraṃśa*), nor a form of licence which poets resort to in dire straits or for literary effect. Rather, such *yati*s consistently occur only at specific metrical positions, and must thus be occasioned by their metrical context. It also seems that the (regrettably understudied) traditional recitation of Sanskrit verse often involves a prolonged or slurred syllable at these very same positions, which allows the performer to restore hiatus in the text. These two phenomena of the musical and textual tradition may both be linked to an underlying cause. The reason for the presence of unusual caesurae in poetical praxis and of unusual articulation in performance may be sought in the abstract metrical schemata underlying the fixed metres of classical Sanskrit verse: both occur in metrical positions where the foot-based schema for the syllable-based classical metre involves catalectic (incomplete) or syncopated (off-beat) feet.

The Caesura in Sanskrit Metrics*

The term 'caesura' in this paper refers to a point that separates one metrical segment (colon) from another within a periodic unit (line) of verse. The Sanskrit term for

* The research behind this paper is linked to my doctoral thesis on Viśākhadatta's play the *Mudrārākṣasa*, supported in part by the Rabindranath Tagore Research Fellowship awarded by the

what in English I call a caesura is *yati*, 'restraint'. Theoretically, the caesura is expected to fall at a boundary between two words, allowing the reciter of a poem to realise it as an audible (*śravya*) pause (*virāma);* another common term for the *yati* is *viccheda*, 'split'.[1] These synonymous terms are employed in Sanskrit poetics not only for in-line caesurae, but also for the ends of verse quarters (*pāda*s), which thus seem to be regarded as qualitatively non-different from the former. Even if this is so, there is a perceivable quantitative difference between the two, of which the theoreticians are also aware. A brief text called the *Yatyupadeśopaniṣad* (cited in its entirety by several commentators on poetical *śāstras*[2]) begins with a list of the positions where a *yati* can occur. This treats the ends of quarters separately from in-line caesurae and emphasises that a *yati* is especially required at the ends of half-verses.[3] The distinctiveness of the half-verse *yati* is traditionally said to consist of the non-application of *saṃdhi* over this boundary and the prohibition of compounds crossing it.[4] Correspondingly, in the praxis of Sanskrit poets, the *yati*s delimiting verse quarters (which I shall call line breaks hereafter) indeed appear to be more marked than those separating one colon of a line from another (to which I refer hereafter as caesurae).[5] In fact, there seems to be at least one practical feature in addition to the absence of *saṃdhi* and the scarcity of compounds stretching over these boundaries. The established metres always call for a heavy syllable at

---

Indian Council of Cultural Relations. The topic of the 'abominable' *yati* was omitted from the dissertation, but I have published about it in Hungarian (Balogh 2015a). My research on epigraphic texts was done under the aegis of the Asia Beyond Boundaries project (https://asiabeyondboundaries.org/), supported by the European Research Council. Throughout this paper, Sanskrit is transliterated according to IAST conventions. I use hyphens and spaces in Sanskrit text to separate compound members and independent words (respectively), unless the boundaries are fused in vowel *saṃdhi*. For prosodic notation I use the standard symbols ⏑ to represent light syllables and – to represent heavy syllables. The sign ⏓ stands for an unregulated (anceps) syllable, while ○ indicates an unfilled metrical position that may be realised as a pause in recitation. A colon (:) represents the caesura in metrical formulae.

1 Thus Hemacandra's *Chando'nuśāsana* 1.15 (Velankar 1949: १४): *śravyo virāmo yatiḥ*; and Halāyudha's commentary on the *Chandaḥsūtra* of Piṅgala 6.1 (Kedāranāth 1938: 100): *vicchidyate vibhajyate pada-pāṭho 'sminn iti vicchedo viśrāma-sthānaṃ, sa ca yatir ity ucyate.*

2 The text of the *Yatyupadeśopaniṣad* (a mere four *ślokas*) is cited (from Halāyudha's commentary on the *Chandaḥsūtra*) and discussed in Weber 1863: 462–466. For several commentaries (on the *Vṛttaratnākara* of Kedārabhaṭṭa) citing and expounding this text (or a variant of it), see Sharma et al. 1969: 23–31. For an in-depth discussion, see Pollock 1977: 20–36.

3 *Yatyupadeśopaniṣad* 1a–c, *yatiḥ sarvatra pādānte ślokārdhe tu viśeṣataḥ / samudrādi-padānte ca ...* Here *samudrādi* refers to the coded numbers (*bhūtasaṃkhyā*) by which traditional metrical definitions identify the length of each colon of verse. For instance, *samudra* is a code for 4, since there are held to be four oceans.

4 Thus, for example, Halāyudha on *Chandaḥsūtra* 6.1 (Kedāranāth 1938: 101) says, *ślokārdhe tu viśeṣataḥ ity atra saṃdhi-kāryābhāvaḥ spaṣṭa-vibhaktitvaṃ ca viśeṣaḥ.*

5 Pollock (1977: 37) advises against using the word *caesura* in the context of Indic poetry, and employs 'pause' for the ends of lines and 'break' for in-line *yati*s. While I accept his reasoning that this feature is not identical to the caesura of classical European poetry, I see no problem in applying familiar terminology in a slightly modified sense.

the ends of lines, but not infrequently such line-final syllables are actually light, yet counted as heavy by a rule corresponding to the tenet of *brevis in longo*. This applies in particular to the ends of the even quarters (i.e. to the half-verse break and the end of the stanza); short syllables at the ends of odd quarters appear to be rare in the longer lyrical metres, though not uncommon in some popular shorter verse forms.[6] Additionally, *brevis in longo* is to my knowledge never invoked before (in-line) caesurae: where a metre prescribes a heavy syllable at the end of a colon (which is almost always the case[7]), that syllable is invariably heavy by nature or by position.

'Abominable' *Yatis*

The lack of a word boundary at a caesura is regarded by Sanskrit theoreticians as a serious defect in poetry (*yatibhraṃśa*).[8] But even such a lack may come in several flavours. To illustrate diverse cases of *yati* transgressions, I reproduce here two stanzas in the *pṛthvī* metre. The formula for this metre is ⏑ – ⏑ ⏑ ⏑ – ⏑ – : ⏑ ⏑ ⏑ – ⏑ – – ⏑ ⏓, with a caesura prescribed after the eighth syllable in several traditional treatises on Sanskrit metrics,[9] yet there are numerous instances in actual poetry where this prescription is ignored. Thus, a notorious example from the *Nītiśataka* of Bhartṛhari[10] goes,

> *labheta sikatāsu tai:lam api yatnataḥ pīḍayan*
> *pibec ca mṛga-tṛṣṇikā:su salilaṃ pipāsārditaḥ /*
> *kadācid api paryaṭañ: śaśa-viṣāṇam āsādayen*
> *na tu pratiniviṣṭa-mū:rkha-jana-cittam ārādhayet //*

6 In the *Mudrārākṣasa*, Viśākhadatta only makes use of *brevis in longo* at the ends of odd *pādas* in the metres *anuṣṭubh*, *upajāti* and *vasantatilaka*, in which he avails of this licence 16, 2 and 14 times (respectively), i.e. in 37, 25 and 37 per cent (respectively) of the total number of odd *pādas* in these metres.

7 A light syllable before a caesura occurs in only three Sanskrit metres, each very rare (Pollock 1977: 99).

8 Thus Daṇḍin in *Kāvyādarśa* 3.125–126 (Dimitrov 2011: 396) says this should be avoided: ... *yati-bhraṣṭaṃ ... iti doṣā ... varjyāḥ kāvyeṣu sūribhiḥ*. Later on (3.152; Dimitrov 2011: 424) he explains that *yatibhraṃśa* is jarring to the ear, *śravaṇodvejanaṃ*. It is possible that some of the early theoreticians, including Bharata, regarded the *yati* as optional, but others, including Piṅgala, viewed it as compulsory and this latter view gained the upper hand in the long run (Velankar 1949: 19).

9 Such as the *Chandaḥsūtra* of Piṅgala 7.17 (Kedāranāth 1938: 158): *pṛthvī jsau jsau yalau g vasu-navakau*.

10 Number 319 in Kosambi 1948. The stanza is also cited as an illustration of the non-observance of *yati* in *pṛthvī* by Pollock 1977: 81 and Ghosh 1978: 631.

Although the third *pāda* of this stanza seems to observe the prescribed caesura, this is probably mere happenstance; in quarter *b* the theoretical break falls between a nominal stem and a declensional ending, while in *a* and *d* it is smack in the middle of a morphologically indivisible word.[11] It is thus fairly certain that whoever composed this particular stanza followed a school of versification that did not stipulate a (compulsory) caesura here. GHOSH (1978) presents an overview of *śāstra*s that do or do not require this caesura and discusses specimens of classical Sanskrit poetry that refrain from observing it. He concludes that several great poets including Kālidāsa occasionally break the caesura in the *pṛthvī* metre, even though they hold to it most of the time in this metre and observe caesurae fastidiously in other metres.

If a poet generally does use a caesura at a particular point, yet sometimes omits it, the rationale for this is most probably a conscious transgression to enhance the poetic effect of the composition. In contrast to the downright lack of caesurae in the above example, in verse 9 the Allahabad *praśasti* of Samudragupta[12] we read,

> *pradāna-bhuja-vikkrama-:praśama-śāstra-vākyodayair*
> *uparyyupari-sañcayo:cchritam aneka-mārggaṃ yaśaḥ /*
> *punāti bhuvana-trayaṃ: paśupater jjaṭāntar-guhā-*
> *nirodha-parimokṣa-śī:ghram iva pāṇḍu gāṅgaṃ payaḥ //*

Here the caesurae in *pāda*s *a*, *b* and *c* are more or less in good order (if any appear otherwise, please bear with me a short while: I shall return to them). In *pāda d*, however, the break is conspicuous by its absence. Expected to fall in the middle of the word *śī:ghram*, 'swift', the omission of a caesura here puts extra emphasis on the rush of 'the pale Gangetic water swift upon its release from confinement in the cavities within Śiva's dreadlocks'. I see this instance as a premeditated transgression by the poet Hariṣeṇa,[13] enhanced further by the torrential enjambment of the compound *jaṭāntar-guhā-nirodha-parimokṣa-śīghram.* What is more, the *yati*s in the first three quarters are made even more prominent by initial alliteration[14] (clearly manifest in *pradāna ... praśama* and *punāti ... paśupater*, and obscured by

11 The *Yatyupadeśopaniṣad* (2) actually permits putting caesurae inside a word, provided that both of the segments are longer than one syllable: *kvacit tu pada-madhye 'pi samudrādau yatir bhavet / yadi pūrvāparau bhāgau na syātām eka-varṇakau //*. This sort of mid-word *yati* seems to be extremely rare in poetic praxis, and in any case the *pṛthvī* stanza cited here stands in violation even of this licence.

12 FLEET 1888: 9, line 30–31.

13 Contrary to my opinion, POLLOCK (1977: 83) mentions this verse as an example of the non-compulsory nature of the caesura in *pṛthvī.*

14 My thanks to Stephen Durnford for pointing out this feature of the stanza, which I had overlooked, and to Jean-Luc Chevillard for noting that such word-initial 'rhyming' (*mōṉai*) is regularly used in Tamil poetry to link words within a colon.

vowel *saṃdhi* in *uparyyupari … ucchritam*), and this emphasis is also conspicuous by its absence in the fourth *pāda*.

So far I have discussed cases where the outright absence of a word boundary at the *yati* can be ascribed to a tradition which does not put stock in a caesura at that position, and cases where a poet deliberately chooses to ignore the caesura to heighten the effect of his poetry. However, a fair number of cases are less than clearly transgressive, since the concept of a word boundary is somewhat fuzzy in Sanskrit.

First, there is a relatively straightforward matter: the issue of nominal compounds (e.g. *vikkrama-:praśama* in *pāda a* of the above stanza). The *Yatyupadeśopaniṣad* makes it clear that a word boundary without a manifest declensional case ending (i.e. a non-ultimate member of a compound) is just as acceptable at a caesura as one with a case ending.[15] This is generally confirmed by the praxis of poets, who have no qualms about putting their caesurae at the boundaries of compounded words.[16]

Less than straightforward is the matter of word boundaries (inside or outside of compounds) obscured by vowel *saṃdhi*, such as *sañcayo:cchritam* in the above example. This can come about in one of two ways. On the one hand, word-final and word-initial vowels may merge in a single long vowel or diphthong; on the other hand, word-final *ĭ*, *ŭ* and *ṛ* change into the approximants *y*, *v* and *r* when followed by a word-initial vowel. The *Kāvyālaṅkārasūtravṛtti* of Vāmana unconditionally allows the breaking of words on account of vowel *saṃdhi*.[17] Contrarily, the *Kāvyālaṃkāra* of Bhāmaha, though it provides no explicit rule for vowel *saṃdhi*, actually illustrates the fault of *yatibhraṃśa* with such an example (and no other).[18] The *Yatyupadeśopaniṣad* is distinctly aware of this twilight zone of caesurae and implicitly accepts it as legitimate, stipulating that a vowel joined in *saṃdhi* is generally to be regarded as the end of the pre-caesura word (*pūrvāntavat*), and only

15 *Yatyupadeśopaniṣad* 1*d*, *vyaktāvyakta-vibhaktike*. Halāyudha (Kedāranāth 1938: 101) explains: *tatra śrūyamāṇa-vibhakty-antaṃ vyakta-vibhaktikam, samāsāntarbhūta-vibhakty-antam avyakta-vibhaktikam.*

16 This is basically a subjective impression, open to refutation on an empirical basis. In the way of statistical figures, I can say for certain that of the 500 caesurae in the verses of the *Mudrārākṣasa*, 42 (i.e. 8%) coincide with compound boundaries, in contrast to 0 caesurae within words. Further details are available in Balogh 2015a: 20–21. Dieter Gunkel (personal communication, September and October 2015) has expressed doubts about compound boundaries at *yati* points being equally acceptable to independent word boundaries. A cursory investigation of the data available to me shows that in-compound *yati*s may indeed be less frequent than one might expect on the basis of the general ratio of in-compound boundaries to independent word boundaries. Poets may thus have felt some degree of aversion to putting a compound boundary at their *yati*s, but nonetheless did so frequently enough for the author of the *Yatyupadeśopaniṣad* to allow this practice explicitly. The matter deserves further analysis, but for my present purposes I feel we can safely deem in-compound *yati*s entirely non-abominable.

17 *Sūtra* 2.2.4 (Jha 1971: 62): *tad* [i.e. *yatibhraṣṭam*] *dhātu-nāma-bhāga-bhede svara-saṃdhy-akṛte prāyeṇa; vṛtti* ad loc.: *svara-sandhy-akṛta iti vacanāt svara-sandhi-kṛte bhede na doṣaḥ.*

18 *Kāvyālaṃkāra* 4.24–25 (Sastri 1956: 169): *yatiś chando-'dhirūḍhānāṃ śabdānāṃ yā vicāraṇā/ tad-apetaṃ yati-bhraṣṭam iti nirdiśyate yathā // vidyutvantas tamālā:sita-vapuṣa ime vāri-vāhā dhvananti.*

occasionally (*kvacid eva*) as the beginning of the post-caesura word (*parādivat*), while an approximant is to be regarded as the beginning of the latter word.[19]

These instructions, however, are rather succinct and imprecise. The words *pūrvāntavat* and *parādivat* are evidently used to distinguish between cases of vowels merged in *saṃdhi* where the caesura falls, respectively, after the merged vowel and those where it falls before.[20] But neither the *Upaniṣad* nor the commentaries I have studied say anything about the circumstances in which the *parādivat* variant is permitted, even though the expression *kvacid eva* implies specific cases rather than a random rareness. The statement that approximants are (always) *parādivat* seems to be a technicality based on the concept of the written *akṣara*, which dictates that a consonant (including the approximants produced in *saṃdhi*) joins the following vowel.[21] All in all, the *upaniṣad* definitely ratifies *yati*s in which the word break is obscured by *saṃdhi*, and seems to say that some of these should be employed only in special cases.

Case in Point: Anomalous Caesurae in the *Mudrārākṣasa*

Curious to see how an actual poet handles his caesurae, I examined the verses of the *Mudrārākṣasa* of Viśākhadatta from this viewpoint. The total number of theoretical *yati*s in the play happens to be exactly 500.[22] Not a single one of these occurs inside a morpheme (as in *śī:ghram* above), nor are there any instances of caesurae between a prefix and a stem (for which see later). There are a fair number (42, to be precise) of caesurae between compounded nouns (as in *vikkrama-:praśama* above).[23] The most interesting finding, however, is that caesurae obscured by vowel *saṃdhi* (as in *sañcayo:cchritam* above), though uncommon, appear in numbers that cannot,

---

19 *Yatyupadeśopaniṣad* 3, *pūrvāntavat svaraḥ saṃdhau kvacid eva parādivat / draṣṭavyo yati-cintāyāṃ yaṇ-ādeśaḥ parādivat //*. The expression *yaṇ-ādeśaḥ* refers to *Aṣṭādhyāyī* 6.1.77 (*iko yaṇ aci*), i.e. the formation of approximants from final vowels in *saṃdhi*.

20 As illustrated, for example, by Halāyudha commenting on Piṅgala 6.1 (Kedāranāth 1938: 102), citing *asthāno:pagatayamunā* (*Meghadūta* 1.54) for *pūrvāntavad-bhāva* and *mahiṣa:syāhito* (untraced) for *parādivad-bhāva*.

21 As explained more specifically in what seems to be an alternative version of the *Yatyupadeśo-paniṣad* in Trivikrama's commentary on *Vṛttaratnākara* 1.11 (Sharma et al. 1969: 24), which does not mention *yaṇādi* as a separate case but says that a consonant attached to a vowel at the beginning of the post-caesural word is to be treated as the beginning of that latter word even if it belongs to the end of the former: *pūrvāntavat svaraḥ saṃdhau parasyādiḥ svarāt paraḥ // parādi-varṇa-saṃbaddhaṃ vyañjanaṃ tu parādivat / prāk-padānta-sthitaṃ sādhu vyavahāreṣu dṛśyatām //*.

22 Here and throughout this paper I rely on the text of the *Mudrārākṣasa* as edited by Alfred Hillebrandt (Hillebrandt 1912). Verses of the *Mudrārākṣasa* are referred to by act and verse number since the consecutive verse numbers in Hillebrandt's edition are incorrect from the beginning of Act 5 onward. See Balogh 2015b: 242–246 for a correspondence of *Mudrārākṣasa* verses in Hillebrandt's and Telang's editions.

23 See Balogh 2015a: 19–23 for further statistics.

Table 1: Caesurae obscured by vowel saṃdhi *in the* Mudrārākṣasa

Metre	*Stanzas*	*Caesurae*	*1. Late*		*2. Early*		*3. Slip*	
			count	*%*	*count*	*%*	*count*	*%*
hariṇī	3	24	0	0%	0	0%	1	4%
mālinī	4	16	0	0%	0	0%	0	0%
mandākrāntā	1	8	0	0%	0	0%	0	0%
praharṣiṇī	3	12	0	0%	0	0%	0	0%
pṛthvī	1	4	0	0%	0	0%	0	0%
rucirā	2	8	0	0%	0	0%	0	0%
śārdūlavikrīḍita	39	156	1	1%	2	1%	3	2%
śikhariṇī	18	72	0	0%	0	0%	0	0%
sragdharā	24	192	5	3%	1	1%	1	1%
suvadanā	1	8	0	0%	0	0%	0	0%
Total	96	500	6	1%	3	1%	5	1%

in my opinion, be written off as the result of chance or sloppy penmanship. These anomalous caesurae (of which there are 14 in the *Mudrārākṣasa*) form the principal subject of the remainder of this study.

To see if there is a pattern underlying caesurae obscured by vowel *saṃdhi*, I have classified them into three distinct types and tallied the occurrences of each type separately by metre. In Table 1 above, the second and third columns show how many stanzas of a particular metre occur in the *Mudrārākṣasa* and how many caesurae this entails (since some metres have two caesurae per line, while others have just one). The next three pairs of columns indicate the number and proportion of anomalous caesurae broken down by type. To make notable figures more conspicuous, the cells for caesura types that do not occur in a particular metre are shaded in grey. My classes of anomalous caesura are as follows:

1. **Late** (*pūrvāntavat*, in the terminology of the *Yatyupadeśopaniṣat*): a caesura *after* a vowel produced by the *saṃdhi* merging of a final and an initial vowel (e.g. *vinayā:laṃkṛtaṃ*);
2. **Early** (*parādivat*): a caesura *before* a vowel produced by *saṃdhi* merging (e.g. *hatakasy:ātyantika*);
3. **Slip** (*yaṇādeśa*): a caesura after an approximant produced by *saṃdhi* from a final vowel before an initial vowel (e.g. *upahasaty: ekānta-bhīrūn*).[24]

24 The *Yatyupadeśopaniṣad* says that this type of vowel *saṃdhi* should be treated as *parādivat*, which implies that both the *saṃdhi*-derived semivowel and the preceding consonant join the next word

Table 2: Details of anomalous caesurae in the Mudrārākṣasa

	Metre	*Stanza*	*Text*
late	*śārdūla*	1.13	*bhartur ye pralaye 'pi pūrva-**sukṛtā:saṅgena** niḥsaṅgayā*
	sragdharā	3.10	*nālaṃkurvanti rathyāḥ: pṛthu-jaghana-**bharā:krānti**-mandaiḥ prayātaiḥ*
	sragdharā	3.24	*sā mayy eva skhalantī: prathayati **vinayā:laṃkṛtaṃ** te prabhutvam*
	sragdharā	3.27	*āruhyārūḍha-kopa-:sphuraṇa-**viṣamitā:grāṅgulī**-mukta-cūḍāṃ*
	sragdharā	3.27	*loka-pratyakṣam ugrāṃ: sakala-ripu**kulo:ccheda**-dīrghāṃ pratijñām*
	sragdharā	4.7	*sotsedhaiḥ skandha-deśaiḥ: khara-kavika-**kaśā:karṣaṇā**tyartha-bhugnaiḥ*
early	*śārdūla*	2.6	*devaḥ svarga-gato 'pi **śātrava-vadhen:ārādhitaḥ** syād iti*
	śārdūla	2.16	*sā Viṣṇor iva Viṣṇugupta-**hatakasy:ātyantika**-śreyase*
	sragdharā	3.19	*cūḍā-ratnāṃśu-garbhās: tava **caraṇa-yugasy:āṅgulī**-randhra-bhāgāḥ*
slip	*śārdūla*	2.13	*skandhe dakṣiṇayā balān **nihitayāpy: aṅkaṃ** patantyā muhuḥ*
	śārdūla	3.5	*śūrebhyo 'bhyadhikaṃ bibhety **upahasaty: ekānta**-bhīrūn aho*
	hariṇī	4.2	*katham idam **ihety: unnidra**sya: prayānty aniśaṃ niśāḥ*
	sragdharā	4.12	*daivāt pūrṇa-pratijñaḥ: punar api na **karoty: āyati**-jyāni-bhītaḥ*
	śārdūla	7.20	*kāryāṇāṃ gatayo vidher api na **yānty: ālocanā**-gocaram*

I must note here that my categories are not mutually exclusive. Some of the instances I classified as 'Slip' could have been assigned to the 'Late' category instead, since they involve the enclitics *api* and *iti*, reduced to consonants and thus possessing no prosodic value when their initial vowel merges with a preceding final vowel, while their final vowel becomes an approximant on account of a following initial vowel.[25]

Although the total number of obscured caesurae is relatively low, the table definitely gives the impression that their distribution among metres is far from random, as they occur in but three of 10 metres, and two of these three metres exhibit all three types of anomalous caesura. The picture becomes even sharper if we take into account the exact location of the anomalies. Of the three metres concerned, the *śārdūlavikrīḍita* (formula: – – – ⏑ ⏑ – ⏑ – ⏑ ⏑ ⏑ – : – – ⏑ – – ⏑ ⏓) has only one caesura per line, but the other metres have two. In *hariṇī* (⏑ ⏑ ⏑ ⏑ ⏑ – : – – – – : ⏑ – ⏑ ⏑ – ⏑ ⏓), it is the first of these two caesurae that behaves 'abominably', although this may not be significant on account of the small number of cases studied. However, the *sragdharā* (– – – ⏑ – – : ⏑ ⏑ ⏑ ⏑ ⏑ ⏑ – : – ⏑ – – ⏑ – ⏓) is represented by no less than 24 specimens in the *Mudrārākṣasa*, and all of the seven anomalies found in these

---

because that is where they find a vowel to which they can attach. Nonetheless I prefer to avail of the opportunities afforded by an alphabetic script and segment such caesurae as *upahasaty: ekānta-bhīrūn* rather than *upahasa:tyekānta-bhīrūn*.

25 These cases are *Mudrārākṣasa* 2.13 and 4.2 (q.v. Table 2 below). Thus *nihitayāpy: aṅkaṃ* (Slip) could, alternatively, be analysed as *nihitayā:py aṅkaṃ* (Late) and *ihety: unnidrasya* (Slip) as *ihe:ty un-nidrasya* (Late). I have chosen to classify these as 'Late' caesurae because they involve enclitics, which are by nature closely linked to the preceding word. This is also the opinion of the *Yatyupadeśopaniṣad* (4*ab*), *nityaṃ prāk-pada-saṃbandhāś cādayaḥ prāk-padāntavat.*

occur at the second caesura of that metre. Table 2 above presents the anomalous caesurae individually, grouped by category and giving a one-line context for each. Caesurae (including the irrelevant ones) are represented by a colon in the text, and the immediate context of each anomalous caesura appears in darker bold type.

More Sightings

Before studying the habits and hypothesising about the evolution of the abominable *yati*, we need to confirm that this elusive creature is not endemic to the *Mudrārākṣasa*. Since first becoming aware of the phenomenon, I have repeatedly noticed caesurae obscured by vowel *saṃdhi* in *sragdharā* and *śārdūlavikrīḍita* verses, but a systematic study of a more substantial corpus of texts is yet to be accomplished. For the purposes of this paper, I have extended my research into two more textual domains, both of which are quite close in literary space-time to Viśākhadatta: the three plays attributed to King Harṣa, and the Mandasor pillar inscription of Yaśodharman.[26]

For the former, I have relied on a previous study by Roland STEINER (1997: 243–253). In his analysis he classified caesurae into categories similar (though not identical) to mine. His findings differ from what I have found in the *Mudrārākṣasa* in that he reports (ibid. 245–246) six instances of a caesura without vowel *saṃdhi* occurring between a prefix and a stem, a phenomenon that is entirely absent from the *Mudrārākṣasa*, but permitted by some theoreticians.[27] However, he also finds numerous (no less than 42) anomalies of the type that interests me here: caesurae occluded by vowel *saṃdhi*. One of these (the only specimen of my 'Slip' type in the Harṣa corpus) may not be quite relevant to the present analysis, since it involves a stanza in the *pṛthvī* metre which, as noted above, does not follow caesura rules very stringently.[28] Of the remaining 41 obscured caesurae, all but one

26 The striking resemblance of some stanzas of Yaśodharman's inscription to some verses of the *Mudrārākṣasa* was first pointed out by ANTANI 1922, but ignored by subsequent scholars. As I discuss in BALOGH 2015b: 228–230, Viśākhadatta may well have been connected to the Aulikara court of Daśapura around, though not necessarily during, Yaśodharman's reign. As for Harṣa, his metrical profile—i.e. the proportions in which he employs various metres in his dramas—is strikingly close to that of Viśākhadatta; see BALOGH 2015b: 217 for details.

27 The *Yatyupadeśopaniṣad* implicitly permits breaks between a polysyllabic prefix and a stem by the more general rule that intra-word breaks are permitted so long as both segments are longer than one syllable. The *Kāvyālaṅkārasūtravṛtti* of Vāmana (*vṛtti* to *sūtra* 2.2.4, JHA 1971: 62) permits all breaks so long as they are not within a verbal or nominal stem: *yati-bhraṣṭaṃ dhātu-bhāga-bhede nāma-bhāga-bhede ca sati bhavati / … dhātu-nāma-bhāga-pada-grahaṇāt tad-bhāgātirikta-bhede na bhavati yati-bhraṣṭatvam /*.

28 The caesura in question is in *pāda b* of *Ratnāvalī* 2.16: *caturbhir api sādhu sādhv: iti mukhaiḥ samaṃ vyāhṛtam*. My reason for classifying this as a 'Slip' caesura (*sādhv: iti*) rather than, as STEINER (ibid. 247–248) sees it, a truly abominable transgression (*sā:dhv iti*) is that all other *pṛthvī* lines in Harṣa's plays have tidy caesurae throughout (three regular lines in this stanza and four in *Ratnāvalī*

Table 3: Anomalous caesurae in Yaśodharman's inscription

	Stanza	*Text*
late	3	*sa śreyo-dhāmni samrāḍ: iti manu-**bharatā:larkka**-māndhātṛ-kalpe*
	4	*ye bhuktā gupta-nāthair: nna sakala **vasudhā:kkrānti**-dṛṣṭa-pratāpair*
	4	*nājñā hūṇādhipānāṃ: kṣitipati-**mukuṭā:ddhyāsinī** yān praviṣṭā*
	4	*vīryāvaskanna-rājñaḥ: sva-gṛha-**parisarā:vajñayā** yo bhunakti*
	5	*ā lauhityopakaṇṭhāt: tala-vana-**gahano:patyakād** ā mahendrād*
	6	*nīcais tenāpi yasya: praṇati-bhuja-**balā:varjjana**-kliṣṭa-mūrddhnā*
	7	*nirddeṣṭuṃ mārggam uccair: ddiva iva **sukṛto:pārjjitāyāḥ** sva-kīrtteḥ*
	7	*tenākalpānta-**kālā:vadhir** avanibhujā: śrī-yaśodharmmaṇāyaṃ*
early	6	*cūḍā-puṣpopahārair: mmihirakula-**nṛpeṇ:ārccitaṃ** pāda-yugmam*
	7	*stambhah stambhābhirāma-:sthira-bhuja-**parigheṇ:occhritiṃ** nāyito ttra*
slip	3	*rājasv anyeṣu **pāṅsuṣv: iva** kusuma-balir: nnābabhāse prayuktaḥ*

occur in the two metres in which Viśākhadatta also repeatedly employs obscured caesurae: *śārdūlavikrīḍita* and *sragdharā*. The single exception is a 'Late' caesura in a *śikhariṇī* stanza (*Nāgānanda* 3.8*d*, cited in Steiner 1997: 246). One further difference from Viśākhadatta's praxis is that Harṣa seems to use such caesurae at the first *yati* of the *sragdharā* metre at least as often as at the second (4 instances at the first, 2 instances at the second caesura in the Harṣa corpus as reported by Steiner).

The Mandasor pillar inscription of Yaśodharman[29] is a *praśasti* composed entirely in *sragdharā* (discounting a colophon consisting of a single *anuṣṭubh* verse) and, as expected, it yields a bounty of 'abominable' *yati*s. As shown in Table 3 above, in a mere seven stanzas one finds eight specimens of 'Late' caesura, two of the 'Early' type, and one 'Slip'. One of the 'Late' caesurae (in 7*c*) and the single 'Slip' is at the first *yati* point of the metre, while all others are at the second. There are in addition two instances (both in verse 1) of a caesura falling between a verbal prefix and the verb, an anomaly found in the Harṣa corpus but not in Viśākhadatta's play, and not involving vowel *saṃdhi* (hence not listed here).

It can thus be amply demonstrated that the caesura obscured by vowel *saṃdhi* is frequent enough in the works of at least some authors to be a consequence of something other than chance negligence or an idiosyncrasy of Viśākhadatta.

4.17). Furthermore, the examples Ghosh (1978) cites for the non-observance of the caesura in *pṛthvī* almost always involve a 'hard' transgression (i.e. the expected caesura falls inside a morpheme by all counts), whereas this example can be explained otherwise if we recognise *saṃdhi*-obscured caesurae as a special case.

29 Fleet 1888: 142–148.

A Tentative Explanation

STEINER (1997: 246–247) theorises that anomalous caesurae could have been realised as a pause in recitation without impeding listeners' understanding of the text, since they generally involve the separation of common and easy-to-grasp morphological elements such as prefixes, common enclitics or the final vowel of a two-syllable declensional ending (*-ena*, *-āya* or *-asya*). He also observes (ibid. 248–249) that anomalous caesurae occur more frequently in certain metres than in others. My findings provide the basis for making this observation more concrete: a particular type of anomalous caesura (namely that obscured by vocalic *saṃdhi*) occurs more frequently (or perhaps, solely) at specific points of specific metres. For this reason I am convinced that the key to understanding this not-so-abominable but definitely intriguing species of *yati* lies in its metrical context rather than in its morpho-syntactic or semantic/pragmatic environment.

A clue pointing this way can be found in the recitational tradition associated with classical poetry. To be sure, the way present-day *paṇḍit*s and other recipients of a traditional education chant Sanskrit verses may not have much in common with the performance techniques that were in vogue a millennium or two ago. However, it does appear that people from diverse linguistic and geographic backgrounds within India often recite a given classical metre using a remarkably similar tune (or chant intonation), which makes it at least plausible that their recitational practice goes back to a single tradition that is both antique and widely prevalent. Modern studies of such performance practices are sadly lacking, and my own knowledge of the field is deplorably deficient,[30] but it is my impression that most performers who chant a *śārdūlavikrīḍita* stanza prolong the syllable preceding the caesura in that metre, and typically elaborate it with a melisma (a slur, a legato shift to a different note in the prolonged syllable). Some performers do the same before the second caesura of *sragdharā*.[31] The slurring or prolongation if the pre-caesural syllable is not, however, ubiquitous: many metres involving caesurae are recited without this feature. Fortuitously, such prolongation (with or without a legato shift) provides an opportunity for the performer to resolve *saṃdhi* (see line B5 in Table 4 below for an illustration), and I think it is hardly an accident that caesurae which can only be realised in performance by restoring a vowel lost in *saṃdhi* occur precisely at such points.[32]

30 What little insight I do have, I owe to Ferenc Ruzsa who long ago shared with me and a few colleagues what he in turn had learned from Sadananda Das at his Spoken Sanskrit course in Heidelberg.

31 For audio examples of prolongation of the precaesural syllable with a melisma in *śārdūlavikrīḍita* (recited by Sadananda Das), see *subhāṣitas* 12–15 at the website DAS n.d. For prolongation (without a melisma) in both *śārdūlavikrīḍita* and *sragdharā* (recited by Ashwini Deo), see DEO n.d. Further illustrations are readily available on YouTube.

32 I must admit that I do not know whether a representative of any currently living recitational tradition would instinctively resolve *saṃdhi* at these points if asked to chant a stanza with such a caesura. This is relatively easy to test, and my prediction is that at least some of those proficient not only in recitation but also in Sanskrit grammar would indeed do so. A confirmation of this would

Even if we can take it as established that there is a connection between the slur in performance and the slurred caesura in a text, this is still but an interesting correlation rather than a causal relationship. I contend that the reason why both these phenomena occur at particular metrical positions and not at others must be sought in the deep structure of the metres of classical Sanskrit poetry.

A ground-breaking paper by Ashwini DEO (2007) has shown that these classical metres can in fact be viewed in terms of generative metrics as particular instantiations of foot-based schemata alike in nature to those of Western classical poetry. In the latter tradition poets selected a schema to follow in a composition, but retained some freedom to implement each foot in a variety of metrical formulae (employing for instance an arbitrary mixture of dactyls and spondees in the first four feet of a hexameter line). But according to Deo the Sanskrit tradition—presumably at a very early stage—solidified at the level of actual instantiations. This hypothesis is appealing in its elegance and intuitively convincing (to me at least). It does, admittedly, go counter to practically all traditional Sanskrit metrical theory, which never admits any flexibility in syllabo-quantitative metres[33] and usually describes metrical schemata as consisting of arbitrary units of three syllables (*gaṇas* or *trika*s) rather than of feet of specific moraic quantity but variable syllable count. It must also be admitted that the minutiae of the derivation of a particular classical metre from a certain foot-based schema remain unproven and for the most part unprovable. Nonetheless, various metrical oddities—including the obscured caesura—may serve as circumstantial evidence to substantiate Deo's hypothesis and may even be useful for reconstructing the schemata hidden behind classical metres.

As to the matter at hand, DEO (2007:102–103) describes two independent functions of the caesura in Sanskrit metres. One of these is to split up cola based on abstract schemata consisting of feet with a different mora quantity; the other indicates 'gaps' where a particular metrical position remains unfilled because the derivation of the metrical formula from the abstract schema involves catalectic (incomplete) or syncopated (off-beat) feet. Any particular caesura may fulfil either or both of these functions. Having described herself as 'a fluent participant' in the recitational tradition (ibid. 70), DEO also notes that in recitational practice the syllable preceding caesurae occurring at unfilled metrical positions is typically prolonged, whereas caesurae performing only the

---

supply further evidence for my hypothesis, though a negative finding would (conveniently) still not falsify my speculation, which pertains to reciters and poets a millennium or two ago.

33 With very few exceptions, such as the variation of heavy or light initial syllables in *upajāti* and *vaṃśamālā*. For exceptions in praxis (not, to my knowledge, provided for in theory), POLLOCK (1977: 210) cites some very interesting early *śārdūlavikrīḍita* stanzas from the *Lalitavistara*, in which the first (heavy) syllable of each line appears to alternate freely with two light syllables. This alternation seems to be an important piece of evidence in favour of the idea that classical syllabo-quantitative patterns are derived from earlier foot-based patterns. Another phenomenon that may be worth studying from this aspect is the occasional nine-syllable line in epic *anuṣṭubh*.

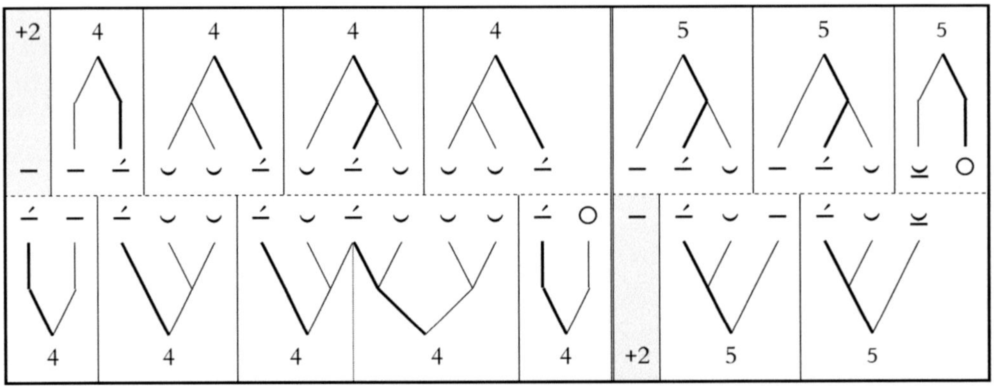

Figure 1: Two ways of parsing śārdūlavikrīḍita.

first function are realised as a pause which 'is brief and never alternates with [...] vowel lengthening' (ibid. 103).

It thus follows logically that the slurred caesurae observed in texts may correspond to empty metrical positions. What remains to be done is to show that such empty positions actually occur in the abstract schemata for the metres where we empirically find slurred caesurae. Deo presents reconstructed schemata for a number of popular Sanskrit metres, yet her proposed parses for *śārdūlavikrīḍita* or *sragdharā* do not include empty metrical positions. Nonetheless, Deo (ibid. 93) is the first to admit that 'there is no sure-fire solution' to the problem of determining whether the derivation of a classical Sanskrit metre involves syncopation or catalexis, since a particular metrical template may be the surface instantiation of several alternative foot-based schemata.[34] The schema which Deo (ibid. 109) proposes for *śārdūlavikrīḍita* consists of iambic feet, tetramoraic before the caesura and pentamoraic after it, with an extrametrical syllable (anacrusis) at the start and a truncated foot (catalexis) at the end. In order to account for the slurred caesura, I propose an alternative reconstruction based on trochaic feet. As in Deo's parsing, the feet are tetramoraic before and pentamoraic after the caesura; however, this schema involves anacrusis at the start of the *second* colon and catalexis at the end of the *first* colon, with the added twist of syncopation at the end of the third foot of the first colon.

These alternative ways of deriving the *śārdūlavikrīḍita* pattern from an abstract schema are illustrated in Figure 1, with the upper half showing Deo's iambic

34 I must, however, stress that this does not imply that a wide variety of arbitrary abstract schemata can be constructed for any given syllabo-quantitative formula. The constraints proposed in Deo's paper may be incorrect in some details, but in general they are plausible and seem to conform well to the observed variety of metrical templates. Staying within these constraints, the array of possible parsings for a given template is severely limited even with quirks like syncopation, anacrusis and catalexis.

schema and the lower half, my proposed trochaic schema. The metrical template (shown in the middle of the figure) is identical except for the hypothesised pauses—before the caesura in my version and at the end of the line in Deo's. The numerals at the top and bottom of the figure show the number of morae in each foot. Feet are separated by vertical lines, a double line indicating the caesura and a dotted line showing the boundary of feet joined by syncopation. Columns shaded in grey indicate extrametrical syllables. Between the numbers and the metrical formula, trees show how the feet branch into metrical positions, each of which may be instantiated as a syllable or subdivided into two syllables.[35] The thicker line in a tree indicates the strong metrical position and syllable (also indicated by an accent in the prosodic formula).

As far as I can tell, the two derivations are equally plausible in theory. In fact, the seven-syllable metrical phrase preceding the caesura of *śārdūlavikrīḍita* (– ⏑ – ⏑ ⏑ ⏑ –) is also found in the rare metre called *candravartma*, for which Deo (2007: 95–96) actually presents a syncopated trochaic derivation like mine here. It is in my opinion generally desirable to attempt to present identical schemata for identical sequences in the surface instantiations, so proposing this derivation for *śārdūlavikrīḍita* makes this application of the theory more parsimonious.

As for practice, Deo's iambic schema certainly fits a regular *śārdūlavikrīḍita* line (illustrated in line A1 of Table 4), but explains neither the melisma or prolongation observable in traditional performance (including Deo's own), nor the anomalous caesurae in poetic praxis. Lines A2 and A3 of Table 4 show the two ways in which a caesura obscured by vowel *saṃdhi* might be realised as a break in performance. The first mutilates a word, while the second is extremely awkward to pronounce.

In my alternative trochaic schema (illustrated in part B of Table 4), the catalectic last foot of the first colon provides the unfilled metrical position that is in my view the underlying cause of both the slurred extension in performance and the slurred caesura in the texts. Early in the prehistory of Sanskrit versification, an empty metrical position before a caesura may have been realised in performance as a bimoraic pause (line B1) or, alternatively, as a prolongation of the preceding syllable, which would thus have been recited as a tetramoraic melisma (line B2).

A *saṃdhi*-obscured *yati* at an unfilled metrical position realised through such a melisma (line B4) remains as abominable as one realised through a bimoraic pause (line B3). However, the extension of the precaesural syllable provides an opportunity for the resolution of *saṃdhi* by reciting two syllables in place of a single melismatic syllable (line B5). I hypothesise that this perceived opportunity opened up a way for poets to compose *śārdūlavikrīḍita* stanzas with a merged

35 I follow Deo (2007: 75–78) in the method of generating syllabic templates from the metrical schemata.

Table 4: Śārdūlavikrīḍita *schemata and examples*

In both parts of Table 4, columns represent feet in the abstract metrical schema. A shaded column indicates extrametrical syllables. Vertical lines show the boundaries of feet; a double line between columns marks the location of the caesura, while a dotted vertical line indicates feet joined because of syncopation. The text samples both come from verse 3.5 of the *Mudrārākṣasa.*

A. Schema in iambic feet

A	–	– –́	⏑ ⏑ –́	⏑ –́ ⏑	⏑ ⏑ –́	– –́ ⏑	– –́ ⏑	⏓ ○
A1	śrī	r labdha	prasare	va veśa	vanitā	duḥkhopa	caryā bhṛ	śam
A2	śū	rebhyo	’bhyadhikaṃ	bibhety u	pahasa	ty ekānta	bhīrūn a	ho
A3	śū	rebhyo	’bhyadhikaṃ	bibhety u	pahasaty	ekānta	bhīrūn a	ho

B. Schema in trochaic feet

B	–́ –	–́ ⏑ ⏑	–́ ⏑ –́	⏑ ⏑ ⏑	–́ ○	–	–́ ⏑ –	–́ ⏑ ⏓
B1	śrīr la	bdhaprasa	reva ve	śavani	tā _	duḥ	khopaca	ryā bhṛśam
B2	śrīr la	bdhaprasa	reva ve	śavani	tā$_{\bar{a}}$	duḥ	khopaca	ryā bhṛśam
B3	śūre	bhyo ’bhyadhi	kaṃ bibhe	ty upaha	sa _	ty e	kāntabhī	rūn aho
B4	śūre	bhyo ’bhyadhi	kaṃ bibhe	ty upaha	sa$_{a}$	ty e	kāntabhī	rūn aho
B5	śūre	bhyo ’bhyadhi	kaṃ bibhe	ty upaha	sat$_{i}$	e	kāntabhī	rūn aho

vowel at the caesura position and for audiences to appreciate such stanzas as metrically correct. If in such cases the reciter restores hiatus and does not realise the caesura as a pause,[36] then this sort of *yati* becomes an interesting variation rather than an abomination.

I believe that it should also be possible to reconstruct a schema for *sragdharā* in such a way that it accounts for the occurrence of slurred caesurae at the second *yati* position of this metre (or possibly at both positions). Despite some effort expended in this direction, I have not succeeded in producing such a derivation, and Deo (2007: 110) also notes that her own schema for *sragdharā* is problematic. For now I can only say that there may be more to *sragdharā* than meets the eye, and the reconstruction of its schema should be attempted with a view to other metres with related templates, such as *mandākrāntā, suvadanā* and *citralekhā.*

Conclusions

To reiterate the main points of my somewhat convoluted argument, there is a twilight zone between clear-cut cases of correct and transgressive caesurae

36 A momentary pause of no substantial moraic duration would be acceptable in the ‘Early’ and ‘Slip’ classes of obscured caesura, but it would fall inside the post-caesura word before the caesura in the ‘Late’ category (e.g. *pūrvasukṛta-ā:saṅgena*).

in Sanskrit syllabo-quantitative verse. This zone is inhabited, among others, by a type of *yati* where the word break is obscured by vowel *saṃdhi*. This type of *yati* is theoretically permitted by the core text on caesurae, and instances of it are found in a variety of poetic texts. An exact study of a small sample of texts and a general impression of a much larger body of literature definitely shows that the frequency distribution of the *saṃdhi*-obscured *yati* peaks in a narrow range of metrical templates rather than being even throughout the gamut of metres. This indicates that the employment of obscured word breaks is not something poets viewed as a transgression of the caesura (done out of clumsiness or to heighten the literary effect of a poem by omitting an expected break). It likewise indicates that we are not dealing with a general sort of licence that allows fuzzy caesurae. In both these cases, *saṃdhi*-obscured *yati*s would not differ markedly in frequency from metre to metre. Therefore there must be something special in the immediate metrical context of the caesurae that allow such slurs. I theorise, adopting the views of Deo (2007), that this something is an unfilled metrical position preceding the caesura in the abstract schema of the metrical template. The unfilled position may be realised in performance as a pause with measurable moraic duration, but it also may (and often is) be realised as a prolongation of the pre-caesural syllable. I believe, though this is probably impossible to prove, that it was this recitational practice of prolonging the pre-caesural syllable that allowed poets to employ covert caesurae in metres that possess such an unfilled position, but not in other metres. In performance, then, the caesura would have become overt when the reciter restored hiatus instead of prolonging the pre-caesural syllable.

It is in my opinion beyond doubt that the distribution of the obscured *yati* across metres is not random. Even if further research should render all my other claims invalid, this in itself is a considerable finding. It shows that there was a pattern or rule to versification which (at least some) classical Sanskrit poets, consciously or instinctively, employed in their works, but which was not articulated in any treatise on poetics, traditional or modern, that I am aware of.

If, in addition, I am correct in my assumption that the obscured caesura is linked to the slurred performance of pre-caesural syllables in certain metres, then this gives us an insight into the process of the composition of classical Sanskrit poetry. It is a concrete manifestation of the primarily aural (*śravya*) nature of this poetry inasmuch as it shows that poets, though they may have committed their products to writing immediately after or already in the course of the creative act, were influenced by performative practice. They probably hummed the lines they were working on and possibly not even noticed consciously that there was anything out of the ordinary with obscured caesurae in metres that allowed for the restoration of hiatus by co-opting a prolonged syllable to this purpose. One can even imagine a sort of coevolution in which the development of the obscured caesura on the textual side and the prolonged or melismatic chanting style on the performative side reciprocally catalysed one another.

Further, if I am right to believe that the root cause of the obscured caesura is an unfilled metrical position in the abstract metrical schema (which may be true or false regardless of whether I am correct about interaction with performance), then we have a practical implication of Deo's claims about the verity of such abstract schemata. The reasoning is admittedly a bit cyclical: if Deo is right, then her hypothesis can be used to explain the obscured *yati*, and if such an explanation works, then Deo's hypothesis is corroborated. However, it is very hard to conceive of concrete evidence for a metrical system that, if it ever existed, was already forgotten by the time of the earliest extant *śāstra*s dealing with classical metres. Therefore, even tenuous evidence merits consideration. There certainly remains much work to do on reconstructing schemata for at least the common classical metres. Such work should pay close attention to metrical phrases that occur with little or no variation in a number of established metres.[37] Should it turn out to be possible to (re)construct schemata that include an empty metrical position in all or most metres which exhibit the obscured caesura in poetical praxis, and to do so in such a way that these schemata are consistently applicable (*mutatis mutandis*) to other metres involving identical or related constituent phrases, this interconnection would be evidence in favour of both the general correctness of Deo's hypothesis and of my hypothesis about the origin of the obscured caesura.

The phenomenon of the obscured caesura should be examined in a much larger corpus of texts, first with an eye to see if it occurs with any regularity in any other metres beside *śārdūlavikrīḍita* and *sragdharā*. On the basis of my studies so far, *pṛthvī* and *hariṇī* may be good candidates for such metres, though the case of the former has the additional complication that it was not universally regarded to require a caesura. Another likely candidate is the *mandākrāntā*, which shares much of its metrical structure with *sragdharā* and which is frequently used (in addition to *śārdūlavikrīḍita* and *sragdharā*) in commentaries to illustrate cases of *saṃdhi*-obscured *yati*. Once the metres prone to exhibit obscured *yati*s are identified more securely, further study of a larger body of texts could be used to determine whether their use is quite universal or peculiar to certain authors, ages, regions or genres. The texts dealt with in this paper suggest that it was quite common in North India in early post-Gupta times. My cursory investigation of Kālidāsa's dramas, however, has yielded a mere two instances of obscured caesurae in the *Abhijñānaśākuntala*[38] and none in the poet's other plays. (There are, however, a number of instances in the

37 Deo has already explored what she calls 'the Sanskrit trochaic tetrameter' (Deo 2007: 72–73) and the *indravajrā* family (ibid. 82–89), but not the constituent phrases of the more elaborate 'courtly' metres. Velankar's compilation of '*vṛtta-ghaṭaka*s' (Velankar 1951) may be a good starting point for studying promiscuous metrical phrases, but needs to be extended to patterns with a shared foot structure.

38 Verses 1.18 and 1.32 in Kanjilal 1980. Neither of these is a *śārdūlavikrīḍita* or *sragdharā* verse, but both involve the separation of a prefix from a stem. Such separation occurs elsewhere in Kālidāsa's plays in contexts not involving vowel *saṃdhi*, so this is probably a phenomenon quite distinct from the case of the abominable *yati*.

mandākrāntā metre in the *Meghadūta*, some of which are even cited in commentaries as examples of the phenomenon.) Obscured caesurae also seem to be uncommon, though not unheard of, in imperial Gupta epigraphs.[39] It remains to be seen whether this type of *yati* is more or less frequent in geographically and temporally more distant texts. A larger dataset may also shed light on whether the three varieties of obscured caesura behave identically or in different ways—perhaps even give meaning to the proviso '*kvacid eva*' for the *parādivat* variety. Another direction for further research would be to examine whether the slurring of the *yati* ever occurs at the ends of odd *pādas*, and if it does, whether it does so in a systematic way.[40]

References

ANTANI, V. J. (1922). The date of the Mudrā-Rākshasa. *Indian Antiquary*, 51: 49–51.

APTE, V. S. (1957–59). *The practical Sanskrit-English dictionary* (3 vols.) Poona: Prasad Prakashan.

BALOGH, D. (2015a). Ördög úr esete a cifra cezúrákkal avagy a szanszkrit időmértékes verselés sormetszetei Viśākhadatta költészetében'. [Strange Caesurae in Sanskrit Metrical Verse: A case study in Viśākhadatta's poetry]. In Kakas, B. & Szilágyi, Z. (Eds.), Kéklő hegyek alatt lótuszok tava – Tanulmányok Bethlenfalvy Géza tiszteletére [Lotus Lake Under Blue Mountains – Essays in Honour of Géza Bethlenfalvy], (pp. 25–43). Budapest: L'Harmattan.

—. (2015b). *A Textual and Intertextual Study of the Mudrārākṣasa* (Unpublished doctoral dissertation). Eötvös Loránd University, Budapest, Hungary. Retrieved from http://doktori.btk.elte.hu/lingv/baloghdaniel/diss.pdf.

DAS, S. (n.d.). Recited Subhashita files. *Devavānī*. Retrieved from http://www.devavani.org/hablado2eng.html (last accessed September 2016)

DEO, A. (n.d.). Classical Sanskrit meters. Retrieved from http://pantheon.yale.edu/~asd49/meters.html.

39 For instance, verses 5 and 8 of the Allahabad inscription of Samudragupta (FLEET 1888: 6, line 9, *amanuja-sadṛśāny: adbhuta°* and line 16, *kavi-mati-vibhavo:tsāraṇaṃ*), verse 1 of the Bilsad pillar inscription of Kumāragupta I (FLEET 1888: 44, line 10, *sphaṭika-maṇi-dalā:bhāsa-gaurāṃ*), and verses 1 and 3 of the Kahaum Pillar of (the time of) Skandagupta (FLEET 1888: 67, line 4, *varṣe ttrinśad-daśaiko: ttaraka-śatatame* and line 12, *giri-vara-śikharā:gropamaḥ kīrtti-karttā*). All of these specimens are in *sragdharā*, and all but one at the second caesura of that metre.

40 The *Mudrārākṣasa* has just a single such instance, found in 5.3, a *śikhariṇī* stanza whose quarter *c* ends with a 'Slip', *bahu-prāpita-phalety / aho*. I have heard verses of this metre recited with a legato extension of the last syllable, and DEO's derivation (2007: 106–107) of the formula involves catalexis in the last foot, so the finding, though isolated, fits the hypothesis proposed in this paper. Commentators' illustrations of *saṃdhi*-obscured line breaks (lumped in with caesurae under the umbrella term *yati*) also include stanzas in *anuṣṭubh* (Halāyudha on *Chandaḥsūtra*, KEDĀRANĀTH 1938: 102), *upajāti* (Halāyudha on *Chandaḥsūtra*, KEDĀRANĀTH 1938: 102; Sulhaṇa on *Vṛttaratnākara*, SHARMA et al. 1969: 28), *mālinī* (Sulhaṇa on *Vṛttaratnākara*, SHARMA et al. 1969: 28) and *śārdūlavikrīḍita* (Somacandra on *Vṛttaratnākara*, SHARMA et al. 1969: 31).

—. (2007). The metrical organization of Classical Sanskrit verse. *Journal of Linguistics, 43*(1): 63–114.

DIMITROV, D. (2011). *Śabdālaṃkāradoṣavibhāga. Die Unterscheidung der Lautfiguren und der Fehler.* Wiesbaden: Harrasowitz.

FLEET, J. F. (1888). *Inscriptions of the early Gupta kings and their successors* (Corpus Inscriptionum Indicarum, vol. 3) Calcutta: Government Press.

GHOSH, A. (1978). Caesura in Pṛthvī metre. *Annals of the Bhandarkar Oriental Institute, 58/59*, 627–634.

HILLEBRANDT, A. (Ed). (1912). *Mudrārākṣasa by Viśākhadatta. Edited from mss. and provided with an index of all Prākrit words.* Breslau: Marcus.

JHA, B. (Ed.). (1971). *Kāvyālaṅkāra Sūtra of Āchārya Vāmana.* Benares: Chowkhamba Sanskrit Series Office.

KANJILAL, D. K. (Ed.). (1980). *A reconstruction of the Abhijñānaśākuntalam.* Calcutta: Sanskrit College.

KEDĀRANĀTH (Ed.). (1938). *The Chhandas Śāstra by Śrī Piṅgalanāga: With the commentary Mṛitasañjīvanī by Śrī Halāyudha Bhaṭṭa.* Bombay: Nirṇaya Sāgar Press.

KOSAMBI, D. D. (Rd.). (1948). *The epigrams attributed to Bhartrhari, including the Three Centuries.* Bombay: Bharatiya Vidya Bhavan.

POLLOCK, S. (1977). *Aspects of versification in Sanskrit lyric poetry.* New Haven, CT: Americal Oriental Society.

PRINCE, Alan. (1989). Metrical forms. In: Kiparsky, P. & Youmans, G. (Eds.), *Rhythm and meter* (pp. 45–80). San Diego: Academic Press.

SASTRI, C. S. R. (Ed). (1956). *Kāvyālaṅkāra of Bhāmaha, vol. 1., paricchedas 1 to 6.* Madras: Sri Balamanorama Press.

SHARMA, A., DESHPANDE, K. & PADHYE, D. G. (Eds.). (1969). *Vrttaratnakara of Sri Kedara Bhatta with four commentaries.* Hyderabad: Osmania University.

STEINER, R. (1997). *Untersuchungen zu Harṣadevas Nāgānanda und zum Indischen Schauspiel.* Swisttal-Odendorf: Indica et Tibetica.

VELANKAR, H. D. (1949). *Jayadāman (A collection of ancient texts on Sanskrit prosody and a classified list of Sanskrit metres with an alphabetical index).* Bombay: Haritosha Samiti.

—. (1951). The Vṛtta-Ghaṭakas. *Journal of the Bombay Branch of the Royal Asiatic Society (New Series), 26*, 150–157.

WEBER, A. (1863). *Ueber die Metrik der Inder.* Berlin: Harrwitz und Gossmann.

What do Sanskrit Adpositions Really Do and What Do They Mean? The Analysis of Prati

Małgorzata Sulich-Cowley

1 Introduction

The classification of parts of speech in Sanskrit grammatical tradition differs slightly from that adopted in Western linguistics. Sanskrit grammarians distinguished four main parts of speech (*padajāta*, lit. 'classes of words'): noun (*nāma*), verb (*ākhyāta*), particle (*nipāta*) and verbal prefix (*upasarga*). This classification was already presented and discussed in Yāska's *Nirukta* in the fifth century BCE. This is not to say that Sanskrit grammarians did not recognise formations such as adjectives (which were usually called *viśeṣaṇa*) or adverbs (which were often considered stems with fixed ending, e.g., accusative, instrumental or ablative singular). They were not, however, characterised by independent structural properties; they shared them with nominal stems and therefore were not enlisted as parts of speech. It might seem interesting that adverbs are not a part of this classification while verbal prefixes are, particularly in view of the fact that the latter are often derived from the former, which precede them in historical development. However, one has to remember that *upasarga*s do not express case relations in Sanskrit; they are for the most part used to express adverbial meanings.[1]

There is no doubt as to whether noun and verb are meaningful units. In later grammatical literature we find discussions regarding their precise semantic value, but they definitely are meaning-carriers. The *upasargas* and *nipātas*, on the other hand, were rather problematic. The issue concerned not only their semantic value, but also whether they possess any meaning in the first place. In the present article I will present the analysis of the adposition *prati* to determine its actual semantic domain, according to Sanskrit grammarians, and how—and to what extent—it influences the verbal roots it occurs with. I will also introduce the standpoint of later philosopher-grammarians on the issue.

1 Nir. 1.66.

2 Terminology

For the purposes of this article, I was aiming to find one term that could be used collectively for all the terms that Pāṇini uses. The term *upasarga* is usually translated as 'preverb' because, according to the Sanskrit grammatical tradition, it is an element connected with an action and attached to a verbal root. At the same time, the same group of words, though designated as *karmapravacanīya*, can also be used separately as postpositions. If we decide to use one term to describe both *upasargas* and *karmapravacanīyas*, which I find prudent in the present article, the term 'adposition' seems appropriate. It is the only term that encompasses the different categories that are assigned to such elements by Sanskrit grammarians. As we will see, most of these elements are basically verbal prefixes, but they also function as postpositions and they occur in nominal compounds. We do not find typical prepositions in Sanskrit. I also occasionally use the term 'verbal prefix' when reference is made to *upasargas* only.

3 Grammatical analysis

Before we look into the particular case of the adposition *prati*, it is worth presenting the views of the two earliest grammarians whose work has come down to us: those of Yāska and Pāṇini on the classification of parts of speech in general, and adpositions in particular. With respect to the latter, Yāska, being the author of the first etymological treatise in India, concentrates on the issue of the meaningfulness of adpositions, while Pāṇini describes mostly their syntactical features.

3.1 *Yāska's* Nirukta

So what does the Sanskrit tradition say about *upasargas*? As mentioned above, Sanskrit grammarians did not doubt that nouns and verbs were meaning-carriers. The issue of their precise semantic value was discussed extensively but the basic premise was never questioned. The situation with *upasargas*, on the other hand, was not that clear. In the *Nirukta*, Yāska presents two viewpoints regarding the meaning of verbal prefixes. He says:

> *na nirbaddhā upasargā arthān nirāhur iti śākaṭayanaḥ / nāmākhyātayos tu karmopasaṃyogadyotakā bhavanti / uccāvacāḥ padārthā bhavantīti gārgyāḥ / tad ya eṣu padārthaḥ prāhur ime taṃ nāmākhyātayor arthavikaraṇam /*
>
> 'Unconnected prepositions', says Śākaṭāyana, 'have no meaning, but only express a subordinate sense of nouns and verbs.' 'They have various meanings', says Gārgya, 'hence whatever their meaning may be, they express that

meaning (which brings about) modification in the sense of the noun and the verb.' (Trans. SARUP 1921–27.)[2]

As Yāska proceeds with enlisting the verbal prefixes along with their respective meanings, one can assume that he agrees with Gārgya and actually thinks that, even unconnected,[3] the *upasargas* possess their own, individual semantic domains. As I will try to show based on the example of *prati*, this semantic domain is not really as obvious and simple as Yāska would have us believe. Most of the verbal prefixes he combines in pairs with opposite meanings. Thus he finds that *prati* is the opposite of *abhi*:

abhi ity ābhimukhyam / prati ity etasya prātilomyam /

Abhi [means] 'towards'; *prati* is its antithesis. (Trans. SARUP 1921–27.)[4]

According to Yāska, then, the basic meaning of *prati* would be 'against, in opposition to, away from'. In other words, it would express the reverse effect, contradiction. From Yāska's work we can also deduce that he did not assign one separate meaning to every single *upasarga*; there are cases of two words expressing the same meaning and, as there is no other reference given, one could assume that they are often synonymous. This is also the case in Pāṇini's *Aṣṭādhyāyī*, where some verbal prefixes can be used in the same meaning, or perhaps it is better to say that they elicit the same meaning from the verb they precede; this situation also occurs with such *upasargas* that would not normally be considered synonymous.

3.2 *Pāṇini's* Aṣṭādhyāyī

Pāṇini lists the adpositions under several headings in the *Aṣṭādhyāyī*. They all appear in the so-called *ekasaṃjñā* section, beginning with the *sūtra* A. 1.4.1 *ākaḍarād ekā saṃjñā* ('[In the section beginning with this *sūtra*] and ending with A. 2.2.38 only one technical term applies [to a given item]').[5] In this section,

2 Nir. 2.29.14–16.

3 KAHRS (2012:116–120) analyses Yāska's term *nirbaddha*, translated as 'unconnected' by many researchers and commentators, and shows the problems arising from such a translation. Given that the *Nirukta* focuses on Vedic Sanskrit, the separate character of *upasargas* can be explained. KAHRS proposes to translate *na nirbaddhā upasargā arthān nirāhur iti śākaṭayanaḥ* in the following manner: '*upasargas* which are unconnected (to nouns and verbs) do not express meanings, according to Śākaṭāyana.' KAHRS translates the following verse, *nāmākhyātayos tu karmopasaṃyogadyotakā bhavanti*, 'But they indicate (*dyotakā bhavanti*) that a noun or a verb has a specific connection with an action.' This leads him to the interesting conclusion that Yāska and Śākaṭāyana actually had in mind the category Pāṇini called *karmapravacanīya*.

4 Nir. 2:29.17–18.

5 All the *sūtras* are given in the translation of KATRE 1989, with occasional modifications.

and in this section only, one linguistic unit gets one designation at a given time. This section is governed by the following *paribhāṣā*: *vipratiṣedhe paraṃ kāryam* ('When there is incompatibility [between two rules which can equally apply in the given domain,] what is provided by the subsequent rule should operate').[6] This further means that these designations are mutually exclusive, which creates a very interesting situation when it comes to the classification of parts of speech.

Western linguistics seems to strive to clearly classify parts of speech, even though these classifications are by no means devoid of problems and contradictions. That means that an element classified as, shall we say, a noun could be used in an expression to perform the function of an adjective. For example, the words 'horse' and 'race' are both nouns. However, in the compound 'horse race' the first element performs an adjectival function. In Pāṇini's *Aṣṭādhyāyī* the same element, in our case an adposition, can fall into different categories depending on its purpose. In other words, its categorisation always depends on the context; it does not seem to be analysed independently unlike other parts of speech, including the particles (*nipātas*). The following are different categories that can apply to *prati* according to Pāṇini. The main class in which adpositions are enlisted is the class of *nipātas*, commonly translated as 'particles'. Pāṇini does not define *nipātas* as a group, nor does he specify the meaning of individual adpositions as Yāska does.[7] The section begins with this rule:

A. 1.4.56 *prāg iśvarāt nipātaḥ*

[The technical term] *nipāta* ('particle') denotes elements specified in the subsequent rules [in the section beginning here] preceding [the rule] A. 1.4.97.

This *sūtra* determines the domain of particles in a very broad sense. The following two *sūtras* introduce the *gaṇas* (i.e., lists of nominal stems) enlisting the elements that fall into the category of *nipātas*. Only in A. 1.4.57 does Pāṇini specify that the elements in question are not supposed to signify objects (*asattva*):

A. 1.4.57 *cādayo 'sattve*

[The technical term *nipāta*] denotes members of the group beginning with *ca* ('and') when they do not signify things.

A. 1.4.58 *prādayaḥ*

[The technical term *nipāta*] denotes the class beginning with *pra* ('forth').

6 This is Pāṇini's rule A. 1.4.2.

7 It is, of course, acceptable that one might define the elements simply by enlisting them. What I mean by the lack of definition here is not so much that Pāṇini does not define them semantically, but that he does not even mention the syntactic function of *nipātas* as a group.

The next term that applies to adpositions is *upasarga*, defined by the author of the *Aṣṭādhyāyī* as an element connected with an action:

A. 1.4.59 *upasargāḥ kriyāyoge*

[The technical term] *upasarga* ('verbal prefix') denotes [the group of particles beginning with *pra*] when there is connection with an action.

In other words, *upasarga*s are proper verbal prefixes. They do not, however, necessarily have to be attached to verbal roots,[8] but they are semantically and syntactically connected with them. Further, Pāṇini introduces *gati*s:

A. 1.4.60 *gatiś ca*

[The technical term] *gati* denotes [the group of particles beginning with *pra* when there is connection with an action].

Both *upasarga*s and *gati*s are elements connected with an action, so the question naturally arises as to the need for their separate classification. The reason for this division is the fact that the term *gati* covers a wider range of elements, not only proper verbal prefixes but also a number of particles.

Another undefined term that Pāṇini uses is *karmapravacanīya*:

A. 1.4.83 *karmapravacanīyāḥ*

[Here begins the section on] *karmapravacanīya*s.

This *adhikāra sūtra* ('governing rule') opens a new section, in which the elements enlisted in the rule A. 1.4.58 mentioned above are designated with the term *karmapravacanīya*. This is also the only section in which Pāṇini decides to define the meanings of individual adpositions in a variety of contexts; unlike Yāska, he does not provide us with the basic meaning of the adpositions in question. It is therefore unclear whether he considers *upasarga*s meaningful units or not. The meanings included in the section on *karmapravacanīya*s, however, lead us to believe

8 Verbal prefixes functioned independently of verbs in the earliest Vedic literature. When we look closely at the wording of the rule A. 1.4.59, we notice that Pāṇini is very careful in its formulation. He does not say that an *upasarga* is attached to a verb, but merely that it is connected with an action. He also recognises the status of prefixes in Vedic literature in several rules: A. 1.4.81 *chandasi pare 'pi* ('In the Vedic literature [those *gati*s and *upasarga*s] also occur after [the verbal stem with relation to which they have the status of *gati* or *upasarga*]') and A. 1.4.82 *vyavahitāś ca* ('[In the Vedic literature *gati*s and *upasarga*s occur] separated [from the verbal stem with relation to which they have the status of *gati* or *upasarga*]').

that the change in the syntactic properties of adpositions results in them changing their semantic properties as well. This issue will be discussed in §8, describing Bhartṛhari's views on adpositions.

4 The adposition prati as a karmapravacanīya

In the section on *karmapravacanīya*s Pāṇini discusses the adposition *prati* in only two *sūtra*s and gives a variety of meanings in which it can be employed:

> A. 1.4.90 *lakṣanetthambhūtākhyānabhāgavīpsāsu pratiparyanavaḥ*
>
> [The technical term *karmapravacanīya* denotes the elements] *prati*, *pari* and *anu* when they are used to indicate a) characteristic (*lakṣaṇa*), b) statement of fact (*itthambhūtākhyāna*), c) division (*bhāga*) and d) repetition, succession (*vīpsā*);
>
> A. 1.4.92 *pratiḥ pratinidhipratidānayoḥ*
>
> [The technical term *karmapravacanīya* denotes the element] *prati* when it is used in the sense of 'representative' (*pratinidhi*) or 'exchange' (*pratidāna*).

When we take into account the meaning of *prati* given by Yāska, which is along the lines of 'against, in opposition to, away from', we notice that there are, at least theoretically, serious discrepancies between the semantic value assigned to *prati* by Yāska and Pāṇini. We can also notice that the second rule, namely A. 1.4.92, does not help us at all in our search for the basic meaning and semantic range of *prati* because it uses expressions containing the very adposition to explain it. One has to remember, however, that Pāṇini does not try to define the adpositions as such in these rules, but rather show in which semantic contexts they could be termed *karmapravacanīya*. It does not have to indicate that the meanings given by Yāska and Pāṇini are mutually exclusive; I think we could provisionally accept that the semantic values proposed by Pāṇini do not exclude the meaning given by Yāska, but rather extend it. The question remains, however, to what extent these additional meanings can be incorporated into the semantic domain of *prati*. Are they basic or secondary? And is *prati* really polysemic?

The following are the examples given by the Kāśikāvṛtti, the first complete commentary on Pāṇini's *Aṣṭādhyāyī*, dated to the seventh century CE:

A. 1.4.90

1) characteristic (*lakṣaṇa*): *vṛkṣaṃ prati vidyotate vidyut* ('lightning flashes on the tree')
2) statement of fact (*itthambhūtākhyāna*): *sādhur devadatto mātaraṃ prati* ('Devadatta is good to his mother')

3) division (*bhāga*): *yad atra māṃ prati syāt* ('whatever be my share in this')
4) repetition, succession (*vīpsā*): *vṛkṣaṃ vṛkṣaṃ prati siñcati* ('he waters every tree')

A. 1.4.92
5) representative (*pratinidhi*): *abhimanyur arjunataḥ prati* ('Abhimanyu is the representative of Arjuna')
6) exchange (*pratidāna*): *māṣān asmai tilebhyaḥ prati yacchati* ('he exchanges his *māṣā* beans for sesame seeds')

These examples under the two rules belonging to the *karmapravacanīya* section show that *prati* is used separately from the verbal root. In some of them (examples 2 and 5) there is no verb with which *prati* could potentially be connected. In examples 1 and 4, the verbs used, i.e., *vidyut* and *sic* respectively, do not appear in usage with this preverb at all, which naturally enforces its connection with a noun. As for the examples 3 and 6, we do in fact find the verbs *as* and *yam* with the preverb *prati*. In the case of *prati-yam,* the meaning would be similar to the one given above; MW offers these alternatives: 'to be equivalent to/worth as much, to grant or bestow perpetually, to return'.[9] The verb *as*, on the other hand, when preceded by the adposition *prati*, has the meaning 'to be equal to or a match for'[10] so it does make a difference whether we connect the adposition with a verb or a noun, as each construction renders a different meaning. The question remains whether Pāṇini's division into *upasarga*s and *karmapravacanīya*s, and consequently assigning them different syntactical functions, is based on semantic criteria. Alternatively, could syntactic constructions have formed the basis for semantic analysis?[11] Regardless of the answer, the result of such a classification is the grammatical behavior of adjacent stems. In the section assigning case endings to different *kāraka*s,[12] Pāṇini states:

A. 2.3.8 *karmapravacanīyayukte dvitīyā*

The second *sUP* triplet (accusative) is introduced [after an item] co-occurring with a *karmapravacanīya*.

9 MW: 669.

10 MW: 676.

11 This is, most probably, an unsolvable problem. We can analyse it thus: sometimes adpositions get the designation *karmapravacanīya*, from which follows a variety of meanings assigned to them in particular contexts. This designation also influences the grammatical behaviour of the nominal stems with which they are connected. On the other hand, this linguistic description is not merely a theoretical concept, but closely follows the usage of the Sanskrit language. This, in turn, would suggest that semantic (and syntactic) analysis of common Sanskrit phrases led Pāṇini to the said description.

12 The *kāraka*s are semantic-syntactic relations between the verb and nouns in a sentence. See §5.

It means that the very fact that an adposition gets the designation of *karmapravacanīya* enforces certain grammatical behaviour. In Pāṇini's system, adding the adposition that was termed *karmapravacanīya*, which in turn might be determined by the meaning in which it appears, determines the grammatical environment. As we can see in the examples 1 to 4 analysed above, all the nouns in direct relation to *prati* bear an accusative ending:

*vṛkṣa**ṃ** prati*
*mātara**ṃ** prati*
*mā**ṃ** prati*
*vṛkṣa**ṃ** vṛkṣa**ṃ** prati*

Rule A. 2.3.8 is a general statement. The *sūtra* A. 2.3.11 establishes that in the case of *prati*, the required case ending is the ablative. This happens only in one case, however, and reference is made directly to rule A. 1.4.92, analysed above:

A. 2.3.11 *pratinidhipratidāne ca yasmāt*

[The fifth *sUP* triplet is introduced after a nominal stem co-occurring with a *karmapravacanīya*] when signifying 'representative' (*pratinidhi*) or 'exchange' (*pratidāna*).

We can see this in examples 5 and 6:

*arjuna**taḥ** prati*
*tile**bhyaḥ** prati*

The above analysis tried to show that the classification of adpositions such as *prati* can be both semantic and functional. The elements enlisted in the *gaṇa prādi* are termed *upasarga* when used as verbal prefixes. On the other hand, they are termed *karmapravacanīya* when connected with a noun (which can be deduced for example from the aforementioned rule A. 2.3.8, but which is never explicitly stated) and also employed in particular meanings; as such they enforce certain grammatical operations. One of the outcomes of this division in classification is the prevention of the ṣ-substitution introduced by the rule A. 8.3.65.[13] This *sūtra* states

13 A. 8.3.65 *upasargāt sunotisuvatisyatistautistobhatisthāsenayasedhasicasañjasvañjām* ('[The retroflex ṣ comes in place of the sound s which is not at the end of a *pada*] of [the verbal roots] *ṣuÑ* ("to press out, extract", DhP III:1), *ṣū* ("to impel", DhP VI:115), *ṣo* ("to terminate", DhP IV:39), *ṣṭuÑ* ("to praise", DhP II:34), *ṣṭubhU* ("to chant, utter", DhP I:421), *ṣṭhā* ("to stand", DhP I:975), *senaya* ("to march with an army"), *ṣidhA* ("to go, move", DhP I:48), *ṣicA* ("to pour out", DhP VI:140), *ṣañjA* ("to attach", DhP I:1036) and *ṣvañjA* ("to embrace, clasp", DhP I:1025) after a prefix [containing the sounds *i* or *u* even with the intervention of the infix *aṬ* in close proximity].')

that the sound *s* is replaced by *ṣ* in a number of verbal roots when preceded by an *upasarga*. This clearly suggests that when an adposition performs other functions than that of an *upasarga* in a sentence with the listed verbs (that is, it might be a karmapravacanīya as in *nāgaraṃ prati senayati* 'he marches with an army towards the city'), the *ṣ*-substitution does not apply.

5 The adposition *prati* and valency

5.1 *The roles in a sentence*

I have examined above the adposition *prati* as a *karmapravacanīya*, but how does it affect verbal roots when this functions as an *upasarga*? I will analyse the role of *prati* in the change of valency of verbal stems. For Sanskrit grammarians, 'an action' expressed by a verbal root is the centre of the whole sentence. Pāṇini describes different roles that can be assigned to participants in this action (e.g., an agent, a recipient, a place etc.). These participants are called *kāraka*s and they form a semantic-syntactic category, which can be expressed by either nominal or verbal endings. The question arises then whether adpositions in any way influence the arguments that a certain verb requires. When describing the functions of different *kāraka*s in the *Aṣṭādhyāyī*, Pāṇini mentions the *upasarga prati* only twice, and in both cases the context is the same. The *sūtra*s in question are:

> A. 1.4.40 *pratyaṅbhyāṃ śruvaḥ pūrvasya kartā*
>
> [The technical term *sampradāna*] denotes the agent (*kartā*) of the previous act (of requesting) in relation to the verbal stem *śru* ('to listen, hear', DhP I: 989) co-occurring with prefixes *prati* or *ā* [and meaning 'to promise'].
>
> A. 1.4.41 *anupratigṛṇaś ca*
>
> [The technical term *sampradāna*] denotes also [the agent (*kartā*) of the previous act] (of uttering a praise) in relation to the verbal stem *gṝ* ('to announce, proclaim', DhP IX: 28) co-occurring with prefixes *anu* and *prati* [meaning 'answer or respond to a praise'].

The examples for these two rules are the following:

> A. 1.4.40 *devadattāya gāṃ pratiśṛṇoti* ('he promises a cow to Devadatta')
> A. 1.4.41 *hotre pratigṛṇāti* ('he responds to the *hotṛ*')

In neither of these two rules do we have the meaning of *prati* stated explicitly. As we can see, however, it influences the verbal root immensely. The action expressed by the verbal stem seems to be reversed. The addition of a prefix thus changes the meaning of the whole verb; it indicates a preceding action that is not directly expressed. In the first example, if a cow is promised to Devadatta, it suggests that it was asked for before. The whole context would therefore be the following:

mahyaṃ gāṃ dehi ('Give me the cow')
devadattāya gāṃ pratiśṛṇoti ('He promises to give the cow to Devadatta')

Thus Devadatta, being an agent of the previous action (i.e., asking) is turned into a recipient of the current action (i.e., promising). In the second example, the response to the *hotṛ* implies that he recited/chanted before. The context is the following:

hotā prathamaṃ śaṃsati ('First the *hotṛ* praises/chants')
hotre pratigṛṇāti ('He responds to the *hotṛ*')

Similarly, the *hotṛ*, being an agent of the previous action (i.e., chanting), becomes a recipient of the current action (i.e., responding). These recipients (*sampradāna*) are expressed by the dative case (*devadattāya* and *hotre* respectively). Although it might seem that Pāṇini merely records the usage of *prati* with the said verbs, it is important to notice how he formulates the rules. He points out that the addition of the preverb *prati* in these two cases influences the roles of participants in the action. The nouns appearing in the sentence do not just take another case ending but they begin to perform a different function. Therefore, I believe we can assume that the addition of the adposition reflects not only on the syntactic level of the sentence but also its semantic one.

These two rules present a very interesting case from the semantic point of view and, in my opinion, contribute massively to our search for the semantic core of *prati*. The use of *sampradāna* in the examples above shows that the action is directed towards Devadatta and *hotṛ* respectively. They are both the recipients of respective actions. That could indicate that the meaning of 'in the direction of' is hidden within the prefix *prati*. Yet at the same time, it means a certain response to a previous action. Therefore, using Yāska as a point of reference, we could say that it means both *ābhimukhya* ('towards') and its *prātilomya* ('opposition [of "towards"]').

5.2 *Verbal endings*

The addition of *prati* can also influence the type of endings added to a verbal stem, that is, whether we add *ātmanepada* or *parasmaipada* endings. The rule A. 1.3.57 *jñāśrusmṛdṛśāṃ sanaḥ*[14] establishes that when the verbal root *śru* ('to listen, hear'),

14 A. 1.3.57 *jñāśrusmṛdṛśāṃ sanaḥ* ('[The *ātmanepada* *l*-substitutes are introduced after the verbal stems] *jñā* ("to know", DhP IX: 36), *śru* ("to hear, listen", DhP I: 989), *smṛ* ("to remember", DhP I: 845) and *dṛś* ("to see", DhP I: 1057) when co-occurring with the desiderative marker *saN*.')

among others, is followed by the desiderative marker *saN*, we add the *ātmanepada* endings. There are a couple of exceptions to this rule, including the situation when this verb is preceded by the prefix *prati*. The addition of *prati* blocks *ātmanepada* and enforces *parasmaipada* endings.

> A. 1.3.59 *pratyāṅbhyāṃ śruvaḥ*
>
> [The *ātmanepada* *l*-substitutes are not] introduced after the verbal stem *śru* ('to hear, listen', DhP I: 989) co-occurring with [the prefixes] *prati* and *āṄ* [and the desiderative marker *saN*].

On the basis of this rule we derive the form *pratiśuśrūṣati* ('he wishes to promise'). The adposition *prati* is considered an *upasarga* for the purpose of this rule; A. 1.3.59 cannot apply if *prati* is considered a *karmapravacanīya*. In the *Nyāsa*,[15] the commentary on the *Kāśikāvṛtti*, we find a counterexample: *devadattaṃ prati śuśrūṣate* ('he desires to serve Devadatta'). In this case *prati* should be construed with the noun *devadatta*, not with the verb *śru*. Therefore, the application of the *ātmanepada* ending by A. 1.3.57 is not prohibited. The commentary says that *prati* should be interpreted in the meaning of *lakṣaṇa* ('characteristic') based on the *sūtra* A. 1.4.90. Interestingly, we could detect the meaning of 'in the direction of, towards' in this adposition as it shows what, or rather whom, the desire to serve is aimed at.

6 Compounds

In the section describing compounds in the *Aṣṭādhyāyī*, we also find a couple of *sūtras* dealing with *prati* and its potential meanings. The rule A. 2.1.9 *sup pratinā mātrārthe* ('An item [ending in] *sUP* triplets [combines with the indeclinable nominal *pada*] *prati* [to form an *avyayībhāva* compound] when it indicates "a bit".') allows us to create compounds such as *śākaprati* ('a little (quantity) of vegetables') or *sūpaprati* ('a little of soup, nothing but soup'). As the noun in these examples has its own distinct meaning, one has to assume that the meaning of 'a little' is conveyed by the adposition *prati* itself. The *Kāśikāvṛtti* gives the synonyms[16] of *mātrā* such as *bindu* ('a drop'), *stoka* ('a bit') or *alpa* ('a little'). Moreover, a compound is allowed only with *prati* used in this particular meaning. Consequently, in the sentence *vṛkṣaṃ prati vidyotate* ('lightning flashes in the direction of a tree'), the compound **vṛkṣaprati* is not possible due to semantic constraints.

A very interesting example is found in the rule A. 2.1.14 *lakṣaṇenābhipratyābhimukhye* ('[The indeclinable nominal *padas*] *abhi* and *prati*

15 KV 1.454.28.
16 KV 2.25.10.

[optionally combine] with [a syntactically connected nominal *pada*] denoting a characteristic mark [to form an *avyayībhāva* compound] when they denote a direction towards (*ābhimukhya*)'). The examples are the following:

> *pratyagni: agniṃ prati śalabhāḥ patanti* ('the moths are falling towards the fire')
> *abhyagni: agnim abhi śalabhāḥ patanti* ('id.').

This rule is directly connected with two *sūtra*s discussed above, namely A. 1.4.90, which assigns the meaning *lakṣaṇa* to *prati* when it is termed *karmapravacanīya*, and A. 2.3.8, which introduces an accusative after a nominal stem that is connected with a *karmapravacanīya*. Of particular interest here is the meaning *ābhimukhya* assigned to both *abhi* and *prati*. As we recall from the *Nirukta* (see **§3.1**), these two adpositions, although in Yāska's classification discussed as *upasarga*s, carry opposite meanings. Yāska claims that *abhi* is used in the meaning of *ābhimukhya* ('towards'), while *prati* is its contradiction. This *sūtra* indicates that the adposition *prati* can express a plethora of meanings that are often mutually exclusive and contradictory.

Both examples from the *samāsa* section show that the combination with the adposition *prati* is definitely semantically conditioned. Apart from the fact that it has great implications with respect to the general role of semantics in Pāṇini's treatise, it also shows a variety of meanings in which *prati* can be used.

7 Semantic analysis[17]

Given all the instances of semantic variations that seem to appear in *prati*, is it possible at all to determine its semantic core? Can we reduce somehow the meaning of this adposition, as the earliest Sanskrit grammarians seem to have done, or are we to accept that it is simply polysemic in nature? The following are all the meanings of the adposition *prati* that we have found in the earliest grammatical literature and we presented so far:

A. Yāska's *Nirukta*

1) opposition to *ābhimukhya*

17 It should be stressed at this point that all the examples analysed in the present article have come from grammatical literature. To an extent, therefore, they are purely theoretical. The analysis of other pieces of literature would definitely prove extremely useful in precisely determining the semantic domain of *prati* and other adpositions.

B. Pāṇini's *Aṣṭādhyāyī*

B1. *karmapravacanīya*

2) characteristic (*lakṣaṇa*) – *vṛkṣaṃ prati vidyotate vidyut*
3) statement of fact (*itthambhūtākhyāna*) – *sādhur devadatto mātaraṃ prati*
4) division (*bhāga*) – *yad atra māṃ prati syāt*
5) distributive function (*vīpsā*) – *vṛkṣaṃ vṛkṣaṃ prati siñcati*
6) representative (*pratinidhi*) – *abhimanyur arjunataḥ prati*
7) exchange (*pratidāna*) – *māṣān asmai tilebhyaḥ prati yacchati*

B2. *samāsa*

8) a bit (*mātrā*) – *sūpaprati*
9) direction towards (*ābhimukhya*) – *pratyagni / agniṃ prati śalabhāḥ patanti*

B3. *upasarga*

10) *devadattāya gāṃ pratiśṛṇoti*
11) *hotre pratigṛṇāti*

Such a variety of meanings would suggest that *prati* is in fact highly polysemic. If we take a closer look at the examples, however, we might find that this is not necessarily the case. In example 2, the tree becomes a mark (*lakṣaṇa*) to indicate where the lightning has struck, but the lightning was '**directed towards**' the tree. Example 3 shows that Devadatta is good '**towards**' his mother, similar to 4, where the share should be mine, that is, '**directed to me**'. Example 5 is problematic even for traditional commentators, who point out that the distributive meaning is actually expressed by the repetition of *vṛkṣa*, while *prati* is termed *karmapravacanīya* only for the sake of blocking the sound *ṣ* in *siñcati* (the situation discussed in **§4**). However, in my opinion we can still deduce the meaning of '**direction**' in this example. Examples 6 and 7 could express a meaning similar to the one presented in verbal formations *pratiśṛṇoti* and *pratigṛṇāti*, where they show the reverse of the action, i.e. the reverse of the direction. In other words, it could be broadly described as the opposition to *ābhimukhya*. Therefore, we could narrow down the meaning of *prati* to two options: *ābhimukhya* and its opposition. The only example that cannot be explained in such a way is example 8, which employs the meaning 'a little' for *prati* when used as the second member of a compound. Unfortunately, the commentaries do not give any additional information regarding these unique compounds. Therefore, I am not able to explain the reasons for such a completely unrelated meaning of *prati*. It is possible that the analysis of the actual usage of such compounds would shed more light on the issue. As far as the remaining examples are concerned, I would argue that whether the meaning expressed is *ābhimukhya* or its opposition, it is always '**direction towards**' something. In my opinion this is what *prati* expresses in the end—the movement towards, be it in response to another action or purely just the first action.

8 Philosophical analysis: Bhartṛhari's *Vākyapadīya*

It was mentioned above, while quoting Yāska's *Nirukta*, that there were two prevalent opinions in ancient India regarding the meaningfulness of *upasargas* (see **§3.1**). Some considered them expressive by themselves, while others thought that they only get their meaning in connection with nouns and verbs. This issue was also discussed in later philosophical literature, starting in the fifth century CE with Bhartṛhari, the author of the *Vākyapadīya*.

Firstly, it should be pointed out that Bhartṛhari distinguishes *upasargas* and *karmapravacanīyas*; he discusses their potential meaningfulness and their functions separately as if they were two distinct parts of speech.[18] The complete presentation of the issue of adpositions as given by Bhartṛhari is outside the scope of the present article, but an outline of his views will be given here. Bhartṛhari enumerates three views regarding the meaning of verbal prefixes:

> *sa vācako viśeṣāṇāṃ sambandhād dyotako 'pi vā /*
> *śaktyādhānāya dhātor vā sahakārī prayujyate //* VP 2.188
>
> This (i.e., an adposition) is expressive due to the relation of attributes (of an action). It is also possible for it to be a manifestor of it. Or it is used as a help to give power to the root (to express its meaning).[19]

Some might consider *upasargas* expressive, that is, independently meaningful (*vācaka*), which means that they possess the meaning the verbal root does not have; others might think that they merely illuminate a meaning that a root can have but does not convey (*dyotaka*). Finally, they might help in obtaining the required meaning, which means that it is conveyed by the combination of a verbal prefix and a verbal root. In the preceding *kārikā* the author explains what it means that verbal prefixes are *dyotaka*:

> *kvacit sambhavino bhedāḥ kevalair anidarśitāḥ /*
> *upasargeṇa sambandhe vyajyante praparādinā //* VP 2.187

18 VP(1):84 *evaṃ nāmākhyātopasarganipātalakṣaṇaṃ padacatuṣṭayaṃ vyākhyātam / atha karmapravacanīyāḥ pañcamaṃ padam abhyupagatam iti* [...]/ ('In this way the characteristics of four parts of speech, namely, a noun, a verb, a verbal prefix and a particle have been explained. Then the *karmapravacanīyas* are agreed to be the fifth.')

19 The translation is based on Subramania IYER's (VP(2)) with some modifications.

> Distinctions already existing in some (roots) but not expressed separately (by them) are brought out when they come into contact with a preverb like *pra* and *parā*.

This is the view held by Bhartṛhari, even though he discusses others as well: *upasarga*s are not meaningful by themselves; they do not express (*vācaka*) a separate meaning that would add to the semantic value of the verbal root. They do, however, help to illuminate the meaning that is already present in the verbal root. According to this view, therefore, all verbs are polysemic, and the variety of meanings expressed by the combination of a root with a prefix is hidden within the root itself.

The elements termed *karmapravacanīya*s, on the other hand, perform a completely different function for Bhartṛhari. They define the relation created by an action that often disappears. Indirectly therefore, *karmapravacanīya*s are also connected with an action, just an action that is no longer mentioned in a sentence. He introduces them thus:

> *janayitvā kriyā kācit sambandhaṃ vinivartate* /
> *śrūyamāṇe kriyāśabde sambandho jāyate kvacit* // VP II.197
>
> Sometimes an action creates a relation and disappears (that is, it is not mentioned). Sometimes, a relation is produced while the verb is actually heard.

He further specifies:

> *sa copajātaḥ sambandho vinivṛtte kriyāpade* /
> *karmapravacanīyena tatra tatra niyamyate* // VP II.199
>
> When the verb is not mentioned, a relation created by it is delimited in some places by the postposition.[20]

Subramania Iyer explains[21] this relation with the help of the example mentioned above, namely, *vṛkṣaṃ prati vidyotate vidyut* ('lightning flashes on the tree'). There are a couple of actions involved here: the action of flashing (mentioned by the verb *vidyotate*) and the action of aiming (not mentioned but implied). The tree is the aim of the flashing. According to Bhartṛhari, what the postposition *prati* specifies is the relation occurring between the action of aiming and the aim itself, and the relation in question is characterised as *lakṣya-lakṣaṇa-bhāva*. We know

20 Kahrs (2012:112) proposes a different translation: 'And this secondarily (*upa*-) produced relation—inasmuch as the word denoting the action has disappeared—is determined in this and that instance by a *karmapravacanīya* [which *has* expressed an action: *karma proktavantaḥ*].'

21 Probably based on the *Vṛtti*, VP(2):86.

that there is the relation because of the accusative ending after *vṛkṣa*, and this relation is merely specified by the *karmapravacanīya*. Kahrs quotes Puṇyarāja's commentary on this verse (Kahrs 2012:113): '[...] it [= the relation] is determined by a *karmapravacanīya*; that is to say, the particular relation is understood through the *karmapravacanīya*. (And) for that very reason they have expressed an action; and (now) they indicate/co-signify [*dyotayanti*] a specific relation created by an action, and so they are called *karmapravacanīyas*.' This brings us to the final verse summarising Bhartṛhari's view on the adpositions termed *karmapravacanīyas*:

> *kriyāyā dyotako nāyaṃ sambandhasya na vācakaḥ /*
> *nāpi kriyāpdākṣepī sambandhasya tu bhedakaḥ //* VP 2.204
>
> It is not a co-signifier/illuminator of an action, nor does it (directly) express a relation, nor does it hint at (an unexpressed) word denoting an action. It specifies (the nature of) the relation.

This particular nature or function of *karmapravacanīyas*, namely specifying the relation, makes them the fifth class of words—the view that is mentioned in the *Vṛtti*.[22]

The solutions proposed by Bhartṛhari raise a lot of questions that go beyond the semantics of adpositions. The author of the *Vākyapadīya* does not seem to explain, for example, how different verbal prefixes are able to bring about particular meanings from the verbal roots they attach themselves to. All that the author of the *Vākyapadīya* seems to be saying[23] is that both *upasargas* and *karmapravacanīyas* contribute to the meaning of the surrounding words and the whole sentence, while remaining meaningless themselves. The question that is worth investigating is whether the classification of parts of speech proposed by Sanskrit grammarians and philosophers could not, in fact, partially be considered the classification of parts of a sentence. The usage and purpose of both *upasargas* and *karmapravacanīyas* described by Indian grammarians seems to indicate this.

9 Conclusion

The above analysis of the adposition *prati* leads to two conclusions. Firstly, we have to notice that the approach to adpositions and their meaningfulness evolved over the centuries. Yāska in his *Nirukta* assigns different meanings to individual verbal

22 VP(1):240 [...] *etasmāc ca vṛttibhedāt pañcamaṃ padajātaṃ karmapravacanīyāḥ kaiścid ācāryāḥ pratijñāyante /* ('And thus, because of this special function, *karmapravacanīyas* are considered a fifth class of words by some teachers.' Trans. Kahrs 2012.)

23 This analysis of Bhartṛhari's *Vākyapadīya* is preliminary. Therefore the conclusions cannot be treated as final by any means.

prefixes (*upasarga*), and although he presents two views regarding their semantic value, or the lack thereof, we can still assume that he himself considered the *upasarga*s at least partially meaning-carriers. It is impossible, in my opinion, to state with certainty what Pāṇini's position on the semantic value of adpositions was. In the section dealing with *karmapravacanīya*s he does prescribe elements used in certain meanings, but that does not necessarily mean that he considered them meaningful by themselves; it might only indicate their usage in particular contexts. Bhartṛhari, on the other hand, most definitely does not consider adpositions—either in the function of *upasarga*s or *karmapravacanīya*s—meaningful by themselves. They play a significant role in bringing about the meaning inherent in a verbal root or indicating the relation between two elements in a sentence, but cannot be considered meaning-carriers in the same way nouns and verbs are. We observe, therefore, a shift in the approach of Sanskrit grammarians and philosophers to adpositions. They evolved from a part of speech that could potentially have an independent semantic value, to one that should not be considered independently at all and should always be analysed with respect to verbs or nouns, meaningless by itself.

Secondly, if we assume, in contrast to the Sanskrit grammatical tradition, that adpositions are actually meaningful elements, we should be able to distinguish their semantic core. Based on the examples found in grammatical literature, we have determined that, regardless of the variety of contexts in which *prati* appears, there is a common meaning in almost all of them. I believe that we can safely say that in most cases *prati* means, or helps bring about the meaning, 'in the direction of'. Thus in Yāska's terms, contrary to his own words, it would mean *ābhimukhya*, be it the direction of an action or the response to a previous action.

References

A = *Aṣṭādhyāyī of Pāṇini*:

- Katre, S. M. (Trans.). (1989). *The Aṣṭādhyāyī of Pāṇini*. New Delhi: Motilal Banarsidass.
- Vasu, Ś. C. (Ed. & Trans.). (1997). *The Aṣṭādhyāyī of Pāṇini* (2 vols.). New Delhi: Motilal Banarsidass. (Original work published 1891.)
- Sharma, R. N. (Trans.). (2002). *The Aṣṭādhyāyī of Pāṇini* (vols. 1–6). New Delhi: Munshiram Manoharlal. (Original work published 1987.)

Kahrs, E. (2012). Bhartṛhari and the tradition: *Karmapravacanīya*. In Voegeli, F., Eltschinger, V., Feller, D., Candotti, M. P., Diaconescu, B. & Kulkarni, M. (Eds.), *Devadattīyam Johannes Bronkhorst felicitation volume* (pp. 107–122). Bern: Peter Lang.

KV = Miśra, S. (Ed.). (1985). *Kāśikāvṛtti of Jayāditya-Vāmana along with commentaries Vivaraṇapañcikā-Nyāsa of Jinendrabuddhi and Padamañjarī of Haradatta Miśra* (vols. 1–6). Varanasi: Ratna Publications. [References are to volume, page and line.]

MW = Monier-Williams, M. (1999). *A Sanskrit-English dictionary.* New Delhi: Munshiram Manoharlal Publishers Pvt. Ltd. (Original work published 1870.)

Nir = Sarup, L. (Ed. & Trans.). (1998). *The Nighaṇṭu and the Nirukta: The oldest Indian treatise on etymology, philology and semantics.* New Delhi: Motilal Banarsidass. (Original work published 1920–1927.) [Reference is made to page and line.]

VP(1) = Subramania Iyer, K. A. (Ed.). (1983). *The Vākyapadīya of Bhartṛhari, kaṇḍa II, With the commentary of Puṇyarāja and the ancient Vṛtti.* New Delhi: Motilal Banarsidass.

VP(2) = Subramania Iyer, K. A. (Trans.). (1977). *The Vākyapadīya of Bhartṛhari, chapter II, English translation with exegetical notes.* New Delhi: Motilal Banarsidass.

Welcome with Open Arms: Iranian Loanwords in the Purāṇic Lexicon

Martina Palladino

In the *Sāmba-* and *Bhaviṣya-purāṇas*,[1] the story of Sāmba—Kṛṣṇa's son, who is cursed by his father and contracts leprosy—is narrated.[2] Sāmba asks the sun god to heal him, and the Sun, satisfied with his fasts and devotion, cures his leprosy. After that, Sāmba, bathing in the river Candrabhāgā, discovers an anthropomorphic statue of the Sun, carved out of the wood of the Kalpa Tree by the god Viśvakarman. He recovers the image and sets it up in Mitravana, but in Jambudvīpa there is no Brahman available to take care of the Sun's image and carry out its worship. Upon Sūrya's advice, Sāmba, having mounted Garuḍa, flies to Śākadvīpa to invite 18 families of Maga Brahmans, created by the Sun himself, to attend his worship. In Śākadvīpa Sāmba finds the society divided into four classes, those of the Maga, Maśaka, Mānasa and Mandaga, respectively.

In the Purāṇas we also find descriptions of the Magas and their ritual practices. These include many Mazdean elements: they wear the *avyaṅga-* (the sacred girdle); they have their 'reversed' Vedas; they must be provided with some ritual objects (*varśman-*, *patidāna-* and *pūrṇaika-*), wear a beard, and respect the five ritual times

1 All the Sanskrit texts come from the edition of STIETENCRON (1966). The manuscripts he used were as follows:

Sāmba-Purāṇa:

SP[I] = *Sāmba Purāṇa.* (1899). Bombay: Śrīveṅkaṭeśvara Press.

SP[II] = *Sāmba Purāṇa.* Ms. India Office Library, No. 3619.

Bhaviṣya-purāṇa (= BhP)*:*

Bhaviṣya Mahāpurāṇa. (1959). Bombay: Śrīveṅkaṭeśvara Press.

Bhaviṣya Mahāpurāṇa. (1897). Bombay: Śrīveṅkaṭeśvara Press.

AUFRECHT = Bhaviṣya Purāṇa Manuskript. In Aufrecht, T. (1859.) *Catalogus Codicum Manuscriptorum Postvedicorum quotquot in Bibliotheca Bodleiana adservantur* (pt. 1) (pp. 30–33). Oxford University.

2 For the comprehensive version of the legend, see the printed editions of the two Purāṇas and STIETENCRON 1966. There are also many articles dealing with the arrival of the Magas in India and the problem of their integration into Indian society: WEBER 1857; HODIVALA 1920; HAZRA 1958; HUMBACH 1978; SRIVASTAVA 1972; THAPAR 1984, 2000.

of the day (Av. *ratu-*, MP *gāh*); and they are not allowed to kill dogs. In *Bhaviṣya-Purāṇa* ('BhP') 1.139, the Magas are described as the descendants of Jaraśatra, the son of the Sun and the goddess Nikṣubhā; the name clearly recalls that of Zaraθuštra.

On the other hand, they exhibit other features that are clearly Hindu: they have *tilaka*s on their foreheads; they have to recite the *Gāyatrī* three times a day; they worship snakes; their social system is typically Indian; and as a matter of fact their Mit(h)raic/solar cult has deeply influenced the Saura branch of Hinduism. Finally, other elements, like the shaven head, the reddish-brown garment and the prohibition of agriculture can easily be ascribed to Buddhism.

In the *Bhaviṣya-Purāṇa* (1.140) we also find the Bhojakas; they are described as the descendants of the Magas, born from their union with the women of the Bhoja family. In the *Sāmba-Purāṇa* ('SP'), the term '*bhojaka*' has generally been replaced with '*yājaka*' (BhP 1.144.26; SP 27.23); '*bhojaka*' survives only in a few later passages, but in general the indiscriminate use of the names 'Maga' and 'Bhojaka' shows that there was probably no serious distinction between them.[3] Some scholars[4] have stated that the discrimination could be due to different periods of migration to India: the Magas probably arrived first, and the Bhojakas came later, claiming to become part of the Maga community; others believe that they were part of the same migratory wave, which then split into two different communities. Especially in the *Bhaviṣya-Purāṇa*, the elements of the ritual strictly related to Mazdean cults are attributed to the Bhojakas. In any case, there is no doubt that the Maga/Bhojaka religious environment was characterized by syncretism and the coexistence of different influences.

The Purāṇic texts affirm that the Magas came from the land of Śākadvīpa, the Iranian Sakastāna (identified with modern Sīstān).[5] Scholars generally agree[6] on their origin: they probably came to India together with the Śaka tribes during the first century CE, even if they cannot totally exclude the hypothesis that they moved to India in early Achaemenid times.[7] In any case, their cultural features are very similar to those of the Śakas, Kūṣānas and all the populations that lived in between India and Iran: their cults, basically Mazdean, had been enriched with Hellenistic

3 See HAZRA 1958, in particular p. 96.

4 See STIETENCRON 1966; HAZRA 1958; HUMBACH 1978; SRIVASTAVA 1972.

5 For references on this topic see DAFFINÀ 1967 and GNOLI 1967.

6 Many scholars have dealt with the hypothesis on the origin of the Magas: STIETENCRON 1966; HAZRA 1958; SCHEFTELOWITZ 1933; HUMBACH 1969 and 1978; and BISWAS 1949.

7 SRIVASTAVA (1972: 246) believes that the Magas should have come to India in the Achaemenid age because a cult needs time to be elaborated and accepted into a new society. For this reason, it is impossible that they would have come along with the Śaka tribes in the first centuries of our era and immediately found a place in the Brahmanical literature of the Purāṇas. HAZRA 1958 had already proposed the theory of their first migration to India in the early Achaemenid period, because they exhibit some features that can be connected to Old Persian and the Medo-Persian environment, starting with their name. See also CHATTOPADHYAYA 1950.

and Indian elements. Probably the Magas, while moving forth to India, progressively 'Hinduized' themselves; perhaps they also contributed to the development of the Saura cult, especially in relation to iconography. In the *Sāmba-* and *Bhaviṣya-Purāṇas*, when Sāmba finds the statue in the river Candrabhāgā, the text itself states that it is the first time that the Sun appears in an anthropomorphic form (SP 29.2–3); in SP 31.15–19, there is a description of the statue, which is evidently the product of a perfect combination of Iranian and Indian elements. The northern iconography of the sun god, characterized by a long garment, boots, the *avyaṅga* and sometimes a beard,[8] definitely recalls typical Kūṣāna dress. In the north of India in this period, the Sun is represented with the typical Iranian features just described; the Iranian influence, maybe even brought by the Magas themselves, deeply modified the elements of the Saura cult in the north, and testifies to the importance of their presence in India.

Varāhamihira, the famous astronomer of the sixth century CE, who himself was a Sun worshipper and probably a Maga, describes the calendar of the Maga Brahmans in the first chapter of his *Pañcasiddhāntikā*; it is undoubtedly based on the Zoroastrian one (cf. PANAINO 1996).

Finally, in 1879, A.F. WEBER published a late poem, the *Magavyakti* by Kṛṣṇadāsa Miśra (ca. sixteenth century), in which Maga families are listed and celebrated: some of the names of the families are clearly Indian, but others can be connected once again with Iranian culture.

Terminology

In the *Sāmba-* and *Bhaviṣya-Purāṇas* (but especially in the latter), we find numerous loanwords drawn from different Iranian languages: the four classes of Śākadvīpa, the ritual terminology and some proper names. Curiously, in these sections of the Purāṇic texts, even the common lexicon employed for describing some features of the Magas is quite unusual: rather than the 'classical' Sanskrit term, the Iranian one is preferred, which is adopted and 'Sanskritized'. The Iranian vocabulary comes from different strata of Iranian languages: we can clearly identify words that easily correspond to stems attested in Old Persian, Avestan, Middle Persian and even Bactrian, although we cannot establish *a priori* the precise linguistic varieties of the dialects through which the loanwords were introduced. Moreover, the loanwords are not exclusively Iranian: an example drawn from Greek represents the further confirmation of the cultural syncretism that characterizes the cult of the Maga Brahmans.

8 The beard is considered a characteristic feature of the Persians: even Kālidāsa, in *Raghuvaṃśa* 4.64, describes the bald bearded heads of the Persians and compares them to honeycombs with bees.

The four classes of Śākadvīpa

magāś ca maśakāś[9] *caiva mānasā*[10] *mandagās tathā* //
magā brāhmaṇabhūyiṣṭā maśakāḥ kṣatriyāḥ smṛtāḥ[11] // 30–73 //
vaiśyās tu mānasā[12] *jñeyāḥ śūdrās teṣāṃ tu maṃdagāḥ* //
na teṣāṃ saṃkaraḥ kaścid varṇāśramakṛtaḥ[13] *kvacit* // 31–74 // (SP 26 ~ BhP 1.139)

Maga (*brāhmaṇa*). These are the Brahmans of Śākadvīpa, priests of the Sun (EWA III, 376; KEWA II, 544). The term is related to the Iranian Magians, and is probably a 'Sanskritization' of OP *magu-* (MP *moγ*, Sogd. *mwγ*, NP *mōγ*), even if the shift of the thematization from *-u* to *-a* is not clear. '*Magu'* is also the title of the rebellious Gaumāta of Darius's Bīsūtūn inscription; in Herodotus, we find the loanword μάγος and the restitution of Ir. **magu-ǰati-* 'killing of the Magians', Gr. μαγο-φονία: Herodotus (3.79) narrates the massacre of the Magoi, when Darius restored his power after Gaumāta's usurpation. The importance of this episode leads some scholars[14] to postulate that the Magians at the Achaemenid court did not have exclusively sacerdotal duties, but that only a small part of them maintained a state of religious purity; the rest of the caste probably had political and administrative assignments. It is very difficult to think that Darius could have ordered the complete extermination of a sacerdotal group in a state of ritual purity.

In the Avesta we never find the corresponding term alone, but in a compound, the hapax legomenon *moγu.ṯbiš-* (*Yašt* 65.7), 'one who is inimical to the Magus', 'der die Magier, die Angehörigen des magischen Stammes, aus dem die Priester hervorgehen, befeindet' (Bartholomae 1961: 1109). Finally, the term can also be related to OIA *maghá-/maghávan-*, Av. *maga-/magavan-*.[15]

The term *magu-* itself is attested twice in the *Bhaviṣya-Purāṇa*: 1.140.32, pl. *magavas*; 1.140.47, *maguḥ*. It is never attested in the *Sāmba-Purāṇa*.

Maśaka (*kṣatriya*). Christensen (1933: 250) explained the name of the second class as being derived from **mas-saγata* < **mas-sakata* 'die große Sakenhorde'. Herodotus (1.215–216) describes the Μασσαγέται as a nomadic population, different from the Scythians. According to him, they possess huge quantities of gold and bronze, they practice promiscuity and cannibalism, and they worship the Sun, to whom they sacrifice horses (cf. Rosén 1987: 137). Scheftelowitz (1933: 316) connects the term with Sak. **masak* 'groß, vornehm', Av. *mas, masan.*

9 SP^I: *māmagāś*; SP^II: *māgadhāś*; BhP: *magagāś*; Aufrecht: *magasa.*
10 BhP: *gānagā*, var.: *mānasā.*
11 SP^I: *kṣatriyās tathā.*
12 BhP: *gānagā.*
13 BhP: *dharmāśrayakṛte.*
14 See for example Panaino (2011, in particular p. 359).
15 On the concept of *maga-/maghá-* see Gnoli (1965).

Mānasa (*vaiśya*). SCHEFTELOWITZ (1933: 316) provides this explanation: it comes from Ir. **māna-za* 'dem Hause entstammend', the literal translation of the Sanskrit word *vaiśya*, in which the Iranian -*z*- turns back into the Indian -*s*-.

Mandaga (*śūdra*). SCHEFTELOWITZ (1933: 316) associates the term with OP *bandaka-*, MIr. *bandag*, MPrth. *bndg*; MPrs. *bng* = *bannag*; Paz. *banda*; NP *bândâh*, 'servant, slave'. They are the class that received from Sāmba eight female slaves to become their wives, while the Magas had the women of the Bhoja family.

The names of the four classes are listed also in the *Agni-Purāṇa* (119.20–21); *Brāhma-Purāṇa.* (20.71-72); *Kūrma-Purāṇa* (1.48, 36–37); *Viṣṇu-Purāṇa* (2.4.69–70); *Varāha-Purāṇa* (177); and in the *Mahābhārata* (6.12.33).

Ritual objects and components of the ceremony

avyaṅga (*abhyaṅga*)

avyaṅgadhāriṇaḥ sarve[16] *vidhidṛṣṭena karmaṇā* / 35–78 / (SP 26 ~ BhP 1.139)
aher aṅgāt samutpanno
hy avyaṅgas tu tataḥ smṛtaḥ // 15b // (BhP 1.142)

This is the sacrificial belt of the Magas (BÖHTLINGK 1879: 133; EWA III, 17). The term is clearly the 'Sanskritization' of the Av. *aiβiiā̊ŋhana-*, the sacred belt of the Zoroastrians (BARTHOLOMAE 1961: 98).

A remark in the *Bhaviṣya-Purāṇa*, 'Because it is made of a part of the serpent, it is known as *avyaṅga*' (BhP 1.142.15b), recalls the para-etymology of the term: *a-vi-aṅga-* 'having non-incomplete limbs' (cf. *Kātyāyana-Śrautasūtra* 6.3.22), with privative *a-* and the particle *-vi-* that indicates separation.

This ritual object is frequently mentioned in the text and is the peculiar attribute of the Magas. The sun god wears it, and every worshipper has to wear it as well. It is also described in BhP 1.141 and 146: it could be of different lengths and is made of snakeskin. This is evidently in contrast with Zoroastrian orthodoxy, because snakes are considered the evil animals *par excellence*—connected with Aṇgra/Aŋra Maiiniu (MP Ahreman), the antagonist of Ahura Mazdā—and Zoroastrians have the duty to kill them. In any case, in Pārsī Zoroastrian orthodox literature we find an exception: the *Mār Nameh*,[17] 'Book of the Snake', in which the encounter with a snake could be considered a good omen.

In India, the serpent is widely worshipped, and figures like the Nāgas have great importance.

varśman

pūrṇaikaṃ[18] *dakṣiṇe pāṇau*

16 BhP: *-dhāriṇaś caiva.*
17 See MODI 1893 and NABARZ 2006.
18 BhP: *pūrṇaika.*

varśma vāmena dhārayan /
patidānena vadanaṃ
pracchādya niyataḥ śuciḥ / 59 / (BhP 1.139)

(Av. *barəsman-*.) This is the Av. *barəsman-*, Paz. *bar(ə)sum*, MP *barsom*: the sacred bundle of twigs used in the divine service (Bartholomae 1961: 947; Nyberg 1974: 44). The sacred twigs were probably taken from the *haoma* plant or the pomegranate; their number varies according to the ceremony being performed. Today brass or silver wires are used in place of twigs.

patidāna (> Av. *paiti.dāna-*). This is the Av. *paiti.dāna-*, a mouth-veil used by the priest for covering his mouth so as not to contaminate the sacred fire while he recites.

pūrnaika: This is an unknown ritual object; Hodivala (1820: 28) identifies it with a kind of tree, but it is more plausible to think of a one-armed (*-eka-*) object for pouring water or other liquids (*pūrṇa-*).

homa (= *sóma-*; > Av. *haoma-*). Av. *haoma-* (Bartholomae 1961: 1732), Skt. *sóma-*, is the name of the plant, twigs and juice of the Haoma. In the text we also find the ***parahoma-*** (Av. *parahaoma-*), the drink obtained from pressing *homa-*, fundamental to some parts of the Zoroastrian liturgy. It also corresponds to the name of the god Haoma/Soma.

Sacred texts ('reversed Vedas') and priests

Veda, **Viśvavada**, **Vidud** and **Aṅgirasa**

ta eva viparītās[19] *tu*
teṣāṃ vedāḥ prakīrtitāḥ /
vedo viśvavadaś caiva
vidud aṃgirasas tathā[20] // 37 // (BhP 1.140)

The sacred texts of the Magas, which probably correspond to the *Yasna*, *Visprad* (*Visperad*), *Vidēvdād* and *Nīrangistān*.

The scripts are related to the Avestan ones for logical reasons linked to the Zoroastrian canon; this connection was first suggested by A.F. Weber (1857: 105).

átharvan

na cātharvā jagannātha
brāhmaṇo nātra vidyate // 18 // (BhP 1.117.18b)

19 The employment of the term *viparīta-* is very curious: the Magas' Vedas are described as 'reversed', probably meaning that they are not the 'original' ones; in other passages of the text, it is specified that the Magas should be learned in the orthodox Vedas too. In *BhP* 1.140.35–36 it is stated that the 'reversed Vedas' were pronounced by Brahmā, who had pronounced those of the Brahmans as well.

20 BhP: *vedo viśvamadaś caiva vidvad vahnirasas tathā.*

(> Av. *āθauruuan-*, *aθaurun-*, *āθrauuan-*.) This is the fire-priest, the priest of Agni (BÖHTLINGK 1879: 28; KEWA I, 28; EWA I, 60). The Av. *āθauruuan-*, *aθaurun-*, *āθrauuan-*, MP *āsrōn* has a more general meaning: it is the general priest who undertakes his ritual functions (BARTHOLOMAE 1961: 65). In *Yašt* 13.88, Zarathuštra himself is celebrated as the first *aθaurun* (*paoiryāi aθaurune*) and honoured as *āθravan* (*Yašt* 13.94), while in the Gāthās he assumes the title of *zaotar*. The term is secondarily connected to **athar-* 'fire'.

Analysis of names

Mihira (> Baktr. μιιρο, Pahl. *mihr*, Av. *Miθra*, Skt. *Mitra*). The god Mithra, the Sun (EWA III, 406; KEWA II; NYBERG 1974: 132). In the *Sāmba-* and *Bhaviṣya-Purāṇa*s the Sun is generally called Mitra, but we also find four occurrences of Mihira (in the *Bhaviṣya-Purāṇa*: 1.78.51–53, 1.143.36–41, 1.71.3 and 1.139.33, of which only the first two have parallels in the *Sāmba-Purāṇa*, 9.1–3 and 36.36–41); they are both names of the god, but the second is probably derived from the 'Sanskritization' of Bactrian μιιρο (or μιορο, μιρο)—seen on the coins of the Kuṣāṇa king Kaniṣka (WEBER 1957: 104)—from Middle Persian *mihr-*. This name of the Sun, mentioned next to Mitra, probably indicates the Iranian concept of the god, the Avestan Mithra of the tenth *Yašt*.

Raśnu and **Saośra** ['Rājña': BhP 1.76.13b and 130.52b, written also 'Rājā' or 'Rājñā'; 'Srauṣa': SP^{I} 6.22a, 29.18b, written 'Stoṣa' in 16.8a, 'Toṣa' in SP^{I} 16.8b and 36.39; SP^{II} always 'Strauṣa'; BhP 1.76.13b, 'Śroṣa'.] (> Av. *rašnu* and *sraoša-*.) The Av. *rašnu-*, MP *rašn*, is the god of justice (BARTHOLOMAE 1961: 1516; NYBERG 1974: 167); the Av. *sraoša-*, MP *srōš* [*slwš*], is one of the *yazdān* and the god of obedience (BARTHOLOMAE 1961: 1634; NYBERG 1974: 179).

In the *Mihr Yašt*, these two figures are the attendants of Mithra on his morning crossing. Sraoša appears in vv. 41 and 100 of the *Yašt*, Rašnu in vv. 41, 79, 81, 100 and 126 (cf. GERSHEVITCH 1967).

Jaraśastra (Jataśastra, Jaraśabda)
tasmān mattaḥ[21] *samutpannas*
tava[22] *putro bhaviṣyati* //
jaraśastra[23] *iti khyāto*
vaṃśakīrtivivardhanaḥ // 43 // (BhP 1.139)

(> Zaraθuštra-.) This term is probably the Indian name of Zaraθuštra-; the etymology of the name is related to **zaraṇt-* 'old' (Ved. *járant-*) + *uštra-* 'camel' (BARTHOLOMAE 1961: 420; MAYRHOFER 1977: 416 – I/105).

---

21 AUFRECHT: *sa tu.*

22 BhP: *na ca.*

23 AUFRECHT: *jalagaṃvu.*

Other terms

sāramya

eṣa sāraś ca sāramyo[24] // 15a // (BhP 1.142)

(> Av. *zarənya-*.) This recalls Av. *zarənya-*, an adjective meaning 'golden' (Bartholomae 1961: 1683). Instead of the Sanskrit *sauvarṇa-*, *kāñcana-* or *rukmavat-*, the Iranian loanword is preferred.

āsura

hy āsuras tena saṃsmṛtaḥ // 9b // (BhP 1.142)

(> Av. *ahura-*.) In this context, this word is certainly connected to Av. *ahura-* 'lord' (Böhtlingk 1879: 195; KEWA I, 65; Bartholomae 1961: 285). This choice is very interesting, because the term *āsura-* directly refers to the Iranian type of deity (cf. Ahura Mazdā). In the later tradition of the Purāṇas, the *āsuras* have already been turned into demonic entities; probably the terms referring to the deities, *devá-/daēuua-* and *ásura-/ahura-*, were characterized by an amphipolarity[25] that the two cultures had developed in one direction or another, losing this double polarity. The choice of the term is particularly significant, because it reflects the intent to connect the Purāṇic text with the Iranian cultural environment.

heli

sa muktaḥ sarvapāpebhyo
yāti helisalokatām // 29 // (BhP. 1.74)

The choice of the very unusual term *heli-* (MW 1305; EWA III, 545)—clearly drawn from the Gr. ἥλιος and also attested in Sanskrit in the form *kheli-* —instead of the numerous other names of the Sun is very interesting. Greek loanwords confirm once again the religious syncretism that characterized the populations settled in the Indo-Scythian lands.

Conclusion

The massive presence of Iranian loanwords in the Purāṇic sections related to the Maga Brahmans underlines the connection between this class and the Iranian

24 Aufrecht: *sāramyā*, *BhP*: *sā ramyā*.

25 See Kellens 2010. In particular, Kellens writes: '[...] Tant les mots indiens que leurs équivalents iraniens ont conservé des traces plus ou moins accusées de leur caractère amphipolaire originel. Ces traces sont en tout cas suffisantes pour signifier que les deux domaines linguistiques ne se différencient pas par des inversions de polarité, mais par la perte progressive et parfois inverse de l'amphipolarité. [...] L'amphipolarité est un phénomène qui affecte un vaste secteur du vocabulaire culturel' (2010: 191).

cultural environment, in particular with the populations that settled in the lands between India and Iran. Many scholars have dealt with the names of the classes of Śākadvīpa, the 'reversed' sacred texts and the unusual Purāṇic lexicon, but nobody has systematically pointed out the multi-layered scenario that characterized the cultural environment of the Maga Brahmans; the analysis of vocabulary can potentially shed light on the controversial historical presence of this class in India throughout the ages. The links with many aspects of Iranian tradition could be a sign of the constant presence of this social group, perhaps since Achaemenid times, on Indian soil. HUMBACH (1978: 248) suggested that these loanwords could have been later additions drawn from some Pārsī Zoroastrians' teachings in India; this possibility cannot be excluded, especially because we are dealing with Purāṇic materials, which have been subjected to continuous additions. Nevertheless, the presence of these Iranian influences testifies to the importance of the relationship with Iranian culture and in a certain sense qualifies and legitimises the Magas within Indian society. They possess peculiar features, which raised them to the high rank of Brahmans, and in the meantime they contributed to the development of the Saura cult. Even if the Iranian terms are the product of later additions, there is no reason to doubt that those people really came from Indo-Scythian lands; their origin is testified not primarily by loanwords, but by deep-rooted evidence such as their calendar, based on the Zoroastrian one. In any case, their origin or pretended origin was the key factor in their arrival and acceptance in India, where they were celebrated as Brahmans.

Their peculiar cult, customs and language made their popularity grow, and they imposed themselves on Saura culture, especially in the sixth to seventh centuries. In turn, they were welcomed with open arms in Indian society, probably also due to some aspects of their common Indo-Iranian heritage, traits perceived as familiar by the Indians (starting from Mithraic solar cult).

Today in India we find communities of Śāka(l)dvīpīya Brahmans, mainly settled in Rājasthān and Bihār, who still base their religious practices on Sāmba legend and on the Magas' practices; they don't recognize Bhojakas as part of their background, but they relate themselves to the Purāṇas, to the Magas and to Iranian culture in order to define their own identity.

References

BARTHOLOMAE, C. (1961). *Altiranisches Wörterbuch*. Berlin: de Gruyter. (Original work published 1904.)

BISWAS, D. K. (1949). The Maga ancestry of Varāhamihira. *Indian Historical Quarterly, 25*(3), pp. 175–183.

BOYCE, M. (2011). ĀΘRAVAN-. In *Encyclopaedia Iranica* III/1 (pp. 16–17). Retrieved from http://www.iranicaonline.org/articles/atravan-priest. (Original work published 1987.)

Chattopadhyaya, S. (1950). *The Achaemenids in India.* Calcutta: Sarkhel.

Christensen, A. (1933). Die Iranier. In Götze, A. & Christensen, A. (Eds.), *Die Iranier, Kulturgeschichte des alten Orients* (vol. 3:1). Munich: Beck.

Daffinà, P. (1967). *L'immigrazione dei Saka nella Drangiana.* Rome: Istituto italiano per il Medio ed Estremo Oriente.

Gershevitch, I. (1967). *The Avestan hymn to Mitra.* Cambridge: Cambridge University Press.

Gnoli, G. (1965). Lo stato di maga. *Annali dell'Istituto Universitario Orientale di Napoli, 15,* pp. 105–117.

—. (1967). *Ricerche storiche sul Sīstān antico.* Rome: Istituto italiano per il Medio ed Estremo Oriente.

Hazra, R. C. (1958). *Studies in the Upapurāṇas* (vol. 1). Calcutta: Sanskrit College.

Hodivala, S. K. (1920). *Parsis of ancient India.* Mumbai: Author.

Humbach, H. (1969). Iranische Sonnenpriester in Indien. *ZDMG Supplementa, 1*(3), pp. 882–884.

—. (1978). Miθra in India and the Hinduized Magi. In *Études Mithraiques, Actes du 2e Congrès International, Téhéran, du 1er au 8 september 1975* (pp. 229–253). Tehran: Bibliothèque Pahlavi.

Kellens, J. (2010). Pôle indien, pôle iranien. In Shulman, D. (Ed.), *Language, Ritual and Poetics in Ancient India and Iran* (pp. 187–191). Jerusalem: Israel Academy of Sciences and Humanities.

MacKenzie, D. N. (1971). *A concise Pahlavi dictionary.* London: Oxford University Press.

Mayrhofer, M. (1956). *Kurzgefasstes etymologisches Wörterbuch des Altindischen.* [= **KEWA**]. Heidelberg: Winter.

—. (1977). *Iranisches Personennamenbuch, I: Die altiranischen Namen. Faszikel l, Die Avestischen Namen* Vienna: Österreichische Akademie der Wissenschaften.

—. (1986–2002). *Etymologisches Wörterbuch des Altindoarischen.* [= **EWA**]. Heidelberg: Winter.

Mayrhofer, M. & Brandenstein, W. (1964). *Handbuch des Altpersischen.* Wiesbaden: Harrassowitz.

Modi, J. J. (1893). *The Persian Mâr-nâmeh; or, The book for taking omens from snakes.* Bombay: Education Society's Steam Press.

Monier-Williams, M. (2005). *A Sanskrit-English dictionary.* [= **MW**]. Oxford: Clarendon. (Original work published 1899.)

Nabarz, P. & Taqizadeh, S. H. (2006). The Persian 'Mar Nameh': The Zoroastrian 'Book of the Snake', omens and calendar. Oxford: Twin Serpents.

Nyberg, H. S. (1974). *A manual of Pahlavi, part II: Glossary.* Wiesbaden: Harrassowitz.

Panaino, A. (1996). The year of the Maga Brāhmaṇas. In *Convegno internazionale sul tema: La Persia e l'Asia Centrale da Alessandro al X secolo (Roma, 9–12 novembre 1994)* (pp. 569–587). Rome: Accademia Nazionale dei Lincei.

—. (2011). Erodoto, i Magi e la storia religiosa iranica. In Rollinger, R., Truschnegg, B. & Bichler, R. (Eds.), *Herodot und das Persische Weltreich = Herodotus and the Persian Empire: Akten des 3. Internationalen Kolloquiums zum Thema 'Vorderasien im Spannungsfeld klassischer und altorientalischer Überlieferungen,' Innsbruck, 24.–28. November 2008* (pp. 343–370). Wiesbaden: Harrassowitz.

PINGREE, D. & NEUGEBAUER, O. (1970–1972). *The Pañcasiddhāntikā of Varāhamihira* (2 vols.). Copenhagen: Munksgaard.

ROSÉN, H. B. (1987). *Herodoti Historiae, 1: Libros 1.–4.* Leipzig: Teubner.

SCHEFTELOWITZ, I. (1933). Die Mithra-Religion der Indoskythen und ihre Beziehung zum Saura- und Mithras-Kult. *Acta Orientalia, 11*(4), pp. 293–333.

SRIVASTAVA, V. C. (1972). *Sun-worship in ancient India.* Allahabad: Indological Publications.

THAPAR, R. (1984). *Ancient Indian social history: Some interpretations.* New Delhi: Orient Longman.

—. (2000). *Cultural pasts: Essays in early Indian history.* New Delhi: Oxford University Press.

WEBER, A. F. (1857). *Indische Skizzen: Vier bisher in Zeitschriften zerstreute Vorträge und Abhandlungen.* Berlin: Dümmlers.

—. (1879, June). Über die Magavyakti des Kṛishṇadâsa Miçra. *Monatsberichte der Königlichen Akademie der Wissenschaften zu Berlin*, pp. 446–488.

VON BÖHTLINGK, O. (1879). *Sanskrit Wörterbuch im kürzerer Fassung.* St. Petersburg: Kaiserliche Akademie der Wissenschaften.

VON STIETENCRON, H. (1966). *Indische Sonnenpriester. Sāmba und die Sākadvīpīya-Brāhmana: Eine textkritische und religionsgeschichtliche Studie zum indischen Sonnenkult.* Wiesbaden: Harrassowitz.

Speaking of the Little Traditions

Agency and Imposition in 'Sanskrit-Speaking' Villages in North India

Patrick McCartney

While some linguists consider Sanskrit (ISO 639-3 SAN) a dead or post-vernacular language, it is spoken with varying degrees of fluency, vitality and 'purity' in small, rural language nests across the India. Several anecdotal news reports suggest that in some of these remote villages upwards of ninety to one-hundred percent of the inhabitants have adopted Sanskrit as their preferred vernacular. These nests were established by the Sanskrit revival movement with the assistance of Samskrita Bharati and its parent organisation, the Rashtriya Svayamsevak Sangh (RSS). They hold a fascinating position in the Hindu nationalist (*deśabhakta*) imaginary. More broadly, the idea of a 'Sanskrit-speaking village' generates cultural pride through the social imaginary. The 'Sanskrit-speaking village' is a fable that allows the Indian citizen and transglobal yoga practitioner to cultivate romantic tendencies about a glorious golden 'Vedic' age that exists in the present.

India is a multilingual landscape with a highly diverse linguistic ecology. Wagdi (ISO 639-3 WBR) and Malvi (ISO 639-3 MUP) are two less prestigious languages that are being pushed aside to make more room for Sanskrit in relatively remote villages in Rajasthan and Madhya Pradesh. Sanskrit, as the *devabhāṣā* ('language of the gods'), is fundamental to the utopian aspirations of the *deśabhakta* ('patriot') who envisages a cultural and moral renaissance facilitated by increasing the number of Sanskrit speakers.

This article serves as an entrée to a prospective sociolinguistic survey of Sanskrit amidst these less prestigious languages in the Hindi-speaking belt of North India. The methodology focuses on analysing the encroachment of this prestigious language by identifying sites where Sanskrit is spoken so that issues of linguistic vitality, intergenerational transmission, language contact and convergence, including code-mixing and switching, can be explored (Masica 1991: 9, Phillips 2012: 23).

The aims of this paper are to highlight some of the issues surrounding the reclamation of Sanskrit as a vernacular language and provide some introductory evidence of vernacular Sanskrit in Indian villages (cf. ZUCKERMANN & WALSH 2011, 2014). This paper presents only part of the 'Imagining Sanskrit Land' project's broader aim. The sociolinguistic aim is to address the lack of empirical data and put this phenomenon in proper perspective by conducting ethnographic research in some of these rumoured 'Sanskrit-speaking' villages.

While this project is still in its infancy, the first step in this broader research project will be to identify viable 'Sanskrit-speaking' villages. The following questions are beyond the limited scope of this paper. Ultimately, however, I seek to know whether Sanskrit is spoken in these villages and, if so, how is it spoken? What is the level of substrate interference from the community's mother tongue? What is the prognosis for a successful 'reclamation' or 'adoption' of Sanskrit? Why do these communities aspire towards becoming Sanskrit-speaking communities?

This paper is an extension of previous research into Sanskrit-speaking communities that began with ARALIKATTI (1989, 1991), HOCK (1983, 1991, 1992a, 1992b, 1992c), NAKAMURA (1973) and PANDHARIPANDE (1996). HANNEDER (2002) and HASTINGS (2004, 2008) have continued this research in the current century. The most current research has been conducted by MCCARTNEY (2011, 2014).

The antonymic concepts of Sanskritisation and oralisation (or Deshification, from *deśi* 'local') are a good place to begin with generating a theoretical framework. SRINIVAS (1952, 1955, 1956, 1959, 1966, 1989) first proposed the idea of Sanskritisation. This theory ultimately seeks to explain 'upward mobility'. PANDHARIPANDE (1992: 260) described how Sanskritisation facilitates linguistic and cultural assimilation that can allow a community to 'move up' in society (cf. CHARSLEY 1998, JAFFRELOT 2000, MARRIOTT & BEALS 1967, SRINIVAS 1956, 1989). This is a means for lower caste groups to raise their status through adopting the cultural practices of Sanskritic Hinduism, which also might include the shift to speaking Sanskrit (STAAL 1963). While Sanskritisation does have its critics (GOULD 1961, CHARSLEY 1998, SHRIVASTAVA 2008), the process by which less prestigious individuals or communities adopt the language and practices of the dominant group as a strategy to gain legitimacy is still a viable framework for understanding the social forces at play in South Asia, especially with regards to the use or adoption of Sanskrit as a preferred vernacular. GOULD explained that:

> Srinivas's concept rests ultimately on the notion that the caste system, like all status hierarchies, causes the low to invidiously compare themselves with the high and to try in every way they can to soften, modify, reduce, and even eliminate altogether the basis for these status differences. (GOULD 1961: 945)

In contrast, DONIGER (2009: 5–9) referred to Deshification as the localising force that subsumes the Sanskritic world *into* the local traditions, stating that, 'Sanskrit and oral traditions flow back and forth, producing a constant infusion of lower-class words and ideas into the Brahmin world, and vice versa'. THOMPSON (2016) explained how POLLOCK (2001, 2006) envisaged a hieratic binary between the ideas of Sanskritisation and vernacularisation (*née* Deshification) that does not fully appreciate the agency of subaltern groups in their appropriation and expression of prestigious cultural artifacts.

In a linguistic sense, we can appreciate that when the high register of 'pure' Sanskrit is adopted at the local village level, it will go through a process of Deshification. One of my hypotheses is that this isolated and unchecked local influence by the community's mother tongue on Sanskrit will at least initially, but probably permanently, result in the formation of creoloid-type 'inter-languages' (SELINKER 1972, THOMASON 2009, TARONE 2010, GROSJEAN 2012, AL-KHRESHEH 2015). While Sanskrit *might* be spoken, it will be heavily influenced by the local vernacular.

Contests over who ought to have access and the legitimate right of expression are not new. This co-opting of tradition is no more obvious than in the various ways the epic Rāmāyaṇa has been used by different groups throughout Asia; and more locally, how the Mahābhārata and Bhagavad-Gītā are used to justify particular restrictive and conservative ideologies and social structures (cf. KOSAMBI 1962, RAMANUJAN 1991, PANDIT 1992, AMBEDKAR & REGE 2013, GATADE 2015, MURTHY 2015b, NIGAM 2016). The vetting of alternative realities and stories not in line with the current Brahminical hegemony has grown considerably in the last few decades through State-supported censorship and violence (cf. DASGUPTA 2006, PRAKASH 2007, FRADKIN 2015, ISLAM 2015).

Sometimes this culture of Brahminical 'Sanskritic' Hinduism is willingly adopted. At other times it is due to the proselytising of groups like Samskrita Bharati (discussed below) amongst some of the poorest and remotest villages of India that vernacular Sanskrit is *reclaimed* (I prefer the concept of 'adoption') in communities that historically have had nothing, or at least very little to do with speaking this language. This has just as much to do with pragmatic politics and vote banks as it does with religion and ideology. Some religious activists have openly claimed to have very little regard for the welfare of the people they were apparently helping. For example, Swami Asseemanand is currently serving a jail sentence. He admitted to caring little for the welfare of the people he worked amongst and was only interested in getting them to become Hindu and vote for the Bharatiya Janata Party (BJP) (REGHUNATH 2014).

Both Sanskritisation and Deshification refer to linguistic and semiotic interplays or absorptions between local, popular and Sanskritic traditions. Part of this paper's broader anthropological focus urges us to consider the 'little and Great traditions'. This is an anthropological concept first proposed by REDFIELD & SINGER (1955: ix) to understand the complex interplay between any great civilisation and an anthropological study of local village life. MARRIOTT (1955a, b) further developed this original universal idea of Redfield and Singer, specifically locating it within the South Asian cultural and geographical sphere to create ethno-sociological models premised on local ideas and concepts. MARRIOTT (1955b) referred to the upward and downward movements observed when the little and Great traditions interact respectively as 'universalization' (Sanskritisation) and 'parochialisation' (Deshification) (MARRIOTT & INDEN 1977, MARRIOTT 1989).

BERGER (2012) considered SRINIVAS's (1955) study of village life to be representative of the Structuralist-Formalist paradigm that explored the 'social structure' of an Indian village. In a similar style, MAYER (1960) produced a seminal example of the 'Indian village ethnography' in Madhya Pradesh. The location of his research was quite close to where I have already conducted a brief ethnography in one of the rumoured 'Sanskrit-speaking' villages, namely Jhiri. BERGER (2012: 328) also highlighted GOUGH (1955), who criticised the 'village' as a 'meaningful unit of study' due to it not being a 'well-defined structural entity'. This idea was further developed by NANDY (2001), who discussed how the rise in technology has made the journey between the 'village' and the 'city' ambiguous, while also creating even more porous boundaries.

These contrasting ideas about the larger social, economic and political forces at play in India and the structural integrity of the 'village' as an analytical unit need to be considered when fleshing out the possible ways in which to calibrate this research regarding 'Sanskrit-speaking' villages. Having laid out a theoretical floor plan this paper now bifurcates into two sections. In section 1, the scene is set through an explanation of some of the more pertinent ethno-political and religious features of the Sanskrit reclamation movement. Section 2 highlights some of the various communities where it is rumoured that Sanskrit is in the process of replacing less prestigious languages in remote rural areas of North India. Some of these communities are where I might conduct further research. Section 2 also provides the phonemic charts of respective languages, demonstrating their similarity.

1 Setting the Scene

While linguists marvel at its grammatical purity, Sanskrit is considered by millions of devout Hindus and yoga practitioners to be a 'sacred' language, capable of facilitating a salvific promise of liberation (*mokṣa*). It is the language's perceived symbolic capital as the 'language of the gods' (*devabhāṣā*) that has helped sustain its millennial usage in a post-vernacular state, beyond its usage as a mother tongue. This transition from a first language to a post-vernacular language occurred about 2500 years ago (DESHPANDE 1979a, 1979b, 1986, 2013). Sanskrit's 'purity', which is a highly problematic concept for sociolinguists, is related largely to the grammatical ossification that occurred around the time of the transition from the late Vedic period to the classical period (DESHPANDE 1978, 1986).

Languages are constantly evolving. Earlier versions are often considered more 'pure', but as languages come into contact and influence each other, their perceived purity is questioned. The quest to retain both the perceived grammatical and spiritual purity of Sanskrit presents several difficulties for the Sanskrit revival movement. This is particularly so because of the multilingual context of India.

Across the internet one can find rumours of villages in remote parts of India where it is claimed that 'everyone speaks only fluent Sanskrit' (NAGRAJ 2003, KUSHALA 2005, GHOSH 2008, DEOPUJARI 2009, TRIVEDI 2010, Hindutvainus 2011, ANSELL 2012, DASA 2012, *Good Governance* 2013, SINGH 2013, VISWANATHAN 2013, 'Indian Village', 2014, SREEVATSAN 2014, *admirableindia* 2015, *News Minute* 2015, 'A Village Whose Denizens', 2009, *Dailybhaskar.com* 2016). Most of the people whom I have met that have mentioned these somewhat mythic communities have not visited these villages. Nor do they really know where they might be located. Instead, they rely on the anecdotal stories and rumours presented in the media that fertilise the social imaginary through what Appadurai referred to as the mediascape (APPADURAI 1990, 1996, 2013). This concept refers to the way the world is presented and perceived through and by mass media. The Indian media is particularly responsible for promoting the idea that these 'Sanskrit villages' exist. The result is that these rumours are either uncritically accepted as factual or, alternatively, they are rejected outright.

Samskrita Bharati is a global organisation that focuses on popularising spoken Sanskrit. It is the linguistic wing of the Sangh Parivar, a collection of Hindu nationalist organisations organised by the Rashtriya Svayamsevak Sangh (RSS). Hindu nationalists, or rather *deśabhaktas* (*deśa* 'country' + *bhakta* 'faithful'), value the instrumental and symbolic power of Sanskrit for its possible sanitising and redemptive capacities that will, it is assumed, result in the development of a Hindu nation through a cultural and moral renaissance (samskrit101 2009, MCCARTNEY 2014). Sanskrit is deeply ensconced in the Hindu nationalist agenda (known as *Hindutva*, which conveys the sense of Hinduness) of Sanskritising India in order to create an imagined community they refer to as *Bhāratavarṣa*, the 'divine Hindu kingdom' (*rāṣṭra*) (cf. ANDERSON 2006). ANDERSON's idea of *imagined communities* is a broader concept that does not specifically refer to the utopian aspirations of the *Sanghis* (the colloquial term and collective noun used to identify the constituent organisations of the Sangh Parivar).

This utopian-imaginary community is similar to what ALTER (2014) described using ANDERSON's concept, that there exists a relationship between the environment, the body, yoga (and Sanskrit) and nationalism. At its core, the Sangh Parivar aims to create a Hindu theocratic state at the expense of the current constitutionally secular democracy of India (NANDA 2005, WASKEY 2007, REDDY 2011, SHARMA 2011). This way of life can be understood as a 'framework of global modernity' and as an expression of a trans- and post-national universal morality, which is an attempt to find a new form of the modern state that is not a direct product of the post-Enlightenment, secularised, Christian world (CHATTERJEE 1998: 64, 67–68). A clear example is an article that proposes that studying Sanskrit is good for the nation, as it has supposed moral benefits, but is also an expression of modernity by not precluding people from becoming IT engineers (PAL 2016).

This paper is the beginnings of an attempt to explore a continuum of political and religious expressions and identities that perhaps consists, as PAUWELS (2010: 509) mused, of porous boundaries. Smith's definition of an *ethnie* (ethnic community) is based on much older cultural groups that can be used to define the boundaries of modern nations. These attributes are: a) a collective proper name; b) myths of common origins and ancestry; c) shared historical memories; d) one or more differentiating elements of a common culture such as language, customs or religion; e) an association with a specific 'homeland' or historic territory; and f) a sense of solidarity amongst most members of the community (SMITH 1991: 21). As Witzel explained, 'The distant past seemed to represent a "whole" intact and undamaged world' (WITZEL 2015: 14). It is through the promotion of Sanskrit that this 'undamaged world' might be created. Creating wholeness in a majoritarian sense includes creating not only a Hindu nation, but also a pan-global Hindu world where Sanskrit will replace English as the next global *lingua franca* and all the global citizens will follow a Hindu 'way of life' (MANTHAN 2015). This lifestyle is commonly referenced by the concept of *sanātana dharma* ('eternal moral principles') (*Sanâtana Dharma* 1903, KASTURI 2010, FRAWLEY 2016).

Since ancient times, India has had a long-running battle over language and national identity (SCHUESSLER 2015). Sanskrit and the texts composed in it are one of the hallmark ingredients used by the Hindutva movement in its attempt to create a homogenous majority under the concept of 'the Hindus' at the exclusion of 'others'. It exhibits overtly fascist tendencies (PATNAIK 1993, PUNIYANI 2006, HASAN 2015). Both the aforementioned RSS and the World Hindu Council (*aka* the Vishwa Hindu Parishad) are the extra-parliamentary wings of the current ruling party, the BJP (HARMAN 2004). SEN (2015: 690–691) explained that due to the size and diversity of India, Hindutva's particular brand of fascism is open to contestation and mitigation by the deployment of alternative imaginaries of ethnicity and nationhood. KHALIDI (2008) suggested that the Hinduisation of the state is not the sole focus of the Sangh, yet is a state program in which the Congress party has been just as actively involved in promoting Hindu assimilatory practices at the expense of other religious and minority groups. SEN (2015: 692) cogently asserted that the centre of fascism is the 'identification of blood as a restraining principle' that locates the nation through relationships between (Hindu) blood, the crowd and the state. BANAJI's analysis is worth quoting at length:

> The distinctive feature of India's fascism is that it has had to grow in a society where the mass of the population remains committed to democracy and no agenda for the overthrow of democracy can ever be affirmed overtly in those

> terms. Thus Arendt's characterization of fascist movements using/abusing democratic freedoms to abolish them is, paradoxically, more true of India than it ever was of Europe. In India fascist tendencies are currently at work in two forms, one direct, the other more insidious. The more direct form consists chiefly in the mobilisation of a communal mass base which fluctuates in intensity but is clearly seen by the RSS as the organic strategy, and the one most directly linked to its ideology of extreme nationalism. That ideology was not a product of the RSS specifically, since the Hindu Mahasabha played an equally seminal role in forging its main elements. I'm referring of course to the fanatically extreme nationalism that was embodied in different ways in Savarkar and Golwalkar and encapsulated India's version of a fascist utopia ethnically cleansed or purged of its 'alien' elements. Everyone knows that both propagandists were deeply influenced by the Nazi extermination of the Jews and took that as their model for the way Muslims would have to be dealt with, in principle anyway. But mass communalism and sustained communal propaganda have been supplemented by more insidious subversions of democracy that combine the elements of a war of position with a war of movement. Thus progressive control of the media by the extreme right which includes the mainstreaming of the extreme Right by the media, so that overtly communal elements are repeatedly projected as normal and innocuous (note the repeated presence of hard-core RSS elements on the prime time talk shows of channels like NDTV and CNN-IBN) and the BJP's relentless parliamentary agitations, consciously calculated to induce a breakdown in the functioning of parliament and project that as the bungling of a corrupt and ineffectual government, both have the character of a war of position, that is, a protracted war of attrition against India's democracy that legitimises fascist politics and creates a dispersed revulsion against 'the parliamentary system'. A vital part of this trench warfare has been a widespread infiltration of the state apparatuses, a molecular penetration of the police, the bureaucracy and the intelligence agencies, which creates a state within the state, and one that is barely camouflaged when investigations into the criminal activity of the RSS underground (into the RSS cadre who have drifted into groups like Abhinav Bharat) are sabotaged by the state itself, or when the police are overtly implicated in communal carnages such as the explosion of violence led by the Shiv Sena in Bombay in January 1993. (BANAJI 2013)

The country's foreign minister Sushma Swaraj has called for the Bhagavad-Gītā, a Sanskrit religious text, to be designated as the national scripture (*'Sushma Pushes for BhG'*, 2015). In contrast to the apparently sacrosanct view espoused in the text and by its ardent supporters, B. R. AMBEDKAR and D. D. KOSAMBI are of the opinion that Brahmins composed this text in an attempt to reclaim their power base during the early Gupta period (320–550 CE) against the Buddhists. This was done to give ideological and moral support to their counter-reformation and to acquire wealth and power in a new central government (Kosambi 1962: 37, Pandit 1992, Murthy 2015a, b). Based on Ambedkar, according to Pandit (1992), the Bhagavad-Gītā is neither a book of religion nor a treatise on philosophy. Instead, it dogmatically defends the Brahminical religion on philosophical grounds while incorporating into its ideology popular ideas from Buddhism and Yoga (cf. Madsen 2013).

Supporters of this movement to install the Bhagavad-Gītā as the national 'holy book' also believe that it is through the study of Sanskrit that the Indian citizen will gain a deeper sense of cultural pride and patriotism. Furthermore, it is thought that this will help to right the historical wrongs and sense of past injustices committed during the colonial and Mughal periods through unmediated access to the original texts (McCartney 2014). The Bhagavad-Gītā is one book in the epic 18-book Mahābhārata. Both texts, due to their canonical status, are particularly suited for stressing the symbolic value of the rational choice of the BJP in its majoritarian political use of this dominant canon to promote a particular national-moral imagination. It serves as the basis for a feeling of cultural superiority and is instrumental to the rejection of rational arguments against a particular interpretation of history that is thoroughly contested (cf. Patnaik 1993: 69, Visvesvaran, Witzel et al. 2009).

The implications for Samskrita Bharati's ambitious project reside in its vision and mission. This is explicitly stated on their website as a desire to 'revive a language, rejuvenate a culture, and revolutionise the world' ('Vision and Mission', 2014). This ideology is based on linguistic, cultural and religious purity. Samskrita Bharati does not tolerate any sort of hybridity. Samskrita Bharati's aim—through the promotion of Sanskrit as a spoken, 'living' and ultimately first language—is to bring about linguistic and cultural purification, religious-moral edification and a Hindu theocratic state. However, South Asian Languages (SALs) have been in long and intense contact with each other, so the idea of linguistic purity is somewhat flawed due to this contentious and fluid topic, which has presented a typological problem for both ancient and modern linguists alike (Drocco 2012). Any hybridisation of a revived language should be expected and tolerated. The sociolinguist has an interesting opportunity to explore the revitalisation of a 'dead language' within the interdisciplinary framework of political science, sociolinguistics and the sociology of religion. This is because in South Asia, multilingualism is the norm and not the exception (Agnihotri 2008). Phillips (2012) suggested that the multilingual nature of South Asian society makes the task of identifying the so-called mother tongue often impossible. Magier (1983: 4) observed that 'each of the numerous codes (a speaker) controls will be appropriate to a different set of contexts that arise routinely in daily life'. Multilingualism implies intense language contact resulting in characteristic features being transferred through convergence (Subbarao 2008). This *Sprachbund* or linguistic area has led to contact between languages and language families (Emeneau 1956, Errington 2008). It is, and ought to be considered, a facilitator and not an obstacle to linguistic diversity and language revival (Pandit 1972).

However, this idea of linguistic and cultural pluralism is antithetic to the Hindu nationalist agenda. Setting the tone of this paper, the possible reinstitution of Sanskrit as a dominant national and even international *lingua franca* is fraught, tenuous and divisively sectarian. Moreover, the practice of imposing Sanskrit on other isolated communities at the expense of their own languages seems somewhat unethical as well as unconstitutional (cf. the Official Languages Act, 1963 and the Eighth Schedule to the Constitution of India). Religious as well as linguistic boundaries are actively contested, and while boundaries remain open and fluid, the powerful continue to assert and maintain dominance in local, national and regional communal politics. Low-caste and low-prestige communities seek to assert their right to a different identity than the one imposed by more powerful and dominant sections of society (MARTIN 2013: 239). Even within Rajasthan itself, which has a multitude of languages and dialects, there are internal problems with one linguistic community asserting itself in an attempt to impose its language on others ('Imposition of Marwari', 2007). This might just be media hype, and in reality perhaps little imposition is actually occurring. As asserted by DEOPUJARI in the English-language RSS magazine, the *Organiser*, the specious apparatus involved in imposing Sanskrit on minority groups is subtly performed through positioning it as an integral component of development and cultural unity in rural areas.

> Due to the Sanskrit language caste discrimination between so-called lower and upper castes has reduced. Those who speak the language can hold his head high in the society. The oneness of the society leads to the development of the village. One more medium of imbibing virtues like a sense of duty, integrity, devotion, faith, etc., is the Sanskrit language. By speaking consistently in [*sic*] devvani [*sic*], the so-called downtrodden or the depressed class of society also feels elevated. They not only feel confident but also develop samskars [*sic*], which is the very base of any developmental activity. Therefore, Sanskrit Sambhashaṇ [*sic*] is one of the prominent aspects of rural development, the work being undertaken by swayamsevaks [*sic*] across the country. There are a number of villages in the country where all daily activities of life are conducted only in Sanskrit. The prominent villages in this group are Muttoor and Hosahalli in Karnataka and Jhiri and Mohad in Madhya Pradesh where Sanskrit has truly become language of the masses. More than ninety-five percent of the people of Muttoor and 100 percent of the people in Jhiri speak Sanskrit. (DEOPUJARI 2009)

As a symbol, the Sanskrit village signifies an ideological example of the potential moral benefits a community can accrue through choosing to speak Sanskrit over another language. This has anecdotally led to entire communities renouncing alcohol, the consumption of meat and other vices such as fornication, gambling and smoking (GHOSH 2008, Hindutvainus 2011, Press Trust of India 2015). I have witnessed this rhetoric promoted by Samskrita Bharati in their intensive language camps as the main reason people should switch to Sanskrit. Some villages, as alleged by organisations like Samskrita Bharati, have even rejected their first language in favour of Sanskrit (Nagraj 2003, 'Is the Sanskrit Spoken', 2011, *Firstpost* 2011, Ansell 2012, Dasa 2012, *Good Governance* 2013, Singh 2013, *News Minute* 2015, 'A Village Whose Denizens', 2009). The founder of Samskrita Bharati, Chamu Krishna Shastry, believes:

saṃskṛta-karaṇena	***jīvana-parivartanam***
sanskrit-do.INS	life-reformation

'Through the work of Sanskrit lives are reformed.' (samskrit101 2009)

(Glossing conventions throughout this article follow the 'Leipzig Glossing Rules', https://www.eva.mpg.de/lingua/resources/glossing-rules.php.) In an effort to increase the Hindu vote bank, one proselytising strategy of the Sanskrit revival movement is to establish Sanskrit language nests in remote and often tribal-dominated (*ādivāsin* = *ādi* 'original' + *vāsin* 'inhabitant') villages and districts. This post-vernacular language, which is no longer spoken by people as a first language (cf. Shandler 2008), and the language nests where this occurs, share a unique position within the Hindutva imaginary. I describe these villages as 'nodes of Sanskritic purity', which generate romanticised notions of the idyllic, rural backdrop that is the imagined glorious and golden 'Vedic age' alive in the present (ca. 1750–500 BCE). This age is seen as the antithesis and antidote to the perceived polluting influences of modernity and Western culture upon a narrow and high-jacked definition of 'core Indian' values. This use of a traditional vector for redefining the individual or collective identity by adopting the floating lexical signifier of the 'Vedic' lifestyle leads to such comments as those made by RSS chief Mohan Bhagwat regarding sexual assault: that 'such crimes hardly take place in Bharat, but they occur frequently in India', and that 'all of this is happening due to exposure to Western values'. His remedy relies heavily on the cultural and linguistic impact that Sanskrit is said to provide, as 'it is important to go back to core Indian values' ('Rapes Happen in India', 2013). The assertion is that the core of these values is found in Vedic culture, which is underwritten by the Sanskrit language.

One advertisement that I found on YouTube promoted a fuel-efficient motorbike set to the backdrop of an idyllic Sanskrit village (Sharma 2009). This advertisement is set in the village of Mattoor, Karnataka, which is famous for being the model 'Sanskrit-speaking village'. In the advertisement, as the traveler passes by, various villagers from different castes try warning him of the impending fallen tree that has blocked the road, shouting:

bhoḥ	***mārgaḥ***	***na-asti***	***āvṛtaḥ***
VOC	road	NEG-is.3.SG.AUX	conceal.PST.PTCP

'Hey, the road isn't open, it's blocked.'

In the last moments the protagonist takes the lexifying *-am* particle and adds it to the English *wonderful* to make the Sanskritised adjective 'wonderful-*am*'. This is a common feature of hybridised spoken Sanskrit and substrate interference (cf. McCartney 2011). The rest of this paper focuses on four of the 'Sanskrit-speaking' villages where it is anticipated that the proposed research will be conducted.

2 Sanskrit Villages and Local Languages

I propose to conduct comparative sociolinguistic research across a number of 'Sanskrit-speaking' villages in order to determine: the level of linguistic vitality of Sanskrit; the number of speakers of Sanskrit; the amount of substrate interference from each communities' mother tongue; and how this creates a hybrid interlanguage during the stage of second-language learning known as the 'imperfect stage'. Ideally, I would spend a minimum of 12 months in each village. A smaller amount of time would create the risk of collecting only anecdotal evidence. Spending 12 months in any village, however, seems unlikely. Regardless, I would like to compare three or four villages from different geographic regions where a different mother tongue is used. Currently, the intention is to take a 'one village at a time' approach, and hopefully have the next several years to conduct what is likely to be a very interesting project for many reasons. However, before I choose the first village in which to spend 12 months, I would like to at least visit as many as possible of the villages mentioned in Figure 1 below, so as to better assess the options for this proposed research.

Figure 1 provides a list of purported 'Sanskrit-speaking' villages. This is a composite list that I have developed through a prolonged internet search over a few years. At the time of writing. I have visited only two of the villages on this list in an exploratory attempt to find viable sites to conduct future research. I have been to the villages of Gamiri Gaon, in Assam, and Jhiri in Madhya Pradesh. Gamiri Gaon is a difficult field site due to the multilingual nature of the community. There are over ten languages spoken by a composite group of ethnic communities. I first

1. Gamiri Gaon, Assam
2. Mattur, Karnataka
3. Hoshahalli, Karnataka
4. Jhiri, Madhya Pradesh
5. Mohad, Madhya Pradesh
6. Bhagwat, Madhya Pradesh
7. Shyamsundapur, Odisha
8. Ganoda, Rajasthan
9. Kaperan, Rajasthan
10. Khada, Rajasthan
11. Bawali, Uttar Pradesh
12. Bantola, Uttarakhand
13. Kimoda, Uttarakhand
14. Mandal, Uttarakhand
15. Dholakha, Nepal

Figure 1: List of 'Sanskrit-speaking' villages.

came to know of this village through an article found on the Samskrita Bharati website (Ansell 2012). Unfortunately, there are hardly any speakers of Sanskrit in this village of approximately 5000 people. It would be a rather unproductive option for conducting research on spoken Sanskrit. It is the Nepali community that speaks Sanskrit. However, Sanskrit is at least the third language of the Nepali community, as they are bilingual in Assamese. In the week I spent in Gamiri, I met perhaps only ten people who could hold a conversation in Sanskrit without needing to change to English or Hindi.

Prior to going to Assam, I spent one month in Jhiri. I first came across a mention of this village while reading Ghosh's (2008) article. At the time of writing, I have produced four short documentary films about life in this village (McCartney 2015, 2016a, b, c). While there are speakers of Sanskrit in this village, the reasons are unclear as to why the teaching of Sanskrit in this village has not continued since 2011. It began in 2002, but abruptly stopped. The use of Sanskrit as a daily vernacular is waning to the point that it is certainly not the superordinate language of this community. It seems that it never was, despite the best efforts of the community and the media to present it as such. The excerpt below explicitly refers to the Sanskritisation process whereby indigenous peoples are allegedly adopting the imposed language. Nagraj suggested that the adoption of Sanskrit is increasing literacy and turning the village from a 'non-descript entity' into a newsworthy phenomenon the nation can be proud of.

> In this tribal-dominated village, Sanskrit is slowly becoming a way of life. Slogans in Sanskrit mark the village walls, the language is spoken in practically every house and every school-going child is rattling off a few sentences. The entire process actually started by default. Until about 10 years ago, Ganoda village was like any other in Banswada district of Rajasthan. Tribal dominated, average literacy levels and a nondescript entity. But the growing number of students passing out of the government Sanskrit college in Ganoda changed all that. Over 100 students in the three Sanskrit institutions of the village—a primary school, middle school and the college—have joined hands with a group of their teachers to try and make Sanskrit the second language of the Wagdi speaking population. (Nagraj 2003)

The following four villages are interesting for many reasons. Why have they been chosen for this experiment to create 'Sanskrit-speaking' villages? My assumption is that, due to the relatively isolated locations and potentially limited multilingual communities in Ganoda, Jhiri, Mohad and Bhagwat, the likely success of Sanskrit taking root is perhaps higher than in more diverse linguistic ecosystems such as densely populated urban areas.

Wagdi (ISO 639-3 WBR) and Malvi (ISO 639-3 MUP) are two less prestigious languages that are in the process of having another prestigious language imposed on them. Deopujari asserted that '[s]preading awareness for Sanskrit can abolish the linguistic differences of the country' ('Sanskrit Can End Differences', 2015). The intention to reduce the linguistic complexity of India to a monocultural ecology is clear. In his ideal world, people will only speak Sanskrit. The districts of Banswada (Wagdi-speaking) and Rajgarh (Malvi-speaking) are part of a dialect continuum where the lexical and grammatical influence of Gujarati and Rajasthani produce strong similarities.

The prevalence and convergence toward a standard Hindi increases in urban areas as a result of education. Methodologically, due to often unconscious code-switching or code-mixing that occurs in multilingual domains, the acquisition of 'pure' dialect samples presents a challenge for how best to approach language elicitation in social and geographical space. Whereas tribal villages located further from urban centres are less vulnerable to the pressure of conforming to urban standards of speech, this makes the task of the ethnographer no less problematic (cf. Naik 1969: 23–24, Phillips 2012: 27–28). I posit that this is one reason why Samskrita Bharati chooses to cultivate Sanskrit villages in remote areas, where it is easier to impose the use of Sanskrit due to the apparently less complicated sociolinguistic factors in tribal villages that are more likely to be monolingual.

Figure 2 provides basic census data comparing three of India's 640 districts. The districts are ranked according to population size. The three districts in which these villages are located show a literacy range of 56–76% (Office of the Registrar General and Census Commissioner 2015).

Depending on where the lines between various dialects are drawn, Wagdi is said to have between 2.5–4.5 million speakers (Ishtiaq 1999: 27, Lewis, Simons & Fennig 2016c). Malvi has approximately 1.1–5.5 million speakers (Lewis, Simons & Fennig 2016a). Sanskrit, on the other hand, is reported to have 14,000 mother-tongue speakers and approximately 200,000 second-language users (Lewis, Simons & Fennig 2016b); the official language of India, Hindi (ISO 639-3 HIN), has 422 million speakers (Office of the Registrar General and Census Commissioner 2011). Now the discussion will move on to a closer look at the languages spoken in the four villages of Ganoda, Jhiri, Mohad and Bhaguwar.

Ganoda, Banswada District, Rajasthan

In Banswada District in southeastern Rajasthan, the Bhili dialect of Wagdi is the language of the majority. Wagdi is a non-tonal Indo-Aryan language with an SOV

Ranking	*District*	*Population*	*Growth*	*Sex Ratio*	*Literacy*
267	Banswara, Rajasthan	1,797,485	26.53%	980	56.33
322	Rajgarh, MP	1,545,814	23.26%	956	61.21
419	Narsinghapur, MP	1,091,854	14.01%	920	75.69

Figure 2: Census Data for Three Districts.

syntactic structure that uses postpositions. It is mutually intelligible with languages in Gujarat and Rajasthan. It is written using the Devanāgarī script of Hindi (LEWIS, SIMONS & FENNIG 2016c). ZOGRAF (1982: 65) identified more than 20 subdialects of Wagdi spread over more than 50 districts across four states, including Gujarat, Rajasthan, Madhya Pradesh and Maharashtra. PHILLIPS (2012: 24) explained in his sketch grammar that present-day Wagdi incorporates features of Gujarati and southern Rajasthani dialects such as Mewari and Malvi, as well as some aspects of Hindi. The village of Ganoda is dominated by *ādivāsins* who are referred to as 'tribals' (NAGRAJ 2003). This would suggest that the subdialect, Adivasi Wagdi, predominates in Ganoda. CAIN (2013: 45–6) mentioned that researchers who know both Hindi and Gujarati reported having difficulty being understood. This suggests that Wagdi must be learnt in order to communicate in this language nest. The phonemic inventory of Wagdi shares similarities with other Indo-Aryan languages. Figure 3 displays the phonemic inventory of Wagdi, which has eight vowels and 34 consonants.

The consonant inventory also shares common features with Indo-Aryan languages influenced by Rajasthani and Gujarati. The affricated stop [c] is often lost in 'pure' Wagdi, and while pronounced as [t͡ʃ], it has shifted to [s] and then also to [h]. Examples include [ca] 'tea', which is often pronounced [*sa*] or [*ha*], just as [*so*] 'hundred' is pronounced [*ho*] (MASICA 1991: 94–95, PHILLIPS 2012: 63).

Vowels

	Front	*Central*	*Back*
Close	i		u
Close-mid	e	ə	o
Open-mid	ɛ		ɔ
Open	(æ)	ɑ	

Consonants

	Bilabial	*Labio-Dental*	*Dental Alveolar*	*Retroflex*	*Palatal*	*Velar*	*Glottal*
Stops		p b	t d	ʈ ɖ	tʃ dʒ	k g	
Aspirated		p^{h} b^{h}	t^{h} d^{h}	t^{h} d^{ɦ}	tʃ^{h} dʒ^{h}	k^{h} g^{h}	
Fricatives			s	ʃ			ɦ
Nasals	m		n	ŋ		ɳ	
Laterals			l	ɭ			
Trill/Flap			r	ɽ			
Semivowel	w	ʋ			j		

Figure 3: Phonemic Inventory of Wagdi.

Jhiri, Rajgarh District, Madhya Pradesh

Roughly 600 kilometres northeast of Ganoda in the neighbouring state of Madhya Pradesh is another 'Sanskrit-speaking' village called Jhiri. Jhiri is a small hamlet in Sarangpur Tehsil, Rajgarh District. It is located 27 kilometres east of the district headquarters of Rajgarh, and 104 kilometres from the state capital, Bhopal. Both Hindi and the regional variant of Umawadi Malvi are spoken in Jhiri. Figure 4 shows the phonemic inventory of Hindi, which consists of eleven vowels and 26 consonants (SHAPIRO 2003).

Over the past decade, residents of this hamlet of approximately 600 people initially resisted the work of Samskrita Bharati (Hindutvainus 2011). During a conversation at the Samskrita Bharati 14-day language camp in New Delhi in 2009, the head of Samskrita Bharati, Chamu Krishna Shashtry, informed me, 'only ten percent of the village speak Sanskrit' (MCCARTNEY 2014). Figures 5 and 6 are two common web images asserting Jhiri's credentials as a traditional Sanskrit-speaking village. In Figure 5, the graffiti, reading from top-left to bottom-right, says:

वदतु	संस्कृतम्	मम	भाषा	संस्कृत	भाषा
vadatu	***saṃskṛtam***	***mama***	***bhāṣā***	***saṃskṛta***	***bhāṣā***
speak.2.IMP	sanskrit	my.1.GEN	language	Sanskrit	language

'Speak Sanskrit, my language is the Sanskrit language.'

Vowels

	Front	*Central*	*Back*
Close	i		u
	ɪ	ʊ	
Close-mid	e	ə	o
Open-mid	ɛ		ɔ
Open	(æ)		ɑ

Consonants

	Bilabial	*Labio-Dental*	*Dental Alveolar*	*Retroflex*	*Palatal*	*Velar*	*Uvular*	*Glottal*
Stops	p b		t̪ d̪	ʈ ɖ	tʃ dʒ	k g	(q)	
Aspirated	p^h b^h		t̪^{h} d̪^{h}	t^h d^{ɦ}	tʃ^h dʒ^h	k^h g^h		
Fricatives	f	s z			ʃ	(x) (ɣ)		ɦ
Nasals	m		n	(ŋ)		ɳ		
Laterals			l	ɭ				
Trill/Flap			r	ɽ ɽ^h				
Semivowel	w	ʋ			j			

Figure 4: Phonemic Inventory of Hindi.

Figure 5: Men sitting in street in front of Sanskrit Graffiti in Jhiri, MP (Ghosh 2008).

Figure 6 contains only partial sentences. The top left word is *namo*, which is part of a common Sanskrit salutation derived from the verbal root √*nam* 'submit, bend'. *Namo namaḥ* ('hail') is a distributed noun phrase that consists of an interjective plus dative construction. Due to external sandhi rules, when a *visarga* (*aḥ* [əh]) is positioned at the end of the word and meets a *na*, it changes to -*o*, thus *namaḥ namaḥ* becomes *namo namaḥ*. The sentence under the window is:

मम	माता	दवता
mama	**mātā**	**devatā**
my.1.GEN	mother	god

'My mother is god.'

Figure 6: Sanskrit Graffiti (Ghosh 2008).

What is interesting about these villages is that, according to the media, even though some Sanskrit is spoken, basic facilities and amenities like toilets in homes and schools are lacking. This is a common problem across India, not restricted to isolated rural environments. As Doron & Jeffrey (2013) demonstrated, India now has over 900 million mobile phone subscriptions but less than half the population of 1.2 billion has access to a toilet in their home. Even though people might be able to speak Sanskrit and use a mobile phone, urinating while talking or walking goes against an ancient injunction (cf. Manu 4.47). How does an emphasis on speaking Sanskrit help the rural masses and other marginalised groups when an absence of necessary infrastructure and sanitation are certainly more pressing issues? Perhaps it is not meant to. Perhaps the aim of getting indigenous peoples and rural folk to speak Sanskrit says more about the production of a nationalist-religious fantasy (which I refer to as 'Sanskrit Land') that still holds the traditional village lifestyle as core to its ideology. If speaking Sanskrit really helps facilitate development there is little evidence of this in Jhiri.

Mohad and Bhaguwar, Narsinghpur District, Madhya Pradesh

Mohad and Bhaguwar are two villages approximately ten kilometres west of the district centre and town of Narsinghpur. Both villages are located in Kareli Tehsil. The language spoken in this area is Malvi. Its classification is Indo-European, Indo-Iranian, Indo-Aryan, Western-Central zones, Rajasthani-Marwari, Rajasthani, Malvi ('Malvi Language', 2015). According to the 2001 census, the second-language

Vowels

	Front	*Central*	*Back*
High	i i:		u u:
Mid	e e:	ə	o o:
Low		ɑ ɑ:	

Consonants

	Bilabial	*Labio-Dental*	*Alveolar*	*Retroflex*	*Palatal*	*Velar*	*Glottal*
Stops	p b		t d	ʈ ɖ	tʃ dʒ	k g	
Aspirated	p^h b^h		t^h d^h	t^h d^{ɦ}	dʒ^h dʒ^h	k^h g^h	
Fricatives			s		ʃ		ɦ
Nasals	m		n				ŋ
Laterals			l				
Trill/Flap			r	ɽ			
Semivowel		w			j		

Figure 7: Malvi Phonemic Inventory.

literacy rate in Hindi was 75 percent. 55 percent have high proficiency and twenty percent have routine proficiency (Lewis, Simons & Fennig 2016a). At an official level Malvi is used as an oral medium, but Hindi is relied upon for written communication (Baskaran 2015: 6). Baskaran (2015: 205) provided a workable sketch grammar for Malvi, from which Figure 7 presents a phonemic inventory. Malvi has 11 vowels and 31 consonant phonemes.

Comparing these phonemic charts, it is obvious that there is a general phonemic similarity among the various Indo-Aryan languages of Sanskrit, Hindi, Wagdi and Malvi. This affinity also extends into a grammatical and lexical affinity. There is very little information available specifically on these villages. They are difficult not only to get to but also, in some instances, quite difficult to locate.

Concluding Remarks

In this paper some of the universal constraints, global mechanisms, local peculiarities and idiosyncrasies of this particular language context have been explored. Sanskrit has had an illustrious history as a dominant religious, scientific and literary language. It is the principal language of religious worship for hundreds of millions of people. Yet, just like its counterpart Latin, its use and vitality as a spoken language, while still prestigious within particular social domains, has waned considerably from its apogee a millennium ago.

Whom does Sanskrit belong to? Samskrita Bharati will tell us it is the language of the people (*jānabhāṣā*) and also of the gods (*devabhāṣā*). But the ancient texts, particularly the *dharmaśāstra*s, and the historical sociolinguistic evidence points to a rather different situation. Samskrita Bharati's objective to teach more people Sanskrit is admirable because there is a mountain of untapped knowledge in the form of untranslated manuscripts literally rotting away on shelves across the subcontinent. But teaching a simplified Sanskrit to an overwhelmingly illiterate mass of rural folk will do nothing to help in the preservation and translation of abstract philosophical texts written in Sanskrit. The appropriation of Sanskrit by the Hindu right, the linguistic-cultural diversity, the sheer size of India, and the religio-political complexities make the revitalisation of Sanskrit, or any other minority language, a challenging prospect. This is because, for many people in India, it represents an antiquated and intolerant cultural hegemony. For some, however, even though they are part of the majority, and identify with Sanskritic heritage, inside their community only a fraction of the people speak the language. Furthermore, the common (neo-liberal) opinion is that there is very little profit to be made from pursuing studies or contemplating a career in Sanskrit, as the jobs are quite limited.

As a sociolinguist, I am interested in the aspirations of communities. I am interested in how meaning, identities and practices accrete around various signs and, in this case, languages. What motivates people to speak Sanskrit or to try and persuade others to join them? It is clear that the answer involves a utopian aspiration to become a better individual and citizen through belief in a politico-religious ideal.

Samskrita Bharati is deeply committed to revitalising 'their' language. This leads us to ask: for which language should we be focusing on helping to create pedagogical material? I would argue that Wagdi and Malvi are just as 'divine' as Sanskrit and just as deserving when it comes to promoting increased literacy and cultural pride in these languages and communities. Samskrita Bharati already produces ample pedagogical material, from children's textbooks and videos to facilitating spoken Sanskrit camps across India and among the Indian diaspora in other countries. Sanskrit may share just a tiny portion of India's language pie, however it has stood the test of time in proving itself to be durable and to some extent 'eternal' as well. While the Sanskrit canon is an intangible cultural heritage representative of the Great tradition, the languages of the little traditions are also intangible. Therefore, they ought to have state support in ensuring their continued use while promoting pride in these cultures.

References

A village whose denizens speak in Sanskrit. (2009, February 19). *Webindia123.com.* Retrieved from http://news.webindia123.com/news/articles/India/20090219/1180717.html.

admirableindia. (2015, August 17). Sanskrit speaking villages in India. *Admirable India.* Retrieved from https://admirableindia.wordpress.com/2015/08/17/sanskrit-speaking-villages-in-india/.

Agnihotri, R. K. (2008). Orality and literacy. In Kachru, B. B., Kachru, Y. & Sridhar, S. N. (Eds.), *Language in South Asia* (pp. 271–284). Melbourne: Cambridge University Press.

Al-Khresheh, M. H. (2015). A review study of interlanguage theory. *International Journal of Applied Linguistics & English Literature, 4*(3): 123–131.

Alter, J. S. (2014). Nature cure and Ayurveda: Nationalism, viscerality, and bioecology in India. *Body & Society, 21*(1), pp. 3–28.

Ambedkar, B. R. & Rege, S. (2013). *Against the madness of Manu: B. R. Ambedkar's writings on Brahminical patriarchy.* New Delhi: Navayana.

Anderson, B. (2006). *Imagined communities: Reflections on the origin and spread of nationalism.* New York: Verso.

Ansell, V. (2012). A Sanskrit-speaking village in Assam. *Samskrita Bharati.* Retrieved from http://samskritabharati.in/archives/2535.

Appadurai, A. (1990). Disjuncture and difference in the global cultural economy. *Public Culture, 2*(2): 1–24.

—. (1996). *Modernity at large: Cultural dimensions of globalisation.* Minneapolis: University of Minnesota Press.

—. (2013). *The future as a cultural fact.* London: Verso.

Aralikatti, R. N. (1989). *Spoken Sanskrit in India: A study of sentence patterns.* Tirupati: Kendriya Sanskrit Vidyapeetha.

—. (1991). A note on the word order in Modern Spoken Sanskrit and some positive constraints. In Hock, H. H. (Ed.), *Studies in Sanskrit syntax* (pp. 13–17). Delhi: Motilal Banarsidas.

Banaji, J. (2013). Trajectories of fascism: Extreme-right movements in India and elsewhere. (The fifth Walter Sisulu Memorial Lecture, Jamia Millia Islamia, New Delhi, 18 March 2013) [PDF file]. Retrieved from http://eprints.soas.ac.uk/16825/1/Jamia%20lecture%20(fascism).pdf.

Baskaran, S. G. (2015). Malvi. In *Linguistic Survey of India* (pp. 199–246). New Delhi: Government of India.

Berger, P. (2012). Theory and ethnography in the modern anthropology of India. *HAU: Journal of Ethnographic Theory, 2*(2), pp. 325–357.

Cain, B. (2013). A sociolinguistic profile of Garasia dialects [PDF file]. *SIL.* Retrieved from https://www.sil.org/resources/archives/54606.

Charsley, S. (1998). Sanskritization: The career of an anthropological theory. *Contributions to Indian Sociology 32*(2), pp. 527–549.

Chatterjee, P. (1998, Autumn). Beyond the nation? Or within? *Social Text, 56,* 57–69.

Dailybhaskar.com. (2016). Did you know: People of this village only speak in 'Sanskrit'! *Daily Bhaskar.* Retrieved from http://daily.bhaskar.com/news/JM-RIT-sanskrit-speaking-village-5332274-PHO.html.

Dasa, B. C. (2012). Five Indian Villages where Sanskrit is Spoken. *Centre for Traditional Education.* Retrieved from http://globalvarnasramamission.blogspot.com.au/2012/01/five-indian-villages-where-sanskrit-is.html.

Dasgupta, S. (2006). Gods in the sacred marketplace: Hindu nationalism and the return of the aura in the public sphere. In Meyer, B. & Moors, A. (Eds.), *Religion, media, and the public sphere* (pp. 251–272). Bloomington: Indiana University Press.

Deopujari, S. (2009, September 6). Sanskrit can become the language of the masses in rural areas. *Organiser, 61*(9). Retrieved from http://organiser.org/archives/historic/dynamic/modules24bf.html? name=Content&pa=showpage&pid=307&page=29.

Deshpande, M. M. (1978). Pāṇinian grammarians on dialectal variation in Sanskrit. *Brahmavidyā: Adyar Library Bulletin,* 61–114.

—. (1979a). History, change and permanence: A classical Indian perspective. In Krishna, G. (Ed.), *Contributions to South Asian studies* (vol. 1). Delhi: Oxford University Press.

—. (1979b). *Sociolinguistic attitudes in India: An historical reconstruction.* Ann Arbor, MI: Karoma Publishers.

—. (1986). Sanskrit grammarians on diglossia. In Krishnamurti, B., Masica, C. P. & Sinha, A. J. (Eds.), *South Asian languages: Structure, convergence and diglossia* (pp. 312–321). Delhi: Motilal Banarsidass.

—. (2013). Aryan origins: Brief history of linguistic arguments. In Thapar, R. (Ed.), *India: Historical beginnings and the concept of the Aryan* (pp. 98–156). Delhi: National Book Trust.

Doniger, W. (2009). *The Hindus: An alternative history.* London: Penguin Press.

Doron, A. & Jeffrey, R. (2013, October 25). When nature calls in India, phones are on hand. *Sydney Morning Herald.* Retrieved from http://www.smh.com.au/comment/when-nature-calls-in-india-phones-are-on-hand-20131024-2w467.html.

Drocco, A. (2012). Eternal Sanskrit and the meaning of the tripartite Prakrit terminology *tatsama, tadbhava* and *deśī. Linguistica e Filologia,* 32, 119–136.

Emeneau, M. B. (1956). India as a linguistic area. *Language, 32*(1), 3–16.

Hasan, M. (Presenter). (2015). Is Modi's India flirting with fascism? *Al Jazeera: Head to Head.* Retrieved from https://www.youtube.com/watch?v=m1W-oXZ_31U.

Errington, J. (2008). *Linguistics in a colonial world: A story of language, meaning, and power.* Melbourne: Blackwell Publishing.

Lewis, M. P., Simons, G. F., & Fennig, C. D. (Eds.). (2016a). Malvi: A language of India. Ethnologue: Languages of the World (19th ed.). Dallas, TX: SIL International. Retrieved from https://www.ethnologue.com/language/mup/.

—. (2016b). Sanskrit: A language of India. Ethnologue: Languages of the World (19th ed.). Dallas, TX: SIL International. Retrieved from https://www.ethnologue.com/language/san/.

—. (2016c). Wagdi: A language of India. Ethnologue: Languages of the World (19th ed.). Dallas, TX: SIL International. Retrieved from https://www.ethnologue.com/language/wbr/.

Firstpost. (2011, November 22). Rajasthan town folk communicate in Sanskrit to keep it alive. *Firstpost.* Retrieved from http://www.firstpost.com/fwire/rajasthan-town-folk-communicate-in-sanskrit-to-keep-it-alive-137566.html.

Fradkin, A. (2015, Summer). Modi's India: Caste, inequality, and the rise of Hindu nationalism. *Wilson Quarterly.* Retrieved from http://wilsonquarterly.com/stories/modi-hindu-politics-caste-india/.

Frawley, D. (2016, January 12). Essential facts of Sanatana Dharma. *IndiaFacts Research Centre.* Retrieved from http://indiafacts.org/essential-facts-of-sanatana-dharma/.

Gatade, S. (2015, March 10). Goodbye secularism! Enter theocracy!! *Kafila.* Retrieved from https://kafila.online/2015/03/10/goodbye-secularism-enter-theocracy/.

Ghosh, A. (2008, September 21). Sanskrit boulevard. *Hindustan Times.* Retrieved from http://www.hindustantimes.com/india-news/sanskrit-boulevard/article1-339234.aspx.

Good Governance. [sri9011]. (2013, July 19). @taslimanasreen Sanskrit isnt really a dead language. Still spoken in a village in Karnataka and on Indo-Nepal border [Tweet]. Retrieved from https://twitter.com/sri9011/status/358480346272108545.

Gough, K. (1955). The social structure of a Tanjore village. In Marriott, M. & Beals, A. R. (Eds.), *Village India: Studies in the little community* (pp. 36–52). Chicago, IL: Chicago University Press.

Gould, H. A. (1961, June). Sanskritization and westernization: A dynamic view. *The Economic Weekly* (pp. 945–950).

Grosjean, F. (2012). An attempt to isolate, and then differentiate, transfer and interference. *The International Journal of Bilingualism, 16*(1), 11–19.

Hanneder, J. (2002). On 'The death of Sanskrit'. *Indo-Iranian Journal, 45*(4), 293–310.
Harman, C. (2004). The Hindutva and European fascism – Some comparisons and some lessons. *Marxists' Internet Archive.* Retrieved from https://www.marxists.org/archive/harman/2004/xx/hindutva.htm.
Hastings, A. M. (2004). *Past perfect, future perfect: Sanskrit revival and the Hindu nation in contemporary India* (Unpublished doctoral dissertation). Chicago, IL: University of Chicago.
—. (2008). Licked by the mother tongue: Imagining everyday Sanskrit at the home and in the world. *Journal of Linguistic Anthropology, 18*(1), 24–45.
[hindutvainus]. (2011, May 22). Sanskrit village – Jhiri, Madhya Pradesh [Video file]. Retrieved from https://www.youtube.com/watch?v=lHLIy-WHDew.
Hock, H. H. (1983). Language death phenomena in Sanskrit: Grammatical evidence for attrition in contemporary spoken Sanskrit. *Studies in the Linguistic Sciences, 13*(2), 21–35.
—. (1991). Review of R. N. Aralikatti (1989). Spoken Sanskrit in India: A study of sentence patterns. *Studies in the Linguistic Sciences, 21*(1), 161–165.
—. (1992a). A Note on English and Modern Sanskrit. *World Englishes, 11*(2–3), 163–171.
—. (1992b). Is Sanskrit dying? *Seminar, 391*, 17–24.
—. (1992c). Spoken Sanskrit in Uttar Pradesh: Profile of a dying prestige language. In Kelley, G. B., Dimock, E. C., Kachru, B. B. & Krishnamurti, B. (Eds.), *Dimensions of sociolinguistics in South Asia: Papers in memory of Gerald B. Kelley* (pp. 247–260). New Delhi: Oxford & IBH.
Imposition of Marwari may foment language riots. (2007). *The Hindu.* Retrieved from http://www.thehindu.com/todays-paper/tp-national/tp-otherstates/imposition-of-marwari-may-foment-language-riots/article1832920.ece.
Indian village where people speak in Sanskrit. (2014). *BBC India.* Retrieved from http://www.bbc.com/news/world-asia-india-30446917.
Is the Sanskrit spoken natively in pockets in India changing? (2011). *Stack Exchange: Linguistics.* Retrieved from http://linguistics.stackexchange.com/questions/369/is-the-sanskrit-spoken-natively-in-pockets-in-india-changing.
Ishtiaq, M. (1999). *Language shifts among the scheduled tribes in India: A geographical study.* Delhi: Motilal Banarsidass.
Islam, S. (2015). *Hindu nationalism and Rashtriya Swayamsevak Sangh.* Delhi: Media House.
Kasturi, M. (2010). 'All Gifting is Sacred': The Sanatana Dharma sabha movement, the reform of dana and civil society in late colonial India. *Indian Economic and Social History Review, 47*(1), 107–139.
Khalidi, O. (2008). Hinduising India: Secularism in practice. *Third World Quarterly, 29*(8), 1545–1562.
Kosambi, D. D. (1962). *Myth and reality: Studies in Indian culture.* Mumbai: Popular Prakashan.
Kushala, S. (2005, August 13). This village speaks God's language. *Times of India.* Retrieved from http://timesofindia.indiatimes.com/articleshow/msid-1199965,curpg-1.cms.
Madsen, B. (2013). *Why yoga? A cultural history of yoga.* London: Madzen Press.
Magier, D. (1983). *Topics in the grammar of Marwari* (Unpublished doctoral dissertation). University of California, Berkeley, CA.

Malvi language. (2015). *World Heritage Encyclopedia.* Retrieved from http://community.worldheritage.org/articles/Malvi_language.

Manthan, V. [Vichar Manthan]. (2015, December 15). VICHAR MANTHAN Ma. Krishna Shastry on 'Samskrita Movement – Its relevance & necessity in USA'. Retrieved from https://www.youtube.com/watch?v=lKljhDp9boU&feature=youtu.be.

Marriott, M. (1989). Constructing an Indian ethnosociology. *Contributions to Indian Sociology 23*(1), 1–38.

Marriott, M. & Inden, R. B. (1977). Toward an ethnosociology of South Asian caste systems. In David, K. H. (Ed.), *The new wind: Changing identities in South Asia* (pp. 227–238). The Hague: Mouton.

Martin, N. M. (2013). Fluid boundaries and the assertion of difference in low-caste religious identity. In Kassam, T. R. & Kent, E. F. (Eds.), *Lines in water: Religious boundaries in South Asia* (pp. 239–268). Syracuse, NY: Syracuse University Press.

Masica, C. P. (1991). *The Indo-Aryan languages.* New York, NY: Cambridge University Press.

Mayer, A. C. (1960). *Caste and kinship in Central India: A village and its region.* Berkeley: University of California.

McCartney, P. (2011). Spoken Sanskrit in a Gujarat ashram. *Journal of the Oriental Society of Australia, 43*, 61–82.

—. (2014, February 27). The sanitising power of spoken Sanskrit. *Himal Southasian.* Retrieved from http://himalmag.com/sanitising-power-spoken-sanskrit/.

—. [patrick mccartney]. (2015, August 13). Episode 3: Jalam ≠ Chillum [Video file]. Retrieved from https://www.youtube.com/watch?v=cLZeuCT_mwQ.

—. [patrick mccartney]. (2016, April 6). Episode 1: Imagining Sanskrit Land [Video file]. Retrieved from https://www.youtube.com/watch?v=pJy_Oqnqag8.

—. [patrick mccartney]. (2016, March 2). Episode 2: Total-am [Video file]. Retrieved from https://www.youtube.com/watch?v=7tAp8m9RHPU.

—. [patrick mccartney]. (2016, September 8). Episode 4: Imaging Sanskrit Land: It's Time to get Married [Video file]. Retrieved from https://www.youtube.com/watch?v=_B3un7aHEAc.

Murthy, B. S. (2015a). (2011, July 22). Mundane distortions in the divine discourse. *Boloji.com.* Retrieved from http://www.boloji.com/index.cfm?md=Content&sd=Articles&ArticleID=11241.

—. (2015b). (2012, January 7). On 'Ambedkar and the Bhagawat Gita'. *Boloji.com.* Retrieved from http://www.boloji.com/index.cfm?md=Content&sd=Articles&ArticleID=11758.

Nagraj, A. (2003, March 14). Tribal village in Banswada district of Rajasthan switches to ancient language, spreading the good word. *Indian Express.* Retrieved from http://www.chitrapurmath.net/sanskrit/sanskrit_lifestyle.htm.

Naik, J. P. (1969). *Education planning in a district.* New Delhi: Asian Institute for Educational Planning and Administration.

Nakamura, H. (1973). *A companion to contemporary Sanskrit.* Delhi: Motilal Banarsidass.

Nanda, M. (2005). *The wrongs of the religious right: Reflections on science, secularism and Hindutva.* Gurgaon: Three Essays Collective.

Nandy, A. (2001). *An ambiguous journey to the city: The village and other odd ruins of the self in the Indian imagination.* New Delhi: Oxford University Press.

News Minute. (2015, March 21). An entire village that talks in Sanskrit. *News Minute.* Retrieved 21/11, 2015, from http://www.thenewsminute.com/lives/527.

Nigam, A. (2016, August 3). Cow-gangs of Akhand Bharat and the Dalit revolt – Hindutva unravels. *Kafila.* Retrieved from https://kafila.online/2016/08/03/cow-gangs-of-akhand-bharat-and-the-dalit-revolt-hindutva-unravels/.

Office of the Registrar General and Census Commissioner, India. (2011). Statement 1: Abstract of speakers' strength of languages and mother tongues—2001. *Census of India.* Retrieved from http://www.censusindia.gov.in/Census_Data_2001/Census_Data_Online/Language/Statement1.aspx.

—. (2015). 2011 District Census Hand Book. Census of India. Retrieved from http://www.censusindia.gov.in/2011census/dchb/DCHB.html.

Pal, S. (2016, August 17). This tiny Sanskrit speaking village in Karnataka has at least one IT engineer in every family! *The Better India.* Retrieved from http://www.thebetterindia.com/65046/sanskrit-village-mattur-shimoga-karnataka/.

Pandharipande, R. (1996). Language shift with maintenance: The case of Sanskrit in India. In Verma, S. K., Siṃha, D., Śrīvāstava, R. N. (Eds.), *Perspectives on language in society: Papers in memory of Prof. Srivastava* (pp. 183–205). Delhi: Kalinga.

Pandit, N. (1992, May 16–23). Ambedkar and the 'Bhagwat Gita'. *Economic and Political Weekly, 27*(20/21), 1063–1065.

Pandit, P. B. (1972). *India as a sociolinguistic area.* Poona: University of Poona.

Patnaik, P. (1993). The fascism of our times. *Social Scientist, 21*(3/4): 69–77.

Pauwels, H. (2010). Who are the enemies of the bhaktas? Testimony about 'śāktas' and 'others' from Kabīr, the Rāmānandīs, Tulsīdās, and Harirām Vyās. *Journal of the American Oriental Society, 130*(4), 509–539.

Phillips, M. P. (2012). *Dialect continuum in the Bhil tribal belt: Grammatical aspects* (Unpublished doctoral dissertation). London: School of Oriental and African Studies.

Pollock, S. (2001). The death of Sanskrit. *Comparative studies in society and history, 43*(2), 392–426.

—. (2006). *The language of the gods in the world of men: Sanskrit, culture, and power in premodern India.* Berkeley: University of California Press.

Prakash, G. (2007). Secular nationalism, Hindutva, and the minority. In Needham, A. D. and Rajan, R. S. (Eds.), *The crisis of secularism in India* (pp. 177–190). Durham: Duke University Press.

Press Trust of India. (2015, June 28). Sanskrit should be propagated to purify minds of people: Sushma Swaraj. Indian Express. Retrieved from http://indianexpress.com/article/india/india-others/sanskrit-should-be-propagated-to-purify-minds-of-people-sushma-swaraj/.

Puniyani, R. (2006). *Contours of Hindu Rashtra: Hindutva, Sangh Parivar, and contemporary politics.* New Delhi: Kalpaz Publications.

Ramanujan, A. K. (1991). Three hundred Rāmāyaṇas: Five examples and three thoughts on translation. In Richman, P. (Ed.), *Many Rāmāyaṇas: The diversity of a narrative tradition in South Asia* (pp. 22–49). Berkeley: University of California Press.

Rapes happen in India, not Bharat: RSS Chief. (2013, January 4). CNN-News18 Retrieved from http://www.news18.com/videos/politics/mohan-split-quote-bhupen-phoner-529804.html.

Reddy, D. (2011). Capturing Hindutva: Rhetorics and strategies. *Religion Compass, 5*(8), 427–438.

Redfield, R. and Singer, M. (1955). Foreword. In Marriott, M. & Beals, A. R. (Eds.), *Village India: Studies in the little community.* Chicago, IL: Chicago University Press.

Reghunath, L. G. (2014, February 1). The believer: Swami Aseemanand's radical service to the Sangh. *The Caravan.* Retrieved from http://www.caravanmagazine.in/reportage/believer/.

[samskrit101]. (2009). Samskrita Bharati ITV Interview Sri Chamu Krishna Shastry and Sowmya Joisa [Video file]. Retrieved from https://www.youtube.com/watch?v=VhpRKY4a3ds.

Sanâtana Dharma: An advanced text book of Hindu religion and ethics. (1903). Benares: Central Hindu College.

Sanskrit can end linguistic differences in country: Expert. (2015). *Hindustan Times.* Retrieved from http://www.pressreader.com/india/hindustan-times-ranchi/20150706/281685433510139/TextView.

Schuessler, J. (2015, January 2). Literature of India, enshrined in a series. *New York Times.* Retrieved from http://www.nytimes.com/2015/01/03/books/murty-classical-library-catalogs-indian-literature.html.

Selinker, L. (1972). Interlanguage. *International Review of Applied Linguistics, 10,* 209–241.

Sen, S. (2015). Fascism without fascists? A comparative look at Hindutva and Zionism. *South Asia: Journal of South Asian Studies, 38*(4), 690–711.

Shandler, J. (2008). *Adventures in Yiddishland.* Berkeley: University of California Press.

Shapiro, M. C. (2003). Hindi. In Jain, D. & Cardona, G. (Eds.), *The Indo-Aryan languages* (pp. 250–285). London: Routledge.

Sharma, G. [GOVIND SHARMA]. (2009, October 6). Bajaj Discover Add in sanskrit [Video file]. Retrieved from https://www.youtube.com/watch?v=8FTVGNdDp2o.

Sharma, J. (2011). *Hindutva: Exploring the idea of Hindu nationalism.* New Delhi: Penguin Books.

Shrivastava, M. (2008). Power and contestation: India since 1989. *Labour, 62,* 291–297.

Singh, S. (2013, June 9). New life, old death for Sanskrit in Uttarakhand. *Indian Express.* Retrieved from http://archive.indianexpress.com/news/new-life-old-death-for-sanskrit-in-uttarakhand/1126773/.

Smith, A. D. (1991). *National identity.* Reno, NV: University of Nevada Press.

Sreevatsan, A. (2014, August 10). Where are the Sanskrit speakers? *The Hindu.* Retrieved from http://www.thehindu.com/news/national/where-are-the-sanskrit-speakers/article6299433.ece.

Srinivas, M. N. (1952). *Religion and society among the Coorgs of South India.* Oxford: Clarendon Press.

—. (1955). The social system of a Mysore village. In Marriott, M. & Beals, A. R. (Eds.), *Village India: Studies in the little community* (pp. 1–35). Chicago, IL: Chicago University Press.

—. (1956). A Note on Sanskritization and westernization. *Far Eastern Quarterly, 15*(4), 481–496.

—. (1959). The dominant caste in Rampura. *American Anthropologist, 61*(1), 1–16.

—. (1966). *Social change in Modern India.* Hyderabad: Orient Longman.

—. (1989). *The cohesive role of Sanskritization and other essays.* Delhi: Oxford University Press.

Staal, J. F. (1963). Sanskrit and Sanskritization. *Journal of Asian Studies, 22*(3), 261–276.

Subbarao, K. V. (2008). Typological characteristics of South Asian languages. In Kachru, B. B., Kachru, Y. & Sridhar, S. N. (Eds.), *Language in South Asia* (pp. 49–80). Melbourne: Cambridge University Press.

Sushma pushes for declaring Bhagavad Gita as national scripture. (2015). *The Hindu.* Retrieved from http://www.thehindu.com/news/national/sushma-pushes-for-declaring-bhagwad-gita-as-national-scripture/article6670252.ece.

Tarone, E. (2010). Interlanguage. In Berns, M. (Ed.), *Concise encyclopedia of applied linguistics* (pp. 134–139). Oxford: Elsevier.

Thomason, S. G. (2009). How to establish substratum interference. *Issues in Tibeto-Burman historical linguistics, 75*, 319–328.

Thompson, A. (2016). *Engendering the Buddhist state: Territory, sovereignty and sexual difference in the inventions of Angkor.* London: Routledge.

Trivedi, A. (2010, January 19). Sanskrit is second official language in Uttarakhand. *Hindustan Times.* Retrieved from http://www.hindustantimes.com/india/sanskrit-is-second-official-language-in-uttarakhand/story-wxk51l8Re4vNxofrr7FAJK.html.

Vision and mission. (2014). *Samskrita Bharati.* Retrieved from http://samskritabharati.in/about-us-2/mission.

Visvesvaran, K., Witzel, M, Manjrenkar, N., Bhog, D. & Chakravarti, U. (2009). Hindutva view of history. Rewriting textbooks in India and the United States. *Georgetown Journal of International Affairs, 10*(1), 101–112.

Viswanathan, T. S. (2013, April 4). Tale of two villages. *The Hindu.* Retrieved from http://www.thehindu.com/features/friday-review/history-and-culture/tale-of-two-villages/article4581221.ece.

Waskey, A. J. (2007). The political theory of theocracy. *National Social Science Journal, 28*(1), 116–129.

Witzel, M. (2015). Textual criticism in Indology and in European philology. *Electronic Journal of Vedic Studies, 21*(3), 1–82.

Zograf, G. A. (1982). *Languages of South Asia: A guide.* London: Routledge.

Zuckermann, G. & Walsh, M. (2011). Stop, revive, survive: Lessons from the Hebrew revival applicable to the reclamation, maintenance and empowerment of Aboriginal languages and cultures. *Australian Journal of Linguistics, 31*(1), 111–127.

—. (2014). 'Our ancestors are happy!' Revivalistics in the service of indigenous wellbeing. In Heinrich, P. & Ostler, N. (Eds.), *FEL XVIII Okinawa: Indigenous Languages: Their Value to the Community* (pp. 113–119). Bath: Foundation for Endangered Languages.

Nature and Character Emotions in the *Śrīgovindavilāsamahākāvya, Sarga* 1

Judith Unterdörfler

The description of nature in classical Indian literature is a topic that has drawn particular scholarly attention in the last two decades. Thus several articles on this have been published, focusing for example on different motifs of natural symbolism.[1] The delicate and artful description of nature used by classical poets can be seen very vividly in the medieval Sanskrit poem *Śrīgovindavilāsamahākāvya.* The following paper comprises an introduction to this as yet unpublished Vaiṣṇava work, some thoughts on nature in classical Indian literature in general and an analysis of the poem's first chapter with special attention to the use of natural symbolism. The aim is to show two things: first, how closely the description of nature is intertwined with the feelings of the poem's main characters (the *gopīs* and Lord Kṛṣṇa), and second, how the poet uses descriptions of nature in this way as a means of establishing the right atmosphere for what is going to take place afterwards, i.e. Lord Kṛṣṇa's descent and his amusements with the cowherdesses.

The poem *Śrīgovindavilāsamahākāvya*

The *Śrīgovindavilāsamahākāvya* is a yet unpublished[2] Vaiṣṇava poem, most likely written in the middle of the sixteenth century. As the title itself suggests, we are dealing with the genre *mahākāvya,* literally 'great poem', also called *sargabandha,* 'an arrangement of chapters'.[3] It is indeed quite an extensive work, containing in total nine sargas with approximately 60 to 80 stanzas each.

1 A treasure trove of such articles are the proceedings of the Pandanus workshops held in Prague and Milano since 1998. Similarly inspiring for anyone dealing with plants in Indian literature is the Pandanus Database of Plants (PADA).

2 A critical edition, translation and annotation of the poem are part of my dissertation, which will be submitted in 2017.

3 For general information on the genre, see LIENHARD 1984, chapter 4.

According to my current knowledge, the text is transmitted in only two manuscripts, one kept in Jodhpur (Rajasthan Oriental Research Institute, Acc. No. 12259) and the other in Bikaner (Anup Sanskrit Library, Acc. No. 3009). While the latter claims to have been written in Saṃvat 1614 (= 1557 CE), the colophon of the first one gives the date of transcription as Saṃvat 1602 (= 1545 CE).

Unfortunately we do not know very much about the author, but one finds some biographical hints about him in the ninth and last canto of the *mahākāvya* as well as at the end of each chapter. These chapter-colophons resemble the chapter-colophons of Śrīharṣa's *Naiṣadhīyacarita* (tenth century) not only structurally and metrically—in that they are both composed in the *Śārdūlavikrīḍitam* metre, and the first hemistich of each colophon is identical—but there are also striking similarities with regard to content: in *pāda*s a and b, i.e. the first hemistich, the author tells us his name, in this case Bhoja, as well as the names of his mother (Mandodarī) and father (Śrīmalla). Furthermore, he stresses his descent from a family of carpenters (*vardhaki*), which is unusual for a Sanskrit poet (9.90):

> *śrīmallaḥ sa vidagdhavardhakiśiro'laṃkāraratnāṅkuro*
> *mandodary api yaṃ kavīndratilakaṃ prāsūta bhojaṃ sutam /*
> *tasyāsmin racite 'rjitelavaraṇādhīśaprasādāvaleḥ*
> *śrīgovindavilāsanāmni navamaḥ sargo 'gamat pūrṇatām //*[4]

> (a/b) This Śrīmalla, a jewel-sprout from the head ornament of skillful carpenters, and Mandodarī have brought forth that one Bhoja as a son, who is an ornament of the best poets. (c/d) In this poem named *Śrīgovindavilāsa*, which he [Bhoja] who acquired a series of favours from the king of Ilavaraṇa composed, the ninth chapter has reached completion.[5]

The city Ilavaraṇa or Iḍādurga, as it is named elsewhere in *sarga* 9, is today known as Idar, situated in Gujarat about 100km northeast of Ahmedabad. An inscription that includes a genealogy of the royal family and is dated to Saṃvat 1612 (= 1555–56 CE) says that Idar was ruled by king Bhāramalla in the middle of the sixteenth century.[6] From the multiple references to king Bhāramalla in the ninth chapter as

---

4 Cf. the first chapter-colophon of the *NaiC*: *śrīharṣaṃ kavirājarājimukuṭālaṃkārahīraḥ sutam śrīhīraḥ suṣuve jitendriyacayaṃ māmalladevī ca yam / taccintāmaṇimantracintanaphale śṛṅgārabhaṅgyā mahākāvye cāruṇi naiṣadhīyacarite sargo 'yam ādir gataḥ //* 1.145 //. '(a/b) Śrīhīra, who is the diamond [made as an] ornament for the crown of the lines of great poets, and Māmalladevī have brought forth Śrīharṣa as their son, who [is intelligent, for he] subdued the heap of sense-powers. (c/d) In this *mahākāvya Naiṣadhīyacarita*, which is beautiful with the erotic mode of *śṛṅgāra* [the utmost *rasa*], and which is the fruit of his meditation on the sacred formula *cintāmaṇi*, the first chapter has come to an end.'

5 With one exception, which is indicated (footnote 28), all translations in this article are mine and I take full responsibility for possible mistakes or misinterpretations.

6 Archaeological Survey of India 1936: 96. He was enthroned by the sultan in 1514 (DOSÁBHAI 1986: 99).

well as the mention of favours from the king of Ilavaraṇa in the colophons, we can draw the likely conclusion that the text was written during his reign in the early to mid-sixteenth century. The available manuscripts must then have been copied very close to the time of the poem's composition. With respect to the very last colophon in *sarga* 9, mentioning the king's grace towards Bhoja, we can furthermore deduce that he was probably a court poet of king Bhāramalla.

Concerning the content of the poem, the title *Śrīgovindavilāsa* again gives us further information: the story is about Lord Kṛṣṇa's amorous amusements, which take place in the forest of Vṛndāvana. To depict these pleasures, the first *sarga* presents a scene in which the spring, friend of the love god Kāma, slowly manifests on earth, permeating the whole world. The following cantos begin with the beautiful Vanadevatā (forest deity of Vṛndāvana), who is sitting with Kṛṣṇa on Mount Govardhana and who shows and explains to him the beauty of nature. With the proper mood having been set, Kṛṣṇa performs the famous *rāsa* dance with the *gopīs* as well as the *jala-krīḍā*, the amorous frolic in the river Yamunā. Finally, we have Rādhā, Kṛṣṇa's most beloved cowherdess, coming onto the scene, which ends in her and Kṛṣṇa's union in a creeper-house. During their amorous *tête-à-tête*, the other *gopīs* are desperately searching for their Lord all over the forest and almost dying from the pain of separation.

As mentioned above, my paper will focus on the first chapter, in which the *gopīs*' yet unfulfilled love and their growing longing is depicted hand in hand with the arrival of the personified spring on earth. But before turning to the concrete Sanskrit example verses, it will be helpful to have a short look at how nature can be described with words in general as well as how it is depicted in classical Indian literature before the middle of the sixteenth century.

Nature in Literature

As soon as we are surrounded by nature—let us suppose we're entering a beautiful forest or walking through a lovely mountain region—we usually perceive nature directly with all our senses. When we then describe nature and thus try to grasp it with words, we must choose a particular register or mode of expression, which may be everyday language, scientific language, even poetic language. As is often maintained, scientific language tries to see the world 'as it is', i.e. in an objective way. Poetic language, by contrast, 'tries to maintain the uniqueness of the individual view, the uniqueness of the perspective proper to a concrete human being in a concrete historical period and geographical space'.[7] Of course we must be aware

7 Michalovic 2003: 22. When we later take account of the *rasa* theory and the 'aesthetic experience' of the connoisseur, the poem's specific time and space are transcended in a way when the recipient recalls his own memories of similar experiences he has had. During the reception of the poem, this certainty of a *conditio humana* is exactly what makes the reader/listener enjoy the text.

that there is no clear-cut dichotomy and often descriptions in Sanskrit rely on a precise understanding of how nature works according to *śāstra*, the scientific treatises, and with *śāstric* vocabulary. What I want to draw attention to here is another phenomenon, namely the paradox which the poet has to solve when describing nature, which is 'embedded in the conflict between a unique view and a universal language'.[8] This conflict can only be mediated with symbols (whether verbal or based on imagery), which primarily operate by conveying one meaning through another meaning. The symbol simultaneously refers to both its symbolic and its primary meaning.[9] In Sanskrit terms, we would talk in this context about the function of *vyañjanā* 'suggestion'. Thus we can say that it is fundamental to the poet's process of invoking a symbol—and also for the understanding of the reader/listener—to keep up this interplay of literal and metaphorical meaning.[10] When the poet depicts nature, he subjects it to his or her intentions in a way that nature, which itself has no intentions, becomes a symbol that serves to express emotions, ideas, values and so on. We will observe this more clearly with the help of the examples from the *Śrīgovindavilāsamahākāvya.*

In the Indian literary tradition, it is said that the frequency of nature symbols seems to be much higher than in European traditions.[11] Not being an expert in this field, I don't want to judge the truth of this statement, though surely some doubts arise when thinking for example of Greek bucolic literature (Theocritus, Bion, Moschus) or Vergil's *Eclogues*, in which the natural symbolism is obvious. In any case, we can agree that the idea of a kind of *unio mystica* or the unity of all creatures (*ātman-brahman*) in Indian thinking certainly favours natural symbolism.[12]

Already in early Indian literature we find examples of symbolic correspondences between man and nature.[13] One of these is the man/tree comparison in *Bṛhadāraṇyaka-Upaniṣad* 3.9.28.1–6, which says:

yathā vṛkṣo vanaspatis tathaiva puruṣo 'mṛṣā /
tasya lomāni parṇāni tvag asyotpāṭikā bahiḥ // 1 //
tvaca evāsya rudhiraṃ prasyandi tvaca utpaṭaḥ /
tasmāt tad ātṛṇṇāt praiti raso vṛkṣād ivāhatāt // 2 //
māṃsāny asya śakarāṇi kināṭaṃ snāva tat sthiram /
asthīny antarato dāruṇi majjā majjopamā kṛtā // 3 //
yad vṛkṣo vṛkṇo rohati mūlān navataraḥ punaḥ /

8 Ibid.

9 Zuska 2003: 12.

10 Michalovic calls it a 'game of replacement of the literal by the metaphorical, [which] is the basis for the creation of new meanings' (Michalovic 2003: 22).

11 Knotková-Capková 2000: 103.

12 Ibid.

13 On the following verse, see Mishra 2004: 222, who despite the initial *yathā* interprets even the quoted verses as naturalistic identification.

martyaḥ svin mṛtyunā vṛknaḥ kasmān mūlāt prarohati // 4 //
retasa iti mā vocata jīvatas tat prajāyate /
dhānāruha iva vai vṛkṣo 'ñjasāpretya sambhavaḥ // 5 //
yat samūlam āvṛheyur vṛkṣaṃ na punar ābhavet /
martyaḥ svin mṛtyunā vṛknaḥ kasmān mūlāt prarohati // 6 //

(1) As is a mighty tree so, indeed, is a man—his body hairs are its leaves and his skin is its outer bark. (2) His blood flowing from his skin is the sap flowing from its bark. Therefore, this juice flows out of a wounded man as sap from an axed tree. (3) His flesh is its sapwood, his sinew is [the tree's] bast fibre, that is certain. The bones are its heartwood and his marrow resembles its pitch. (4) A tree which is cut down, grows anew from its root; a mortal man, when he is cut down by death, from what root does he grow? (5) Do not say 'from the seed', for it is produced while he is alive; and just like a tree growing from a seed, he instantly takes birth before he dies. (6) A tree, when its root is eradicated, will never grow again; when a mortal man is cut down by death, from what root does he grow?

Similarly, in the *Śāntipārva* of the *Mahābhārata* Bhṛgu tells Bharadvāja that trees are like men in the sense that they are conscious living beings.[14] He explains their essence as consisting of the five elements (*mahābhūtas*) by analyzing their tactile, auditory and visual senses and so on.[15]

Of course one finds literary references to natural images not only in the Upaniṣads and epics, but also in early Sanskrit poetry, where nature often plays a crucial role. The most famous example is possibly Kālidāsa's *Meghadūta*, a poem students of Sanskrit are likely to be familiar with. As the title already points out, a cloud plays the role of a messenger in the poem. A Yakṣa addresses the cloud and asks it to deliver his message to his beloved, who is far away. For more examples of natural symbolism, one could name other works of Kālidāsa, like the *Kumārasaṃbhava* and the *Raghuvaṃśa*, or works of other famous early poets like Māgha, Bhāravi or Śrīharṣa, not to mention the *Ṛtusaṃhāra*, of course.[16] The examples are manifold, since descriptions of nature are an integral part of *mahākāvya* according to *alaṃkāraśāstra*, the rhetoric and aesthetic treatises, and poets consistently follow this convention.[17]

I will leave it at that for now and instead give some cross-references while explaining the verses of the *Śrīgovindavilāsa*, where we will also find certain nature symbols that clearly belong to the *kavisamaya*, i.e. the poetic conventions. First

14 *Jīvaṃ paśyāmi vṛkṣāṇām acaitanyaṃ na vidyate* (*MBh* 12.177.17c).

15 *MBh* 12.177.6–18. That Indian people felt, and still feel, a strong proximity to and respect for plants can even be observed in some rituals, in which practitioners accept plants as their own blood relations, a phenomenon that Mishra calls 'kindredation' (MISHRA 2004: 222).

16 For the descriptions of the seasons in Sanskrit literature in general, see RAGHAVAN 1972.

17 See e.g. Daṇḍin's *Kāvyādarśa*, *KĀ* 1.16.

of all we might name the lotus flower, which is compared with the face, eyes, hands or feet and serves as a symbol of beauty. Sometimes it is used so excessively that one could even talk of a 'lotification' of the person being described.[18] Another *kavisamaya* is the creeper embracing a tree just as a woman embraces her man, of which Urvaśī in Kālidāsa's *Vikramorvaśīyam* is a famous example. And of course the *dohada*s, the tree's cravings,[19] are a popular topos in classical Sanskrit poetry as well, which can be understood as the 'exquisite notion that sudden blossoming of trees in the spring is a kind of birth, preceded by a pregnancy fancy'.[20]

Examples of nature depiction in *Śrīgovindavilāsa, sarga* 1

Turning now to the verses of the *Śrīgovindavilāsamahākāvya*, let us start with a very simple, straightforward example of a nature symbol, the moon-like face of a *gopī* (stanza 22):

> *śaśimukhī śvasitoṣmahatādharā*
> *vigalitasmaraṇānimiṣekṣaṇā* /
> *kṛtahavā bahuśo'pi sakhījanaiḥ*
> *prativaco hum iti vyatarac cirāt* //
>
> (a/b) The woman with the moon-like face, whose lip was afflicted by the heat of her sighs, whose memory had slipped away and whose eyes were hardly blinking anymore—(c/d) although she had been called by her girlfriends so many times, her only answer was a 'hum', and that after a long while.

This verse occurs in a sequence about the different behavioural patterns of the girls longing for Kṛṣṇa (they tremble, cry, fall down etc.), a passage that recalls a similar one-by-one-description of women in *Bhāgavatapurāṇa* 10.32.3–9, although these women are happy to see Kṛṣṇa again. *Śaśimukhī*, 'the one with the moon-like face' (f.), serves as a mere embellishment in this verse, pointing to the beauty of the girl and underlining the feeling at the very heart of natural images in *kāvya*: 'that the human body (especially the female human body) is not fundamentally different

---

18 Pieruccini 2000: 175.

19 There are four trees whose cravings are satiated exclusively by women: the *bakula* tree, whose craving is satiated when sprinkled with wine from a woman's mouth; the *aśoka* tree, when kicked by a woman's feet; the *kurabaka* tree, when embraced by a woman; and the *tilaka* tree, when looked at from the corner of a woman's eye. In the *Śrīgovindavilāsa*'s first *sarga* we find at least one verse dedicated to each of the four trees. On *dohada* in its primary form, i.e. the craving of a pregnant woman, with many references especially to Jaina and Buddhist literature, see Bloomfield 1920.

20 Bloomfield 1920: 2.

from vegetation'.[21] The term is later used for other girls as well, or even for Kṛṣṇa himself. Thus we can regard it as a standard attribute that evokes beauty in Sanskrit poetry; in some places it might even be a verse-filler.

The metre of this first verse and of almost the whole first *sarga* is the beautiful *Drutavilambitam*. As its name indicates, it progresses in alternately fast and slow motion, and thus on a structural level fittingly imitates the gradually but continuously approaching spring season. Of course it's no coincidence that Bhoja uses this metre, since both Kālidāsa and Māgha used the *Drutavilambitam* in their descriptions of spring in the *Raghuvaṃśa* (9.24–48) and *Śiśupālavadha* (6.2–21).[22]

A famous element in the depiction of the spring season and of nature in general is the bee, which also plays a major role in the following two examples. We can see very clearly here how Bhoja uses the bee as a symbol in different ways depending on the emotion he wants to establish (stanza 48):

> *navanipītalatāmadhur unmadāṃ*
> *madhukarīṃ vicucumba madhuvrataḥ /*
> *mṛdu jugañja dudhāva ca pakṣatī*
> *paṭu nanāda muhur muhur abhramat //*
>
> (a/b) Just after imbibing the honey of the creeper, the one devoted to honey [i.e. the big black 'he-bee'] heartily kissed the intoxicated honey-maker [i.e. the 'she-bee']; (c/d) he gently hummed and shook his wings, strongly buzzed and flew around constantly.

In the structural centre of the verse—as well as in the centre with regard to content—stands the word *vicucumba*: the kiss between male and female bee marks their union.[23] Furthermore, the bees are in a chiastic structure in *pāda*s a and b, and modified with one *bahuvrīhi* each, indicating their state of high euphoria. That the intoxication is crucial in this verse is nicely demonstrated by the threefold repetition of the keyword *madhu*,[24] whose sound varies in the following *mṛdu* (c). In addition, the verse is distinguished by a sophisticated phonetic device based on the alliteration of *m* throughout the verse (eleven times) and of the vowel pair *a*/*u* in *madhu* (42 of the 48 syllables have an *a* or *u*).

---

21 Pieruccini 2000: 184. To be specific, here of course it is not vegetation but the cosmic sphere.

22 Cf. also Raghavan 1972: 63–64.

23 While it is not an actual union, a similar image—a male and female bee drinking *madhu* out of the same calyx—is found in *Kum.* 3.36ab: *madhu dvirephaḥ kusumaikapātre papau priyāṃ svām anuvartamānaḥ / śṛṅgeṇa ca sparśanimīlitākṣīṃ mṛgīm akaṇḍūyata kṛṣṇasāraḥ //.* '(a/b) The "he-bee" followed his beloved ["she-bee"] and drank [with her] honey from the same calyx; (c/d) and the black "he-antelope" scratched the "she-antelope" with his horn, while she had her eyes closed because of this touch.'

24 *Madhu*, clearly in the meaning 'honey, intoxicating liquor' here, is the word most often used elsewhere in the first *sarga* to denote the spring season.

As a result of kissing the 'she-bee', we see the 'he-bee' flying around and buzzing, which—although it is of course his natural behaviour—can be interpreted here as an expression of his excitement. This image of the *sambhoga-śṛṅgāra* ('successful love, union') of the happy bee-couple surely intensifies the *gopīs*' suffering in their *vipralambha-śṛṅgāra* ('disappointed love, separation'), and also increases their longing for Lord Kṛṣṇa. In this way nature functions as what the Indian aestheticians call a *vibhāva*, specifically an *uddīpana-vibhāva*, a 'stimulative determinant'.[25]

Furthermore, the scene might be understood proleptically as foreshadowing the actual union with Kṛṣṇa that is going to take place in the later chapters.

In sharp contrast to the happy bee-couple of verse 48 stands the poor single bee of the next example, stanza 38:

> *ciranibaddharasām iha mālatīṃ*
> *kvacid api bhramaro na gaveṣayan /*
> *virahaduḥkham asahyam avāpya kiṃ*
> *samapatad dahanatviṣi kiṃśuke //*

> (a/b) Since the bee could nowhere find the *mālatī* flower, which he had loved for so long,[26] (c/d) he suffered so much from the unbearable separation that he suddenly plunged into the *kiṃśuka* flower, which had the brilliance of fire.

In contrast to the previous verse, the bee in his state of suffering from separation is depicted here in a situation parallel to that of the *gopīs*: he cannot find (*na gaveṣayan*) his beloved—which in this case is not a female bee but a specific plant, the *mālatī* flower.[27] For this reason, he feels such hopeless despair that he even appears to commit suicide as a last resort. Crucial to the image is the red colour of the *kimśuka* flower. *Butea frondosa*, as it is called among the botanists, interestingly bears the English name 'flame of the forest', which very nicely takes account of the flowers' outstanding red refulgence.[28] Not only can the comparison of the flower's redness with fire be seen as a poetic convention (cf. *Rām.* 6.62.19, *Kirāt.* 16.52,

---

25 For Bharata's definition of *vibhāva* 'determinant', see the introduction to *NŚ* 7.4: *vibhāvaḥ kāraṇaṃ nimittaṃ hetur iti paryāyāḥ / vibhāvyate 'nena vāgaṅgasattvābhinaya ity ato vibhāvaḥ /*. '*Vibhāva* is synonymous with *kāraṇa, nimitta, hetu.* As words, gestures and the representation of the temperament are determined by this, it is called "determinant".' Cf. also Ingalls's explanation: 'By determinants are meant those factors which make the realization of the emotion and the *rasa* possible. They are of two sorts, objective determinants (*ālambanavibhāva*) and stimulative determinants (*uddīpanavibhāva*)' (Ingalls 1990: 16). Though I know that those terms need further explanation, discussing the aesthetic theories in greater detail unfortunately exceeds the scope of this paper.

26 *Ciranibaddharasām* could also be translated as 'on which nectar had been stuck for some time'.

27 *Jasminum grandiflorum* is an evergreen plant with small, white, sweet-smelling buds, which open in the evening. In India the *mālatī* flower is commonly used as ornamental plant, while in literature we often find descriptions of the bees' preference for the *mālatī* over all other flowers (for references see Syed 1990: 498–502; *PADA* s.v. *mālatī*).

28 See Image 1.

MSS 7956), but so can the scene of the bee's apparent suicide as a whole: a similar description is found for example in *Sūktimuktāvalī* 59.11:

> *mālatīvirahākrāntāḥ paśya bhṛṅgā mumūrṣavaḥ* /
> *ātmānaṃ prakṣipantīva kiṃśukaprabhavāntale* //
>
> See these bees, overwhelmed by the separation from their *mālatī*, wishing to end their lives; they seem to throw themselves into the fire which arises out of the *kiṃśuka* [flower].

The *utprekṣā*, often translated as 'poetic fancy',[29] is indicated in part by *iva* in the latter example, and in the *Śrīgovindavilāsa* by the fact that the verse is in the form of a question. For the *gopī*s, who see the bee as sharing in their own feelings and ascribing their own motivations and reasoning to the animal, it seems straightforward to interpret the bee's falling into the *kiṃśuka* flower as suicide. Nature helps, unintentionally, to substantiate the superimpositions of the humans by having a flower that looks like fire, which is the crucial point of the image here.

A variation on this image is found in stanza 754 of Hāla's *Sattasaī*,[30] where the 'he-bee', who is separated from his beloved, jumps in despair into a grove of flowers, red as fire. At first sight it seems like another masculine *satī*, but afterwards the bee immediately enjoys them. Thus it clearly corresponds to the canonical comparison of bees with frivolous lovers, enjoying the nectar of the flowers (women) and then leaving them.[31]

In the next example, stanza 40, we find a similar situation—a desperate, abandoned being apparently committing suicide—with the same protagonists (bee and plant) but in different roles:

> *alam anīdṛśasaurabhayā śriyā*
> *mama jahau bhagavān yadi śaṃkaraḥ* /
> *iti viṣaṇṇam ivātanu ketakaṃ*
> *nijamukhe nyadhitālihalāhalam* //
>
> (a) 'To hell with my beauty, my incomparable fragrance! (b) Now that Lord Śiva has abandoned me …' (c) Thinking thus, the *ketaka* flower, as if really depressed, (d) poured the deadly poison, the black bees, into her own mouth.

29 For example, as in Ingalls 1990 and Milanetti 2000. For a detailed explanation of this figure of speech, see Gerow 1971: 131–138.

30 *hā hā kiṃ teṇa kayaṃ mālaïvirahammi putti bhasaleṇaṃ / kaṃkellikusumamajjhe jalaṇo tti samappio appā* // 754 //. 'Do you know, my daughter, what the poor bee did in the absence of the jasmine flower? He threw himself into the red *aśoka* flowers as if into a fire.' Translation from Khoroche/Tieken 2009: 185.

31 Rossella 2000: 202, 205.

If we divide nature symbols into the two categories of 'semantic universals', i.e. natural phenomena that are quite universally understandable, and other similes in which the semantics are not so obvious to the 'cultural outsider',[32] this verse clearly belongs to the latter group. It alludes to a Purāṇic mythos which gives an explanation for Śiva's anger at the *ketaka* flower: when Brahmā, Viṣṇu and Śiva were fighting for hegemony, Śiva transformed himself into a fire pillar (*jyotirliṅga*) and commanded both of them to find the pillar's beginning and end. By telling Viṣṇu that Brahmā had found the upper end of the *liṅga*, the *ketaka* flower lied in favour of Brahmā. Śiva was so enraged that he cursed the *ketaka* and excluded her from the *liṅga-pūjā*.[33]

Again this is not the first verse to talk about the *ketaka* being rejected by Śiva. For example, in *MSS* 7660, the flower might be depressed as well but the tone of the verse is still more comforting than hopeless. Its focus is on the wordplay of *nirguṇa*, 'being without good qualities' or 'having no qualities' at all, which designates the character of Śiva in his aniconic *liṅga* form:

> *ekena cet parihṛto 'si maheśvareṇa*
> *kiṃ khedam āvahasi ketaka nirguṇo 'sau* /
> *anye na kiṃ jagati santi paraṃ guṇajñā*
> *ye tvāṃ vahanti śirasā naradevadevāḥ* //

> (a/b) If you are abandoned by the one great god (Lord Śiva), why do you feel sorry, o *ketaka*?—For he is [himself] without (good) qualities. (c/d) Aren't there others on earth who can greatly appreciate good qualities, who bear you on their heads, kings and gods?

Going back to *Śrīgovindavilāsa* 1.40 and the image of the disappointed *ketaka* lover, we find that the word *halāhalam* stands out both as a mythological reference to Śiva and as the deadly alliterative conclusion to the verse. In addition, *halāhalam* creates a kind of ring composition by repeating the same sounds of the initial word, *alam*. Its onomatopoeic sound, imitating the noise of swallowing, is also intensified here by the triple *la* in the *rūpakasamāsa ali-halāhalam*. In contrast to *viṣaṃ* or other synonyms for 'poison', *halāhalam* is usually explicitly used for the poison which was produced at the churning of the milk-ocean and which Śiva drank to save the gods. Thus this term relates the scene to Śiva by alluding to another mythos, one that depicts this very image of swallowing a deadly liquid.

The important characteristic of the bee, who actually constitutes the poison in this image, is not his bustling, erratic movements, which in other verses often serves as a comparison with the unsteady eyes of the *gopīs*. Here it is simply the

32 Vacek 1998: 137, 142.
33 *ŚiPu*, Vidyeśvara Saṃhitā 7.19. See also Syed 1990: 230–6.

dark, black colour which it shares with this kind of toxic substance in the Indian poetic imagination.

Furthermore, the *ketaka* flower is usually described by poets with emphasis on the strong fragrance that gives it the botanical name *Pandanus odoratissimus*. That is not the case here, where Bhoja had something different in mind. It would be probably more appropriate to translate the adjective *viṣaṇṇa* not as 'depressed' but more literally as 'downcast' (derived from *vi-sad*). When we look at pictures of this flower, we can see that our poet got the idea of ascribing the feeling of depression ('hanging the head down') to the *ketaka* flower by directly observing of the actual plant.[34]

After discussing the fame and fragrance of the *ketaka* flower, let us now turn to an example which appeals not only to the olfactory but also to the auditory senses. Moreover, 'poison' plays a role here as well (stanza 54):

> *iti vadanty api kāpi nitambinī*
> *priyatamāgamane samayīkṛtam /*
> *pikarutaṃ paripīya yathā viṣaṃ*
> *bhuvi papāta nimīlitalocanā //*

> (a) While saying this, some woman with beautiful hips (c) fully drank in the cuckoo's call (b) which had been made the signal for her lover's coming. (c) [She drank it] as if it were poison (d) and hereupon fell on the ground with her eyes closed.

The introductory *iti vadantī* refers to the two preceding verses, in which the *gopī* had condemned the moon for his painfully burning (though essentially cold) rays. Central to verse 54 is the call of the cuckoo, herald of spring,[35] which here does not cause pleasant anticipation, as is usually the case. This clearly positive connotation is predominant for example in *Kum.* 3.32, where the cuckoo's 'lovely sound' becomes the call of the love god Kāma:

> *cūtāṅkurāsvādakaṣāyakaṇṭhaḥ puṃskokilo yan madhuraṃ cukūja /*
> *manasvinīmānavighātadakṣaṃ tad eva jātaṃ vacanaṃ smarasya //*

> (a/b) The male cuckoo, whose voice had become impassioned by the taste of the mango sprouts, uttered a sweet sound (c/d) that became the voice of the love god, and was able to break the pride of the reluctant women.

The cuckoo communicating Kāma's will to young women in *Raghu.* 9.47 is another example of the bird's call as favourable sign in Sanskrit *kāvya*:

---

34 See Image 2.

35 Together with the mango buds, the call of the cuckoo is the first harbinger of the spring season; see SYED 1993: 152, 173.

> *tyajata mānam alaṃ bata vigrahair na punar eti gataṃ caturaṃ vayaḥ /*
> *parabhṛtābhir itīva nivedite smaramate ramate sma vadhūjanaḥ //*
>
> '(a/b) Give up your pride, enough of your quarrels! This pleasant age [of yours], once it is gone, will not come back'. (c/d) As if the will of the love god had thus been made known by the cuckoos, the women engaged in sporting.

In contrast to Kālidāsa's usage, the voice of the cuckoo in *Śrīgovindavilāsa* 1.54 is directly connected with the disappointed hopes of the cowgirl. Instead of serving as the voice of Kāma, the call is considered by Bhoja a sign of the arrival of the lover, who does not actually appear. Thus the natural phenomenon again functions as an *uddīpana-vibhāva*, 'stimulative determinant', i.e. an object evoking a certain emotion.[36] This emotion, in our case the sentiment of love amid separation (*vipralambha-śṛṅgāra-rasa*), is successfully amplified by the spring and its signs, which intensified the *gopī*'s wish for coming together with her beloved in the first place. As we see here, it is elevated to such an extent that the *gopī*'s mental and physical suffering culminates in her apparent death.

For the last example we return to the very first verse of the *Śrīgovindavilāsa*, in which one again finds the image of a face as the moon, though this time not merely as a means of embellishment but also with a deeper symbolic meaning:

> *smitamiṣonmiṣadaṃśutaraṅgita-*
> *vrajavadhūjanarāgapayonidhiḥ /*
> *śamanabhītitamaḥśamano harer*
> *mudam udañcayatān mukhacandramāḥ //*
>
> (d) The moon that is Hari's face (a/b) causes the ocean that is the passion of the Vraja women to swell up in waves by the spreading rays that are disguised as his smile. (c) It destroys the darkness that is the fear of death. (d) May that moon cause joy to arise!

The subject *mukhacandramas*, the moon-face, is not only a common *epithetum ornans* for Kṛṣṇa, just as *śaśimukhī* was in our first example, but completes the natural image here by combining with the long *bahuvrīhi* of *pāda*s a and b. On the level of natural phenomena, we have the moon, causing the waves of the sea to move with his rays. In Bhoja's fancy it is Hari's face that excites the passion of the women of Vraja. The rays, *aṃśu*, are his smile, *smita*, which stands prominently at the beginning of the verse and thus at the beginning of the whole poem. Again this analogy between smile and rays can be regarded as *kavisamaya* in Sanskrit poetry.[37]

36 Cf. note 25.

37 A comparison between moonlight and teeth is found for example in *Kum.* 6.25: *atha mauligata-syendor viśadair daśanāṃśubhiḥ / upacinvan prabhāṃ tanvīṃ pratyāha parameśvaraḥ //*. 'Then the

In his *Kāvyādarśa*, Daṇḍin cites *smitam mukhendor jyotsnā*, 'the smile is the shine of the moon-face', as example for a compounded (*mukhendu*) and at the same time uncompounded (*smitam, jyotsnā*) *rūpaka*, i.e. a metaphorical identification (*KĀ* 2.68). Furthermore, the canonical connection of *smita* and *sita* (the white colour of the smile) is important here not only because of its beautiful, repetitive sound, but also for establishing the dichotomy of light and dark. On the one hand we have the white moon rays, and on the other the dark colour of the ocean, with which passion, *rāga*, also having a dark colour in the Indian poetic imagination, matches well. A similar image, in which a woman with her moon-like rays stirs up her beloved, can be found in the Jaina *mahākāvya Ādipurāṇa* by Jinasena (12.62):[38]

> *tadvaktrendoḥ smitajyotsnā tanvatī nayanotsavam /*
> *bhartuś ceto'mbudheḥ kṣobham anuvelaṃ samātanot //*
>
> (a/b) This shine, the smile of her moon-like face, which was producing a festival for the eyes, (c/d) constantly caused agitation for the ocean, the heart of her husband.

The dark aspect is not explicitly focused on here, whereas in *Śrīgovindavilāsa* 1.1 it is repeated in *pāda* c: the common comparison or even identification of darkness (*tamas*) with fear (*bhīti*) or death (*śamana*) is combined in the metaphorical compound *śamanabhītitamaḥśamana*, whose wordplay is based on the two meanings of *śamana*, 'destroyer' and 'death'. Thus at the literal and metaphorical level Kṛṣṇa is depicted as the one who turns the darkness into light.

Conclusion

As the examples have shown, nature is used in the *Śrīgovindavilāsamahākāvya* as an expressive tool to describe the situation of desperate longing that the *gopīs* find themselves in. For the most part, the poet focuses on one natural phenomenon per verse, which he then relates to one of the human senses. As we have seen in the examples, these can be visual (1.1, 1.22, 1.38, 1.48) as well as auditory (1.54) and olfactory (1.40) sensations. The bees, the cuckoo, the blooming flowers, trees etc., all heralds of the spring season, assume a specific symbolic role in this scenery, and in doing so convey the full breadth of human emotions, joy as well as sorrow.[39] They become a means of expressing as well as deepening and in some places even

highest God answered, while he was increasing the tender brilliance of the moon, which he wore in his crown, with the white rays of his teeth.'

38 The Sanskrit verse is cited in Gupta 1993: 92.

39 Chettiarthodi 2005: 21–22.

Image 1: Skt. kiṃśuka, Butea frondosa

Image 2: Skt. ketaka, Pandanus odoratissimus

establishing the feelings of love and deep longing in the characters. Bhoja for his part neither randomly links different natural phenomena with emotions nor simply copies standard images from other *kāvya*, but bases his images on the direct observation of plants, animals etc., as we have seen most clearly in the case of the downcast *ketaka* flower (1.40).

What the scholar Murali says about the tradition of *aintiṇai*, the fivefold categorization of the environment in Tamil poetry, could similarly apply to the *Śrīgovindavilāsa*: we find here 'an environmental aesthetics, where the human *bhāva* [i.e. the state of being/emotion] seeks its correspondence in the natural *vibhāva* ['determinant', which makes the realization of emotion and *rasa* possible]'.[40]

Not only are the *gopīs* affected by the surrounding natural phenomena, but so is Kṛṣṇa himself, as becomes clear at the end of the chapter. This was actually the plan of the love god Kāma when he sent his *svasuhṛt* (1.26, 1.32), his 'friend' spring, who is known as the 'season of love par excellence'.[41] Thus *sarga* 1 ends with the fulfillment of Kāma's intention when, after the completion of the spring season (*surabhisamṛddhi*, 1.62), Kṛṣṇa descends to Vṛndāvana—not for nothing is the love god called *bhūmipati*, 'lord of the earth', more than once in the first canto (1.39, 1.49). The right atmosphere is created and the scene set for the subsequent amusements, which is accomplished by the poet's skillful compilation of various illustrative natural images. Bhoja knows so precisely how to use nature as a symbol that he also enables the reader/listener of his poem to relish the evoked *rasa* with the same intensity as the characters of his play.

40 Murali 1998: 157–158.

41 Feller 1995: 110. In contrast to other *mahākāvyas* where spring often appears as beautiful lady (*śrī*), here it keeps its original male gender. For further references see Feller 1995: 94–96.

References

Primary Literature

BhP = *Bhāgavatamahāpurāṇa*. Śrīkṛṣṇadāsa, K., Sharma, R. N. & Singh, N. Ś. (1987). *Śrīmad Bhāgavatamahāpurāṇaṃ* (4 vols.). Delhi: Nag.

Bṛhadāraṇyaka-Upaniṣad = Olivelle, P. (1998). *The early Upaniṣads: Annotated text and translation*. New York: Oxford University Press, 1998.

KĀ = *Kāvyādarśa*. von Böhtlingk, O. (1890). *Dandin's Poetik (Kâvjâdarça)*. Leipzig: Haessel.

Kirāt. = *Kirātārjunīya*. Cappeller, C. (1912). *Bharavi's poem Kiratarjuniya, or, Arjuna's combat with the Kirata*. Cambridge, MA: Harvard University.

Kum. = *Kumārasaṃbhava*. Kāle, M. R. (1967). *Kālidāsa's Kumārasaṃbhava, cantos I–VIII, complete*. Delhi: Motilal Banarsidass.

Megha. = *Meghadūta*. Hultzsch, E. (1998). *Kālidāsa's Meghadūta. Delhi: Munshiram Manoharlal. (Original work published 1911.)*

MBh = *Mahābhārata*. Sukthankar, V. S., Balasaheb, P. P., Belvalkar, S. K. & Vaidya, P. L. (1933–72). *The Mahābhārata* (21 vols.). Pune: Bhandarkar Oriental Research Institute.

MSS = *Mahā-subhāṣita-saṃgraha*. Sternbach, L. & Bhaskaran Nair, S. (1974–1987). *Mahā-subhāṣita-saṃgraha. Being an extensive collection of wise sayings and entertaining verses in Sanskrit* (vols. 1–6). Hoshiarpur: Vishveshvaranand Vedic Research Institute.

NaiC = *Naiṣadhīyacarita*. Ācārya, N. R. (1952). *Śriharṣaviracitaṃ Naiṣadhīyacaritam*. Mumbai: Nirṇayasāgara Presa.

NŚ = *Nāṭyaśāstra*. *GRETIL*. Retrieved from http://gretil.sub.uni-goettingen.de/gretil/1_sanskr/5_poetry/1_natya/bharnatu.htm.

Raghu. = *Raghuvaṃśa*. Scharpé, A. (1964). *Kālidāsa-lexicon. Vol I: Basic text of the works. Pt. IV: Raghuvaṃśa*. Bruges: De Tempel.

Rām. = *Rāmāyaṇa*. Bhatt, G. H. (1960–1975). *The Vālmīki-Rāmāyaṇa: The national epic of India*. Baroda: Oriental Institute.

Ṛtu. = Roberts, J. T. (1990). *The seasons: Kālidāsa's Ritusaṃhāra*. Tempe: Arizona State University, Center for Asian Studies.

ŚiPu = *Śivapurāṇa*. (1920). Mumbai: Veṅkateśvara Steam Press.

Śiśu. = *Śiśupālavadha*. Vetāl, A. S. (1929). *The Śiśupālavadha: With two commentaries, the Sandehaviṣauṣadhi by Vallabha Deva, and the Sarvaṅkaṣā by Mallinātha*. Benares: Jai Krishnadas-Haridas Gupta.

Śrīgovindavilāsamahākāvya = Unterdörfler, J. (2017). *Śrīgovindavilāsamahākāvya by Bhoja, edited with an introduction and annotated translation*. (Manuscript in preparation.)

Sattasaī = Weber, A. (1881). *Das Saptaçatakam des Hâla*. Leipzig: Brockhaus.

Sūktimuktāvalī = Krishnamacharya, E. *The Sūktimuktāvalī*. Baroda: Oriental Institute.

Vikramorvaśīyam = *Vikramorvaśīyam of Kālidāsa: With three commentaries*. (1966). Hyderabad: Sanskrit Academy, Osmania University.

Secondary Literature

Archaeological Survey of India. (1936). *Annual report.* Calcutta: Office of the Superintendent of Government Printing.

BLOOMFIELD, M. (1920). The dohada or craving of pregnant women: A motif of Hindu fiction. *Journal of the American Oriental Society, 40*, 1–24.

CHETTIARTHODI, R. (2005). Humanizing nature—A study in the imagery of Kālidāsa. In L. Sudyka (Ed.), *Love and nature in kāvya literature: Proceedings* (pp. 19–28). Kraków: Jagiellonian University, Institute of Oriental Philology.

DOSÁBHAI, E. (1986). *A history of Gujarat: From the earliest period to the present time.* New Delhi: Asian Educational Services. (Original work published 1894.)

FELLER, D. (1995). *The seasons in mahākāvya literature.* Delhi: Eastern Book Linkers.

GEROW, E. (1971). *A glossary of Indian figures of speech.* The Hague: Mouton.

GUPTA, P. (1993). *Rasa in the Jaina Sanskrit* mahākāvyas: From 8th to 15th century A.D. Delhi: Eastern Book Linkers, 1993.

INGALLS, D. H. H. (Ed.). (1990). *The Dhvanyāloka of Ānandavardhana with the Locana of Abhinavagupta* (D. H. H. Ingalls, J. Moussaieff Mossan & M. V. Patwardhan, Trans.). Cambridge: Harvard University Press.

KNOTKOVÁ-CAPKOVÁ, B. (2000). The motif of water/river in the poetry of Sunīl Gaṅopādhyāy. In J. Vacek (Ed.), *Pandanus 2000: Natural symbolism in Indian literatures* (pp. 103–117). Prague: Signeta.

KHOROCHE, P. & TIEKEN, H. (2009). *Poems on life and love in ancient India: Hāla's Sattasaī.* New York: Excelsior Editions.

LIENHARD, S. (1984). *A history of classical poetry: Sanskrit – Pali – Prakrit.* Wiesbaden: Harrassowitz.

MICHALOVIC, P. (2003). Nature, 'the view' and poetic language. In J. Vacek (Ed.), *Pandanus 2003: Nature symbols in literature* (pp. 21–26). Prague: Signeta.

MILANETTI, G. (2000). Wonder and multiple meanings: The description of nature in Avadhi poetry. In J. Vacek (Ed.), *Pandanus 2000: Natural symbolism in Indian literatures* (pp. 131–147). Prague: Signeta.

MISHRA, A. K. (2004). Man's psychological relationship with nature as reflected in the Sanskrit literature: A symbolic note. In G. U. Thite & M. R. Deshpande (Eds.), *Problems in Vedic and Sanskrit literature* (pp. 222–225). Delhi: New Bharatiya.

MURALI, S. (1998). Environmental aesthetics: Interpretation of nature in akam and puram poetry. *Indian Literature, 41*(3), pp. 155–162.

PADA = *Pandanus Database of Plants.* (1998–2009). Retrieved from http://iu.ff.cuni.cz/pandanus/database/.

PIERUCCINI, C. (2000). Human body and vegetation in early kāvya. In J. Vacek (Ed.), *Pandanus 2000: Natural symbolism in Indian literatures* (pp. 159–190). Prague: Signeta.

RAGHAVAN, V. (1972). *Ṛtu in Sanskrit literature.* Delhi: Shri Lal Bahadur Shastri Kendriya.

ROSSELLA, D. (2000). Animals and women (nāyikās) in Hāla's Sattasaī. In J. Vacek (Ed.), *Pandanus 2000: Natural symbolism in Indian literatures* (pp. 191–209). Prague: Signeta.

SYED, R. (1990). *Die Flora Altindiens in Literatur und Kunst* (Unpublished doctoral dissertation). Ludwig Maximilian University of Munich, Germany.

—. (1993). *Kālidāsa's Kumārasaṃbhava.* Reinbek: Wezler Verlag für Orientalistische Fachpublikationen.

VACEK, J. (1998). A neytal feature to be found in the Meghadūta? In J. Vacek (Ed.), *Pandanus 1998: Flowers, nature, semiotics; Kāvya and sangam* (pp. 137–165). Prague: Signeta.

ZUSKA, V. (2003). Symbolic meaning as a figure against the background of nature's horizon. In J. Vacek (Ed.), *Pandanus 2003: Nature in literature, art, myth and ritual* (pp. 11–20). Prague: Signeta.

How to Teach Sanskrit Grammar

The Case of the Perfect System in the *Bhaṭṭikāvya*

Lidia Szczepanik-Wojtczak

The *Bhaṭṭikāvya* is the earliest known Sanskrit didactic poem. Bhaṭṭi (ca. 6/7 CE), the legendary composer of the work, sets out to illustrate the rules governing the Sanskrit language, as well as its poetry, while at the same time retelling the well-loved exploits of Rāma. The subsequent *sarga*s (22 in total) vary significantly in style and have been grouped by recognised commentators into four distinct *kāṇḍa*s: *Prakīrṇa*, *Adhikāra*, *Prasanna* and *Tiṅanta*. *Tiṅanta kāṇḍa*, which spans over cantos 14–22, is a topical-structural illustration of the Sanskrit verbal system, each *sarga* exemplifying a different tense or mood.

This paper attempts to place the *Bhaṭṭikāvya* within the framework of Sanskrit poetics and aims to show how the author of the *Bhaṭṭikāvya* went about teaching grammar, specifically the perfect tense (*liṭ*), which is the 'subject' of the 14 canto of the epic poem. The perfect tense according to the *Aṣṭādhyāyī* of Pāṇini is then presented with the purpose of demonstrating that Bhaṭṭi's synthesis and prescriptive approach to teaching was perhaps meant to supplement the Pāṇinian tradition, or maybe even function as a disparate method. The final section of the paper deals with the *Bhaṭṭikāvya*'s functionality and purpose as an educational aid.

*Bhaṭṭikāvya**

The *Bhaṭṭikāvya*, 'Bhaṭṭi's Poem'—also known as *Rāvaṇavadha*, 'The Death of Rāvaṇa'—is one of the great Sanskrit *sargabandha*s, epic poems. Due to the relative paucity of secondary sources on this valuable work, this paper will first be an attempt at placing the *Bhaṭṭikāvya* (henceforth BhK) within the genealogical framework of pre-modern Indian literary theory. I will then move on to discuss

* This publication was made possible in part by the J. Gonda Foundation of the Royal Netherlands Academy of Arts and Sciences and the International Institute for Asian Studies in Leiden.

the functionality of the BhK as an educational poem, taking the exposition of the perfect tense in *sarga* 14 as an example.[1] I will consider the perfect tense as it is presented in Pāṇini's *Aṣṭādhyāyī* and discuss whether the widely accepted assumption that the BhK is a handbook of grammar belonging to the Pāṇinian school of thought is entirely accurate.

The BhK is the earliest example of an entire Sanskrit belletristic work composed with a didactic purpose—*śāstrakāvya* or *kāvyaśāstra* depending on the author of the definition. Lienhard explains how he sees the distinction between the two terms—*śāstrakāvya* is poetry that happens to also be didactic, and *kāvyaśāstra* is a scientific text that also happens to be poetic (LIENHARD 1984: 225). Modern scholars traditionally ascribe the term *śāstrakāvya* to the BhK.[2] In fact, most Indian theoreticians seem to define *śāstrakāvya* and *kāvyaśāstra* as quite the opposite. Raghavan notices that Bhoja, the eleventh-century king and poetician, cites the BhK as one of the examples of the *kāvyaśāstra* type of composition, whereas treatises like the work on polity *Kāmandakīya Nītisāra* belong to the *śāstrakāvya* type[3] (RAGHAVAN 1963: 628).

The Kashmiri polymath Kṣemendra, who was roughly contemporaneous with Bhoja, also discusses the categories of *śāstrakāvya* and *kāvyaśāstra* at the beginning of the third book of his *Suvṛttatilaka*. He says:

> *śāstraṃ kāvyaṃ śāstrakāvyaṃ kāvyaśāstraṃ ca bhedataḥ /*
> *catuṣprakāraḥ prasaraḥ satāṃ sārasvato mataḥ //* 3.2
>
> *Śāstra, kāvya, śāstrakāvya* and *kāvyaśāstra*—
> this is the division of literature into four modes as it is understood by the wise.
>
> *śāstraṃ kāvyavidaḥ prāhuḥ sarvakāvyāṅgalakṣaṇam /*
> *kāvyaṃ viśiṣṭaśabdārthasāhityasadalaṅkṛti //* 3.3

1 This line of inquiry is strongly inspired by Lidia Sudyka's paper 'What Does the Bhaṭṭi-kāvya Teach?' (SUDYKA 2000), as well as her outstanding book, *Od Ramajany do Dydaktyki czyli Zagadki Poematu Bhattiego* (SUDYKA 2004), which focuses mainly on the *Prasanna-Kāṇḍa* of the BhK.

2 NARANG 1969, FALLON 2009, LIENHARD 1984 and SUDYKA 2000, for instance.

3 The other is the *Mudrārākṣasa*; cf. Bhoja's *Śṛṅgāraprakāśa* 11 (lines 14–17 on pg. 470 in volume 2 of the Joyser edition):

> *yatrārthaś śāstrāṇāṃ kāvye 'bhiniveśyate mahākavibhiḥ /*
> *tad bhaṭṭikāvyamudrārākṣasavat kāvyaśāstraṃ syāt //*
> *śāstraṃ yatra kavīnāṃ rahasyam upakalpanty analpadhiyaḥ /*
> *tad ratavilāsakāmandakīyavac chāstrakāvyaṃ tu //*

Bhoja was likely inspired by the categories of *kāvya* expounded by Bhāmaha (*Kāvyālaṃkāra* 1.17):

> *vṛttadevādicaritaśaṃsi cotpādyavastu ca /*
> *kalāśāstrāśrayaṃ ceti caturdhā bhidyate punaḥ* // KĀ 1.17

'And again, [*kāvya*] is divided into four [types]: the deeds of the gods and others, themes invented [by the poet], subjects related to the arts, and subjects related to the sciences.'

Those who know poetry say:
'*Śāstra* is that, which presents all of the features of poetic works.
Kāvya is the well-ornamented, excellent union of words and meanings.[4]

śāstrakāvyaṃ caturvargaprāyaṃ sarvopadeśakṛt /
bhaṭṭibhaumakakāvyādi kāvyaśāstraṃ pracakṣate // 3.4

Śāstrakāvya, which refers to the four aims of existence, is instructive for everyone.
It is said that poetry of Bhaṭṭi, Bhaumaka[5] and others is called *kāvyaśāstra*.'

Thus, according to Kṣemendra, *śāstrakāvya* is a kind of instructive text on the four *puruṣārtha*s which is characterised by an exceptional poetic style, and *kāvyaśāstra* as exemplified by the BhK must refer to works of poetry which carry educational benefits but are not technical (poetry in science vs. sciences in poetry).[6] In light of the material cited above and in the footnotes, it seems that it would be more justifiable to use the term *kāvyaśāstra* for works like the BhK rather than *śāstrakāvya*.

What is particularly important in the scope of this paper is that the oldest commentators do not use these terms to describe the BhK at all. Jayamaṅgala

4 The idea in the first line—that *śāstra* carries the hallmarks of poetry—may be a reference to the notion famously expressed in Mahimabhaṭṭa's *Vyativiveka*, namely that all *kāvya* is indeed *śāstra*, i.e., all of the *belles lettres* have the capacity for instruction (see RAJENDRAN 2001).

Kṣemendra clearly follows Bhāmaha's definition of *kāvya*: *śabdārthau sahitau kāvyaṃ* (*Kāvyālaṃkāra* 1.16.a).

5 Bhaumaka was a poet hailing from Kṣemendra's homeland of Kashmir and the author of the *Arjunarāvaṇīya* (or the *Rāvaṇārjunīya*), a didactic poem which exemplifies the *Aṣṭādhyāyī* in order, while retelling the story of Rāvaṇa's fight with Arjuna as it is depicted in the *Rāmāyaṇa*. In his monograph, Lienhard claims that this poem was 'rightly identified as a *śāstrakāvya* by Kṣemendra', (LIENHARD 1984: 226) but as we can see, Kṣemendra clearly identifies it as *kāvyaśāstra* (which is differentiated from *śāstrakāvya*)!

6 It may also be worth referencing Rājaśekhara's thoughts on this topic, which he presents in his treatise, the *Kāvyamīmāṃsā*:

bhavati prathayann arthaṃ līnaṃ samabhiplutaṃ sphuṭīkurvan /
alpam analpaṃ racayann analpam alpaṃ ca śāstrakaviḥ // Ch. 2, p. 5, lines 9–10.
'The *śāstra* poet: reveals hidden meanings, makes clear what has been obscured,
lengthens that which is short and arranges that which is too long into shorter [compositions].'

Also:

tatra tridhā śāstrakaviḥ / yaḥ śāstraṃ vidhatte, yaś ca śāstre kāvyaṃ saṃvidhatte, yo 'pi kāvye śāstrārthaṃ nidhatte / Ch. 5, p. 17, lines 15ff.

'There are three types of *śāstra* poet—those who compose the *śāstra* texts, those who employ *kāvya* in the *śāstra* and those who lay down the [teachings of] *śāstra* in [the form of] *kāvya*.'

So, according to Rājaśekhara, there was a threefold division which depended on the amount of scientific material that was found in the text or, perhaps, on its technicality. Purely scientific texts, *śāstra*s, were also poetry of sorts; then there were the *śāstrakāvya*s, which were clearly poetic works on particular branches of science; and then there were the *kāvyaśāstra*s, which were poems in which the meanings of the sciences were explicated (like the BhK).

(ca. 10 CE) does not expressly mention the author's overarching educational objectives, and Mallinātha (14/15 CE) instead writes:

> *rāmakathāṃ āśritya pāṇinīyasūtrāṇām udāharaṇaṃ kāvyaṃ cikīrṣur* / (*ad.* BhK 1.1)
>
> 'Having chosen the story of Rāma, [Bhaṭṭi] desired to create a poem of examples on the *sūtras* of Pāṇini.'

In fact, all of the commentators known to me cite the *sūtras* of the *Aṣṭādhyāyī* when they are discussing the grammatical aspects of a given BhK verse.

The poem and its author

As the title suggests, the poem was written by Bhaṭṭi, who is said to have flourished in 7 CE in Vallabhi.[7] On the narrative level of the BhK we are presented with the feats of Rāma, from his illustrious birth to his reunion with Sītā. The plot follows Vālmiki's text faithfully; however, it omits the *Uttarakāṇḍa* completely and ends with Rāma happily winning back his beloved wife.[8] On the instructive level we are given examples-in-use of most of the rules governing Sanskrit literary production.

In the final verses of his *mahākāvya*, in the *kāvyapraśasti*, Bhaṭṭi evaluates his poem and explains its purpose:

> *idam adhigatamuktimārgacitraṃ*[9] *vivadiṣatām vadatāṃ ca sannibandhāt* /
> *janayati vijayaṃ sadā janānāṃ yudhi susamāhitam aiśvaraṃ yathāstram* //
> BhK 22.32
> When this [poem]—stunning in its modes of expression—is studied,
> then, because of its proper composition,
> it brings victory to those desirous of speaking [publicly] and those [already] debating.

7 On the time and place of Bhaṭṭi, see SUDYKA 2004, NARANG 1969, KARANDIKARS 1982 and TRIVEDI 1898 (Introduction). The discussion revolves around the information found in the last verse, in which Bhaṭṭi states that he wrote the BhK in 'Valabhī' under the rule of king Dharasena (*śrīdharasena-narendra*). Historians have established that there were four rulers from Vallabhi called Dharasena, and they ruled between 495 CE and around 650 CE. Based on the title of *narendra* used by Bhaṭṭi to describe his patron, it is generally accepted that the fourth Dharasena was his benefactor because it was this last king who was powerful enough to wield such a high-ranking title.

8 For a comprehensive list of the alterations that Bhaṭṭi made to the Rāmāyaṇa story, see NARANG 1969: 9–15 and LEONARDI 1974 ('Capitolo primo: Rāmāyaṇa e Bhaṭṭikāvyam').

9 This is a punned verse; the translation incorporates both readings. The string *adhigatamuktimārgacitraṃ* can be divided two ways: *adhigatam ukti-mārgacitraṃ* and *adhigata-mukti-mārgacitraṃ*.

Like a beautifully adorned and mighty weapon produces victory for men in battle,
when they have learnt the ways it can be thrown.

dīpatulyaḥ prabandho 'yaṃ śabdalakṣaṇacakṣuṣāṃ /
hastāmarśaṃ ivāndhānāṃ bhaved vyākaraṇād ṛte // BhK 22.33
This poem is akin to a lamp for those who recognise the marks of correct speech.
Without grammar [we] would fumble like the blind.[10]

vyākhyāgamyam idaṃ kāvyam utsavaḥ sudhiyām alam /
hatā durmedhasaś cāsmin vidvatpriyatayā mayā // BhK 22.34
It is enough that this poem, accessible through a commentary, is a celebration for the wise.
Here, I have made the ignorant miserable because of my love for the learned.

Though according to some interpretations of verse 22.33, the BhK was supposed to have been intended for both beginners and proficient users of Sanskrit (see footnote 10), Bhaṭṭi himself says that it is a source which can only be understood with the help of a commentary (or a teacher's instruction—*vyākhyāgamyam*),[11] and that studying it makes fools miserable. This would in fact indicate that the BhK was a more advanced text meant for students who already possessed a working knowledge of the language and wanted to expand their repertoire. One of the keys to understanding the didactic functionality of the poem seems to lie in Bhaṭṭi's statement in 22.32, namely that his *kāvya* is targeted towards those who wish

10 Diwekar's interpretation of these two verses ought to be referenced here. According to him, those who already know grammar will broaden their horizons thanks to the BhK, whereas those who have no knowledge of grammar whatsoever will at least come to know the forms that appear in the poem itself—like the visually impaired, who may not be able to see everything, but can make out the objects they touch with their hands. So, according to Diwekar, the poem is meant for both those who are proficient in using Sanskrit, as well as for those who are not (Diwekar 1929: 829). Fallon's edition has *hastādarśa* instead of *hastāmarśa* in BhK 22.33c, and his translation 'hand mirror' also evokes Diwekar's understanding of this metaphor.

11 Sudyka gives a list of 12 complete and identified Sanskrit commentaries of the BhK, as well as many others that are incomplete or in the vernaculars (Sudyka 2004: 26–28). Narang lists 22 commentators; the majority of his list comprises names and titles that were found in manuscript catalogues (Narang 1969: 25–32).

Conversely, Bhāmaha says in his definition that a *mahākāvya*, or *sargabandha*, should not rely heavily on a commentary/teacher's instruction—*nātivyākhyeyam* (KĀ 1.18). In reference to this, we should also note KĀ 2.20, where Bhāmaha famously adds that if *yamaka* poems and *prahelikās* (riddles) are difficult enough to require a commentary (like the scientific texts—*vyākhyāgamyāni śāstravat*), then the wise rejoice, while the dull-witted suffer. This pair of very similar verses from the BhK (22.34) and the KĀ (2.20) has, of course, been the basis of the discussion on which of the two writers preceded the other.

to learn how to speak publicly (or take part in debates) and those already doing so (*vivadiṣatām vadatāṃ ca*). This implies that the poem could be seen as a text for orators[12] or, more probably, for poets—composing their *kāvyas*, taking part in discussions among their peers of cosmopolitan men of letters, and reciting their work at *goṣṭhīs*.

The BhK is divided into 22 cantos, or *sargas*; commentarial tradition, starting with the oldest extant commentary—*Jayamaṅgalā* by Jayamaṅgala—additionally divides it into four large sections, *kāṇḍas*, based on the subject taught in each:

Prakīrṇa-Kāṇḍa: 1.1–5.96
Adhikāra-Kāṇḍa: 5.97–10
Prasanna-Kāṇḍa: 10.1–13
Tiṅanta-Kāṇḍa: 14.1–22[13]

It is because of the assumption that Bhaṭṭi explains different topics with variegated language[14] and does not follow the order of Pāṇini's *sūtras* that the commentators called the first *kāṇḍa prakīrṇa*, 'scattered, mixed'. The explanations of the Sanskrit commentators and modern scholars regarding the rationality behind the 'mixed' nature of this *kāṇḍa* are not convincing, and Bhaṭṭi's intent in this part of the poem must be the subject of further study. The *Adhikāra-Kāṇḍa* exemplifies the governing rules of Pāṇinian grammar (*adhikāras*), but omits a number of *sūtras*, most noticeably those concerning Vedic Sanskrit.[15] The *Prasanna-Kāṇḍa*, the 'clear' or 'gracious' chapter, encompasses four cantos which are conventionally thought to expound the *śabda* and *artha alaṃkāras* (canto 10); the quality of sweetness—*mādhurya guṇa* (canto 11); 'realism'—*bhāvikatva* (canto 12); and the simultaneous use of two languages—*bhāṣāsāma* or *bhāṣāśleṣa* (canto 13).[16] The languages used

12 This point has been very well-argued by Lidia Sudyka, who first proposed to treat the BhK as a handbook for poets wishing to take part in debates; see Sudyka 2000 and Sudyka 2004: 160ff.

13 Jayamaṅgala writes that the BhK has two levels of description: the first is the illustrative layer in which the poem is divided into the four *kāṇḍas*; the second is the narrative level in which the story of Rāma is told in 22 *sargas* (*tasya copanibandhanaṃ kavinā dvidhā kṛtam / ekaṃ lakṣaṇasūcakaiḥ prakīrṇādhikāraprasannatiṅantakāṇḍaiś caturbhiḥ / dvitīyaṃ lakṣyasūcakai rāmasaṃbhavādibhir dvāviṃśatya sargaiḥ*). He further notices that the illustrative level may be seen as comprising two categories: one illustrating grammatical rules and consisting of the *prakīrṇa*, *adhikāra* and *tiṅanta* chapters; the other illustrating '*kāvya*', the *prasanna kāṇḍa* (*tatra lakṣaṇaṃ dvividham / śabdalakṣaṇaṃ kāvyalakṣaṇaṃ ca / tatra prathamasya trīṇi prakīrṇādhikāratiṅantakāṇḍāni, dvitīyasya tv ekaṃ prasannakāṇḍam*) (*Jayamaṅgalā* ad. BhK 1.1).

14 *Jayamaṅgalā* ad. BhK 1.1: *yatroccāvacena bahūnāṃ lakṣaṇānāṃ prakaraṇaṃ tat prakīrṇakāṇḍam.*

15 See Narang 1969: 85–87, Karandikars 1982: xxvii–xxxvi or the notes of Fallon's 2009 translation for a detailed list of the *adhikāras* and *sūtras* illustrated and omitted in the BhK.

16 Very broadly speaking, Sudyka has convincingly argued a much more coherent interpretation that cantos 11, 12 and 13 ought to be treated as expositions of the *guṇas madhurya*, *prasāda* and *ojas* respectively. These are the (only) three qualities of poetic language mentioned by Bhāmaha in his

by Bhaṭṭi in the thirteenth canto are Sanskrit and Prakrit (it is unclear which Prakrit).

The *Tiṅanta-Kāṇḍa* includes nine cantos and illustrates nine tenses and moods[17]: canto 14 exemplifies the perfect tense; canto 15, the aorist tense; canto 16, the simple future; and so on. The order of tenses seems to be arbitrary and appears to depend on which tense happened to best suit the narrative of the poem. This *kāṇḍa* is so different in style to those preceding it that Leonardi has claimed that it must have been composed by a different author.[18] The metres of the *Tiṅanta* cantos are simple (mainly *anuṣṭubh*) and poetic figures are few and far between compared to the earlier *sargas*. The organisation of the text in this *kāṇḍa* is particularly significant because Bhaṭṭi clearly departs from the Pāṇinian system of grammatical elucidation.

It is worth noting that Bhaṭṭi also abandons Pāṇini's order in the *Prakīrṇa-Kāṇḍa*, hence the label 'mixed'. However his motives for this remain unclear—in the *Prakīrṇa-Kāṇḍa*, Bhaṭṭi's approach to teaching seems haphazard and the story takes centre stage. In attempting to impose Pāṇinian categorisation in the first, 'mixed' *kāṇḍa*, it appears that the commentators were trying to fit square pegs into round holes, as it were. This tendency is also evident in the BhK sections on poetics, for instance when commentators (beginning with Jayamaṅgala again) try to impose the sequence of *alaṃkāras* from Bhāmaha's *Kāvyālaṃkāra* on canto 10 of the BhK. This exercise was destined to fail, however, as the two texts most certainly do not overlap in this respect. Yet the opinion that Bhaṭṭi was expounding *śabda-* and *arthālaṃkāras* in Bhāmaha's order appears repeatedly in the Sanskrit commentaries and in modern publications. Apart from Sudyka (2004), Hooykaas

---

Kāvyālaṃkāra. Simultaneously, these three cantos seem to teach budding bards how to present erotic, political and heroic themes in poetry. (Sudyka 2004: 260ff.)

17 Mallinātha introduces the entire *Tiṅanta Kāṇḍa* thus:

iha sauśabdyaṃ nāma kāvyaśobhākaro guṇaḥ / sa ca 'supāṃ tiṅāṃ ca vyutpattiḥ sauśabdyaṃ parikīrttitam' iti dvividha uktaḥ / tatra subantā vyutpāditāḥ / athedāmīṃ tiṅāṃ lādeśatvāt tatrāpi leṭaś chāndasatvād anyān nava laṅādivilāsān navabhir uttaraiḥ sargair vyutpādayiṣyann asmin sarge liṭvilāsam utpādayati / tata ityādi // (ad. BhK 14.1).

'Here is the quality called *sauśabdya* which makes poetry beautiful. There are two ways in which it is explained: *sauśabdya* is the [correct] derivation of items ending in nominal endings (*sup*) or verbal endings (*tiṅ*). Here [in this poem] the inflection of nouns (*subanta*) has already been discussed. Now because *tiṅ* are substitutes for *l*-affixes (*lādeśatvāt* [see: A.3.4.77–78]) and due the archaic nature of Vedic subjunctive (*leṭ*), the beauty of nine tenses and moods [not 10] like the imperfect (*laṅ*) and others will be portrayed in the following nine cantos. In this one [14], the grace of the perfect tense (*liṭ*) will be illustrated.'

18 'Risultano pertanto elementi che avvalorano il sospetto che l'ultima parte de BHK siasi amalgamata con le precedenti' (Leonardi 1974: 29). Leonardi further claims that since the poem had so many various titles—it was called *Bhaṭṭikāvya*, *Rāmacarita*, *Rāmakāvya* and *Rāvaṇavadha*—these titles must have referred to different parts of the poem. That is, according to Leonardi, the title *Rāvaṇavadha*, 'The Slaying of Rāvaṇa', can only refer to the contents of the *Tiṅanta-Kāṇḍa* in which the battle of Rāvaṇa and Rāma takes place and the death of the demon king actually occurs. However, this logic is untenable if we take into consideration titles such as *Kumārasambhava* or *Śiśupālavadha*, which also only signal the finale of the narrative.

seems to have been one of the few who have actually analysed and compared the two works, and he came to the conclusion that Bhaṭṭi was by no means following the arrangement of the *Kāvyālaṃkāra*.[19]

Coming back to the *Tiṅanta-Kāṇḍa*—in the case of this section, there can be no confusion as to the poet's intent and means. He set out to present his audience with a set of nine cantos illustrating all of the important verbal forms of the nine tenses and moods in Sanskrit. Each *sarga* illustrates exactly one tense or mood and narrates one characteristic *Rāmāyaṇa* episode; there is no overlapping on either the illustrative or narrative layers.

Canto 14 and the perfect system

In terms of subject matter, the 113 verses of *sarga* 14 deal with the first battle between Rāma and the demons. It might seem that 113 verses composed solely with the use of the perfect tense can hardly be palatable, yet the accumulation of verbal forms causes the action to flow faster, the battle scenes come alive before the readers' eyes like in a flip book of rapidly changing images. To give an example of the style of the *sarga* (perfect formations in bold):

> ***tastanur jahvalur mamlur jaglur luluṭhire*** *kṣatāḥ* /
> ***mumūrcchur vavamū*** *raktaṃ* ***tatṛṣuś*** *cobhaye bhaṭāḥ* // BhK 14.30
> *sampātinā prajaṅghas tu* ***yuyudhe*** *'sau drumāhataḥ* /
> ***cakampe*** *'tīva* ***cukrośa*** *jīvanāśaṃ* ***nanāśa*** *ca* // 14.31
> ***uccakhnāte*** *nalenājau sphuratpratapanākṣiṇī* /
> *jambumālī* ***jahau*** *prāṇān grāvṇā mārutinā hataḥ* // 14.32
> *mitraghnasya* ***pracukṣoda*** *gadayāṅgaṃ vibhīṣaṇaḥ* /
> *sugrīvaḥ praghasaṃ* ***nebhe*** *bahūn rāmas* ***tatarda*** *ca* // 14.33

> Wounded warriors on both sides **were thirsty** and **tired**; they **spit up blood**, **stumbled**, **fainted**, and they **suffered**, **cried** and **blundered** in pain.
> Prajaṅgha **clashed** with Sampāti and was hit by him with a tree.
> Prajaṅgha **shrieked**, **shuddered** then **died**.
> Nala **tore out** Pratapana's glistening eyes.
> Jambumālin **died**, hit with a boulder by Mārutin.
> Vibhīṣaṇa **crushed** Mitraghna's body with a bludgeon,
> Sugrīva **injured** Praghasa and many **were destroyed** by Rāma.

19 While Hooykaas agrees that using the terminology of Bhāmaha (and Daṇḍin) in the BhK commentaries was the right course of action, according to him the commentators were 'wrong in clinging too strictly to the sequence in which they found the *arthālaṅkāras* dealt with there' (Hooykaas 1957: 358).

Canto 14 does not really have main characters (perhaps Indrajit, the son of Rāvaṇa, could be the exception). Because of the constant encounters between Rāvaṇa's demon host and Rāma's ape and human companions, we meet a whole troupe of individuals. There are also broad descriptions of armies marching out to war and the auspicious and inauspicious signs that they may see. A whole arsenal of weapons is used by the warriors, from swords, arrows and nooses, to trees and boulders hurled by the mightiest. The *sarga* is composed in the *anuṣṭubh* metre, apart from the first and last verses, which are in *upajāti*. The predominating *alaṃkāra* is *svabhāvokti*, natural description.[20]

Although the main body of text intended to demonstrate the perfect system is the fourteenth canto of Bhaṭṭi's poem, verses 5.104 to 6.4 illustrate the formation of the periphrastic perfect.[21] In verses 5.104 to 6.4, there are 15 occurrences of the periphrastic perfect and, unexpectedly, one example of the reduplicated perfect. However in the data below I will refer only to the forms found in the *Tiṅanta-Kāṇḍa*.

In the canto 14, there are 433 occurrences of perfect forms: 396 reduplicated perfect formations, 35 periphrastic perfect and two perfect participles, both in the active voice. There are 141 verbs in the third-person singular *Parasmaipadam* ('P'), and 84 in the third-person singular *Ātmanepadam* ('Ā'); 156 verbs in the third-person plural P, and 37 in the third-person plural Ā; and 11 in the third-person dual (two of which in *Ātmanepadam*). There are also two instances of the second-person singular P used, and a total of 27 of all of these verbal forms are in the passive voice. Among the periphrastic forms in canto 14, there are 13 verbs in the causative mood, seven in the desiderative and one rare occurrence of the perfect intensive (*śaṃśamāñ cakruḥ* in verse 14.67). The remaining 14 are instances of the periphrastic perfect in the indicative mood, formed either because the roots are of the tenth conjugational class, or according to the rules given in *Aṣṭādhyāyī* 3.1.35–3.1.40.[22] All of the periphrastic perfect forms in canto 14 are made with the

20 *Kāvyālaṃkāra* 2.93.b: *arthasya tadavasthatvaṃ svabhāvo 'bhihito yathā*. Bhāmaha does not seem to actually count *svabhāvokti* as an *alaṃkāra*. See also Daṇḍin's take on *svābhavokti* in *Kāvyādarśa* 2.8.

21 These few *ślokas* are part of a larger portion of text that illustrates the use of the affix *-ām*.

22 *kās-pratyayād ām amantre liṭi* (A.3.1.35)
ij-ādeś ca gurumato 'nṛcchaḥ (A.3.1.36)
daya-aya-āsaś ca (A.3.1.37)
uṣa-vida-jāgṛbhyo 'nyatarasyām (A.3.1.38)
bhī-hrī-bhṛ-huvāṃ śluvac ca (A.3.1.39)
kṛñ ca anuprayujyate liṭi (A.3.1.40)

From these *sūtras* we learn that roots beginning with any heavy (*guru*) vowel found in the *pratyāhāra* iC (that is, *i u ṛ ḷ e o ai au*), apart from the root √*ṛcch*, form the periphrastic perfect. We get a list of roots that form the periphrastic perfect as an exception (√*kās*, √*day*, √*ās*, √*ay*) and also discover that derived verbal forms (those formed with the use of affixes, such as the causative) take up the *-ām* periphrastic affix. Additionally, the periphrastic affix may be added to the roots √*uṣ*, √*vid* and √*jāgṛ*. As regards the roots √*bhī*, √*hrī*, √*bhṛ*, √*hu*, Pāṇini says that they are reduplicated in order

auxiliary root √*kṛ*, as *sūtra* A.3.1.40 prescribes. The most common roots in canto 14 are √*luṭh*, √*hā*, √*han*, √*bandh*, √*dru* and √*jñā*, each appearing four times, while the popular root √*gam* appears only once.

The sheer number and diversity of the forms presented by Bhaṭṭi are of note (an average of nearly four verbal forms per *śloka*!), and this approach is continued in the following *sarga*s when he illustrates the other tenses and moods. It is clear that great deal of thought was put not only into the aesthetic qualities of the poem and its narrative layer, but also into its function as a didactic aid. For instance, as the above data shows, Bhaṭṭi clearly presented his readers with an abundance of the most useful forms, such as the third-person singular, but also made sure to give examples of rarer verbs and roots. A close reading of the chapter shows that there was absolutely no arbitrariness in his process.

To give some examples: in verse 14.6, two subsequent finite verbs are from roots beginning in the cluster *sph* and terminating in a consonant (*pusphuṭuḥ* : √*sphuṭ* and *pusphuruḥ* : √*sphur*); verse 14.7 exemplifies the rule that both *g* and *h* reduplicate with *j* (*jagarjuḥ* : √*garj* and *jahṛṣuḥ* : √*hṛṣ*); verse 14.60 demonstrates not only that in roots with a terminal *-ai*, this diphthong is reduplicated with *a*, but also that in the third-singular P the verbal termination is omitted and *au* is used in its place (*jaglau* : √*glai* and *dadhyau* : √*dhyai*); verses 14.112–113 contain four weak forms made with the substitution of the medial root vowel *a* with *e* (*neśuḥ* : √*naś*, *jeruḥ* : √*jṝ*, *pheluḥ* : √*phal* and *bhejuḥ* : √*bhaj*). This meticulous approach is seen throughout the whole fourteenth canto, as well as in the entire *Tiṅanta-Kāṇḍa*; all of the verbal forms are purposefully placed in relation to each other and, most of the time, appear to have been arranged in 'thematic' sub-groups.

Teaching Sanskrit grammar

Pāṇini's *Aṣṭādhyāyī* is a demanding resource for many reasons; while the *sūtra* form facilitates memorisation, it is also makes the text all but incomprehensible without an external interpretative system. Pāṇini uses a meta-language of codes, like the *pratyāhāra*s or the so-called *IT* markers, denoting particular linguistic, phonological and grammatical phenomena. What is more, he follows the rules of euphonics, so while his *sūtra*s are supremely concise when it comes to the technical side of the matter, there are letters added solely for the sake of abiding by, or bypassing, the rules of *sandhi*. An additional hurdle may be the *anuvṛtti*, or elliptical, style of the work, which means that the *sūtra*s are context-sensitive and must be learnt, and referred to, more or less in order.

to form a verbal stem and therefore are treated like the *hvādi*, or third class of roots (and the *śap* affix, or 'thematic *a*', is elided through *ślu* elision). Finally, the appropriate perfect form of √*kṛ* is attached to the affixed root in order to form the periphrastic perfect.

The way the *Aṣṭādhyāyī* is organised[23] means that a student who wished to refresh his knowledge of a particular verbal formation to use in a composition potentially had to scour all eight books. A perfunctory search shows that we can find data on the perfect tense in at least six of the eight chapters of Pāṇini's work. For instance, in the first book, there are rules regarding the *guṇa* and *vṛddhi* that can or cannot take place when personal verb terminations are added to reduplicated perfect stems (A.1.2.5, 6). The second book contains *sūtras* concerning the substitution that occurs when certain roots are in the perfect tense (e.g. A.2.4.41 on √*ve* ~ *vavau/ uvāya*). The third book of the *Aṣṭādhyāyī* is where the most information about the *liṭ* can be found. Among other things, Pāṇini teaches about the function of the perfect and when it is used, the creation of the periphrastic perfect and perfect participles and the personal endings.[24]

In the sixth book, we can find *sūtras* on the reduplication of the root when the perfect tense is used (A.6.1.8) and on *samprasāraṇa* (A.6.1.15–17, the vocalization of semivowels when they are reduplicated, thus *vac*⟶*uvāca*). There are many very specific rules in this book regarding individual roots and their irregularities in the perfect tense (e.g., A.6.1.38 on √*vay*, 6.1.46 on √*vye* or 6.4.88 on √*bhū*), as well as information on the creation of weak verb stems by substituting the medial *a* of the root with an *e* (e.g. A.6.4.120: √*tan*⟶ weak form: *ten*).

The seventh book gives the general rule about the *iṭ* augment (A.7.2.13), and the fact that certain roots are *aniṭ* in perfect tense, while all others are *seṭ* (also A.7.2.37, A.7.2.57). In the eighth book, there are a few miscellaneous rules on the subject of the *liṭ*, which are very specific and also relate to the modifications that must be applied to the root in order to form the perfect stem (such as A.8.3.78 on cerebralisation in certain cases).

It is understandable that the *Aṣṭādhyāyī* could not function on its own as a resource for students of the Sanskrit language, and the idea of elaborating on the prodigious work was born long before the times of Bhaṭṭi.[25] Kātyāyana's

---

23 From Misra 1966: 22–23:

1. General definition and rules of interpretation.
2. Substitution and purpose of declension.
3. Primary suffixes.

4./5. Suffixes addable to the non-verbal stem forming secondary stem and declensional suffixes.

6./7. Morphophonemics at the word (*pada*) level.

8. Miscellaneous.

24 The most general definition of the perfect tense in the *Aṣṭādhyāyī* is *parokṣe liṭ* (A.3.2.115), which says that the perfect tense is used to denote an action in the past not observed by the speaker.

The personal endings of the *ātmanepadam* perfect tense can be found in A.3.4.81, *liṭas ta-jhayor eś-irec*: that is, *e* is substituted for the *-a*, *-i*, *-am* terminations, and *ire* replaces the *-jha* ending from the universal set found in A.3.4.78. As for the *parasmaidapam*, Pāṇini gives the list of personal verb endings in A.3.4.82: *prasmaipadānāṃ ṇal-atus-us-thal-thus-aṇal-va-māḥ*.

25 We may find traces of the purposeful demonstration of grammar formation in one of the earliest extant Sanskrit *mahākāvyas*, Aśvaghoṣa's *Saundarananda* from 2 CE. In the second chapter of the epic poem, in 'stanzas 7–11 we find the perfect, in 13–23 the s-aorist, in 24–25 the a-aorist, in 27–39

Vārttikas, the first great commentary known to us (4/3 BCE), supplement only 1245 of Pāṇini's 4000-odd *sūtras*. The *Vārttikas* are, of course, encapsulated in the *Mahābhāṣya* of Patañjali (2 BCE), which is simultaneously a commentary on both the *Aṣṭadhyāyī* and *Vārttikas* and, significantly, introduces the novel *bhāṣya* style, i.e. a form based on the dialogue between a student and, in this case, two teachers—one who is capable and one who is not. It is only as late as 7 CE that the idea of closely following Pāṇini's order and explaining the *sūtras* one by one arose with the most frequently used commentary, the *Kāśikā* by Vāmana and Jayāditya. One of the most imperative tasks of the commentators on the *Eight Books* was providing their students with examples and counter-examples of the rules in application (what is understood to be *vyākhyāna* by Patañjali),[26] thus it is no wonder that the BhK and other grammatical *kāvyaśāstras* like it were seen to complement this tradition.

This brings us to the question of the purpose and usefulness of the BhK as an educational tool. It is worth mentioning that many scholars both ancient and modern express the opinion that the BhK was, first and foremost, an exposition of the *Aṣṭādhyāyī*.[27] However this view does not take into consideration the *Prasanna-Kāṇḍa* on aesthetics, as Lidia Sudyka has noted;[28] the *Prakīrṇa-Kāṇḍa*, in which the correspondence with the *Aṣṭādhyāyī* is not entirely clear; and, in my opinion, the *Tiṅanta-Kāṇḍa*.

In the case of the *Prasanna-Kāṇḍa*, Bhaṭṭi clearly abandoned any intention of illustrating grammatical rules and instead elaborated on the aesthetic aspects of poetry, such as *alaṃkāras*, *rasas* and *guṇas*. The difficulties in understanding the instructive nature of the *Prakīrṇa-Kāṇḍa* were mentioned earlier. Finally, while the *Tiṅanta* is an explication of grammatical phenomena, and thus its forms can obviously be explained using the most comprehensive grammar of the Sanskrit language, the *Aṣṭādhyāyī*, it is governed by the distinctly non-Pāṇinian organising principle of a decided topical synthesis into tenses and moods.

The explanation for why Bhaṭṭi chose this approach in the *Tiṅanta* section and decided to compose the last cantos in this manner may be found in his own

---

the reduplicated aorist and in stanzas 40–44 examples of the rarely-used passive aorist' (LIENHARD 1984: 169). SUDYKA (2004: 67) notices that Rājaśekhara calls Aśvaghoṣa the 'poet of nouns and verbs'; this can be found in *Kāvyamīmāṃsā* chapter 5, p. 18, line 7ff. In this part of his treatise, Rājaśekhara cites different types of poets, and under the nickname of *nāmākhyātakavi* he quotes verse 25 from the canto 8 of *Buddhacarita*.

26 *udāharaṇaṃ pratyudāharaṇaṃ vākyādhyāhāraḥ iti etat samuditam vyākhyānam bhavati* | ((Pas_14) KA_I,11.14-12.27 Ro_I,42-47 {14/59}): 'Examples, counterexamples, supplementing based on [previously taught] rules—that is known as *vyākhyānam*.' Patañjali's *vyākhyāna* may have been implied in BhK 22.34 (*vyākhyāgamyam idaṃ kāvyam*). I thank Yuto Kawamura for this reference.

27 See the already mentioned commentary of Mallinatha on BhK 1.1. All of the commentators known to me cite the *sūtras* of the *Aṣṭādhyāyī* when they are explaining grammatical formations. See also FALLON 2009, KARANDIKARS 1982, WARDER 1983, LIENHARD 1984 and NARANG 1987.

28 SUDYKA 2000.

suggestion that the poem was meant for aspiring poets (those who want to take part in discussions or recite their work in a public forum). Sanskrit poets had to know grammar, of course, yet first and foremost, this had to be a working knowledge of grammar in use. They had to be able to 'think in verse' and not refer to the monumental grammar books or their teachers whenever in doubt. Moreover, they had to compose poetry that pleased the audience and earned them their livelihood, whether they were working on a full-blown *kāvya* for their patrons or competing at a poets' competition (*kavigoṣṭhī*). Therefore the *kavi*s had to have at their fingertips a myriad of forms which were not only correct grammatically and prosodically in any given context, but also simply sounded the best. Listening to and memorising *kāvyaśāstra*s on popular *purāṇic* topics, such as the BhK, must have been very practical in this respect because these poems provided ready-made forms in a *kāvya* framework.

Bhaṭṭi gives such importance to the exemplification of verbal formations and subject-predicate constructs in the *Tiṅanta-Kāṇḍa* because this was useful for his intended target, budding poets. If we take into consideration the whole poem, especially the *Prasanna-* and *Tiṅanta-Kāṇḍas*, we may conclude that *Bhaṭṭi's Poem* is not merely a grammar book, nor is it is a *kāvyaśāstra* solely in the technical sense of genre described in the first part of this paper—it is quite literally a textbook (*śāstra*) of poetry itself.

References

Primary Sources

Bhatti Kavya. A Poem on the Actions of Rama. With the commentaries of Jayamaṅgala and Bharatamallika. (1828). Calcutta: Sanskrit College.

Dalal, C. D. & Sastry, R. A. (Eds.). (1916). *Kāvyamīmāṃsā of Rājaśekhara.* Baroda: Oriental Institute.

Fallon, O. (Trans.). (2009). *Bhaṭṭi's Poem: The Death of Rāvaṇa.* New York: New York University Press.

Joyser, G. R. (Ed.). (1955). *Maharaja Bhojaraja's Śringara prakasha: The great 10th century work on Samskrit and Prakrit rhetoric* (vols. 1–4). Mysore: Coronation Press.

Karandikar, M. A. & Karandikar, S. (Eds. & Trans.). (1982). *Bhaṭṭi-kāvyam.* Delhi: Motilal Banarsidass.

Kielhorn, F. (1880–1885). *The Vyâkarana-Mahâbhâshya of Patanjali* (rev. ed.). Bombay: Government Central Book Depôt. Retrieved from http://gretil.sub.uni-goettingen.de/gretil/1_sanskr/6_sastra/1_gram/pmbhassu.htm.

Naganatha Śastry, P. V. (Ed. & Trans.). (1991). *Kāvyālaṃkāra of Bhāmaha.* Delhi: Motilal Banarsidass.

Rāghavāchārya, E. V. V. & Padhye, D. G. (Eds.). (1961). *Minor works of Kṣemendra (Kṣemendralaghukāvyasaṅgrahaḥ).* Hyderabad: Osmania University.

TRIVEDI, K. P. (Ed.). (1898). *The Bhaṭṭi-kâvya; or, Râvaṇavadha, composed by Śri Bhaṭṭi.* Bombay: Government Central Book Depot.

VASU, S. C. (Ed. & Trans.). (1981–1989). *The Aṣṭādhyāyī of Pāṇini* (vols. 1–8). Delhi: Motilal Banarsidass.

Secondary Sources

ABHYANKAR, K. V. & SHUKLA, J. M. (1986). *A dictionary of Sanskrit grammar.* Baroda: Oriental Institute.

DIWEKAR, H. R. (1929). Bhāmaha, Bhaṭṭi and Dharmakīrti. *Journal of the Royal Asiatic Society of Great Britain and Ireland, 4,* 825–84.

GEROW, E. (1971). *A glossary of Indian figures of speech.* The Hague: Mouton.

HOOYKAAS, C. (1957). On Some 'arthālaṅkāras' in the 'Bhaṭṭikāvya' X. *Bulletin of the School of Oriental and African Studies, 20*(1/3), 351–363.

LEONARDI, G. G. (1974). *Tre studi sulla struttura e natura del Bhattikavyam.* Treviso: Canova.

LIENHARD, S. (1984). *A history of classical poetry: Sanskrit–Pali–Prakrit.* Wiesbaden: Otto Harrassowitz.

MISRA, V. N. (1966). *The descriptive technique of Pāṇini. An introduction.* The Hague: Mouton.

NARANG, S. P. (1987). *Bhaṭṭi-Kāvya: A study.* Delhi: Motilal Banarsidass.

RAGHAVAN, V. (1963). *Bhoja's Śṛṅgāra prakāśa.* Madras: Punarvasu.

RAJENDRAN, C. (1989). Mahimabhaṭṭa's concept of poetry as a śāstra. *Adyar Library Bulletin 53,* 113–120.

SUDYKA, L. (2000). What does the Bhaṭṭi-kāvya teach? *Studia Indologiczne,* 7, 271–282.

—. (2004). *Od Ramajany do dydaktyki czyli zagadki Poematu Bhattiego.* Kraków: Księgarnia Akademicka.

Vaṇṇam

Tracing an Ancient Tamil Music Tradition

Prakash Venkatesan

It is generally considered that early musical practices, developed by bards and employed by poets, were integral to the rituals of the ancient Tamils (THANINAYAGAM 1956: 109). There is, however, no direct evidence to be found in ancient Tamil literature to suggest that any particular musical formulae were used either by priests or by bards. What we instead have are references to such practices in the *caṅkam* literary corpus. The *Tolkāppiyam*, the ancient Tamil grammatical treatise, while classifying forms of Tamil poetic conventions, discusses a set of forms called *vaṇṇam*s, which could be understood as musical formulae followed by the bards. I will argue in this paper that the *Tolkāppiyam*, while setting out to create a grammar for literary Tamil, also attempted to adapt the bardic musical formulae to Tamil poetic composition. I will also discuss the structure of the *vaṇṇams*, how they operate in practice and their formulaic characteristics.

I

*Pāṇar*s ('bards') occupy a significant place in the *caṅkam* literary corpus, yet there are only scattered references to them. Still, it is possible for us to infer their social presence in *caṅkam* society, despite the lack of any archaeological or epigraphical evidence, from the literature alone. In fact, among the various *caṅkam* poets, we may surmise that at least a few belonged to the bardic community. These bards belonged to nomadic communities[1] who earned their livelihood by singing the praises of chieftains and kings. *Kūttar*s (dancing actors) and *viṟaliyar*s (dancers) were also part of such communities. There were female bards too, mentioned as '*pāṭiṉi*' (*Puṟam.* 11, 15). *Pāṇar*s used to sing at royal courts, public assemblies and battlefronts. They were close to the chieftains and

1 Cf. *Puṟanāṉūṟu* (hereafter 'Puṟam.') 152; 22–23.

kings, as their friends[2] and well-wishers, and also remained closely connected to society at large.

The root of *pāṇar* is *paṇ*.[3] *Paṇ* means 'music' and applies generically to all forms of music. *Pāṇars* were of two kinds: *ciṟupāṇar* and *perumpāṇar*, each expert in particular forms of music (THANINAYAGAM 2009: 42). The *Tolkāppiyam* identifies four fundamental sounds in music: *akaval*, *ceppal*, *tuḷḷal* and *tūṅkal*.[4] *Pāṇars* predominantly used *akaval*, and in this respect THANINAYAGAM remarks: 'The word *akaval* by itself means a call, an appellative utterance, and refers in this context to the custom of the priests of calling upon the gods and spirits. This usage led to the designation given to the earliest Tamil poetic meter which originally must have been a recitative chant like the religious chant of early ritual' (THANINAYAGAM 1956: 109). This is possibly why female bards (*pāṭiṉis*) and female fortune tellers were also called *akaval makaḷ*[5] ('woman singing *akaval*' or 'woman who calls'). Rituals such as the *veṟiyāṭal*[6] (dance of a priest possessed by Murukaṉ) and practices such as *teivam parāval*[7] ('to worship') find mention in *caṅkam* literature. But the songs of these rituals are not known with any exactitude.[8] The voices of the *pāṇars*, in the period when these rituals were performed, were considered equal to a divine voice (*mutuvāy*).[9] Moreover, there seems to be a strong relationship between *akaval* and ritual. The defining characteristic of the *akaval* sound is its aim of addressing someone, calling out or sending a message, which does not necessarily entail a response. This explains why *akaval* is often employed in rituals invoking the divine. THANINAYAGAM mentions that *pāṇar* songs were derived from the ritual songs of priests in ancient Tamil society (2009: 41). Although we do not know the relation between the *akaval* sound and *vaṇṇam*, it is known that all the songs in *caṅkam* literature employ the *akaval* (*āciriyappā*) sound[10] (the *Tolkāppiyam* clearly defines the sound of *āciriyappā* metre as *akaval* and formulates the grammar of the *āciriyappā*[11]).

2 The friendship (it may also be just a story or a myth) between King Athiyaman Neduman Anchi and Auvaiyar would be an excellent example of the relation of kings and *pāṇars*. For more information see Puṟam. 69, 135 and 212.

3 *TL* 5(1): p. 2596, s.v. *pāṇ*.

4 *Tolkāppiyam*, *Ceyyuḷiyal* (hereafter 'Tol. Cey.') 393, 394, 395 and 396. The sounds mentioned here are used in conjunction with metres in Tamil. *Akaval* is the sound for *āciriyappā*, *ceppal* for *veṇpā*, *tuḷḷal* for *kalippā* and *tūṅkal* for *vañcippā*.

5 *Kuṟuntokai* (hereafter 'Kuṟu.') 23

6 Kuṟu. 53:3, 318:3; *Akanāṉūṟu* (hereafter 'Akam.') 98:19, 370:14.

7 Akam. 98.

8 *Veṟiyāṭal* and *teivam parāval* could possibly have been performed to musical songs with different notations. As *akaval* is closely linked to the rituals, it would have been the prime musical sound used by *pāṇars* and/or *pāṭiṉis* on the basis of *vaṇṇam*. Since we cannot identify the exact songs sung by them, but only the rituals, we cannot look to *caṅkam* poetry to find the exact form used by the *pāṇars*. The *Tolkāppiyam* only gives evidence for *vaṇṇam* in literature.

9 Puṟam. 70:5, 180:9, 319:9; Akam. 22:7, 98:8.

10 ZVELEBIL 1973: 63; Tol. Cey. 393.

11 Tol. Cey. 359, 362, 368–370, 373–375, 386.

In its introduction ('Pāyiram', hereafter 'Tol. Pāyi.'), the *Tolkāppiyam* specifically mentions its objective, which is to define a grammar of the written language.[12] In its first chapter, 'Nūṉmarapu', the *Tolkāppiyam* also mentions that it does not deal with the grammar of music.[13] Yet in the chapter on verses ('Ceyyuḷiyal'), the *Tolkāppiyam* takes up *vaṇṇam* as a category and transforms it into a codified feature of written verse. It could therefore be argued that *caṅkam* poetry, while not an oral tradition, definitely contains elements of an oral tradition (such as *vaṇṇam*). In other words, *caṅkam* poems were not necessarily the oral compositions of the *pāṇar*s, but may rather have been songs composed by *pulavar*s following the *pāṇar* tradition.[14] The *Tolkāppiyam* never formulates a rule for metrical lines in *vaṇṇam* songs, yet the place *vaṇṇam* occupies in the *Tolkāppiyam* deserves our attention. Before defining *vaṇṇam,* the author of the *Tolkāppiyam* addresses the issue of meters that have metrical line limits (i.e., those sung by *pulavars*), followed by those with no such limits[15] (i.e., those sung by local people—*pāṇars*). Thus it would seem that *vaṇṇam* is considered a form that could be sung either with or without metrical line limits.

II

Historically, *vaṇṇam* has been discussed in literature in relation to music. The 'Araṅkēṟṟukkātai' chapter of the *Cilappatikāram* (ca. 5 CE), one of the five great epics of Tamil literature, explains various aspects of music and its performance. In this context, certain commentators mention *vaṇṇam* in connection with beat (*tāḷam*)[16] (both commentators of the *Cilappatikāram*, Arumpata urai āciriyar and Aṭiyārkkunallār, relate *vaṇṇam* to beat). In another chapter, in a discussion of different varieties of songs, *vaṇṇam* is also mentioned.[17] In the seventh-century *Tēvāram*, sung by Saint Tiruñāṉacampantar, there is a verse that mentions people who were competent in *vaṇṇam* and could sing in Tamil.[18] In the twelfth-century *Periyapurāṇam*, *vaṇṇam* is classified into three categories: *peru vaṇṇam, iṭai vaṇṇam* and *vaṉappu vaṇṇam.*[19] (These may be translated as 'primary' or 'extended

12 Tol. Pāyi. 8.

13 *Tolkāppiyam, Eḻuttatikāram* (hereafter 'Tol. Eḻu') 1.1.33, 1928; Tol. Pāyi. 8.

14 Hart 2002: xxiv; Gros 2009: 46.

15 Tol. Cey. 466 discusses the fact that the songs don't have metrical line limits. So using the poetic conventions formulated by Tolkāppiyar, one can sing songs with limitless metrical lines. This gives the singer license to use his imagination and perception.

16 *Cilappatikāram* (hereafter 'Cila.') 3.26 and 6.35 with commentary.

17 Cila. 6.35 with commentary.

18 *Vaṇṇam mūṉṟum tamiḻil terintu icai pāṭuvār* (*Tēvāram* 2290.3).

19 *Eṇṇiya nūl peru vaṇṇam iṭai vaṇṇam vaṉappu eṉṉum*
vaṇṇa icai vakai ellām māturiya nātattil
naṇṇiya pāṇiyum iyalum tūkkum naṭai mutal katiyil
paṇ amaiya eḻum ōcai emmaruṅkum parappiṉār (*Periyapurāṇam*, 3–15–28).

vaṇṇam', 'medial *vaṇṇam*' and 'rhythmic *vaṇṇam*'.) But we do not find any other substantial information about these categories in the texts, nor what they mean. THIRUMURUGAN, a scholar of Tamil musical tradition, says that songs composed or sung in a particular rhythm could also be called songs with *vaṇṇam* (1987: 9). We could consider *vaṇṇam* as '*oli oḻuṅku*', meaning 'rhythm', but further research is required for a better understanding of what exactly was meant by *vaṇṇam*.

References to the concept of beat occur in various places in *caṅkam* poetry.[20] Akam. 98 in particular merits our attention. This song talks about the expertise involved in producing music that combines various musical instruments while performing a ritual in honour of Lord Murukaṉ; the poet mentions the unique way in which a beat pattern orchestrates the song in a beautiful manner. From this we may divine how *vaṇṇam* may have been employed in songs to produce rhythm.

Vaṇṇam comes into being when different sounds join together in a pattern determined by certain musical norms. Short and long sounds, along with plosives, nasals, approximants and *āytam*, a phoneme in Old Tamil,[21] combine musically to produce *vaṇṇam*. These produce sound variations in a song, and when arranged in various combinations could become a formula for making music. It may thus be possible to suppose that *vaṇṇam* could occur in the oral tradition either as an independent song or as part of a song to create sound variations. We can assume that, in literary Tamil, *vaṇṇam* does not occur as a separate verse but acts within a verse to produce variations in sound. The bardic performers, the *pāṇar*s, followed a rhythm of a particular kind. They seem to have used this as a formula in composing and singing songs.

> still I decided that I would sing a song (*vaṇṇam*)
> and I said to my dancing women, 'Now I will sing. You spread the clay
> over the *mrdaṅgam* drum, pluck the *rāga* on the strings of the *yāḻ*
> and blow on the trumpet that is open at one end like an elephant's trunk,
> play on the *ellari* drum, play on the *ākuḷi* drum
> place in my hand the black staff that foretells the future
> (Puṟam. 152:13–19. Trans. HART 1975.)[22]

20 Puṟam. 209.5, 17, 302.5; Akam. 98.17, 105.9; Kuṟu. 59.1, 136.5; *Naṟṟiṇai* 104.5, 132.10.

21 See KUIPER 1997: 17; RAJAM 1992: 44.

22 *pāṭuval viṟali ōr vaṇṇam nīrum*
maṇmuḻā amaimiṉ paṇyāḻ niṟumiṉ
kaṇviṭu tūmpiṉ kaḷiṟṟu uyir toṭumiṉ
ellari toṭumiṉ ākuḷi toṭumiṉ
patalai yorukaṉ paiyeṉa iyakkumiṉ
matalai mākkōl kaivalam tamiṉ eṉṟu
iṟaivaṉ ākaliṉ collupu kuṟuki (Puṟam. 152:13–19)

In the above verse there is clear indication of the way in which *pāṇar*s used *vaṇṇam* and of the kind of instruments used as accompaniment. The regularity in the rhythm of *vaṇṇam* is brought into the realm of literary Tamil by Tolkāppiyar to denote variations in meter within a verse. The first commentator of the Tolkāppiyam, Iḷampūraṇar (eleventh century CE), did not define *vaṇṇam* at all. Another commentator, Pērāciriyar (thirteenth century CE), defined *vaṇṇam* as '*cantam*', which is not to be understood as equivalent to Sanskrit *chandas.*[23] *Cantam* here means the rhythmic movement of a verse.[24] However, *vaṇṇam* was the basis upon which the concept of *cantam* was developed. As early as the thirteenth century, *vaṇṇam* was already identified with *cantam* in spite of the differences between them, probably because rhythm constituted the basis of both.

III

Tolkāppiyar identifies 20 kinds of *vaṇṇam* (Tol. Cey. 525). He explains every *vaṇṇam* in one or two lines and never classifies them into groups; nor do the commentators. SUNDARAM, a musicologist, considers that *vaṇṇam*s may be classified into many categories according to their nature; however, he provides only four categories, namely those measuring the period, nature and celerity of sounds and sounds varied by modes of versification (1994: 34). In this research, however, we classify *vaṇṇam*s into two categories and one sub-category according to their nature and their function in songs.[25]

Sound category

The eight *vaṇṇam*s of the 'sound' category constitute the 'basic' *vaṇṇam*s because they can occur independently as well as in combination to produce other kinds of *vaṇṇam.* The sound categories of *vallicai* ('plosives'), *mellicai* ('nasal') and *iyaipu* ('approximants') are associated with the sounds of consonants in Tamil. *Āḷapeṭai* ('lengthening of sound') is an elongation of vowel and consonant sounds in metrical composition. *Kuṟuñcīr* ('short'), *neṭuñcīr* ('long') and *cittira* ('both long

---

23 *Chandas* is a general term designating metres in Sanskrit; for more information. cf. MARTINS 2013 and MITRA 1989.

24 *Cantam* is a formulaic rhythmic movement used to compose songs, not a general term for metre (*yāppu* is the general term for prosody in Tamil). It has eight basic formulas and eight extended formulas derived from the basic ones needed to compose a song. But there are controversies amongst scholars regarding the root of the name. Some believe this name was derived from Sanskrit *chandas* (cf. LŌCCAṈ 1989); others, that it emerged from domestic language (SUNDARAM 2006).

25 Prof. SUNDARAM's discussion (1994) was based on the nature of the sounds of *vaṇṇam.* Following his method, I divide *vaṇṇam* into two main categories: sound and formulaic rules. Further, as a sub-category of formulaic rules, two *vaṇṇam* have been separated from it and called formulaic rules (*cīr*) based on their function in a song.

Table 1: Varieties of vaṇṇam

Sound	*Formulaic rules*	*Formulaic rules* (cīr)
vallicai (plosives)	*akappāṭṭu* (variation in ending)	*pā* (*cīr*)
mellicai (nasals)	*puṟappāṭṭu* (variation in ending)	*tā* (using mode of versification)
iyaipu (approximants)	*oḻuku* (free flow of sound)	
aḷapeṭai (lengthening of sound)	*orūu* (non-uniform intervals?)	
neṭuñcīr (longer period, two mātras)	*eṇṇu* (uniformity of numbers)	
kuṟuñcīr (shorter period, single mātra)	*akaippu* (sound intervals)	
cittira (mixture of long and short periods, yet with regularity)	*tūṅkal* (?)	
nalipu (a phoneme)	*ēntal* (uniformity of repeating words)	
	uruṭṭu (uniformity of jumps while using short sounds)	
	muṭuku (uniformity of jumps while using short sounds)	

and short') are associated with vowels as well as with the period of the sound. *Āytam* (a phoneme used to represent the voiceless velar fricative[26]), *nalipu vaṇṇam,* is a distinct sound in Tamil. Pērāciriyar and other grammarians and commentators interpret *cittiram* (in *cittira vaṇṇam*) as 'many'. If a song is composed with many (or more than one) *vaṇṇam,* then we consider it a *cittira vaṇṇam.* As SUNDARAM says, 'if a part of a line in a song is written equally with long and short letters then we can consider it as *cittira vaṇṇam*' (1994: 40). Sundaram divided these eight again into two types based on the way they operate in the context of the Tamil musical tradition: 1, those measuring the period of sound (*kuṟil, neṭil, kuṟilneṭil, aḷapeṭai*); 2, those describing the nature of sound (*vallicai, mellicai, iyaipu, nalipu*) (SUNDARAM 1994: 34).

Formulaic rules: *Cīr* category

In this category there are two *vaṇṇams*: *pā vaṇṇam* and *tā vaṇṇam.* These two *vaṇṇams* occur through *cīr* (a 'metrical foot') in a poem (Tol.Cey. 526, 527).

Based on the unit of *mātrās* (a unit of metrical quantity), a syllable or '*acai*' may be formed in a poem. These syllables are named *ōracai, īracai* or *mūvacai* when the unit is present. A *cīr* can be created by adding these syllables. For example:

> *nāḷ* — *ōracai* or one syllable in a *cīr*;
> *murukoḷir* — *īracai* or two syllables in a *cīr*;
> *coṟcīrāy* — *mūvacai* or three syllables in a *cīr.*

26 Cf. RAJAM 1992: p. 44.

A foot in a poem should have more than one *cīr*. If a *cīr* occurs as a foot, it is named '*coṟcīr*'. These *coṟcīr* are the basis for *pā vaṇṇam*. The *Tolkāppiyam* mentions three categories of *coṟcīr* (Tol.Cey. 206):

1. If a *cīr* occurs following an enumeration.
   Example: *nilanīr vaḷivicum peṉṟa nāṉkiṉ / aḷappariyaiyē* (Pati. 14)
   The *cīr* '*aḷappariyaiyē*' occurred as a foot after four elements were counted, and formed *pā vaṇṇam*.
2. If a line has four *cīr*, then it will be called a 'perfect line' or *aḷavaṭi*. If the number of *cīr* in a line lessens, then it forms *pā vaṇṇam*.
3. If there is a separate word apart from the perfect line, then it is called *pā vaṇṇam*.

From these we may list the categories of *pā vaṇṇam*. *Pā vaṇṇam* occurs after the counting of words, when *cīr* lessens, as a separate *cīr* in a complete line. We thus understand *pā vaṇṇam* as creating a difference in a particular form of flowing sound in a song or poem to indicate a change in meaning or sound. Sound variation plays the vital role of alerting the listener to a change of subject. Most *coṟcīr*s act as a final note of a poem or draw attention to a change of meaning in a poem. We may therefore consider *pā vaṇṇam* within the oral tradition as a formula that marks the changes occurring in a song for the listener.

Tā vaṇṇam is closely related to *toṭai* ('mode of versification'), yet differs from it. *Toṭai* usually occurs within a line (Tol.Cey. 34) in a poem and plays a vital role in balancing the rhythmic value of a song. We do not, however, understand the relation between these two in a song.

Formulaic rule category

Ten *vaṇṇams* fall under this category.

1 *Akappāṭṭu vaṇṇam* and *puṟappāṭṭu vaṇṇam*

These two *vaṇṇams* are basically intervals in a song (Tol.Cey. 536, 537). The *ē* sound denotes the end of a song and acts like a formula in the oral tradition.[27] This *vaṇṇam* would have been very useful when a singer wanted to praise multiple characteristics of a chieftain or king. Within a poem, the sound *ē* is used as a note at the end of a line to indicate a change of meaning. *Puṟappāṭṭu vaṇṇam* occurs as a formula when a singer uses *ē* to indicate notes more than once in a song. Sundaram says that this *vaṇṇam* helps to express one's apparent feelings (1994: 47), such as here in *Patiṟṟuppattu* 14:3–15, 22:

Nāḷkōḷ tiṅkaḷ ñāyiṟu kaṉaiyaḻal
Aintoruṅku puṇarnta viḷakkat taṉaiya

27 A poem or song should end with *ē* whenever it written in the *akaval* sound. This character of *akaval* is the basis for *akappāṭṭu* and *puṟappāṭṭu vaṇṇam* (*Yāpparuṅkalam* 1916: 69).

Pōrtalai mikutta vīraim patiṉmaroṭu
Tupputtuṟai pōkiya tuṇivuṭai yāṇmai
Yakkura ṉaṉaiya kaivaṉ mai**yē**
Amarkaṭantu malainta tumpaip pakaivar
Pōrpī ṭaḻitta ceruppukaṉ muṉpa
Kūṟṟuvekuṇṭu variṉu maṟṟumāṟ ṟalai**yē**
Eḻumuṭi keḻīiya tiruñema rakalattu
Nōṉpurit taṭakkaic cāṉṟōr meimmaṟai
Vāṉuṟai makaḻir nalaṉikal koḷḷum
Vayaṅkiḻai karanta vaṇṭupaṭu katuppi
ṉoṭuṅkī rōtik koṭuṅkuḻai kaṇava
[...]
Tavāa liyaṭōviv vulakamō ṭuṭa**ṉē**

The sound *ē* occurs three times in this song: in lines 7, 10 and 22. In lines 7 and 10 the sound occurs at the end of the line, and in line 22 at the end of the song. These three lines indicate changes of meaning in the praise of a person.

If a song ends with anything other than an *ē* sound, then it uses another formula. For example:

Pulliṉ māyvatu evaṉkol aṉṉāy (Kuṟu. 150)
Uṇkaṇ pacappatu evaṉkol aṉṉāy (*Aiṅkuṟunūṟu* 21)
Iyainta vaikal uḷa ākiyarō (Puṟam. 190)

The closing line of a poem ends not with the sound *ē* but with other sounds instead. These songs give a sense of continuity even after they end. This formula is called *akappāṭṭu vaṇṇam*. These two *vaṇṇam*s explicitly show the relation between singer and listener in the oral tradition.

2 *Oḻuku vaṇṇam*[28]

This *vaṇṇam* has the quality of water flowing in a river without hindrance. Tolkāppiyar defines its grammar using just two words: *ōcaiyiṉ oḻukum*, meaning 'the flowing sound' (Tol.Cey. 538); beside this, we have no information about this *vaṇṇam*. Kumarasamy Pulavar, a commentator on the *Yāpparuṅkala Kārikai* (ca. 10 CE), another grammatical treatise, says that *oḻuku* means 'linearity' (explained

28 The musical notations of the songs given here as examples cannot be described in words, but can be experienced and understood only through performance. Many *vaṇṇam* songs can be understood only in performance; this is why I have explained some of the songs in words. We cannot give visual cues to these songs as is done in western and classical music. These are all oral compositions based on beat, not on *rāga*. *Cantam* is the formula for rhythmic beats, but these songs are of much earlier date and are the basis for the creation of *cantam*.

as '*oḻukutal nērē cellal*' in the commentary).[29] When the sound flows uniformly without any variation in a song, it is called *oḻuku vaṇṇam*. Uniformity of rhythm as a formula in composing a song becomes *oḻuku vaṇṇam*, as is evident from the following song from the *Cilappatikāram*:

uḻava rōtai matakōtai yuṭainī rōtai taṇpataṅkoḷ
viḻava rōtai ciṟantārppa naṭantāy vāḻi kāvēri
viḻava rōtai ciṟantārppa naṭanta vellām vāykāvā
maḻava rōtai vaḷavaṉṟaṉ vaḷaṉē vāḻi kāvēri (Cila. 7:4)

3 *Orūu vaṇṇam*

The root word for *orūu* is *oruvu*, a verb, and it means 'an interval'. *Orūu vaṇṇam* indicates that a particular interval occurs in a song which has a sound like the flowing of water (Tol.Cey. 539). For example:

Yāṉē yīṇṭai yēṉē yeṉṉalaṉē
Āṉā nōyoṭu kāṉa laḵtē
Tuṟaivaṉ ṟammū rāṉē
Maṟaiya rāki maṉṟat taḵtē (Kuṟu. 97)

Uḷḷiṉeṉ allaṉō yāṉē uḷḷi
Niṉaintaṉeṉ allaṉō peritē niṉaintu
Maruṇṭaṉeṉ allaṉō ulakattup paṇpē (Kuṟu. 99)

The sounds occurring in these songs are examples of *orūu vaṇṇam*.

The sound *ē* marks an interval in every line and creates a distinct variety of sound in a song. In the first song three *ē*'s occur in the first line and one in other lines, breaking the continuity of sound and creating intervals. The *ē* sound in *orūu vaṇṇam* appears only as a sound interval and occurs many times in a song; it has no bearing on the meaning of the song, but only on the sound.

4 *Eṇṇu vaṇṇam*

The word *eṇ* means numbers (Tol.Cey. 540). This formula is used for singing songs with numbers. For example:

Nilam nīr vaḷi vicumpu eṉṟa nāṉkiṉ ('four')
Aḷappariyaiyē
Nāḷkōḷ tiṅkaḷ ñāyiṟu kaṉaiyaḻal
Aitoruṅku ('five') ***puṇarnta viḷakkat taṉaiyai*** (*Patiṟṟuppattu* 14:1–4)

29 Kumāracuvāmip Pulavar 2004: 214.

In this song the words are followed by a count. The five elements (other than fire) and celestial objects (star, planet, moon, sun and fire) are mentioned with the king being compared to all of them. This formula, presumably, could be used to praise a king or chieftain with music.[30]

5 *Akaippu vaṇṇam*

When regular intermittent breaks occur in a flowing sound, it becomes *akaippu vaṇṇam* (Tol.Cey. 541). Such breaks may be created by variations in periods of sound, for example a long period immediately followed by a short one, as found in the following song from the *Cilappatikāram*:

> *Nāka nāṟu narantai nirantaṉa*
> *Āvu māramu mōṅkiṉa veṅkaṇum*
> *Cēvu māvuñ ceṟintaṉa kaṇṇutal*
> ***Pāka māḻuṭai yāḻpali muṉṟilē*** (Cila. 12.2).

When a long and short period come in opposition to each other, as if in confrontation, this becomes a formula for the *vaṇṇam*: 1–2 1–2 1–1 2–1 2–2 ... In such a series, variations in *mātrā*s among words in each line of a song, or even in a single line, may mark the character of this *vaṇṇam*. 'Sound intervals' of this kind constitute the basis for this *vaṇṇam*. Tolkāppiyar defines the grammar for this *vaṇṇam* in only two words: '*aṟuttaṟuttu oḻukum*', meaning 'occurring in uniform intervals'.

6 *Tūṅkal vaṇṇam*

We cannot define this *vaṇṇam* exactly. *Tūṅkal* is a variety of musical sound of the *vañci* metre, one of the four metres of Tamil, but we are not able to relate this sound to *vaṇṇam*. This topic requires further research.

7 *Ēntal vaṇṇam*

The word *ēntal* means 'having more' (*mikutal*[31]) (Tol.Cey. 543). A singer can use a word two or three times in a song according to his needs and as the mood demands. By using a word more than once, a singer commits himself to expressing the mood that he wants to convey. For example:

30 Scholars like Sundaram and Thirumurugan believe that some *vaṇṇams* were employed in songs based on content rather than sound. *Eṇṇu vaṇṇam* thus possibly represents an attempt at a *vaṇṇam* employed according to this criterion. Scholars believe that *akappāṭṭu vaṇṇam* and *puṟappāṭṭu vaṇṇam* were also employed based on the content of the song. We don't yet have any evidence of *vaṇṇam* in practice; further research may help us to understand it better.

31 Tol.Cey. 231, with Pērāciriyar's commentary (Kaṇēcaiyar 1943).

Nōm eṉ neñcē nōm eṉ neñcē (Kuṟu. 4:1,4; 202:1,5)
Kāmaṅ kāmam eṉpa kāmam (Kuṟu. 136:1; 204:1,5)

Nōm and *kāmam* are used twice and bring the listener into harmony with the singer's mood.

8 *Uruṭṭu vaṇṇam*

This is characterized by a fast rhythm. Tolkāppiyar defines its grammar in two words: '*arākam toṭukkum*' (Tol.Cey. 544). *Arākam* is a component of two metres, *kali* and *paripāṭal*, and *arākam* gives these meters such a rhythm that the verses which employ them can immediately be identified as such. Within a partial verse or an entire verse, when short periods occur continuously in two to six lines, this is called *arākam*. The *Cilappatikāram* contains one such example:

Cuṭaroṭu tiritaru muṉivaru mamararum
Iṭarkeṭa varuḷuni ṉiṇaiyaṭi toḻutēm
Aṭalvali yeyiṉarni ṉaṭitoṭu kaṭaṉitu
Miṭaṟuku kurutikoḷ viṟaṟaru vilaiyē (Cila. 12:18)

Tuḷḷal, a kind of jumping sound, characterizes the *kali* metre. Since *arākam* is a component of this metre, we may consider it as a *tuḷḷal* sound. Continuously occurring short sounds with regular jumps in uniformity becomes the formula for *uruṭṭu vaṇṇam*. Plosives, nasals and approximants should occur in short periods with regular uniform jumps. Even when a long *mātrā* sound occurs, it should be at the end of the line with a shortened *mātrā*.

9 *Muṭuku vaṇṇam*

The word *muṭuku* means 'running fast'. *Muṭuku vaṇṇam* (Tol.Cey. 545) is defined as frequent short vowels with five to seven metrical feet in a line. It doesn't, however, follow the rule of *arākam*.[32] This *vaṇṇam* will act as *muṭukiyal*, a part of *kali* metre, and so we consider it a *tuḷḷal* sound. For example:

Maṇimaru ṭakaivakai neṟiceṟi yolivari nimirkūntaṟ
ṟuṇaiteḷi yoḷitikaḻ teriyalar makiḻuṇkaṇ vāṇutalār
maṇimayiṟ ṟoḻileḻil kaluḻmali kataḻkaṭuṅ kaṭakkaḷiṟ ṟaṇṇalavarō
ṭaṇimika valla vikappap piṇinīṅka
vallavai yellā miyaitarun tolcīr
varaivāy taḻuviya kalcēr kiṭakkaik
kuḷavā yamarntāṉa kar (*Paripāṭal Tiraṭṭu* 1:60–67)

32 Tol.Cey. 63, comm. Vᴇḷḷᴀɪᴠᴀ̄ʀᴀṇᴀṉ 1989: 320 fn.

In this song. the first two lines have five metrical feet; the next line has six metrical feet continued by four; the last line has three. *Muṭuku vaṇṇam* is used only in the first three lines to show the fast pace of the song.

IV

The preceding discussions pose a few important questions. When a literary grammatical treatise absorbs a grammar of music into its fold and transforms it, what are the problems that we may face when we search for the techniques of bardic compositions?

- When we do not have a comprehensive grammar for musical Tamil, how do we discern the musical qualities of *vaṇṇam*?
- How do we approach the variations of *mātrās* in letters in verse and song?
- How do we understand the significance of *cīr* as it occurs in a metrical foot in verse, on the one hand, and as a rhythmic movement in song on the other?
- *Akaval* constitutes the basis of the *pāṇar* musical tradition. How do we understand the relationship between *vaṇṇam* and *akaval*?
- If *akaval* requires four metrical feet in a line, does the same apply to *vaṇṇam*?
- *Tuḷḷal* and *tūṅkal* are sounds of musical qualities. What role do they play in *vaṇṇam*?

Distinct sounds are important to *vaṇṇam*. Tolkāppiyar's approach to grammar used both letters and metrical feet as the basis of prosody. It is usually assumed that the use of letters as a basis follows the custom of the ancient poets, and that basis on which *vaṇṇam* operates is similar. Interestingly, Tolkāppiyar treats *vaṇṇam* as common to both literary poetic compositions (defined by conventional prosodic forms) and to bardic compositions. If rhythm universally constituted the basis for bardic compositions, would *vaṇṇam*-based formulaic classifications help us to understand such traditions in other languages as well?

References

Gros, F. (2009). *Deep rivers: Selected writings on Tamil literature* (M. P. Boseman, Kannan M. & J. Clare, Eds.). Pondicherry: Institut Français de Pondichéry.

Hart, G. L. (1975). *The poems of ancient Tamil: Their milieu and their Sanskrit counterparts.* Berkeley: University of California Press.

Hart, G. L. & Heifetz, H. (2002). *The Puṟanāṉūṟu: Four hundred songs of war and wisdom: An anthology of poems from classical Tamil.* New Delhi: Penguin Books.

Kuiper, F. B. J. (1997). *Selected writings on Indian linguistics and philology* (A. Lubotsky, M. S. Oort and M. Witzel, Eds.). Amsterdam: Rodopi.

LŌCCAṈ, Po. Cā. (1989). *Tiruppukalp pāṭalkaḷir cantak kūṟukaḷ. I, Aṅkayaṟkaṇṇi.* Ceṉṉai: Kalaiyakam.

RAJAM, V. S. (1992). *A reference grammar of classical Tamil poetry (150 B.C.-pre-fifth/ sixth century A.D.).* Philadelphia: American Philosophical Society.

SUNDARAM, V. P. K. (1994). *Tolkāppiyattil Icaikkuṟippukkaḷ.* Ceṉṉai: Ulakat Tamiḻārāycci Niṟuvaṉam.

—. (2006). *Tamiḻ icai kalaikkalañciyam.* Tiruchirāppaḷḷi: Baradithasan University.

Tamil Lexicon (vol. 5). (1982). Madras: University of Madras.

THANI NAYAGAM, X. S (Ed.). (1956). *Tamil Culture* (vols. 5–6). Madras: Academy of Tamil Culture.

—. (2009). *Paṇṭait Tamiḻc camūkattil kalvi* [Education in Ancient Tamil Society] (N. Manoharan, Trans.). Ceṉṉai: Māṟṟu.

THIRUMURUGAN, I. (1987). *Kampaṉ pāṭiya vaṇṇaṅkaḷ.* Ceṉṉai: Vāṉati Patippakam.

ZVELEBIL, K. (1973). *The smile of Murugan: On Tamil literature of South India.* Leiden: Brill.

Primary Sources

Akam. = Kuḻuviṉar. *Akanāṉūṟu.* (1958). Ceṉṉai: Es. Rājam.

Kuṟu. = CĀMINĀTAIYAR, U. Vē. (Ed.). (1955). *Kuṟuntokai.* Madras: Kapīr Accukkūṭam.

CĀMINĀTAIYAR, U. Vē. (Ed.). *Patiṟṟuppattu.* (1994). Ceṉṉai: Ṭakṭar U. Vē. Cāminātaiyar Nūl Nilaiyam (Original work published 1904.)

Cila. = CĀMINĀTAIYAR, U. Vē. (Ed.). (2001). *Cilappatikāra mūlamum arumpatavuraiyum aṭiyārkkunallāruraiyum* (10th ed). Ceṉṉai: Makāmakōpāttiyāya Ṭakṭar U. Vē. Cāminātaiyar Nūl Nilaiyam. (Original work published 1892.)

CĀMINĀTAIYAR, U. Vē. (Ed.). (1971). *Puṟanāṉūṟu.* Ceṉṉai: Ṭakṭar U. Vē. Cāminātaiyar Nūl Nilaiyam. (Original work published 1894.)

CĒKKIḺĀR. (1951). *Periyapurāṇam: Eṉṟu vaḻaṅkukiṉṟa Tiruttoṇṭarpurāṇam.* Ceṉṉapaṭṭaṉam: Vittiyā nupālaṉayantiracālaiyil.

CITAMPARAM PIḶḶAI, Va. U. (Ed.). (1928). *Tolkāppiyam: Eḻuttatikāram: Iḷampūraṇar uraiyuṭaṉ.* Thoothukudi: Citamparam Piḷḷai.

KAṆĒCAIYAR, Ci. (1943). *Tolkāppiyam Poruḷatikāram, Pērāciriyamum.* Jaffna: Cuṉṉākam.

KUMĀRACUVĀMIP PULAVAR, A. (2004). *Āciriyar Amirtacākarar ceyta Yāpparuṅkalakkārikai: Uriccol nikaṇṭu iṇaintatu.* Ceṉṉai: Teṉ Puttaka Nilaiyam.

Naṟṟiṇai. (1957). Ceṉṉai: Es. Rājam.

PAṬṬUCCĀMI ŌTUVĀR, Ti. (Ed). (1950). *Tiruñāṉacampanta Cuvāmikaḷ aruḷic ceyta Tēvārap patikaṅkaḷ: Tala muṟai.* Tiruppaṉantāḷ: Śrī Kāci Maṭattu Veḷiyīṭu.

PAVĀṈANTAM PIḶḶAI, Ca. (1916). *Amirtacākaraṉār iyaṟṟiya Yāpparuṅkalam: Mūlam paḻaiya viruttiyuraiyuṭaṉ.* Ceṉṉai: Tāmsaṉ Kampeṉi.

Tolkāppiyam Poruḷatikāram, Iḷampūraṇam. (1961). Tirunelvēli: Caivacittānta Nūṟpatippu Kaḻakam.

VEḶḶAIVĀRAṆAṈ, Ka. (1989). *Tolkāppiyam: Ceyyuḷiyal: Uraivaḷam.* Madurai: Patipputtuṟai Maturai Kāmarācar Palkalaik Kaḻakam.

Kathak as a *Śāstrīya Nṛtya*

The Rediscovery of the *Nāṭyaśāstra* and the Invention of Classicism in Indian Dance[1]

Katarzyna Skiba

The paper traces the process of dance classicization as it accompanied so called 'Indian dance renaissance', launched in the 1930s, and as it is continued today. The project of art classicization is examined along with the tendency of Sanskritization. The paper discusses various definitions and understanding of classicism in Indian dance, drawing from textual data from books and brochures on Indian classical dance, manuals on Kathak, as well as observations and interviews, conducted during fieldwork in India in 2014 and 2015. Focusing on the case of Kathak, the paper investigates the alleged interlinks between contemporary dance praxis and rules from Sanskrit dance literature. It also questions the legitimacy of Sanskrit texts as adequate sources for investigating Kathak past, underlining the discrepancies between the dance theory, and contemporary practice. It seeks to explain the instrumental role of the strategy to refer the dance to the *Nāṭyaśāstra* and *Abhinayadarpaṇa* in Kathak revival, entangled in the processes of national identity formation. It also concerns the current efforts of various artists and dance scholars to perpetuate the Sanskritized framework in Kathak theory and training.

Since the 1980s, anthropological scholarship has highlighted the notion that classicism in Indian dance emerged amid the process of the cultural translation and indigenisation of the European concept of 'classical dance' in the first half of the twentieth century. The phenomenon comprised part of the creation of a modern 'high culture', intended to activate the nationalist imagination (CHATTERJEE 1993: 52). On the wave of cultural revival, selected South Asian dance forms were

1 The project was funded by the National Science Centre (NCN) on the basis of decision no. DEC-2013/09/N/HS3/02108.

refashioned and introduced as 'styles' of Indian classical dance (Hin. *śāstrīya nṛtya*), synonymous with the 'high culture'.

> ... [T]urning specific Indian dance forms into 'classical dance' was part of the movement to reinscribe them into modern artistic practice and provide them with a well-defined status, equivalent to that of classical ballet in the West. These classical 'styles' are, strictly speaking, 'neoclassical', a modern re-creation and re-making based on an earlier tradition deemed to be 'classical'. (Lopez y Royo 2004: 3)

The term 'neoclassical' seems to be deliberately avoided in popular Indian dance histories. The idea of 'classical Indian dance' has been imposed both on the 'revived' dance forms, and on the old dance techniques described in Sanskrit treatises, forming a link between the two traditions. This link helped revivalists to claim the antiquity of the reconstructed forms and reify the idea of the common roots of the various regional dances deemed to be classical. In this way, 'classical Indian dance(s)' came to symbolize India's past, centuries-old traditions and the idea of 'unity in diversity', which were instrumental in the construction and reproduction of national identity.

Whereas much research on Indian dance revival has focused on Bharatanatyam (Allen 1994, Gaston 1996, Coorlawala 2004, O'Shea 2007, Peterson & Soneji 2008, Soneji 2012), other Indian dances considered classical have attracted much less scholarly attention. The aim of this paper is to explore the phenomenon of Kathak classicization, with attention to the prominent tendency to 'Sanskritize' the dance in this process. On one hand, I intend to draw analogies between the Kathak and Bharatanatyam revivals, since the former seems to incorporate similar strategies as the latter. Whereas the transformation of Sadir dance to the classical form of Bharatanatyam was done in the 1930s in South India, the establishment of Kathak as a North Indian classical dance seems to have taken place around two decades later in national dance institutions (preceded by revivalist attempts undertaken by Madame Menaka in the 1930s). Witnessing the successful 'revival' of Bharatanatyam, Kathak modernists in newly founded dance academies in Delhi seem, to some extent, to have introduced similar changes and referred to the same textual authorities and concepts.

On the other hand, in terms of its different historical, geographical and cultural background, as well as its close proximity to new centers of political power, Kathak revival has partly taken its own route, corresponding to trends in the classicization of Hindustani music (examined by Bakhle 2005). Similarly to the modernists of Hindustani music, Kathak reformers had to deal with the issue of the Muslim component in the tradition, and evaluated it variously in the pre-independence, Nehruvian, and post-1991 periods. The social and religious background of the hereditary performers in North India (different from the hereditary dance communities of South India) also determined the process of Kathak classicization. Finally, the concept of Indian 'unity in diversity' appears to have inspired the search for the common basis of all the classical dance 'styles', and the resulting tendency to 'rediscover' Sanskrit legacy in Kathak.

This paper examines to what extent the discourses on Kathak and Sanskrit treatises are similar to analogous discourses in the sphere of Bharatanatyam. It also explores the enduring link between Kathak and Sanskrit texts in contemporary dance praxis and theory writing, with the intention of investigating the importance of this link and the reasons for its reproduction. The analysis is based on the interviews conducted and observations drawn in India in 2014 and 2015. The field data is juxtaposed with the analysis of the discourse predominant in secondary sources, namely books and manuals on Kathak, pointing to the existing disparity between these two domains and the strategies used by dancers to solve this conflict.

Kathak revival: Rewriting the past, aesthetics and functions of a classical dance form

The function of representing the nation was assigned to classical Indian dance from the beginning of its 'renaissance' in the 1930s, primarily launched by Rukmini Devi in the context of Bharatanatyam. In the case of North Indian dance, the pioneering role at that time was played by Madame Menaka, who sought to refashion Kathak as a refined art of a national character. In her opinion, 'dance is a medium for the expression of the life and emotions of a nation [...] Dance revival in any country must per force have the national technique, the technique developed through centuries, as the starting point' (MENAKA 1933). To advance 'the national technique', she emphasized the necessity of mastering the technique extant in Sanskrit texts, old paintings and sculptures and learning from traditional dance *gurus* (ibid.). It seems that her tenets had a considerabe impact on later phases of Kathak revival in the national dance academies, where the authority of the *śāstras* started to counterbalance the dominance of male *gharānedār gurus*.

Both Rukmini Devi and Madame Menaka were Brahman ladies, previously trained in ballet and inspired by Anna Pavlova. They founded their own modern Indian dance schools, in which they implemented some Western methods of stage production, dance education and the systematization of rules of technique, with an emphasis on clear lines in dance figures. The cultural revivalists in India not only borrowed Western models of classical dance education, but also reproduced colonial perceptions of Indian culture and history, with the idea of the cultural riches of India's past ('golden age'). What has been recognized as 'classical', ancient and refined in India by European Orientalists referred primarily to the Sanskrit legacy. Borrowing this narrative, Western-educated Indian nationalists and cultural revivalists turned to Sanskrit and 'Aryan culture' as fundamentals, so to speak, in their search for the common ethno-linguistic ground of the emerging multilingual and multiethnic nation.

Amid the increasing emphasis on the role of Sanskrit sources, the Islamic component of 'national heritage' in North India (as well as other regional cultures of South Asia) was neglected at an early stage of the cultural renaissance. After 1947, the Nehruvian idea of Indian secularism and 'unity in diversity' started to overshadow the concept of the glorious Hindu/Aryan past of India. In this period, Kathak gained popularity as an Indo-Islamic tradition; however, the process of substituting Muslim elements of the tradition with Hindu equivalents and implementing Sanskrit nomenclature continued (Chakravorty 2008). Since the increase of Hindu fundamentalism in the 1990s, the ideology of Hindutva has seemed to influence the dominant nationalist discourse on India's history, cultural heritage and classical Indian dance alike. This is reflected in recent publications on Kathak, propagating the idea of its origin in Hindu religious practices and philosophy (Srivatsava 2004, 2008, Vatsyayan 1997, Saxena 2006) as well as its adherence to Sanskrit treatises on dance (Jyotishi 2009, Bhate 2004, Datye 2010).

The first theories concerning the origin of Kathak appeared in the 1930s; Kathak historiography started to emerge around the 1940s, together with the histories of other classical dance 'styles' in India. the first publications devoted solely to Kathak and its past were written in the 1950s. The dominant discourse of Kathak history also bears the imprint of Orientalist historiography, dividing India's past into the Hindu, Muslim and colonial ('modern') periods.[2] According to the most popular version, Kathak is believed to have originated as a religious art, performed in temples by wandering bards (Brahmans) called *kathaka*s, who received patronage partly from local rulers and thus shifted to the courts. In the Mughal courts, the art became secularized and influenced by Persian culture. It gained great popularity under the patronage of Wajid Ali Shah (1847–56), *nawab* of Lucknow. The dancers who supposedly performed at the *nawab*'s court, Kalka and Bindadin Maharaj, were considered to be great masters of Kathak, who refined the dance and transmitted it to the next generations. Nowadays, their descendants (such as Birju Maharaj) represent the unbroken tradition and are considered the main authority in defining the criteria of authenticity in the *Lucknow gharana* of Kathak.

Therefore, it would be reasonable to trace Kathak history with reference to the textual sources produced in the context of nineteenth-century Lucknow. For this purpose, a number of colonialists' letters or diaries can be examined, along with the Urdu treatises of Wajid Al Shah, such as *Nājo* and *Banī*, describing dance

2 The Muslim period is sometimes presented as the stage of corruption or contamination of Indian culture, decline of Kathak to a form of entertainment (Devi 1972: 166–167; Kothari 1989: 2, 15; Gupta 2004:13–14).

sequences that resemble some Kathak movements.[3] Over the period of the Nehru-Gandhi leadership, these Urdu treatises have been considered by only a few writers of Kathak history, including Maya RAO (1959) and Sunil KOTHARI (1989). Other interesting nineteenth-century Urdu sources—such as *Sarmaya-i 'ishrat*, describing the dance techniques of the courtesans (*tawaifs*)—had been totally ignored in the dominant discourse on Kathak history until the recent research of WALKER (2004, 2013). Instead, dance historians turned primarily to Sanskrit texts in their search for the principles of the classical canon and insight into Kathak past, following similar initiatives in the sphere of Bharatanatyam. It can be speculated that this textual authority provided a set of rules regarded as more 'universal' (pan-Indian) and fixed than the diversified, fluid, orally transmitted conventions and instructions provided by hereditary performers. Therefore, the treatise could be perceived as more effective in the process of standardizing ('stabilizing' the knowledge of) classical dance.

The legacy of these practices is still palpable. Today, artists and scholars emphasize the adherence to Sanskrit treatises on the performing arts as a main feature of classical Indian dances. This is evident when we analyze the dominant discourse in Indian publications and manuals on Kathak, as well as the artists' statements in the media and their opinions as expressed in interviews. This paper primarily explores the internal perspective concerning the use of language and the circulation of concepts among Kathak artists and Indian historians, along with the way in which they insist on the foundational role of *śāstras* in classical Indian dances. However, while the publications simply describe shastric concepts, ignoring the gap between these theories and the actual shape of Kathak art, dance practitioners seem to make more effort to bridge the gap with various reinterpretations of Sanskrit aesthetics. In the context of Bharatanatyam, Sanskrit conventions, such as hand gestures, have been adopted into praxis more than one finds in Kathak. Perhaps the implementation of shastric rules in Kathak training has not been so effective due to the stronger status of hereditary dance *gurus*, who shared (and still propagate) many competing opinions on Kathak aesthetics. In the Bharatanatyam revival, middle-class women more successfully broke the monopoly of hereditary male instructors in teaching.

The Sanskritization of dance

Among dance scholars, COORLAWALA (2004), MEDURI (2005) and PETERSON & SONEJI (2008) have examined the process of 'Sanskritization' in dance as the incorporation of Sanskrit aesthetics into classical Indian dance in order to differentiate classical

3 The third chapter of *Banī* (Hin. *Banī*, Ur. *Musammī ba Banī*) contains descriptions of 16 *gats* with illustrations. *Gat* is a term used in Kathak for a sequence of movements, often a gait imitating everyday activities. Some of the *gats* in *Banī* incorporate typical Kathak movements, for example *ghūṅghaṭ gat, mukuṭ gat* and *salāmī gat*. *Nājo* includes compositions like *ṭhumrī, horī, dādrā, dhrupavad, stuti* and *tarānā*—the genres to which Kathak is danced nowadays.

forms from folk ones. SRINIVAS, who first used this term in the context of sociology, defines Sanskritization as:

> [... T]he process by which a 'low' Hindu caste, or tribal or other group, changes its customs, ritual, ideology and a way of life in the direction of a high, and frequently 'twice-born' caste. Generally such changes are followed by a claim to a higher position in the caste hierarchy then that traditionally conceded to the claimant caste by the local community[.] (1966: 6)

In case of Kathak, it is problematic to attribute this phenomenon to a particular social group, since the art has partly been relocated from one community to others. Due to being taken over by the Brahman elite,[4] the status of the art has been upgraded. COORLAWALA explains a similar phenomenon in Bharatanatyam revival:

> In dance, sanskritization has become a legitimizing process by which dance forms designated as 'ritual', 'folk', or simply insignificant, attain social and politico-artistic status which brings the redesignation, 'classical' [...] In the I970s, almost every dance form claiming antiquity and sophistication, noted references within the canonized Nāṭyaśāstra and texts in regional languages, and demonstrated how postures, movement units and narrative techniques were organized according to this text. (2004: 53)

In parallel fashion, dance scholars and teachers writing manuals on Kathak tended to draw from Sanskrit aesthetics, conventions and nomenclature in the 1950s. Sanskrit nomenclature was already used by Madame Menaka (MENAKA 1933), who referred to some rules from the *Nāṭyaśāstra* (basic standing positions, differences between *tāṇḍava* and *lāsya*). Sanskrit manuals on dance, mainly the *Nāṭyaśāstra* (NŚ)and *Abhinayadarpaṇa* (AD), have been employed in the process of Kathak textualization and homogenization. These texts have provided a set of conventions, along with pan-Indian dance nomenclature, used in numerous books on Kathak theory, in theory classes in dance departments and in special workshops on the *Nāṭyaśāstra*. Thus, the 'Sanskritization' of Kathak seems to be closely interlinked

4 According to Srinivas, in the course of Sanskritization the newly adopted customs often include studying and referring to Sanskrit texts. Sanskritization does not necessarily imply Brahmanisation, but it is generally an assimilation of the practices of the dominant group. The process may be initiated by members of a low caste who aspire to raise themselves to higher levels of the social hierarchy, or it may be imposed on lower classes by a higher one. Nevertheless, the hereditary male masters (identified as *Kathakas*) remained great authorities of Kathak tradition. It is disputable whether the caste of *Kathakas* is a Brahman community (this argument is put forward in various Indian publications on Kathak history). Perhaps it could be examined as a case of 'mystifying' the origin of hereditary performers in order to assimilate them into the high, Brahmanical culture, and an example of imposture of Sanskritized elements from Brahmans' culture into the practices of lower communities.

with its institutionalization, which generated the need to develop uniform standards for dance art.

As part of this research, I have analyzed publications that are used as manuals in dance academies and explored how the particular shastric concepts are referred to in Kathak practice. The manual-type publications include Rashmi VAJPEYI (1992), Bharati GUPTA (2004), Vidhi NAGAR (2011) and Puru DADHICH (2012). The books of Sunil KOTHARI (1989), Shovana NARAYAN (1998), Sikha KHARE (2005) and Tirath Ram AZAD (2005) discuss both historical and theoretical issues, combining shastric conventions with a description of Kathak technique more closely related to its praxis. Sushil Kumar SAXENA (2006) has vastly elaborated the philosophical framework of Kathak technique. Chetana JYOTISHI-BEOHAR's book (2009) focuses entirely on the concept of *nāyikā-bheda* in Kathak. Roshan DATE (2010) presents the movements and gestures codified in the *Nāṭyaśāstra*, illustrating them with numerous photos of Kathak dancers as well as old Indian sculptures and pointing to the their mutual correspondence. Rohini BHATE has elaborated an edited version of the *Abhinayadarpaṇa* called *Kathakdarpandeepika* (2004), an attempt to integrate the Sanskrit text with Kathak technique. Additionally, I refer to books on classical Indian dance that present the shastric conventions as the common feature of all the classical 'styles', such as VATSYAYAN (1974), KHOKAR (1979), BANERJEE (1984) and JYOTISHI-BEOHAR (2015).

The references to the shastric conventions are basically a set of rules selected from the *Nāṭyaśāstra* and *Abhinayadarpaṇa* that are repeatedly recalled by the aforementioned authors. These are as follows (source manual in parentheses):

- the concept of *rasa* theory (both the *Nāṭyaśāstra* and *Abhinayadarpaṇa*);
- the *aṣṭanāyikā-bheda* (*Nāṭyaśāstra*);
- the division of dance into *nāṭya*, *nṛtya* and *nṛtta* (*Abhinayadarpaṇa*);
- the types of dance: *tāṇḍava* and *lāsya* (*Nāṭyaśāstra*);
- the four types of *abhinaya* (*Nāṭyaśāstra*);
- the classification of the limbs into *aṅg*, *pratyaṅg*, *upāṅg*;
- the *hasta* (often called *mudrā* or *hasta-mudrā* in Kathak)—most books refer to the *Abhinayadarpaṇa*, which enumerates 28 *asaṃyuta hasta*s and 24 *saṃyuta hasta*s, as well as the *devahasta*s, *daśāvatāra hasta*s, *jātīya hasta*s, *bāndhava hasta*s and *navagraha hasta*s of the *Abhinayadarpaṇa*, and 30 *nṛtta hasta*s from the *Nāṭyaśāstra;*
- the descriptions of *karaṇa*, *aṅgahāra* and *recaka* (*Nāṭyaśāstra);*
- the positions of the feet (*pāda bheda*): gaits (*cārī*), standing foot positions (*maṇḍala*), jumps (*utplavana*), circular movements (*bhramari*) and postures (*sthānaka*)—not precisely described, and significantly different from the Kathak movements;
- nine types of head movements (*śiro bheda*), eight types of eye movements (*dṛṣṭi bheda*), seven movements of the eyebrows (*bhṛkuṭī bheda*) and four kinds of neck movements (*grīvā bheda*) (*Abhinayadarpaṇa*);
- the usage of anklet-bells (*Abhinayadarpaṇa*);

- the qualities (*guṇa* and *doṣa*) of a female dancer (*Abhinayadarpaṇa*) and male dancer (*Saṅgītaratnākara*).

These conventions are often recalled by dancers, who tend to integrate them into the Kathak technique. In the next sections of this paper, I will question the relevance of some of these concepts to the Kathak praxis, basing my considerations on empirical data from interviews and observations conducted in several Kathak schools in India in 2014 and 2015.

Rasa as the essence of dance

One of the concepts commonly adopted from the *Nāṭyaśāstra* and *Abhinayadarpaṇa* in Indian classical dances is the theory of aesthetic experience, *rasa.* Many Kathak dancers consider *rasa* to be the essence of art and its ultimate purpose. 'Audiences respond to emotions rather than information ... The language of emotions is universal, so emotions are most important in the dance performance', as Nirupama and Rajendra expound (personal communication, March 14, 2014).[5] However, dancers seem to understand this concept in various ways and often confuse the meaning of *rasa,* 'an aesthetic taste', with (*sthāyi*)*bhāva*, an emotion used in art to evoke a particular *rasa.* According to Chetna Jalan, Kathak dance begins when we understand *rasa:* 'No technique is complete without a proper *rasa*; how you interpret the technique is another dimension of art ... It is something that comes from your heart ...' (personal communication, March 10, 2015). From this point of view, *rasa* seems to be a component of dance technique, whereas in the *Nāṭyaśāstra, rasa* is rather an effect of the presentation and 'tasting' emotions.

It is also noteworthy that some Kathak artists talk about *rasa* and *bhāva* in the context of 'abstract dance', which—according to the shastric definition—is devoid of narrative and emotions.

> To us, DANCE is a unique entity with alluring beauty that teaches us to be, to feel & to recreate the Joys of Life. Whether it is the enduring romance in Mythology, the recurring magic of Seasons or just a pure expression of Abstraction, its sole purpose is to create 'RASA'—the true flavor of aesthetics for the spectator. Dance gives impersonal joy, Tranquil joy or the blissful peace to the spectators. (Personal communication, March 15, 2015.)

Usually, Kathak artists and theorists enumerate nine aesthetic 'tastes' called *rasa,*[6] following the Sanskrit texts. Sometimes, they also refer to *vātsalya rasa* and

5 This dance duet studies *Nāṭyaśāstra* with the help of Sanskritist Dr. R. Ganesh.

6 There are many dance productions that explore this concept as their main theme, for instance Rani Karna's *Navrasmalika*, Tina Tambe's *Navarasa* and Kumudini Lakhia's *Bhav Krida* (a reinterpretation of *navarasa*).

bhakti rasa, drawing from *bhakti* traditions and Hindi literature. The idea of *bhakti* ('devotion') has become very significant to the Kathak revival. It was instrumental in the reinterpretation of love motifs, and the consequential spiritualization of dance, which was also important to the Bharatanatyam revival. Because of the rich exploration of the '*Kṛṣṇa-līlā*' theme in Kathak, *śṛṅgāra rasa* (the 'erotic taste') is considered the dominant 'taste' of this dance. However, in the contemporary praxis of Kathak, the depiction of human love is often explained as a metaphor of the soul's longing for union with a god or Absolute. This shift was part of the process of Kathak 'purification', aimed at distancing the dance from its associations with courtesans, similarly to the marginalization of *devadasi*s in South India. The concept of *śṛṅgāra rasa* has been imposed on various *bhakti* lyrics and Hindi songs and 'spiritualized' in the course of Kathak revival.

The presentation of female characters in Kathak is often modelled on the *aṣṭanāyikā-bheda* ('eight states of the heroine', described in NŚ 24). Older songs from the Kathak repertoire evoke mostly *śṛṅgāra rasa* and *vīra rasa*. The predominant genres of the *Lucknow gharana* of Kathak, such as *ṭhumrī* and *dādrā*, are amorous songs, usually depicting a young woman in a state of separation from her lover (she is identified with the Sanskrit *virahotkaṇṭhitā* or *khaṇḍitā* heroine, who is additionally angry with her lover) or being teased by a man (*cheṛ-chāṛ*—a motif absent from the *aṣṭanāyikā-bheda*, but popular in the old repertoire of Kathak dancers). Hereditary Kathak performers also claim that their ancestors danced to heroic songs (for instance, while presenting the valiant deeds of Krishna, such as the *Kaliya-mardana*). It seems that other *rasa*s and types of *nayika*s appeared in Kathak in the course of twentieth-century innovations to the repertoire.

During my stay in a hereditary family dance schoolhouse in Lucknow (April 2015), modelled on the traditional system of *gurukul*, the advanced students of Kathak were studying concepts from Sanskrit treatises, such as the fourfold *abhinaya* or *navarasa*, for university examinations. The material and Sanskrit terminology were new to them, so their guru was expounding particular conventions and classifications, adducing examples from Kathak vocabulary or mythological motifs known to them from dance training. Learning shastric *hasta*s, they also noticed that some of them are similar to the gestures used in Kathak, but the latter have different meanings and names, or no names at all.[7] According to their guru, *Nāṭyaśāstra* is a source of Kathak and teaches the proper way of conveying gestures, although Birju Maharaj performs them in a different way (Arjun Mishra, personal communication, April 10, 2015). Despite the claimed kinship with the established masters, he seemed to assign more credibility and authenticity to the Sanskrit treatise.

It seems that the Sanskrit theory is often neglected in practical training and performance, especially outside the state academies. Dancers depict emotions

7 Personal observation, Kathak Academy, Lucknow, April 2015.

partly by imitating own guru, or through associations with real life images and experiences. Presentation in Kathak is often described as naturalistic, or mimetic, based on associations, so that non-connoisseurs may easily follow the story. The dance language also includes some culturally specific symbols and suggestions. Great masters from hereditary communities, like Birju Maharaj, emphasize the aspects of creativity and improvisation in Kathak. The mastery results from the everyday life observation of people, their interactions, relationships and environment (Birju Maharaj, personal communication, February 18, 2015). Even in the most renowned schools, like Kathak Kendra, the guru does not fully explain to his disciples how to embody a character, but gives them some clues and freedom to imagine and improvise on the motif.[8] This idea of improvisation and self-expression is quite popular in Kathak. Kathak artists often perceive their own style as providing the most possibility to express oneself (compared to other classical dance forms), while the Sanskrit treatises (and manuals on Kathak referring to them) present numerous conventions of *abhinaya*, limiting the creativity of a performer. Nonetheless, contemporary performers often seek to justify the relevance of their practice to the ancient treatise, for example maintaining that the *Nāṭyaśāstra* equally allows improvisation and provides many tools for the artist's creativity in performance (Nirupama and Rajendra, personal communication, March 14, 2014).

It is also argued among Kathak performers whether *rasa* is a part of the artist's experience. Kathak dancers tend to claim that *rasa* is produced both in the performer and the audience. '*Rasa* first comes to me. If I am not experiencing that *rasa*, how am I going to convey [it] to you? ... If I have not put my own heart in it, the correct *bhava* will not come. And if the *bhava* doesn't come, how can the *rasa* come?' clarifies Chetna Jalan, referring to *śloka* 37 of the *Abhinayadarpaṇa*, on *rasa* production (personal communication, March 10, 2015), which is often quoted by Kathak and Bharatanatyam dancers:

> Where the hand goes, eyes should go there.
> There the eyes go mind also should go there.
> Where the mind goes there the State (*bhāva*) should follow,
> *And where there is the State, there the Sentiment* (rasa) *arises.*[9] (Trans. Ghosh 1957: 46.)

Between abstraction and expression

Another concept generally accepted in the theory of Kathak is the classification of dance into *nāṭya*, *nṛtya* and *nṛtta*. Rani Karna pointed to this as the chief convention

8 Personal observation of Kathak classes in Kathak Kendra, April 2015.

9 *yato hastastato dṛṣṭiryato dṛṣṭistato manaḥ*
yatomanastato bhāvo yato bhāvastato rasaḥ (AD 37).

of Kathak (personal communication, March 13, 2015). The common understanding of these terms among Kathak dancers and theorists resembles the division of theatrical art in the *Abhinayadarpaṇa* (emphasis mine):

> *Dance which has this four-fold aspect [of* abhinaya*] is of three kinds*: nāṭya, nṛtya *and* nṛtta, *according to sages like Bharata and others* (AD 11).
> *Nāṭya* or *nāṭaka* which has some traditional story for its theme is for adoration. That [dance] which does not express States (*bhāva*) by means of *abhinaya*, is called *nṛtta*.
> *That [dance] which suggests sentiments* (rasa) *and states* (bhāva), *is called* nṛtya. *This dance is always fit to find a place in the court of great kings.* (AD 14–16. Trans. GHOSH 1957: 40–41.)[10]

In the view of Kathak artists, 'the dance itself can be divided into distinct parts: the "*nritya*" (expressional, mimetic), the "*nritta*" (pure rhythmic portion) and the "*natya*" (dramatic)' (NARAYAN 1998: 54). The 'dramatic element' of *nāṭya* implies a dramatic dialogue, elaborated by more than one dancer, as Rani Karna clarifies (personal communication, March 13, 2015). Karna also names certain abstract and expressive elements as distinctive features of particular *gharanas*: *Jaipur gharana*, exhibiting a variety of rhythms and syllables (*bols*), is dominated by *nṛtta*, contrary to *Lucknow gharana*, which emphasizes *nṛtya* (ibid.).

This classification becomes problematic with reference to particular details of Kathak performance. For example, *kavitta* is a type of composition that combines narrative (most often Krishna stories) with the recitation of rhythmic patterns, often onomatopoeic. It relates a story, constantly interrupted by more abstract sounds and portions of 'pure dance', breaking with the strict division between *nṛtya and nṛtta*. *Bāmāni bol* is a blend of meaningful words and harmonious syllables. To explain this artistic stylization, Saxena adduces the example of a partly representational composition, depicting Radha as she sits on the bank of a river, ceaselessly remembering Krishna, who abides forever in her eyes (SAXENA 1982: 40–41). In this kind of composition, the verbal and the mnemonic cooperate with the rhythmic structure in creating meaning, so that it is difficult to separate the abstract elements from the narrative.

Moreover, according to Birju Maharaj, *bhāva* is the essence of Kathak, transmitted throughout the entire performance, even during rhythmic footwork

10 *etac catuvidhopetaṁ naṭanaṁ trividhaṁ smṛtaṁ*
nāṭyaṁ nṛttaṁ nṛtyam iti munibhir bharatādibhiḥ (AD 11).
nāṭyaṁ tan nāṭakaṁ caiva pūjyaṁ pūrvakathāyutam
bhāvābhinayahīnaṁ tu nṛttam ity abhidhīyate
rasabhāvavyanjnādiyuktaṁ nṛtyam itīryate
etan nṛtyaṁ mahārājasabhāyāṁ kalpayet sadā (AD 14–16).

and the demonstration of technical skills (personal communication, February 18, 2015). In light of this approach, the term *nṛtta,* understood as non-expressive dance (devoid of *bhāva*), seems to be inadequate for any section of Kathak performance. Chetna Jalan, who regularly invites Birju Maharaj to her school Padatik, in Kolkata, shares a similar view: 'Even all the abstract movements are filled with *rasa* if they come from [the] heart, when you revise the movement in your mind ...' (personal communication, March 10, 2015). Rani Karna has also drawn attention to the fact that some artists 'break the rules', blending the three elements. For instance, Lachchhu Maharaj used to introduce expression (*bhāva*) into the pure dance (Rani Karna, personal communication, March 13, 2015). Again, we can notice how the authority of the hereditary guru is compromised by the textual authority, especially at the hands of educated, middle-class women.

In the *Nāṭyaśāstra*, *nṛtta* seems to be equated with *tāṇḍava*, a vigorous dance performed by Śiva (NŚ 4.261). The main purpose of *nṛtta* is to create beauty (NŚ 4.263). *Nṛtta* consists of *aṅgahāra*s and *karaṇa*s. *Tāṇḍava* is performed to praise the gods during the preliminaries of the play (*pūrvaraṅga*). *Tāṇḍava* inspired Parvati to dance a different type of dance with delicacy (*sukumāraprayoga*), producing erotic sentiments. The difference between these two divine dances seems to lie in the function of each dance: *tāṇḍava* focuses on communication with the sacred, *lāsya*/*sukumāra* on human communication: 'The art of *nṛtta* that was created is known as *tāṇḍava* (NŚ 4.261). Whatever part (of a play) is for praising gods, (one) should perform with vigorous *aṅgahāra*s (created by) Maheśvara while a song related to erotic sentiment involving [depending on] man and woman (is sung) it should be performed by *aṅgahāra*s created by Devī' (NŚ 4. 312, trans. Bose 2001: 16).[11] It seems that this distinction has no connection with gender (Bose 2001: 10–11), as it is often understood by classical dancers, who define *tāṇḍava* as a masculine dance, as opposed to *lāsya*, a feminine dance, ignoring their functional distinction.

The contemporary perception of *tāṇḍava* and *lāsya* may be yet another aspect of the 'purification' of Kathak of overt eroticism and sensuality, and the result of the increasing insistence on the spiritual interpretation of the performance. The practitioners do not seem to be very aware of the discrepancy between the nature of the distinction advocated in the *Nāṭyaśāstra* and the later, gender-based distinction, as none of my respondents acknowledged the former one. The association of *tāṇḍava* dance with the figure of Nataraja, popularized in the 'revival' period, could also have influenced the tendency to identify the vigorous dance with the god

11 *nṛttaprayogaḥ sṛṣto yaḥ sa tāṇḍava iti smṛtaḥ* (NŚ 4.261).
devastuttyāśrayakṛtaṃ yad aṅgaṁ tu bhaved atha
māheśvarair aṅgahārair uddhatais tat prayojayet
yat tu śṛṅgāsambandhaṁ gānaṁ strīpuruṣāśrayam
devīkṛtair aṅgahārair lalitais tat prayojayet (NŚ 4.312).

Shiva, and the subtle dance with the goddess Parvati. Some Kathak manuals also describe the two dances as the separate activities of men and women respectively (Gupta 2004: 3–4, Dādhīc 2012: 9). Since many dancers do not know Sanskrit, they rely more on the explanations provided in the dance manuals than on the original Sanskrit scriptures.

The importance of *abhinaya*

Abhinaya is an essential element in the representational aspect of dance. Its four aspects are broadly discussed in the *Nāṭyaśāstra*, including discussions of *bhāva*. One of the types of *abhinaya*, *vācikābhinaya*, refers to the actor's speech or singing. It is rarely done by a dancer in present-day Kathak performance. Senior gurus from hereditary families of *Lucknow gharana* used to sing songs on stage, but currently the dancers only recite rhythmil patterns before presenting them in a dance piece. The song can be delivered by a vocalist or from a tape, but it is not an integral part of Kathak dancers' acting. In particular, singing female dancers evoked associations with courtesans' culture, so middle-class Kathak danseuses deliberately avoid singing.[12]

Another type, *āhāryābhinaya* (conveying expression through costume and jewellery), contradicts the *ekāhāryābhinaya* convention in Kathak, indicated by hereditary performers as the 'traditional' one. According to many dancers, Kathak is a solo form, in which costume and ornaments are not designed for any particular character, and the performer enacts many characters, one after the other. An analysis of archival photos reveals that there were no prescribed dress conventions among Kathak performers in the 1950s. Nowadays, there are specific Kathak costumes, but they do not convey any message in the play (except for innovative group choreographies called 'Kathak ballets'). Instead, they may suggest the social or religious background of the performers, and the values shared by the community (such as female modesty or marital status). Therefore they can indicate more personal information about the performer rather than the character, which was not an objective of *āhāryā* in the *Nāṭyaśāstra*.

Kathak theorists notably explore *aṅgikābhinaya*, conveying expression through gestures and bodily movements. Many manuals on Kathak include a classification of the movements of particular limbs, on the model of the *Abhinayadarpaṇa*: nine types of head movements (*śiro bheda*), eight types of eye movements (*dṛṣṭi bheda*), seven movements of the eyebrows (*bhṛkuṭī bheda*) and kinds of neck movements (*grīvā bheda*). In various Kathak manuals we can also find a classification of foot positions and movements (*pāda bheda*): gaits (*cārī*), standing foot positions (*maṇḍala*), jumps (*utplavana*), circular movements (*bhramari*) and postures (*sthānaka*). However, the

12 Arjun Mishra, personal communication, April 10, 2015.

movements are not described precisely. Most of them are dissimilar to the Kathak movements, so the authors additionally attempt to provide analogies between the two. Books on Kathak also mention units and sequences of movement, like *karaṇa, aṅgahāra* and *recaka*, with reference to the *Nāṭyaśāstra*. These movements are also totally divergent from Kathak technique, so the exploration of this concept is an additional task, undertaken by several artists, middle-class women in particular (Maya Rao, Nirupama and Rajendra, Roshan Date[13]). In the context of Bharatanatyam, a similar exploration of these concepts by Padma Subramanian led to distinguishing a separate 'style' called 'Bharatanrityam', but no analogous term has been introduced in the field of Kathak (to my knowledge).

Special attention has been afforded to hand gestures, i.e. *hasta*s (often termed *mudrā*s or *hasta-mudrā*s by Kathak exponents). They are often regarded as a codified language, common to all classical Indian dance forms. Again, Kathak manuals follow the *Abhinayadarpaṇa* classification rather than that of the *Nāṭyaśāstra*; the former enumerates 28 (sometimes 32) *asaṃyuta hasta*s and 24 (or 23) *saṃyuta hasta*s. Some of the manuals also mention *devahasta*s, *daśāvatāra hasta*s, *jātīya hasta*s, *bāndhava hasta*s and *navagraha hasta*s, as described in the *Abhinayadarpaṇa*, and 30 *nṛtta hasta*s from the *Nāṭyaśāstra*. Except for a few *asaṃyuta hasta*s, these gestures and their meanings are not broadly disseminated among Kathak dancers. There are some teachers (like Nirupama and Rajendra) who teach students the formula from the *Abhinayadarpaṇa*, chanting and making the gestures, as is done in many Bharatanatyam schools. A particular gesture may exist in Kathak but communicate different messages than described in the Sanskrit texts; however, not many researchers have explained these discrepancies.

Maya Rao has related Kathak gestures and movement sequences to *hasta*s in the *Nāṭyaśāstra*.[14] She explained that *hasta*s are used in Kathak (*gat*s) to depict a certain idea, imitate a gait or narrate a story (Rao 1959). She enumerated the gestures used by Kathak dancers (such as *patāka, tripatāka, śikhara, kapittha, kaṭakāmukha, catura* and *hamsāsya*) to denote objects or characters, identical with those mentioned in the Sanskrit texts. However, as she argued, dancers use them rather instinctively, in various combinations, creating visual associations. Rao identified many of the *hasta*s that constitute typical Kathak movements as one element of a larger sign.[15] The meaning of a hand gesture is usually completed or

13 Interviews with teachers and students of the Natya Institute of Kathak and Choreography and Abhinava Dance Studio were conducted in Bangalore, January to March 2014; fieldwork notes were taken from personal observation of workshops on *karaṇa*s and *aṅgahāra*s in Kathak given by Roshan Date to BHU students (Varanasi, April 2015).

14 Following the shastric format, she classifies all the *asamyukta* (single hand gestures), *samyukta* (combined hand gestures, and *nṛtta hasta*s used in Kathak and mentioned in the *Nāṭyaśāstra*, *Abhinayadarpaṇa* and *Bharatarnava*.

15 For example, *ardhapatākā* and *kaṭakāmukha* in *ghūṅghat kī gat* (the stylized gait with a veil); *mṛgaśīrṣa* and *kaṭakāmukha* in the image of Radha embracing Krishna; *kapittha* and *śikhara* in the figure of Rama; *sandamśa* in the act of plucking flowers.

modified by the configuration of the whole body. For instance, based on the flow, broadness or speed of the movement, hands in *patāka* can signify different things, especially various natural phenomena, like strong or delicate winds or waves. To depict a *chakora* bird as a metaphor for a *nāyikā* in separation, the hands in the *kartarīmukha* are manipulated, supplemented by the movements of the eyebrows, each imitating the flapping of wings. The meaning of gestures in Kathak sometimes correspond to those described in *Abhinayadarpaṇa*, but the treatise neglects to describe these meaningful modulations.

Books, dancers and critics sometimes recall the qualities and defects (*guṇas* and *doṣas*) of a female dancer, described in *Abhinayadarpaṇa*, and a male dancer according to *Saṅgītaratnākara*.

> Characteristics of a dancing girl (*pātra*). She should be slender-bodied, beautiful, young, with full round breasts, self-confident, witty, pleasing, knowing well when to begin [a dance] and when to stop, having large eyes, able to perform in accompaniment of vocal and instrumental music, and to observe the proper time-beats (*tala*), having splendid dresses and possessing a happy countenance. A girl having all these qualifications is called a dancer.
>
> Her disqualifications: The ten kinds of women that should be avoided in the *natya* are: women with white specks in their eyeballs, or women who have scanty hair, or have thick lips or pendant breasts, or who are either very fat or very thin, or are either very tall or very short, or hunch-backed, or have no voice (AD 23–27, trans. Ghosh 1957).

These prescriptions seem to be ignored by today's Kathak exponents, who do not pay so much attention to their own physical appearance or bodily condition. This negligence was pointed out by dance critic Leela Venkataraman:

> We quote verses from the *Nāṭyaśāstra* or *Abhinayadarpaṇa* upholding comments made on the dance, but keep silent when it comes to a dancer whose girth negates the physical attributes prescribed for a dancer in the *śāstras*. In fact, some performers would seem to sport those very qualities mentioned as disqualifications. (Venkataraman 2005)

Many gurus perform until old age, at which time it is actually difficult to meet the *Abhinayadarpaṇa* criteria. Such dancers are usually considered the best masters, due to their life experience and better *abhinaya* skills. Excellence in Kathak is defined as the ability to transcend one's own gender and corporeality, and enter the character more on the psychological level. Hereditary Kathak gurus have been admired for the fact that they could perfectly create the illusion of being a young maiden, despite their male attire, wrinkled skin, big belly or dense moustache (Jagdish Gangani, personal communication, February 12, 2014; Jaikishan Maharaj, personal communication, April 18, 2015). They are also more admired for their *abhinaya* skills. Thus, in this case the shastric theory fails to determine perceptions of the mastery of Kathak dancers.

Senior dancers often complain that the art of *abhinaya* is totally neglected by the new generation of dancers, who focus on the high speed of *tatkār*, multiple *cakkar*s, and group choreographies in which geometrical patterns and coordination play a crucial role. This is also a consequence of the transfer of dance from private gatherings to big concert halls. In auditoriums, it is difficult to admire the details of an individual dancer's acting and technique, therefore solo dance is sometimes judged as monotonous and boring. Limited in *bhāva*, the dance fails to evoke *rasa* within the viewer. Besides, the members of the audience are mostly far from the Sanskrit ideal of *rasika*, so the *rasa* aesthetics rather remain solely a matter of theory in the context of contemporary popular Kathak performance.

In search for fundamentals and continuity in classical Indian dance

Despite the numerous incongruities between shastric theory and Kathak praxis, dance historians emphasize the prevalence of this general structure of dance movements in all the classical dance forms of India. VATSYAYAN claims that the division of movement into *tāṇḍava* and *lāsya*, and into units such as *karaṇa*s, *maṇḍala*s, *cari*s, *khaṇḍa*s and *aṅgahāra*s, are common principles in all classical dance styles (1974: 15–16). Describing the technique of Kathak, she recalls various names of *hasta*s (*hamsāsya, muṣṭi, śikhara, candrakalā, alapadma*). She indicates *samapada*[16] as a basic position in Kathak (drawing analogies to positions in Western ballet), and uses terminology from the *Nāṭyaśāstra* and *Abhinayadarpaṇa* to name jumps (*utplavana*), pirouttes (*bhramarī*) or side-to-side movements of the neck (*sundarī*) in Kathak (ibid. 89–90).

Shovana Narayan also argues that the conventions of *Nāṭyaśāstra* are commonly used in Indian dance forms (not only classical):

> In Kathak most of the 60–70% of the *karana*s are utilized, all the *hasta mudra*s are utilized, single and double, and at least four or five of seven *bhramari*s. We don't utilize *akash bhramari*; that is done by Manipuri dancers. Only

16 Standing on straight legs, flat feet, and with the knees not flexed.

> Kathak uses *chakra bhramari* described in *Nāṭyaśāstra*. You cannot tell the whole story (in *gatbhav*) if you do not utilize the complete *Nāṭyaśāstra*. *Nāṭyaśāstra* is like a biology lesson; it applies to all: both the folk and classical forms. The terminology may be different, but even Wajid Ali Shah's treatises follow *Nāṭyaśāstra*. For example, they mention *talwar gat*, while *Nāṭyaśāstra* talks about *mushti*; the gesture is similar, only the name is different. (Personal communication, February 1, 2014.)

The insistence on the transmission of the shastric tradition through various historical periods and cultural contexts has been also articulated by Maya Rao. As the first student of Kathak in Bharatiya Kala Kendra, Rao conducted research on the Kathak past with reference to both Sanskrit and Urdu textual sources. She analyzed the similarity between the *gat*s described in nineteenth-century Urdu texts (*Ghuncha-e-raag*, *Saut-ul-Mubarak*, *Naghmat-ul-Hind*, *Madan-ul-Musiqi*) and the *aṅgahāra*s mentioned in *Nāṭyaśāstra*, suggesting that there is a continuity between these traditions (RAO 1959). She focused on hand gestures (*hasta*s), noting:

> ... there is a definite system of representing objects and ideas through the *hasta*s, which conforms to the rules laid down in the ancient texts on dance and dramaturgy. Unfortunately these *hasta*s are not known to the Kathak dancers by their textual names. However we can infer that in the history of Kathak, there must have been a stage when the gestures were studied in accordance with the shastras. But later on, the teachers must have drifted away from the texts retaining only the usages of the gestures which they handed down to their disciples. (RAO 1959: 45)

In the opinion of Shovana Narayan, 'traditional gurus [of Kathak] were not well educated, but they knew *Nāṭyaśāstra*, as the tradition was transmitted orally. They used movements from *Nāṭyaśāstra*, performing to both Sanskrit and local languages' (personal communication, Feb 1, 2014). Numerous dancers confirm that older gurus did not rely on any text in practice, but they simultaneously claim that Kathak is rooted in the *Nāṭyaśāstra*. Apart from theoretical arguments, there are various initiatives to 'discover' the continuity of shastric concepts in Kathak, like special workshops during which students try to recreate or reinterpret them. These kinds of discourses and initiatives reveal that there is a constant need to legitimize the presumptuous interconnection and explain the numerous inconsistencies between Sanskrit theory and contemporary dance practice. As is evident from the analysis of the artists' interpretations of Sanskrit aesthetics, these conventions are still not relevant to Kathak praxis and need more systematic and cohesive explanation.

The significance of Sanskrit texts in Kathak classicization and standardization

The dissimilarities between the technique of Kathak, as it is used in praxis, and the dance forms described in the Sanskrit treatises calls into question the legitimacy of tracing Kathak's past through these texts. There is no firm evidence to justify the assumption that hereditary Kathak dancers were familiar with the Sanskrit treatises or the rules described in them in the past. Most of the hereditary gurus whom I have interviewed confessed that they did not refer to any texts in training since their ancestors were illiterate.[17]

The *Nāṭyaśāstra* was rediscovered by British Orientalists in the nineteenth century, and the manuscript published and translated in 1890. The *Abhinayadarpaṇa* became popular thanks to the English translation of Coomaraswamy in 1917. Not many other treatises were available in print or in translation when the Indian dance revival started, generating a need for such texts. The aforementioned Urdu treatises were translated into Hindi only in the 1980s. The approach of Western scholars toward Sanskrit works probably contributed much to upgrading their status in the hierarchy of cultural heritage representative of the Indian nation. It was strategic to select these texts as the basis for the dance forms restituted as classical. Since Sanskrit is not commonly understood by Kathak performers, this subsequently creates the possibility of manipulating the translations. Books and manuals on classical dance theory were produced to reaffirm the legacy of Sanskrit aesthetics in modern classical dance praxis.

What is more, there is no clear evidence that the Sanskrit manuals actually mirrored the living traditions. They might well have had a normative or ideological character (Ganser 2011: 159). Their description of the technique is not precise enough to provide complete instruction for a dance practitioner, and they did not necessarily function as pedagogical tools compatible with praxis. Regardless of this fact, the *Nāṭyaśāstra* has played an important role, providing 'a frame of discourse within which various authorities, textual as well as practical, were made to interact' (ibid. 160). This significance still seems to be relevant in contemporary attempts to systematize the classical canon of dance.

According to the Director of Kathak Kendra, Sushmita Ghosh, the standardization of Kathak is still a work in progress. The attempts to establish a common nomenclature and syllabus for training in Kathak[18] have triggered many controversies and have not brought satisfying results (Sushmita Ghosh, personal

17 Exceptionally, Birju Maharaj maintains that his clan keeps and follows the Kathak scripture, written in Sanskrit, but restricted only to family members (personal communication, February 18, 2015).

18 For example, at Kathak Kendra in 2002 there was a seminar devoted to renaming the movements of Kathak.

communication, April 17, 2015). Birju Maharaj has proposed an alternative classification of dance units and nomenclature in his *Aṅg Kāvya* (2002), an overview of the technique, distanced from the Sanskritized framework. He divides Kathak technique into hand movements (*nṛtta hastak*: basic ornamental, circular wrist emphases), foot positions (*pād bhangimā*), stances (*thāṭ*) and finishing positions (*sam*) using Hindi descriptive nomenclature, explanations and illustrations. This nomenclature partly reflects the terminology used in Kathak dance classes, underlining the figures of major importance in judging the art's virtuosity. The author is considered the unquestionable authority in defining the criteria of authenticity, yet his proposal has not been commonly accepted.

The advisory committee of Kathak Kendra, which endeavors to standardize Kathak, seems to favor Sanskritic nomenclature and concepts. 'Birju Maharaj gave to Kathak movements beautiful, poetic names ... But the question was raised, that [if] many of these movements had already names from *Nāṭyaśāstra*—all the glances, neck movements or standing positions ... What is the need to create the names again?' (Sushmita Ghosh, personal communication, April 17, 2015). On the other hand, there are many Kathak dancers who have studied under Birju Maharaj and inherited his terminology and understanding of Kathak aesthetics, which often contradicts the shastric explanation. The opinions of hereditary masters provide a counter-discourse that weakens the popularity of Sanskritized aesthetics and nomenclature in Kathak praxis. In the context of Bharatanatyam, the voices of hereditary performers (*devadasi*s) and teachers (*nattuvanar*s) were silenced and dominated by middle-class women promoting the dance's Sanskritization. In the field of modern Kathak, an analogous process seems to be occurring.

As I mentioned at the beginning, linking the various classical dance 'styles' to Sanskrit treatises was a strategy to legitimize their 'common source' and reify the concept of 'unity in diversity' supposedly permeating Indian culture. This is still articulated by Kathak artists. For example, the renowned Kathak choreographer Rani Karna emphasizes the importance of the strict codification (primarily of *mudra*s) as a key feature of classical Indian dance. In her opinion, classical Indian dance is a language within which we can distinguish various dialects: Bharatanatyam, Kathak, Odissi etc. (personal communication, March 13, 2015). A similar belief is shared by dancers Nirupama and Rajendra: 'Kathak, Bharatanatyam, and other classical forms became regionalized and acquired different identities. But the mother of all these regional styles is the *margi*—the 'shastric dance', based on universal fundamentals from *śāstra*' (personal communication, March 14, 2014).

Though the modern dance forms were patterned on Western ballet, they were designed to be significantly distinct from it. The *Nāṭyaśāstra* was instrumental in articulating the difference from the West, and simultaneously in demonstrating the similarity between the varied regional traditions of India. Because the correspondence was not so clear, dance theorists 'clarified' it in their publications:

'The preservation of the continuity of the basic principle of the *Nāṭyaśāstra* in these [classical] dance styles is impressive. Its continual change and modification is also significant,' contends Kapila VATSYAYAN (1974:13). Some scholars, like Mandrakanta Bose, who underlines the importance of later Sanskrit works in investigating Kathak past,[19] even maintain that all the classical Indian dances are rooted in the *Nāṭyaśāstra*:

> Our only way to trace the evolution of dancing lies through the rich corpus of Sanskrit manuals on dancing and discussions in musicological literature in general [...] *Nāṭyaśāstra* is unquestionably the ultimate source of all classical styles; but to find their immediate sources we must turn to some other works which followed the *Nāṭyaśāstra* and which presented modifications and additions to the style that was described by Bharata and was subsequently known as *mārga*. Essentially, all the texts follow the *Nāṭyaśāstra* in describing the movements of the different parts of the body, with minor variations and additions. However, in describing the dance-sequences these texts draw upon the *deśī* and the regional traditions. (BOSE 2001: 51–54)

Conclusions

Linking Kathak to Sanskrit literature and aesthetics in the course of the dance revival served the purpose of legitimizing the supposed features of Indian classical dance: antiquity, sophistication, religious roots, spiritual importance and a systematized technique, subject to the precise rules codified in the *śāstras*. Since then, the *Nāṭyaśāstra* has been perceived as a common source of the aesthetics of different regional dance forms, integrating them as varieties of one pan-Indian tradition of classical dance. The constant reproduction of these discourses in recent books and manuals of Kathak betrays the continuing importance of Sanskrit treatises in classical dance theory. Without a doubt, Sanskritization also involves the creation of a common vocabulary and the homogenization of its use. The choice of Sanskrit texts and the set of shastric rules and nomenclature used by Kathak theorists and

19 Bose examines the correspondence between Kathak and some dance forms described in the *Nartananirṇaya* (NN) that are probably proto-Kathak. In her opinion, the historical context of this work (written in the seventeenth century by Pundarika Vitthala for the pleasure of Akbar) is a persuasive argument. Bose compares characteristic elements of Kathak technique—pirouettes (*cakkar*) and steps (*tatkār*)—with the revolving movements *cakrabhramarī* (NN 4.789) and *tirapabhramarī* (NN 4.796) and stamping (*gharghara*, NN 4.841–9), described in NN respectively. In my view, the description of these dance units in NN lacks details that could justify their identification as Kathak. A noteworthy analogy is however drawn between Kathak's *ghūṅghaṭ* and *jakkaḍī* (dances with veils), performed to 'yavana' (Persian) song (NN 4.899–902).

dancers is similar to the Sanskrit conventions and terminology used in the field Bharatanatyam. We may suspect that this is a continuing attempt to emphasize the supposed correspondence between the different regional forms of classical dance as a symbol of India's 'unity in diversity'.

Moreover, Kathak dance technique and nomenclature is still not standardized in practice, partly because of the strong authority of hereditary gurus who promote their own divergent terminology and aesthetics, influencing younger generations of practitioners. Sanskrit conventions are promoted by modernists from the middle-class elite as a kind of homogenizing ground and textual authority that can balance the impact of hereditary gurus. However, in practice, the study of the original texts is often neglected, and the Sanskrit concepts are frequently ignored or not properly understood. Thus, Sanskrit treatises on dance seem to play a more symbolic role in Kathak tradition, 'veiling' its Muslim legacy, relating Kathak to other classical Indian dance forms and equating its status with the 'high' level of Bharatanatyam, as well as providing a testimony for its long history, systematic rules and sophistication, equivalent to that of Western ballet.

References

Allen, M. H. (1997). Rewriting the script for South Indian dance. *The Drama Review, 41*(3): 63–100.

Azad, T. R. (2008). *Kathak Gyaneshwari: A critical study on Indian classical dance.* Delhi: Nateshwar Kala Mandir.

Bakhle, J. (2005). *Two men and music. Nationalism in the making of an Indian classical tradition.* New York: Oxford University Press.

Bharatamuni. (1894). *Nāṭyaśāstra* (Sivadatta & K. B. Parab, Trans.). Mumbai: Nirnaya Sagara Press.

—. (1950). *Nāṭyaśāstra* (vol. 1) (M. Ghosh, trans.). Calcutta: Royal Asiatic Society of Bengal.

Bhate, R. (2004). *Kathakdarpandeepika.* Pune: Akhil Bharatiya Gandharva Mahavidyalaya.

Bose, M. (2001). *Speaking of dance.* New Delhi: D.K. Printworld.

—. (2007). *Movement and mimesis: The idea of dance in the Sanskritic tradition.* New Delhi: D. K. Printworld.

Chakravorty, P. (2008). *Bells of change.* Calcutta: Seagulls Books.

Chatterjee, P. (1999). *The nation and its fragments.* In Chatterjee, P. (Ed.), *The Partha Chatterjee omnibus.* New Delhi: Oxford University Press. (Reprinted from *The nation and its fragments*, 1993, Princeton: Princeton University Press.)

Coorlawala, U. A. (2004). The Sanskritized body. *Dance Research Journal, 36*(2), 50–63.

—. (1992). Ruth St. Denis and India's dance renaissance. *Dance Chronicle, 15*, 123–48.

Dādhīc, P. (2012). *Kathak nṛtya śikṣā* (2 vols.). Indore: Bindu Prakashan.

Datye, R. (2010). *Kathak-Ādikathak.* Mumbai: Indian Education Society.

Dodson, M. S. (2010). *Orientalism, empire, and national culture: India, 1770–1880.* New Delhi: Cambridge University Press.

Khare, S. (2005). *Kathak. Saundaryātmak Śāstrīya Nṛtya.* New Delhi: Kanishka Publishers.

Ganser, E. (2011). Thinking dance literature from Bharata to Bharatanatyam. *Rivista degli Studi Orientali, 84,* 145–161.

Gupta, B. (2004). *Kathak Sagar.* New Delhi: Radha Publication.

Jyotishi-Beohar, C. (2009). *Nāyikā Bheda in Kathak.* Delhi: Agam Kala Prakashan.

Khokar, M. (1979). *Tradition of Indian classical dance.* New Delhi: Clarion Books.

Kothari, S. (1989). *Kathak: Indian classical dance art.* New Delhi: Abhinav Publications.

Lopez y Royo, A. (2003). Classicism, post-classicism and Ranjabati Sircar's work: Re-defining the terms of Indian contemporary dance discourses. *South Asia Research, 23*(2), 153–169.

Maharaj, B. (2002). *Aṅg Kāvya.* New Delhi: Har-Anand.

Meduri, A. (Ed.). (2005). *Rukmini Devi Arundale (1904–1986): A visionary architect of Indian culture and the performing arts.* Delhi: Motilal Banarsidass.

Menaka. (1989). Dance in India. In Joshi, D., *Madame Menaka (53–59).* New Delhi: Sangeet Natak Akademi. (Reprinted from 'Dance in India', September 1933, *Sound and Shadow,* 43–46.)

Nagar, V. (2011). *Kathak nartan* (2 vols.). Delhi: B. R. Rhythms.

Nandikeśvara. (1917). *The mirror of gesture: Being the Abhinaya Darpana of Nandikeśvara* (A. K. Coomaraswamy & G. K. Duggirala, Trans.). London: Harvard University Press.

—. (1957). *Abhinayadarpaṇam* (M. Ghosh, Trans.) Calcutta: Firma K. L. Mukhopadhyay.

—. (2007). *Abhinayadarpaṇa: Text with English translation and notes* (C. Rajendran, Trans.). Delhi: New Bharatiya Book Corporation.

Narayan, S. (1998). *Kathak: Rhythmic echoes and reflections.* New Delhi: Roli Books.

Paṇḍarīkaviṭṭhala. (1998). *Nartananirṇayaḥ* (3 vols.) (R. Sathyanarayana, Trans.). Delhi: IGNCA, Motilal Banarsidass.

Peterson, I. V. & Soneji (Eds.). (2008). *Performing pasts: Reinventing the arts in modern South India.* New Delhi: Oxford University Press.

Rao, M. (1959). Hastas in Kathak. *Marg, 12,* 45–47.

Saxena, S. K. (1982). Representation in Kathak dance. *Journal of the Indian Musicological Society, 3*(2), 37–51.

—. (1991). *Swinging syllables: Aesthetics of Kathak dance.* New Delhi: Sangeet Natak Akademi.

Srinivas, M. N. (1966). *Social change in modern India.* Berkley: University of California Press.

Wajid Ali Shah. (1987). *Banī* (R. Taqi & K. M. Saxena, Trans.). Lucknow: Uttar Pradesh Sangeet Natak Akademi.

Wajid Ali Shah (1989). *Nājo* (Y. Praveen, Trans.). Lucknow: Uttar Pradesh Sangeet Natak Akademi.

Vajpeyi, R. (1992). *Kathak Prasang.* Delhi: Vani Prakashan.

Vatsyayan, K. (1956). Kathak. *Journal of the Music Academy, 27,* 74–88.

—. (1968). *Classical Indian dance in literature and the arts.* New Delhi: Sangeet Natak Akademi.

—. (1974). *Indian classical dance.* New Delhi: Ministry of Information and Broadcasting, Govt. of India.

—. (1997). *The square and the circle of the Indian arts.* New Delhi: Abhinav Publications.

VENKATARAMAN, L. (2005, June 10). A question of weight. *The Hindu.* Retrieved from http://www.thehindu.com/thehindu/fr/2005/06/10/stories/2005061001680200.htm.

WALKER, M. (2004). *Kathak dance: A critical history* (Unpublished doctoral dissertation). Toronto: University of Toronto.

—. (2013). Wounded with the arrow of her eyelashes: Seduction and sensuality in North Indian dance. In Kouwenhoven, F. & Kippen, J. (Eds.), *Music, dance and the art of seduction.* Delft: Eburon Academic Press.

Charting the Sāṃkhya Commentarial Literature

A Study of the Lists of Types of Supernatural Power (*aiśvarya*)

Jooyoung Lim

1 Introduction*

The majority of the commentaries on verse 23 of the *Sāṃkhyakārikā* (hereafter 'SK'; fourth or fifth century) provides and comments upon a list of different types of *aiśvarya* ('supernatural power'). In this study I limit the range of commentaries that I take into consideration to those composed between the fifth and tenth centuries. These are the first eight extant commentaries of the SK, composed in the so-called classical period of Sāṃkhya (see, for instance, Hulin 1978). They are: the *Suvarṇasaptati* ('SS', 金七十論);[1] the *Sāṃkhyasaptativṛtti* ('V1'); the *Sāṃkhyavṛtti* ('V2'); the *Gauḍapādabhāṣya* ('GB'); the *Māṭharavṛtti* ('MV'); the *Yuktidīpikā* ('YD'); the *Jayamaṅgalā* ('JM'); and the *Tattvakaumudī* ('TK').

Studying how these commentaries deal with the varieties of *aiśvarya* offers us a better understanding of the relationship among the commentaries themselves, both in terms of the different ways in which they interpret the contents of SK and, possibly, in terms of their relative chronology, which is still partly unclear.

2 The function of *aiśvarya* in Sāṃkhya

Before moving further into the varieties of *aiśvarya*, we need to contextualise *aiśvarya* within the Sāṃkhya metaphysical system. First of all, we should be familiar with the concept of *buddhi* ('the Intellect'), here a synonym of the term

* I would like to thank an anonymous reviewer for providing me with insightful remarks on an early version of this paper. All mistakes are of course mine.

1 This text is currently available only in its Chinese translation.

mahat ('the Great').[2] *Buddhi* is the first among the 23 *tattvas* ('principles') that manifest from (*mūla-*)*prakṛti* ('the original matter') and which then evolves into *ahaṃkāra* ('the conceptualisation of I'). Verse 23 of the SK introduces the eight functions of *buddhi*, which emerge variously according to the ratio of its *guṇas* ('qualities'):

> *adhyavasāyo buddhir dharmo jñānaṃ virāga aiśvaryam /*
> *sāttvikam etadrūpaṃ tāmasam asmād viparyastam //* SK 23 //
>
> The Intellect is determination. Virtue, knowledge, dispassion, and supernatural power are its forms when *sattva* abounds; the opposite of these, when *tamas* abounds.

Buddhi is characterized by determination and has four functions, namely *dharma* ('virtue'), *jñāna* ('knowledge'), *virāga* ('dispassion') and *aiśvarya* ('supernatural power') when *sattva* abounds—i.e. when it predominates over the other two qualities, namely *rajas* and *tamas*. *Aiśvarya*, which is at the centre of this paper, is thus one of the functions of *buddhi*.

3 The qualities or constituents of *aiśvarya* in the commentaries of SK

While commenting upon verse 23, the commentaries of SK list several varieties of supernatural power, adding some explanatory remarks on the nature of these abilities. The only exceptions in this respect are YD and MV, which just provide lists of these varieties without offering any explanations.

First in the list is *aṇimā*,[3] which is the ability to become very small (*aṇu*). Some commentaries explain that he who possesses such a power can wander (in the sky or world) after becoming small.

Second, *laghimā*[4] is the ability to become light and move like the wind. GB mentions that one who has such a supernatural power is so light as to be able to

2 The term *buddhi* is usually used in epistemological contexts, whereas the term *mahat* is used in ontological ones.

3 V1: *aṇimeti sūkṣmo bhūtvā ākāśaṃ vicarati bhavaty adṛśyaḥ* / V2: *tatrāṇimā aṇūḥ bhūtvā sūkṣmāṇi śarīrāṇi kṛtvā vicarati* / SS: 一者微細極隣虚 GB: *aṇor bhāvo'ṇimā, sūkṣmo bhūtvā jagat vicaratīti* / JM: *tatrāṇimāṇutvaṃ yena guṇena sūkṣmo bhūtvā vicarati* / TK: *aṇimā bhavaty aṇuḥ* /.

4 V1: *laghimeti laghur bhūtvā vāyuvadākāśe vicarati* / V2: *laghimā nāma laghuḥ bhūtvā vāyuvad vicarati* / SS: 二者輕妙極心神 GB: *laghimā mṛṇālītūlāvayavād api laghutayā puṣpakesarāgreṣv api tiṣṭhati* / JM: *laghimā laghutvaṃ yena vāyuval laghutaro bhavati* / TK: *laghimā lagur bhāvati yataḥ sūryamarīcīn ālambya sūryalokaṃ yāti* /.

stand even on the tip of the filament of a flower. TK states that he who is endowed with this ability can reach the sun with a ray of sun as his support. Interestingly, the explanation of SS is that one who has such a supernatural power can reach the mind and spirit of people.

Third, *mahimā*[5] is the ability to become infinitely large. According to SS, one who has such a supernatural power can reach the sky. However, V1 and V2 explain that one possessing this power is honoured and respected by everyone in the three worlds. In this case, we could say that *mahimā* has a mental or spiritual connotation rather than a physical one, as is instead pointed out by the other commentaries.

Fourth, *prāpti*[6] is the power of obtaining whatever one thinks. GB, however, describes it as the ability by which one can obtain any object he thinks about, wherever that object is located. TK explains *prāpti* as the ability of to touch faraway items with great ease, as for instance the moon with the tip of a finger. The same definition is also found in the *Amarakośabhāṣya* of Maheśvara (seventeenth century).[7]

Fifth, *prākāmya*[8] is the ability to create whatever one wishes or wants. Interestingly, SS explains it as the ability to use objects at will simultaneously. TK describes *prākāmya* with examples that entail extraordinary actions: emerging from the earth or sinking into it as if into water.

Sixth, *īśitiva*[9] is the ability to be lord of the three worlds. According to SS, the holder of such a power can in fact obtain victories everywhere. TK explains that one can control the production, arrangement and loss of anything material.

Seventh, *vaśitva*[10] is the ability to subdue other beings. Furthermore, one who has this power does not belong to anything and is totally independent. SS adds that one who has this power can let beings transmigrate to any of the three worlds.

---

5 V1: *mahimeti triṣu lokeṣv arcitaḥ sarvair mānito bhavati* / V2: *mahimā nāma triṣu lokeṣu arcitaḥ pūjito bhavati* / SS: 三者遍滿極虛空 GB: *mahimā mahān bhūtvā vicaratīti* / JM: *mahimā mahattvaṃ yena bhuvaneṣu* / TK: *mahimā mahān bhavati* /.

6 V1: *prāptiriti yaṃ yaṃ manasi cintayati taṃ taṃ prāpnoti* / V2: *prāptir nāma yaṃ yaṃ manasā prārthayati taṃ taṃ prāpnoti* / SS: 四者至得如所意得 GB: *prāptiḥ abhimataṃ vastuyatratatrāvasthitaṃ prāpnoti* / JM: *dharmādi prāptir yena guṇeneṣitasya prāpaṇam* / TK: *prāptir aṅgulyagreṇa spṛśati candramasam* /.

7 *prāptir aṅgulyagreṇa candrādeḥ* / 1.38.

8 V1: *prākāmyam iti kāma icchāyāṃ yāvanti rūpāṇīcchati tāvanti nirmiṇoti* / V2: *prākāmyaṃ nāma pracurakāmo bhavati viṣayān upabhoktuṃ prakāmaṃ samarthaḥ* / SS: 六者隨欲塵一時能用 GB: *prākāmyaṃ prakāmato yadevecchati tadeva vidadhāti* / JM: *prākāmyaṃ pracurakāmitā yenaikamanekaṃ prākāmyate'nekaṃ caikam* / TK: *prākāmyam icchānabhighāto yato bhūmāv unmajjati nimajjati ca yatho 'dake* /.

9 V1: *īśitvam iti sarvajanato'syā jagadiśā gaṇā prabhur bhavati svavargadhiyā vimalacinte ramo bhavati* (?) / V2: *īśitvaṃ nāma trailokyasya prabhur bhūtvā vicarati* / SS: 五者三世間之本主 一切處勝他故 GB: *īśitvaṃ prabhutayā trailokyam apīṣṭe* / JM: *īśitvaṃ prabhutā yena sthāvarādīni bhūtāni sandeśakārīṇi bhavanti* / TK: *īśitvaṃ bhūtabhautikānāṃ prabhavavyūhavyayānām īṣṭe* /.

10 V2: *vaśitvaṃ nāma anyāni vaśamānayati bhūtāni* / SS: 七者不繫屬他 能令三世間衆生隨我運役 GB: *vaśitvaṃ sarvaṃ vaśī bhavati* / JM: *vaśitvaṃ vaśitā yena svatantraś carati* / TK: *vaśitvaṃ bhūtabhautikaṃ vaśī bhavaty avaśyam* /.

Lastly, *yatrakāmāvasāyitva*[11] is the ability to exist in any of the three worlds at will, according to whether one wants to be a god, a human being or an animal. According to verses 53 and 54[12] of SK, the creation of beings (*bhautikaḥ sargaḥ*) caused by transmigration is characterised by three levels: the level of gods, which is of eight kinds; the level of human beings, which is of one kind; and the level of all other beings (animals etc.), which is fivefold.

In all the commentaries of SK, supernatural power is said to have eight qualities (*aṣṭaguṇam aiśvaryam*) or to be of eight kinds (*aṣṭavidham aiśvaryam*). Surprisingly, a ninth type of supernatural power is mentioned in MV, GB and YD, namely *garimā*, despite the fact that all three of them still describe the list as eightfold. None of these commentaries explains what *garimā* is, but we can intuitively understand it to be the ability to become infinitely heavy by contrasting it with the explanation for *laghimā*. Why the term is not explicitly commented upon remains unclear.

4 Four classes of commentaries

It is important to note that the various kinds of supernatural powers are presented in different ways throughout the commentaries. Some texts only give a list without commenting on its members (YD and MV); others offer a list followed by an explanation section in which every member (or almost every member) is described individually (V1, V2, GB and JM). Finally, some commentaries do not give mere lists, but proceed directly to the explanation of the various kinds of supernatural power (SS and TK).

Furthermore—and this is the main focus here—the commentaries vary among themselves in terms of the order in which the kinds of supernatural powers are presented and, as mentioned before, their total number. Remarkably, the actual list and the explanation section differ from one another in both V1 and GB.[13] Such

11 V1: *yatra kāmāvasāyitvam iti brahmādisthāne yatra yathā vastum icchati tatra tathā vasati* / V2: *yatrakāmāvasāyitvaṃ nāma brahmādiṣu sthāvarānteṣu yatrayatrecchati tatratatrāpratihato bhavati* / SS: 八者隨意住 謂隨時隨處隨心得住 GB: *yatrakāmāvasāyitvaṃ brahmādistambaparyantaṃ yatra kāmas tatraivāsya svecchayā sthānāsanavihārānācaratīti* / JM: *yatrakāmāvaśāyitvaṃ kāmenecchayāvaśetuṃ śīlaṃ yasya sa yatrakāmāvaśāyī* / *tasya bhāvaḥ yatrakāmāvaśāyitvam* / *anekārthatvāddhātūnāṃ śī tiṣṭhatau vartate* / *yena guṇena divyantarikṣe bhūmau vāvasthāyitvam ity arthaḥ* / TK: *yatrakāmāvasāyitvaṃ satyasaṅkalpatā yathāsya saṅkalpo bhavati bhūteṣu tathāiva bhūtāni bhavanti* /.

12 *aṣṭavikalpo daivastairyagyonyaś ca pañcadhā bhavati* /
mānuṣyaścaikavidhaḥ, samāsato bhautikaḥ sargaḥ // SK 53 //
ūrdhvaṃ sattvaviśālastamoviśālaś ca mūlataḥ sargaḥ /
madhye rajoviśālo, brahmādistambaparyantaḥ // SK 54 //.

13 V1 mentions *vaśitva* in the list, but skips it in the explanation section, and GB does the same with garimā. For more on the latter, see below.

variations are not justified by the texts themselves, and one has to assume that they are the result of the idiosyncratic activity of each commentator.

However, I argue that some of the variation in the order of the list members and in the explanation sections can actually be explained. These latter cases concern the order in which *aṇimā*, *laghimā* and *mahimā* are presented, also including *garimā* where it appears.[14] In fact, it is the inclusion or exclusion of *garimā* which, in my view, triggers the modification of the order of the list members.

The eight commentaries of SK can be divided into four classes according to the differences they exhibit in listing the supernatural abilities.

Class 1

A first list is found in the oldest commentary, namely the *Suvarṇasaptati* (SS, 金七十論),[15] the *Sāṃkhyasaptativṛtti* (V1)[16], the *Sāṃkhyavṛtti* (V2)[17] and the latest commentary, namely the *Tattvakaumudī* (TK)[18, 19]:

(1) *aṇimā*	(3) *mahimā*	(5) *prākāmya*	(7) *vaśitva*
(2) *laghimā*	(4) *prāpti*	(6) *īśitva*	(8) *yatrakāmāvasāyitva*

It is important to remember that SS and TK do not give separate lists of the abilities, but only contain the sections with their explanations. It is thus possible

14 The following table summarises the variants that occur in the order of the members of the mere lists and of the explanation sections but that I do not take into consideration in this article. The data are from V1, V2, SS and TK.

Commentary	*V1*	*V2*	*SS*	*TK*
Variant	No explanation of *vaśitva*	*īśitva* ↕ *prākāmya*	三世間之本主(*īśitva*) ↕ 隨欲塵一時能用 (*prākāmya*)	*vaśitva* ↕ *īśitva*

15 自在有八種。一者微細極隣虛。二者輕妙極心神。三者遍滿極虛空。四者至得如所意得。五者三世間之本主。一切處勝他故。六者隨欲塵一時能用。七者不繫屬他。能令三世間衆生隨我運役。八者隨意住。謂隨時隨處隨心得住。

16 *aiśvaryam īśvarasya bhāvaḥ / tat punar aṣṭavidhaṃ vākye varṇayanti śiṣṭās tad yathāṇimā laghimā mahimā prāptiḥ prākāmyaṃ īśitvaṃ vaśitvam yatrakāmāvasāyitvam iti /.*

17 *tac ca aiśvaryam aṣṭaguṇaṃ varṇayanti / aṇimā laghimā mahimā prāptiḥ prākāmyam īśitvaṃ vaśitvam atha yatrakāmāvasāyitvam iti /.*

18 *aiśvaryam api buddher dharmo yato'ṇimādiprādur bhāvaḥ / aṇimā bhavaty aṇuḥ / laghimā laghur bhavaty yataḥ sūryamarīcīn ālambya sūryalokaṃ yāti / mahimā mahān bhavati / prāptir aṅgulyagreṇa spṛśati candramasam / prākāmyam icchānabhighāto yato bhūmāv unmajjati nimajjati ca yatho'dake / vaśitvaṃ bhūtabhautikaṃ vaśī bhavaty avaśyam / īśitvaṃ bhūtabhautikānāṃ prabhavavyūhavyayānām īṣṭe / yatrakāmāvasāyitvaṃ satyasaṅkalpatā yathāsya saṅkalpo bhavati bhūteṣu tathāiva bhūtāni bhavanti /.*

19 As for the dates of composition of SS and TK, see §5 of this article.

to follow the order of these explanations in order to understand in which position the abilities are listed.[20]

Class 2

A second list is only found in the *Māṭharavṛtti* (MV)[21]:

(1) *aṇimā*	(4) *mahimā*	(7) *īśitva*
(2) *laghimā*	(5) *prāpti*	(8) *vaśitva*
(3) *garimā*	(6) *prākāmya*	(9) *yatrakāmāvasāyitva*

The list contains nine elements instead of eight since *garimā* is also included. This latter feature of the list stands in stark opposition to the description of the list found in all the commentaries, i.e. that it has eight qualities (*aṣṭaguṇam aiśvaryam*) or that it is of eight kinds (*aṣṭavidham aiśvaryam*).

Class 3

A third list is found in the *Gauḍapādabhāṣya* (GB)[22] and the *Yuktidīpikā* (YD)[23]:

(1) *aṇimā*	(4) *garimā*	(7) *īśitva*
(2) *mahimā*	(5) *prāpti*	(8) *vaśitva*
(3) *laghimā*	(6) *prākāmya*	(9) *yatrakāmāvasāyitva*

If we compare this list to that of classes 1 and 2, we can easily notice that the order of *laghimā* and *mahimā* is inverted. Furthermore, as in class 2, here too *garimā* is included, so that class 3 also lists nine powers. Nevertheless, both GB (list and explanation section) and YD (list only) explicitly refer to the number of supernatural powers as eight—*aṣṭaguṇam* and *aṣṭavidham*, respectively. Interestingly, however, GB does not include *garimā* in its explanation section: whether this was done intentionally in light of the discrepancy of the supposed number of list members and the actual number is hard to tell.

20 As for the order of *īśitva* and *prākāmya* in SS and the order of *vaśitva* and *īśitva* in TK, see fn. 15.

21 *aiśvaryam īśvarabhāvenety aṣṭavidham / aṇimā, mahimā, garimā, laghimā, prāptiḥ, prākāmyam, īśitvaṃ, vaśitvaṃ, yatrakāmāvasāyitvam iti /.*

22 *aiśvaryamīśvarabhāvaḥ / tac cāṣṭaguṇam aṇimā, mahimā, garimā, laghimā, prāptiḥ, prākāmyam, īśitvaṃ, vaśitvaṃ, yatrakāmāvasāyitvaṃ ceti /.*

23 *aiśvaryam apratīghātalakṣaṇam / tat punar aṣṭavidhaṃ aṇimā mahimā laghimā garimā prāptiḥ prākāmyam īśitvaṃ vaśitvaṃ yatrakāmavasāyitvam iti /.*

Class 4

Finally, a fourth list is taught by the *Jayamaṅgalā* (JM)[24]:

(1) *aṇimā*	(3) *laghimā*	(5) *prākāmya*	(7) *vaśitva*
(2) *mahimā*	(4) *prāpti*	(6) *īśitva*	(8) *yatrakāmāvasāyitva*

Here, the order of *laghimā* and *mahimā* corresponds to that found in class 3, but the powers listed are now again eight and there is no *garimā* in the list, just like in class 1. Note that JM has an explanation section in which the order of the powers is different from that of the mere list, which is here labelled as class 4. I will come back to this discrepancy below.

5 Questions about the four classes and clues from other texts

A few questions can be asked about the composition of the above-mentioned four classes:

1. Why is there a different order of *laghimā* and *mahimā* across the classes?
2. Why does *garimā* appear only in classes 2 and 3?
3. Why do classes 2 and 3 list nine elements even though their lists are explicitly said to be eightfold?

Clues to answering these questions can be found in several non-Sāṃkhya texts that also contain lists of the various types of supernatural power. These sources can be divided according to the kind of textual variation that they exhibit. To this end, two versions of the list are attested. Version 1, of which there are two sub-variants (here called 1a and 1b), includes *yatrakāmāvasāyitva* but excludes *garimā*, whereas version 2 includes *garimā* but excludes *yatrakāmāvasāyitva*.

Version 1a lists *laghimā* before *mahimā* and *yatrakāmāvasāyitva*. This version of the list is found in the *Yogasūtrabhāṣya*[25] (fourth or fifth century),

24 *aiśvaryam aṣṭaguṇam animā, mahimā, laghimā, prāptiḥ, prākāmyam, īśitvaṃ, vaśitvaṃ, yatrakāmāvaśāyitvaṃ ceti* /.

25 *tato aṇimādiprādurbhāvaḥ kāyasampat taddharmānabhighātaś ca / tatr**āṇimā** bhavaty aṇuḥ / **laghimā** laghur bhavati / **mahimā** mahān bhavati / **prāptir** aṅgulyagreṇāpi spṛśati candramasam / **prākāmyam** icchānabhighātaḥ / bhūmāv unmajjati nimajjati yathodake / **vaśitvaṃ** bhūtabhautikeṣu vaśī bhavaty avaśyaś cānyeṣām / **īśitṛtvaṃ** teṣāṃ prabhavāpyayavyūhānām īṣṭe / **yatra kāmāvasāyitvaṃ** satyasaṃkalpatā yathā saṃkalpas tathā bhūtaprakṛtīnām avasthānam / na ca śakto'pi*

the *Mārkaṇḍeyapurāṇa*[26] and in a commentary of the *Pāśupatasūtra*, namely Kauṇḍinya's *Pañcārthabhāṣya*[27] (fourth or fifth century):

Version 1a

(1) *aṇimā*	(3) *mahimā*	(5) *prākāmya*	(7) *vaśitva*
(2) *laghimā*	(4) *prāpti*	(6) *īśitva*	(8) *yatrakāmāvasāyitva*

Version 1b, which also includes *yatrakāmāvasāyitva*, can be distinguished from version 1a because of the different order in which *laghimā* and *mahimā* are presented, with the latter preceding the former. Such a list is found in Śaiva texts such as the *Mahārthamañjarī*[28] (fourteenth century) and the *Īśānaśivagurudevapaddhati*[29] (twelfth century):

Version 1b

(1) *aṇimā*	(3) *laghimā*	(5) *prākāmya*	(7) *vaśitva*
(2) *mahimā*	(4) *prāpti*	(6) *vaśitva*	(8) *yatrakāmāvasāyitva*

On the other hand, version 2 includes *garimā* and excludes *yatrakāmāvasāyitva*. It is interesting to observe that whenever *garimā* occurs in a list, *mahimā* always

padārthaviparyāsaṃ karoti / kasmāt / anyasya yatra kāmāvasāyinaḥ pūrvasiddhasya tathā bhūteṣu saṃkalpād iti // (*Yogasūtrabhāṣya* 3.45).

Even though the list comes from the *Yogasūtra* (*tato 'ṇimādiprādurbhāvaḥ kāyasaṃpat taddharmānabhighātaś ca //* 3.45), I took into consideration for my analysis the *Yogasūtrabhāṣya*, since it explicitly mentions and explains all the members of list.

26 ***aṇimā laghimā*** *caiva* ***mahimā prāptir*** *eva ca /* ***prākāmyaṃ*** *ca tathe**śitvaṃ vaśitvaṃ*** *ca tathāparam //* ***yatrakāmāvasāyitvaṃ*** *guṇān etāṃs tathaiśvarān /* (*Mārkaṇḍeyapurāṇa* 40.29).

27 *tad ucyate kāryakaraṇaviśuddhilakṣaṇāḥ tatra kāryaviśuddhis tāvad yadaitad devaśarīraṃ jvalantaṃ bhāsā dīpyantaṃ divi bhuvyantarikṣe ca rukmadaṇḍavad ucchritamātmānaṃ paśyati tadā divi* ***aṇimā laghimā mahimā*** *iti trayaḥ kāryaguṇā bhavanti // antarikṣe ca yasmāddharmaviśeṣāt // tathā karaṇaviśuddhirapi garimādibhiḥ bāhyairantaḥ karaṇena ca dūraviṣayagrāhakatvālocanasaṃkalpādhyavasāyābhimānādayo bhavanti // kasmāt // dharmādivacanāt // api ca* ***prāptiḥ prākāmyam īśitvaṃ vaśitvaṃ*** *ca* ***yatra kāmāvasāyitvam*** *iti pañca karaṇaguṇā bhavanti // ity evaṃ yad anyeṣām aṇimādyaṣṭaguṇaṃ catuḥṣaṣṭivikalpaṃ dharmakāryam aiśvaryaṃ tad iha śāstre harṣa iti saṃjñitam //* (*Pañcārthabhāṣya* 2.12:18–24).

28 *tatra ca tāḥ siddhayo yadā prakāśarūpatayā sarvapadārthāntarbhāvasāmarthyam* ***aṇimā***, *tathaiva vyāpakatvaṃ* ***mahimā***, *bhedarūpagauravavyudāso* ***laghimā***, *svātmaviśrāntilābhaḥ* ***prāptiḥ***, *vedyavilāsopalālanaṃ* ***prākāmyam***, *anavacchinnaiśvaryaśālitvam* ***īśitṛtvam***, *vimraṣṭṛtayā sarvasahatā* ***vaśitvam***, *pūrṇāhambhāvabhāvanā* ***yatrakāmāvasāyitvam*** *iti /* (*Mahārthamañjarī* 51).

29 ***aṇimā mahimā*** *caiva* ***laghimā prāptir*** *eva ca /*
prākāmyaṃ *ca tathe**śitvaṃ vaśitvaṃ*** *ca tataḥ param //*
yatrakāmāvasāyitvam *ity aiśvaryaguṇāṣṭakam //* (*Īśānaśivagurudevapaddhati* 19–4.5).

appears before *laghimā*. Given the position of the powers in the list, one could say that those texts that include *garimā* regard *aṇimā* and *mahimā* as one set of qualities, and *garimā* and *laghimā* as another distinct set. We find this pattern in the *Amarakoṣa*[30] (date not fixed), the *Brahmāṇḍapurāṇa*[31] (fourth century), the Śaiva texts *Tantrāloka*[32] (ca. tenth century) and *Merutantra*[33] (date unknown), Govindbhagavatpāda's Āyurvedic text *Rasahṛdayatantra*[34] (ca. ninth century) and the *Mahāsubhāṣitasaṃgraha*[35] (date not fixed):

Version 2

(1) *aṇimā*	(3) *laghimā*	(5) *prāpti*	(7) *īśitva*
(2) *mahimā*	(4) *garimā*	(6) *prākāmya*	(8) *vaśitva*

6 Establishing some temporal references

Scholars disagree about the date of composition of the SK commentaries, which were composed by several anonymous authors and which do not offer explicit temporal evidence.

The only exceptions are SS, which was translated by the Buddhist monk Paramārtha and is considered to be the earliest of all the SK commentaries, and TK, which is said to be the most recent among the commentaries under investigation her. Here is a chart of references to the different attempts at dating these two texts which can be found throughout the secondary literature:

Chakravarati (1975: 159–168)	SS	557 to 569
	TK	841
Solomon (1974: 171–179)	SS	557 to 569
	TK	Ninth century

30 *vibhūtir bhūtir aiśvaryam aṇimādikam aṣṭadhā / aṇimā mahimā caiva garimā laghimā tathā / prāptiḥ prākāmyamīśitvaṃ vaśitvaṃ cāṣṭa siddhayaḥ //* (*Amarakoṣa* 1.1.38–87).

31 *aṇimā mahimā caiva laghimā garimā tathā / īśitvā vaśitā caiva prāptiḥ siddhiś ca saptamī // prākāmyamuktisiddhiś ca sarvakāmābhidhāparā //* (*Brahmāṇḍapurāṇa* 3.19.4).

32 *aṇimā laghimā caiva mahimā prāptir eva ca / prākāmyaṃ ca tatheśitvaṃ vaśitvaṃ yadudāhṛtam // yatrakāmāvasāyitvamaṇimādyaṣṭakaṃ smṛtam /* (*Tantrāloka* 8.278).

33 *aṇimā mahimā caiva laghimā garimā tathā // īśitvaṃ ca vaśitvaṃ ca prākāmyaṃ prāptir agrataḥ //* (*Merutantra* 63).

34 *aṇimā mahimā cātha laghimā garimā tathā / prāptiḥ prākāmyam īśitvaṃ vaśitvaṃ cāṣṭabhūtayaḥ //* (*Rasahṛdayatantra* 2).

35 *aṇimā mahimā caiva laghimā garimā tathā / prāptiḥ prākāmyam īśitvaṃ vaśitvaṃ cāṣṭa siddhayaḥ //* (*Mahāsubhāṣitasaṃgraha* 481).

HULIN (1978: 138–143)	SS	557 to 569[36]
	TK	Probably tenth century
LARSON (1987: 20–22)	SS	500 to 600
	TK	Mid-ninth or mid- to late tenth century
BURLEY (2006: 22–26)	SS	Sixth century
	TK	841–976 or ninth or tenth century

Thus, even though the dates of other commentaries are not clear, we can roughly assume that the period of their composition can be established on the basis of the textual similarities and differences with SS and TK, the dates of which are relatively clear.

It is no surprise that earlier texts influence later ones and this holds true also for the Sāṃkhya commentarial literature, especially during its classical period. Whether the author of a commentary belongs to the Sāṃkhya school or not,[37] he would definitely refer to former commentaries available to him when composing a new commentary. Such a textual practice is evident from the many similar, or at times identical, passages and quotations that are found across the Sāṃkhya commentaries. In this respect, we can assume that a more intimate relationship occurs among commentaries that share similar features in term of the number and order of components characterising the list of varieties of *aiśvarya*.

7 Analysis of the data

As mentioned in section 2, my analysis focuses only on *aṇimā*, *laghimā*, *mahimā* and *garimā*. The remaining five powers are included in all Sāṃkhya classes. Their order may vary, but for the time being I assume that this is due to the idiosyncratic character of each commentary rather than to a precise reason. On the other hand, I argue that the variation of the order of *laghimā*, *mahimā* and *garimā* can be accounted for.

Class 1 (SS, V1, V2 and TK)

aṇimā *laghimā* *mahimā*

↓

Class 2 (MV)

aṇimā *laghimā* ***garimā*** *mahimā*

↓

36 As for the dating of SS, Hulin refers to TAKAKUSU 1904.

37 For instance, it is not sure whether the authors of JM and MV were members of the Sāṃkhya school or whether they belonged to other philosophical schools that were interested in becoming acquainted with the Sāṃkhya doctrine.

Class 3 (GB)

aṇimā *mahimā* ***garimā*** *laghimā*

↓

Class 3 (YD)

aṇimā *mahimā* *laghimā* ***garimā***

↓

Class 4 (JM)

aṇimā *mahimā* *laghimā*

7.1 From class 1 to classes 2 and 3

Class 1 includes the majority of Sāṃkhya commentaries and can thus be understood as representing the main Sāṃkhya list. One of the main differences between class 1 and classes 2 and 3 is the inclusion of *garimā* in the latter ones.

As both classes 2 and 3 still describe the list of powers as eightfold, one can assume that the inclusion of *garimā*, which adds a ninth member to the list, should have marked a rupture within the Sāṃkhya tradition. It is possible that the texts belonging to classes 2 and 3 were aware of the different traditions that included *garimā* in their list of types of supernatural power. Reflections of such traditions can be observed in the texts containing version 2 of the list, which is eightfold as it includes *garimā* but excludes *yatrakāmāvasāyitva*.

The inclusion of *garimā* is a plausible explanation for the change in position of *laghimā* and *mahimā* between classes 1 and 2 and class 3. The innovation of class 3 can be explained as the attempt to match *mahimā* with the first element of the list, namely *aṇimā*. *Mahimā* is in fact defined in the class-3 commentaries of SK as the physical ability to become great or massive (incidentally, this is also the opinion of SS, in class 1). On the other hand, as I have already mentioned above, according to V1 and V2 (class 1) the meaning of *mahimā* has a spiritual or mental connotation rather than a physical one.[38] We can thus assume that, on the basis of their interpretation of the term *mahimā*, commentaries belonging to class 3 may have found it more reasonable to place *mahimā* after *aṇimā* in order to create the pair *aṇimā-mahimā*, with both items referring to physical abilities that allow modifying the size of the body.

Consequently, the difference in the ordering of *garimā* and *laghimā* between the two commentaries of class 3, namely GB (*garimā-laghimā*) and YD (*laghimā-garimā*), should not be seen as meaningful. What is relevant is the matching of *aṇimā-mahimā* on the one hand, and *garimā-laghimā* (or *laghimā-garimā*) on the other.

As for the issue of the total number of supernatural powers, one can assume that it was probably difficult for the texts of classes 2 and 3 to ignore the content of the commentaries belonging to class 1, and that they felt compelled to retain *yatrakāmāvasāyitva* in the list, contrary to the texts of version 2. For this reason,

38 See fn. 6.

the texts of classes 2 and 3 have both *garimā* and *yatrakāmāvasāyitva* in their lists, thus totalling a number of nine elements, even though they state that *aiśvarya* is eight-fold (*aṣṭavidha* or *aṣṭaguṇa*). In other words, it seems that the texts of classes 2 and 3 accommodated a blatant mistake in their lists in an attempt to integrate two different traditions.

7.2 Secondary literature on classes 2 and 3 listing nine elements

Secondary literature is aware of the problem concerning the different number of types of *aiśvarya*. For instance, in his French translation of SS, TAKAKUSU writes (1904: 1009, fn. 10):[39]

> Although it is said that there are eight categories, Gauḍapāda enumerates nine. Wilson does not seem to have realised it. I think *garimā* was added by mistake or as a synonym for *mahimā*, because that word is not explained below.

In this passage, Takakusu only mentions the *Gauḍapādabhāṣya*'s comments on *garimā*, since he did not know the other commentaries, which were not published yet. He was not sure about the reason of the occurrence of *garimā* in the list and his explanation is not very convincing.

Another relevant observation is found in Bhaṭṭācārya's *Jyotiṣmatī*, a Hindi commentary of TK (BHAṬṬĀCĀRYA 1976: 177):

> (For the sake of establishing the total of eight), if *garimā* is read, *yatrakāmāvasāyitva* is not read. Otherwise, if *yatrakāmāvasāyitva* is read, then this is understood as a synonym of *īśitva* or *vaśitva*. Or alternatively these supernatural powers can be counted in a different manner. All these views are not understood.[40]

Here it is noted that, had *garimā* been included in the list, *yatrakāmāvasāyitva* would not have been. However, the *Jyotiṣmatī* is also uncertain about those cases in which both abilities occur, and assumes that *yatrakāmāvasāyitva* could be a synonym of *īśitva* or *vaśitva*. However, this cannot be the case if one takes into account the explanations of *īśitva*, *vaśitva* and *yatrakāmāvasāyitva* given in the various SK commentaries.

39 'Bien que disant qu'il y a huit catégories, Gauḍapāda en énumère neuf. Wilson ne semble pas s'en être aperçu. Je pense que garimā a été ajouté par erreur ou comme synonyme de mahimā, parce que ce mot n'est pas expliqué plus bas.'

40 *jo garimā kā pāṭh karte haiṃ, ve yatrakāmāvasāyitv kā pāṭh nahiṃ karte* (*aṣṭasaṃkhyā ko yathāvat rakhne ke liye*), *athavā yatrakāmāvasāyitv kā pāṭh yadi karte haiṃ to īśitv aur vaśitv ko paryāyavācī samajhte haiṃ athavā anya kisī rūp se in siddhiyoṃ ko ginte haiṃ / ye sav dṛṣṭiyāṃ asaṃgat haiṃ /*.

Finally, SOLOMON (1974: 54, 179), who edited both V1 and V2, states:

> M, G (and Y) say that there are eight but enumerate the above-mentioned nine, though the Chowkhamba edition of G omits *garimā* and enumerates only eight. V1, V2 and P ['P' here stands for SS] do not mention *garimā*. All explain these except M (and Y). (p. 54)

> It may be noted that all the commentaries say that *aiśvarya* is eight-fold, but Y and M and even T [sic!] enumerate nine, mentioning *garimā* in addition. (p. 179)

Solomon is aware that GB (erroneously confused with TK), MV and YD add *garimā* and list nine elements. However, she does not investigate the reasons of such inconsistency.

In brief, the previous literature does realise that there is a problem with the number of items in the list and simply regards *garimā* as a mistake or as synonymous with some other abilities.

On the presence of *garimā* in the list of varieties of supernatural power, we find a further remark in the *Jyotiṣmatī* (BHAṬṬĀCĀRYA 1976: 177):

> Some editors read supernatural power in the form of *garimā* after *aṇimā*, *laghimā*, *mahimā*. *Garimā* as a form of supernatural power is not accepted in *pātañjala* yoga and other old yoga texts. Stating that while *aṇimā* and *mahimā* occur, *garimā* should be read together with *laghimā* is fallacious. Actually *aṇimā* and *mahimā* do not belong to the same class. This is the same reason why even though *laghimā* is mentioned, the inclusion of *garimā* is logically inadmissible.[41]

This passage informs us that certain—unfortunately unspecified—texts contain a version of the list that includes *garimā*. However, arguing that such an inclusion is due to an attempt at producing a more symmetrical list of abilities (*aṇimā-mahimā* and *garimā-laghimā*) is unsound. In fact, the *Jyotiṣmatī* believes that matching *aṇimā* and *mahimā* would be like matching apples and oranges. As I had pointed out in the previous section, *mahimā* has been interpreted in two ways, spiritually and physically. It seems rather clear that the *Jyotiṣmatī* is aware—or rather adheres—to the former interpretation, an interpretation that prompts it to argue that the inclusion of *garimā* cannot find any formal justification.

---

41 *kuch saṃpādak aṇimā, laghimā, mahimā ke bād garimā rūp siddhi kā pāṭh karte haiṃ / garimā rūp vibhūti kā svīkār pātañjal yog tathā anyānya prācīn yogaśāstroṃ meṃ nahiṃ hai / cūṃki aṇimā aur mahimā hai, ataḥ laghimā ke sāth garimā kā pāṭh honā cāhiye—yah kahā jātā hai, jo ek bhrānt dṛṣṭi hai / vastutaḥ aṇimā aur mahimā ekajātīya nahiṃ haiṃ / yahī kāraṇ hai ki laghimā kā ullekh hone par bhī garimā kā ullekh karnā nyāyataḥ prāpt nahiṃ hotā /*. Note that the word *siddhi* is synonymous with *aiśvarya*.

7.3 From class 3 to class 4

Class 4 is represented by JM, and in particular by its very list of powers, where we find the pair *aṇimā-mahimā* followed by *laghimā* alone: in fact *garimā* in fact is not included here. Interestingly, in its explanation section JM does not have the pair *aṇimā-mahimā*, and enumerates the powers in the order *aṇimā*, *laghimā* and *mahimā*. In other words, the explanation section of JM adheres to class 1.

If we understand this internal change in the order of powers not just as an authorial idiosyncrasy, we can assume that from a typological point of view class 4 stands between class 3, which has the pair *aṇimā-mahimā*, and class 1, where there is no *garimā*.

8 Conclusion

So far we have established that the list of types of supernatural power found in the Sāṃkhya texts of class 1 can be conventionally seen as the main list of the Sāṃkhya school, in particular if we consider how many commentaries have this in common. This class contains the same abilities that we find in version 1a. Then, we have observed that the texts of classes 2 and 3 include *garimā*, possibly under the influence of version 2, but without rejecting *yatrakāmāvasāyitva*. The texts of class 3 in particular seem to have rearranged the order of powers in response to the insertion of *garimā*, also in this case under the influence of the tradition reflected in version 2. Finally, class 4 has the same order of powers as in class 3, but doesn't include *garimā*, thus overlapping with the texts containing version 1b of the list. The relationship among the four classes, version 1 and version 2 is summarised in the following table:

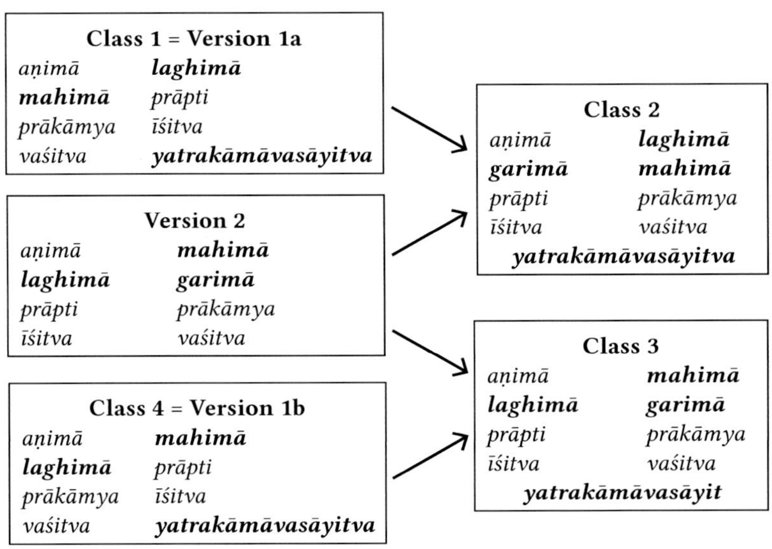

Since we know that two texts belonging to class 1, namely SS and TK, are most probably the first and last in terms of date of composition among the Sāṃkhya commentaries included in this study, we can try to speculate on the chronological implications of the typology established so far.

We can state with a certain degree of confidence that the above-mentioned rupture in the tradition represented by the inclusion of *garimā* in the list—a feature characterising MV, GB and YD (classes 2 and 3) and possibly influenced by the tradition represented by version 2—occurred at a stage in the Sāṃkhya commentarial tradition that is later than the SS. Whether V1 and V2 (class 1) are also older than MV, GB and YD or simply represent another strand of the Sāṃkhya tradition cannot be concluded on the basis of this study.

As far as the actual list of powers in JM is concerned (class 4), the fact that this commentary includes eight members but lists *mahimā* right after *aṇimā* seems to suggest that it may have been composed after the texts of classes 2 and 3 and before TK, which in turn aligns with the main Sāṃkhya tradition, adopting the list as found in the texts of class 1.

In conclusion, the study of the list of types of supernatural power can cast new light on the uncertainties concerning the dates of composition of the Sāṃkhya commentaries. So far, secondary literature has instead focused on the philosophical tenets and technical terms of Sāṃkhya. There are even a few studies that compare mainly the philosophical contents, quotations, similar expressions or parallel passages of the various SK commentaries in an attempt at establishing a possible order for the composition of such texts (Solomon 1974 and Chakravarti 1975). However, they could not establish a definitive sequence because of the difficulty of grouping the different ideas presented in the various commentaries in a chronological order.

Instead, a careful evaluation of the textual variants of similar passages, such as the lists of variants of *aiśvarya* found in the different commentaries, can prove to be a rather fruitful methodology. First, it helps highlight the connections among the various texts and, when possible, compare and connect such texts with relevant non-Sāṃkhya literature. Then, it also opens up the possibility of tentatively arranging significant variants in a chronological order.

References

Primary Sources

Amarakośa. Jhalakikar, V. (Ed.). (1907). *Amarakośa with the commentary of Maheśvara* (6th ed.). Mumbai: Government Central Book Depot.

Brahmāṇḍapurāṇa. Shastri, J. L. (Ed.). (1973). *Brahmāṇḍa Purāna of Sage Kṛṣṇa Dvaipāyana Vyāsa.* Delhi: Motilal Banarsidass.

Gauḍapāda-bhāṣya. MAINKAR, T. G. (Ed.) (1963). *Sāṃkhyakārikā of Īśvarakṛṣṇa. With the commentary of Gauḍapāda.* Delhi: Chowkhamba Sanskirt Prathishthan.

Īśānaśivagurudevapaddhati. GAṆAPATIŚĀSTRĪ, T. (Ed.). (1920–1925). *The Îsânasivagurudevapaddhati* (4 vols.). Trivandrum: Government Press.

Jayamaṅgalā. VĀṄGĪYA, S. (Ed.). (1970). *Sāṃkhya-Kārikā of Śrīmad Īśvarakṛṣṇa with the Jayamaṅgalā of Śrī Satkāriśarmā Vaṅgīya.* Varanasi: Chowkhamba Sanskrit Series.

Māṭhara-vṛtti. ŚARMĀ, V. P. (Ed.), (1970). *Sāṃkhya-Kārikā of Śrīmad Īśvarakṛṣṇa with the Māṭharavṛtti of Māṭharācārya.* Varanasi: Chowkhamba Sanskrit Series Office.

Mahārthamañjari. GAṆAPATIŚĀSTRĪ, T. (Ed.). (1919). *The Maharthamanjarî: With the commentary Parimala of Mahesvarananda.* Trivandrum: Government Press.

Mahāsubhāṣitasaṃgraha. STERNBACH, L. (Ed.). (1974–1981). *Mahā-subhāṣita-saṁgraha: Being an extensive collection of wise sayings in Sanskrit* (5 vols.). Hoshiarpur: Vishveshvaranand Vedic Research Institute.

Mārkaṇḍeyapurāṇa. BHAṬṬĀCĀRYA, J. V. (Ed.) (1879). *Mārkaṇḍeya Purāṇa.* Calcutta.

Merutantra. OJHA, R. N. Ś. (Ed.). (2009). *Merutantram.* Mumbai: Khemarāj Śrīkṛṣṇadās Prakāśan.

Pañcārthabhāṣya. SASTRI, R. A. (Ed.). (1940). *Pāśupatasūtra, with Pañcārthabhāṣya.* Trivandrum.

Rasahṛdayatantra. SHARMA, P. P. (Ed.). (2003). *Rasahṛdayatantra: With 'Mugdhavabodhini' Sanskrit and 'Subodhini' Hindi vyakhya.* Varanasi: Chowkhamba Sanskrit Series Office.

Suvarṇasaptati of Paramārtha (Chinese version). In 大正新脩大藏經.

Sāṃkhya-Saptati-Vṛtti. SOLOMON, E. A. (Ed.). (1973). *Sāṃkhya-Saptati-Vṛtti* (vol. 1). Ahmedabad: Gujarat University.

Sāṃkhya-Vṛtti. SOLOMON, E. A. (Ed.). (1973). *Sāṃkhya-Vṛtti* (vol. 2). Ahmedabad: Gujarat University.

Tantrāloka. SHĀSTRĪ, M. R. and KAUL SHASTRI, M. (Eds.). (1918–1938). *The Tantrāloka of Abhinava Gupta, with commentary by Rājānaka Jayaratha* (12 vols.). Allahabad: Indian Press.

Tattva-kaumudī. SRINIVASAN, S. A. (Ed.). (1967). *Vācaspatimiśras Tattvakaumudī: Ein Beitrag zur Textkritik bei kontaminierter Überlieferung.* Hamburg: Cram, de Gruyter & Co.

Yogasūtrabhāṣyavivaraṇa. RUKMANI, T. S. (Ed.). (2001). *Yogasūtrabhāṣyavivaraṇa of Śaṅkara. Vol. II. Vibhūtipādaḥ and Kaivalyapādaḥ.* Delhi: Mushiram Manoharlal Publishers Pvt. Ltd.

Yuktidīpikā. WEZLER, A. and MOTEGI, S. (Eds.). (1998). *Yuktidīpikā. The Most Significant Commentary of the Sāṃkhyakārikā* (vol. 1). Stuttgart: Steiner.

Secondary Sources

BHATTACHARYA, R. S. (Ed.). (1976). *Sāṃkhyatattvakaumudī.* Delhi: Motilal Banarsidass.

BURLEY, M. (2006). *Classical Sāṃkhya and Yoga. An Indian metaphysics of experience.* London and New York: Routledge.

CHAKRAVARTI, P. (1975). *Origin and development of the Sāṃkhya system of thought* (2nd ed.). New Delhi: Oriental Reprint.

HULIN, M. (1978). Sāṃkhya literature. In Gonda, J. (Ed.), *A history of Indian literature* (vol. 6, pt. 3, fasc. 3). Wiesbaden: Harrassowitz.

LARSON, G. J. & BHATTACHARYA, R. S. (Eds.). (1987). *The encyclopedia of Indian philosophies, Vol. IV: Sāṃkhya, a dualist tradition in Indian philosophy.* Delhi: Motilal Banarsidass.

SOLOMON, E. A. (1974). *The commentaries of the Sāṃkhya Kārikā: A study.* Ahmedabad: Gujarat University.

TAKAKUSU, M. J. (Ed.). (1904). La Sāṃkhyakārikā, étudiée à la lumière de sa version chinoise (II). *Bulletin de École française d'Extrême-Orient, 4*(1): 978–1064

Guṇaratna's Refutation of the Cārvāka Perspective on the Soul

An Argumentative Analysis of *Tarkarahasyadīpikā* 49.98–134

Lucas den Boer

Introduction

Studying the history of the Cārvākas is both fascinating and frustrating. The ideas of these materialistic philosophers, to which authors refer throughout the history of Indian philosophy, are particularly interesting since they strongly oppose central doctrines that were shared by most other thinkers on the Indian subcontinent. Notably, the Cārvākas denied the existence of the soul and an afterlife and argued that everything, including consciousness, is constituted by the four elements. However, the contemporary investigation of this school is severely hampered by the lack of sources. There is no single text that is unanimously accepted as a Cārvāka text, and all extant historical descriptions of Cārvāka philosophy are written by its opponents. We cannot assume that these opponents gave us an accurate account of Cārvāka thought, since they all had their own agendas and might have presented the Cārvāka position as a mere straw man. Since we cannot compare these descriptions with the original Cārvāka texts, it is hard to distinguish the ideas that belonged to the Cārvākas themselves and the ideas that were falsely attributed to them.[1]

Consequently, it seems almost impossible to determine the role Cārvāka thought actually played in the history of Indian philosophy. Yet the notion that the available sources might give a distorted view on the original Cārvāka tenets does not imply that these sources are not worth our attention. So far, most historical

1 One can of course compare the different descriptions to distinguish the ideas that are frequently attributed to the Cārvākas from those that are attributed to them only by a single author. This method has been applied by Ramkrishna Bhattacharya (2002). However, it is evident that without genuine Cārvāka sources, such a method cannot provide definitive answers.

refutations of Cārvāka thought are only consulted in reconstructing the status and ideas of the school of Cārvākas. From this perspective, little scholarly attention has been paid to the strategies that these authors applied in refuting the Cārvāka views. Nonetheless, from a philosophical point of view, it is highly interesting to observe how and why authors refuted the materialist and sceptical position of the Cārvākas.[2] Even though their description of the Cārvākas might be biased, their efforts to refute the Cārvāka standpoint drives these commentators to challenging philosophical argumentations.

An outstanding example of such a source is a passage in the *Tarkarahasyadīpikā* [Light on the Secrets of Reasoning] in which the Jaina author Guṇaratna Sūri (fl. 1412) discusses the Cārvāka perspective on the soul.[3] This passage distinguishes itself from most other sources by giving a rather elaborate and, as it seems, charitable account of the Cārvāka position. Whereas other authors only summarise the Cārvāka tenets, Guṇaratna enters into a debate with them and provides us with arguments and counterarguments from a Cārvāka perspective. Moreover, the view of the Cārvāka opponent is formulated in such a way that it attacks not only Jaina doctrine but also common epistemological standpoints to which other important philosophical schools adhered. Therefore, this passage is certainly worth more scholarly attention than it has hitherto received.[4]

In this article, I will provide an argumentative analysis of this debate. The analysis of this passage serves a double goal. First, by clarifying the arguments in the debate between Guṇaratna and the Cārvāka opponent, one can get a historical insight into the ideas and philosophical tools of a fifteenth-century Jaina philosopher. Second, the analysis will be used as a case study for applying an alternative methodological stance towards the Cārvāka sources. Instead of seeking an answer to the question of which role the Cārvākas played as historical human agents, this article investigates the *argumentative role* of the Cārvāka arguments[5] in the debate itself.

---

2 The Cārvākas are associated with both materialism and scepticism. The label 'scepticism' can be misleading, given the fact that the Cārvākas are usually said to accept perception as a valid source of knowledge. However, the term 'sceptic' does apply to the Cārvākas in the sense that they doubt general presuppositions, especially regarding religious ideas.

3 A discussion of Guṇaratna's biography can be found in the introduction of B.K. Matilal's edition of Śaśadhara's *Nyāyasiddhāntadīpa* (Matilal 1976). Matilal identifies Guṇaratna Sūri as the author of a *Ṭippaṇī* on the *Nyāyasiddhāntadīpa*, the *Tarkarahasyadīpikā* and a book on grammar titled *Kriyāratnasamuccaya*, dated to 1412 CE. This Guṇaratna is praised by a contemporary named Munisundara Sūri for his vast learning and skills in logic and philosophical debate (ibid.).

4 An overview of existing studies on this text can be found in the first section of this article.

5 It remains an open question whether the so-called Cārvāka arguments can be attributed to the historical Cārvākas. In this article I will use the word 'Cārvāka' with reference to the materialist, sceptic position which is usually labelled as Cārvāka philosophy in historical texts such as the *Tarkarahasyadīpikā*.

For this goal, I will mainly restrict my analysis to a conceptual level. Although this choice limits the possible outcomes of this study, it is a suitable approach to the main questions in this article, which can be summarised as follows:

I. How does Guṇaratna refute the Cārvāka arguments against the existence of the soul?
II. Which argumentative role do the Cārvāka arguments play in Guṇaratna's debate with the Cārvāka position?

After a general introduction in the first section, I assess the argumentative role of the Cārvāka arguments in Guṇaratna's *Tarkarahasyadīpikā* 49.98–134. My analysis focuses on the structure of the debate and the impact of specific Cārvāka arguments on Guṇaratna's defence. This analysis is based on the argumentative summary that can be found in the appendix to this article. On the basis of my argumentative analysis, I will conclude that the Cārvāka arguments are a valuable tool for non-Cārvāka philosophers to develop their own ideas and to protect them against obvious criticism.

1 Context and Approach

Cārvākas in the History of Indian Philosophy

Textual sources throughout the history of Indian philosophy discuss materialist doctrines, referred to by such terms as Lokāyata, Cārvāka, Bārhaspatya and *nāstika* (Franco 2011: 629).[6] The first extant source that connects the word 'Cārvāka' with materialism is the *Ṣaḍdarśanasamuccaya* (*ṢDS*) [A Compendium of the Six Philosophies].[7] This work was written in the eighth century CE by the Jain author Haribhadra Sūri (Qvarnström 1999). In seven stanzas of this work, Haribhadra explains the basic Cārvāka/Lokāyata standpoints.[8] These stanzas can be reduced to four main ideas:

6 In some of the sources, such as the Pāli Canon and the *Mahābhārata*, the synonym 'Lokāyata' refers to a branch of Brahmin learning (Franco 2011: 630). This led T. W. Rhys Davids to the hypothesis that the word 'Lokāyata' originally meant 'nature-lore—wise sayings, riddles, rhymes, and theories handed down by tradition [...]' (Rhys Davids 2006: 374).

7 The word 'materialism' is used to refer to the theory that the world consists exclusively of material elements.

In early sources such as the *Mahābhārata*, the word 'Cārvāka' has different meanings, but later references identify Cārvāka thought unambiguously as materialist philosophy. Two centuries before Haribhadra, the term 'Lokāyatika' was already linked to materialism and hedonism by Candrakīrti in the *Prasannapadā* (Franco 2011: 629).

8 In his description of this sceptical, materialistic school, Haribhadra uses the terms 'Cārvāka' and 'Lokāyata' interchangeably. In a commentary on Haribhadra's chapter on Lokāyata thought,

I. There is nothing beyond the objects of the senses. Perception is the only valid means of cognition (*ṢDS* 81, 83).
II. There are four elements (earth, water, fire and air). The body is an aggregate of these elements and consciousness is an epiphenomenon of this aggregate (*ṢDS* 83, 84).
III. The soul is non-existent. Karmic laws and liberation are merely fictions (*ṢDS* 80).
IV. Forsaking worldly pleasure for the sake of something unseen is foolish. The highest goal is sensual pleasure (*ṢDS* 82, 85, 86).[9]

From the eighth century CE onwards, the Cārvākas are described in a fairly consistent way. The main elements in these descriptions usually resemble Haribhadra's account as summarised above.

Even so, it remains a question who these Cārvākas actually were, and it is hard to determine what they really said since there are no extant Cārvāka works.[10] But this does not imply that we can only speculate about Cārvāka thought. Although the different historical descriptions of Cārvāka philosophy since the eighth century CE show some dissimilarities and inconsistencies, there is enough overlap between most descriptions to speak about Cārvāka thought as a distinct, fairly consistent topos in classical Indian philosophy.[11]

Given the strong opposition between the Cārvāka tenets and the main ideas and presuppositions of other Indian philosophers, the Cārvākas have drawn scholarly attention since the beginning of the nineteenth century, when the first attempts to map the history of Indian philosophy were made. In 1837 Henry

---

Guṇaratna writes about its adherents: 300.13, *tannāmāni cārvākā lokāyatā ityādīni* ('Their names [are] Cārvākas, Lokāyatas etc.'). Since Guṇaratna makes no distinction between these names, one can assume that he regards both names as synonyms for the same philosophical school.

The Sanskrit quotations in this article are based on the editions by Luigi Suali and Mahendra Kumar Jain. An explanation of the numbering, symbols and punctuation is included in the references. All translations are mine, unless otherwise indicated.

9 A full translation of the *ṢDS* can be found in Olle Qvarnström's 'Haribhadra and the Beginnings of Doxography in India' (1999).

10 Some scholars, such as Sukhlāljī Saṁghavī & Rasiklāl C. Pārīkh (1940) and Eli Franco (1994), argue that Jayarāśi's sceptical *Tattvopaplavasiṃha* (*TUS*) is a genuine Cārvāka text. However, most ideas that are generally attributed to the Cārvākas are not represented in this text, and Jayarāśi even refutes perception as a valid means of cognition, which is a central element of Cārvāka thought. A recent discussion of this topic can be found in Piotr Balcerowicz's lemma on Jayarāśi in the *Stanford Encyclopedia of Philosophy*. In this article, he describes the *TUS* as 'loosely affiliated with the Cārvāka/Lokāyata school of thought' (Balcerowicz 2011).

11 This does not necessarily imply that there was a distinct school of Cārvāka philosophers who adhered to these ideas, but it does ensure that the term 'Cārvāka philosophy' refers to a historical entity and that the investigation into the role of Cārvāka philosophy in Indian thought does not address an idle question.

Colebrooke mentioned the Cārvākas for the first time in one of his essays. After a brief introduction of the topic, he remarks:

> For want of an opportunity of consulting an original treatise on this branch of philosophy, or any connected summary furnished even by an adversary of opinions professed by the *Chárvákas*, no sufficient account can be yet given of their peculiar doctrine, further than that it is undisguised materialism. (Colebrooke 1837: 402)

Given the scarcity of available sources in Colebrooke's time, it is not surprising that Colebrooke could not say more about the Cārvākas. This situation changed substantially in the decades after Colebrooke's essay, but notwithstanding the growing amount of source materials, the historical status of this school became a point of discussion.[12] An important voice in this debate was Thomas William Rhys Davids, who wrote the following in 1889:

> Throughout the whole story, we have no evidence of anyone who called himself a Lokāyatika, or his own knowledge Lokāyata. After the early use of the word in some such sense as *Nature-lore*, folk-lore, there is a tone of unreality over all the statements we have. And of the real existence of a school of thought, or a system of philosophy that called itself by the name, there is no trace. (Rhys Davids 2006: 375)

It is this view that motivated scholars such as Giuseppe Tucci to show that the Cārvākas did not exist only in the pen of rival authors, and that historical descriptions of Cārvāka thought are based on the ideas of a real philosophical school (Tucci 1925/2006). This project has been carried on by scholars such as Debiprasad Chattopadhyaya, Ramkrishna Bhattacharya and Eli Franco and the majority of publications on this subject are strongly opposed to Rhys Davids's scepticism. In a recent lemma on Lokāyata in *Brill's Encyclopedia of Hinduism*, Franco concludes:

> [B]etween the sixth and ninth centuries, the Cārvāka/Lokāyata was a fascinating, vibrant, and innovative philosophical tradition, which engaged critically with the major philosophies of its time. (Franco 2011: 642)

However, given the absence of undisputed original Cārvāka writings and the blatant lack of objectivity that characterises most descriptions by rival authors, it must be accepted that every conclusion on the historical status of the Cārvākas is partly based on speculative or highly debatable elements.

12 An illustrative example of the growth of sources in this period is an article from 1861 in which John Muir compiles relevant references to Cārvāka thought from the epics and *purāṇas* (Chattopadhyaya & Gangopadhyaya 2006: 351).

The Cārvākas in Guṇaratna's Tarkarahasyadīpikā

The *TRD* is a commentary on Haribhadra's doxographical *ṢDS* and gives a broad overview of the main schools within the Indian philosophical spectrum.[13] In the well-known final chapter of the *TRD*, Guṇaratna comments on Haribhadra's stanzas on the Cārvākas that are mentioned above. However, there is another part of the *TRD* which is also dedicated to the ideas of the Cārvākas but has not received much attention so far.[14] This passage occurs in the chapter on Jaina philosophy, in which Guṇaratna presents an argument for the non-existence of the soul that he attributes to the Cārvākas. Unlike the chapter on Cārvāka philosophy, which is mostly descriptive, this passage has a strong argumentative character. The goal of this passage is of course the refutation of the Cārvāka view, and this debate is an excellent example of the argumentative role that Cārvāka ideas can play in a philosophical text.[15]

Guṇaratna's refutation of the Cārvāka perspective on the soul is a part of his commentary on stanzas 48 and 49 of the *ṢDS*, in which the Jaina concept of the soul is summarised as follows:

> There (i.e. in Jaina philosophy) *jīva* is different and not different from the attributes such as knowledge, etc. [It is] subject to development, the agent of auspicious and inauspicious action and the enjoyer of the fruit of action. ||48|| *Jīva* is characterised by consciousness, and that which is opposed to this is named *ajīva* [...] ||49||[16]

These two stanzas introduce a crucial doctrine of Jainism. According to the Jainas, reality contains two basic categories: *jīva* and *ajīva*. *Jīva* can be translated as soul and *ajīva* is that which is non-soul, i.e. everything except for souls. The central

---

13 The word 'doxography' can be misleading in the Indian context, since Indian doxographies are not necessarily purely descriptive. In *Unifying Hinduism*, Andrew NICHOLSON (2010) has convincingly shown how Indian philosophers used doxographies as a means to innovate existing theories.

14 The *TRD* was edited for the first time in 1905 by Luigi SUALI (1905–1914). A second edition, prepared by Mahendra Kumar Jain, was published in 1970, together with a Hindi translation (JAIN 1970/2009). The passage that will be analysed in this article has been translated into English by CHATTOPADHYAYA & GANGOPADHYAYA (2006), and the first part additionally translated into French by SUALI (1908). Frank VAN DEN BOSSCHE (1998) translated another part of the chapter in which our passage is found. Muneo Tokunaga made an unpublished translation of the first chapter of the *TRD* and prepared an e-text of the entire *TRD*. To my knowledge, no publication discusses Guṇaratna's refutation of the Cārvāka arguments.

15 The *TRD* is a voluminous work of which our discussion with the Cārvākas is only a small part. An evaluation of the role of our passage in the *TRD* would require a study of the entire *TRD*, which goes beyond the limits of the present article.

16 {138.6} *tatra jñānādidharmebhyo bhinnābhinno vivṛttimān* | {138.7} *śubhāśubhakarmakartā bhoktā karmaphalasya ca* ||48|| {138.8} *caitanyalakṣaṇo jīvo yaś caitadviparītavān* | {138.9} *ajīvaḥ sa samākhyātaḥ* [...] ||49||

goal of Jainism is to separate the soul from everything that is non-soul in order to reach the state of liberation. From this perspective, it is not hard to see why a Jaina philosopher can never agree with Cārvāka materialism, which denies the existence of the soul. The whole soteriology of Jainism would collapse if souls were removed from the ontological framework of the Jainas.

In addition to their denial of the soul, the Cārvāka position poses an even bigger threat to Jaina thought by providing an alternative explanation for the existence of consciousness. For the Jainas, consciousness is the hallmark of the soul. If souls are the only entities that can have consciousness, the fact that there is consciousness is already a proof of the existence of the soul. This proof becomes less convincing, of course, if there is an alternative explanation for the existence of consciousness that does not require the existence of souls. The Cārvākas provide such an explanation by saying that consciousness is an epiphenomenon of matter and arises from the mixing of the elements. It is therefore not surprising that Guṇaratna starts his debate with the Cārvāka perspective precisely at the point when he comments on Haribhadra's verses on the Jaina concept of the soul.

Methodological Considerations

The foregoing paragraph has shown the relevance of refuting sceptical ideas regarding the soul, but this does not yet explain why the Cārvākas were selected as targets for this purpose. For example, why did Guṇaratna not address the Buddhist account, which also denies the existence of the soul?

This is a complex question and the answer to it depends heavily on one's methodology, which determines what counts as a motive. To find out the motive that underlies a debate between two schools of thought, one can choose, for example, to examine the social relation between these schools. Alternatively, one can investigate the texts of both schools in order to understand the intellectual motive for the debate. Both approaches may lead to completely different answers, which are not necessarily mutually exclusive.

But in our case, we cannot consult any Cārvāka text, and an investigation of the social encounters between the Cārvākas and Jainas would be idle, since we can reasonably assume that there were no influential thinkers who associated themselves with the Cārvāka tradition in the fifteenth century.[17]

Therefore, I suggest investigating the positions in Guṇaratna's text primarily as conceptual positions. Even without meticulous knowledge of the historical and

17 The first reason for this assumption is that there are no sources that refer to active Cārvāka philosophers in this period. Second, the sources that discuss Cārvāka thought discuss the Cārvākas mostly in a standardised way, and the arguments that are attributed to them barely change. If there were still active Cārvāka proponents engaged in a debate with other schools, one would expect the description of Cārvāka thought to develop over the centuries.

textual context, a contemporary reader can understand the overall argumentation of Guṇaratna's text. The majority of the arguments address general philosophical problems, such as the relation between matter and consciousness and the validity of logical inferences, and these arguments can be assessed in a conceptual way. Instead of asking whether the arguments in the texts are correct renderings of the original Cārvāka arguments, I propose to examine whether the arguments *as given by Guṇaratna* and his refutation of these arguments are useful steps in his overall strategy to establish the existence of the soul.[18]

2 Argumentative Assessment

The general structure of the debate[19] can be summarised as follows: The Cārvākas introduce their argument by claiming that consciousness is caused by the elements and not by the soul. Next, they argue that the soul does not exist. To prove this position, they show that the soul cannot be known by any of the sources of cognition. Maintaining that one can establish the non-existence of entities that are not within the scope of any source of cognition, the Cārvākas conclude that there is no soul.

Guṇaratna responds to this in a twofold way. First, he shows that the soul can be known by several sources of cognition. Strictly speaking, this is enough to invalidate the negative claim that there is no soul. However, Guṇaratna goes one step further by attacking the positive claim of the Cārvākas about the relation between consciousness and matter. His main strategy is to show that this claim cannot be consistently defended from a Cārvāka perspective. By showing that the criticism of the Jaina perspective on the soul is baseless, and by pointing out the problems in a fully material explanation of consciousness, Guṇaratna offers a strong reply to the sceptics.

The Cārvāka Position

The Cārvāka arguments start with the claim that the human body, which exclusively consists of material elements, is the only cause of consciousness. This claim is substantiated by pointing out that consciousness has positive and negative concomitance with the body, i.e. the body is always accompanied by consciousness and consciousness does not occur without a body (A1.3). Apart

18 It would be valuable to complement the present study with a broader historical textual survey. However, such a study cannot be done within the time frame of the current investigation. A plea for an integrated approach that combines history, philology and philosophy can be found in Parimal PATIL's 'History, Philology, and the Philosophical Study of Sanskrit Texts' (2010).

19 Numbers between parentheses in this section, e.g. (A1.1), refer to the numbers used in the argumentative summary of the debate, provided in the appendix to this article.

from this brief argument, the Cārvāka arguments are fully dedicated to their negative claims.

To begin with, the Cārvākas point out that the soul cannot be proved by direct perception (*pratyakṣa-*) (A1). First they claim that sense-perception cannot prove the soul (A1.1). Thereafter, they explain that self-awareness, as a form of direct perception, does not reveal the soul. Instead they claim that self-awareness is just an awareness of the body. At the end of the discussion about direct perception, the Cārvākas briefly indicate that their atomism is not threatened by the fact that atoms are invisible, since atoms acquire visibility when they are assembled, in contrast to the soul, which is *absolutely* imperceptible.

At this point, it becomes clear that writing in the form of a debate, fictional or not, influences the philosophical quality of the discussion. By bringing in the atomistic view of the Cārvākas, the concept of visibility becomes a matter of dispute. Without the Cārvāka perspective, there would be no reason to problematize visibility. From a common-sense perspective, things are either visible or invisible. However, in this passage Guṇaratna demonstrates that visibility is in the end not such a clear-cut quality.

Next, the Cārvākas explain why inference (*anumāna-*) cannot prove the existence of the soul (A2). Apart from the fact that the Cārvākas do not accept inference as a valid means of cognition (A2.1), they point out that one cannot use an inference to prove something that is contradicted by perception (A2.2).[20] For this goal the Cārvākas first explain how a standard inference works:

> [I]nference is in effect preceded by the recollection of the concomitance between the invariable mark and the probandum. For instance, a person who has previously grasped with his eyes the positive and negative concomitance of the invariable mark and the probandum in the case of smoke and fire in the kitchen etc., after at a later time having seen a streak of smoke hanging in the sky, somewhere in a forest, at a mountain ridge, etc., remembers the previously observed concomitance. Then he reasons as follows:
>
> I. 'I have seen that wherever there is smoke there is fire, just as in the kitchen etc.
> II. And smoke is seen here.
> III. Therefore, fire should also be here.'[21]

20 The technical term used to indicate this argumentative fault is *kālātyayāpadiṣṭa-*, often translated as 'fallacy of the mistimed'. It is one of the argumentative fallacies that are covered by the term '*hetvābhāsa-*' or '*pseudoprobans*' (Grimes 1989/1996: 136, 156). It applies to an argument that tries to prove something that is already contradicted by perception or accepted doctrine.

21 A2.3, [49.100]. {141.13[ii]} *yatra yatra dhūmas tatra tatra vahnim adrākṣaṃ, yathā mahānasādau* | {141.14} *dhūmas cātra dṛśyate* | {141.15} *tasmād vahnināpīha bhavitavyam.*

Such inferences only work if there are previous perceptions of the simultaneous occurrence of the invariable mark (e.g. smoke) and the probandum (e.g. fire). However, the Cārvākas point out that the soul is never perceived together with any invariable mark for the simple reason that the soul is imperceptible (A2.3). This entails that one cannot infer the existence of the soul from the presence of, for example, consciousness.

This interpretation of inference implies that inference can never prove the existence of imperceptible entities, and mainly reduces inferential knowledge to an extension of perceptual knowledge. However, the Cārvākas continue their argument with a discussion of another type of inference, named 'inference based on general observation' (*sāmānyatodṛṣṭa-*) (A2.4). Inference based on general observation is a type of inference that allows inferring something about a subject without prior observance of the probandum. For example, a regular inference cannot prove that the sun has movement on account of the fact that it is first seen in the east and later in the south. The problem is that the sun moves too slowly to actually see its movement, hence we cannot perceive the probandum (movement) together with its invariable mark (first here, then there). However, in other cases we can perceive this probandum together with its invariable mark, such as in the case of a walking person. On account of these general observations, we can also infer that the sun has movement. However, according to the Cārvākas, even this type of inference cannot prove the existence of the soul. In the case of the sun, it is perceptible that the sun is first here and then there, but there is nothing that qualifies likewise as an invariable mark for the soul.

The Cārvākas continue their argument by claiming that verbal testimony (*āgama-*) cannot prove the existence of the soul (A3). Indian philosophers who accept verbal testimony as a valid source of cognition only accept testimonies that are 'conveyed by a credible person (*āpta-*) whose words are not contradictory'.[22] The Cārvākas claim that there is no trustworthy person who can claim that he has perceived the soul without contradicting himself. To this argument they add that verbal testimony cannot be used as a source of cognition, since verbal testimonies are mutually contradictory. In the words of the Cārvākas:

> [All] verbal testimonies are characterised by mutual contradiction. In consequence of that, the credibility of verbal testimony is indeed licked by the flames of the forest fire of the following doubt: 'Which verbal testimony is a source of cognition and which verbal testimony is not a source of cognition?' And therefore, there is also no proof of the soul based on the source of cognition named 'verbal testimony'.[23]

22 A3.1, [49.102], {142.6}.

23 A3.2, [49.102]. {142.9} *kiṃ cāgamāś ca sarve parasparaviruddhaprarūpiṇaḥ* | {142.10} *tatas ca kaḥ pramāṇaṃ kaś cāpramāṇam iti samdehadāvāna-lajvālāvalīḍham evāgamasya prāmāṇyam* | {142.11} *tataś ca nāgamapramāṇād apy ātmasiddhiḥ.*

Next, the Cārvākas explain why it is impossible to prove the existence of the soul by analogy (*upamāna-*) (A4). If two objects have a high degree of similarity, one might claim to know something about one of these two on the basis of existing knowledge about the other. However, the Cārvākas point out that there is no analogue which is comparable to the soul (A4.1).

Likewise, the Cārvākas state that postulation (*arthāpatti-*), which is the last option, is not a suitable means of proving the existence of the soul (A5). Indian philosophers who accept postulation as a valid means of knowledge claim that, if one perceives something that cannot be explained without the assumption of a specific entity, one can postulate the existence of that entity. With regard to this source of cognition, the Cārvākas claim that there is nothing in perception which cannot be explained without the assumption of the soul, hence there are no grounds for proving the soul via postulation (A5.1).

Finally, the Cārvākas conclude that, since the soul is not in the range of one of the sources of cognition that give affirmative knowledge (*samupalambhakapramāṇa-*), the soul has become an object of the source of cognition named 'negation' (*abhāva-*),[24] which implies its non-existence (A6.1). It goes without saying that negation as a separate source of cognition is a highly problematic issue.[25] To claim that something is non-existent on the basis of the fact that human beings cannot know it is a bold claim. Nevertheless, accepting that one cannot negate the existence of an entity even when there are no grounds that prove its existence is undesirable too. In the end, most of us are convinced that there are no phoenixes, even though it is complicated to give watertight evidence for their non-existence. Therefore, the idea that one can accept the non-existence of things that cannot be proven by one of the sources of cognition that give affirmative knowledge is surely not far-fetched from a commonsensical point of view.

Refutation of the Negative Cārvāka Claim

The overall Cārvāka argument is a serious attack on the idea that human beings are endowed with souls. However, to invalidate the Cārvāka claim, Guṇaratna is not obliged to address every single argument of the Cārvākas. If he can show that there is at least one source of cognition that can prove the existence of the soul, the whole argument of the Cārvākas collapses. This is precisely Guṇaratna's strategy. In this paragraph, I will comment on several significant steps in Guṇaratna's refutation of the negative claim that the existence of the soul cannot be proven.

24 Literally, '*abhāva-*' means non-existence.

25 Most references to the Cārvākas claim that the Cārvākas only accept direct perception as a source of cognition. It is remarkable that the Cārvākas in Guṇaratna's text accept negation as a source of cognition. This supports the idea that Guṇaratna actually addresses a hypothetical position.

First of all, Guṇaratna states that direct perception can prove the existence of the soul (B1). For Guṇaratna, just as for the later Naiyāyikas, direct perception is not limited to perception via the external senses, such as vision and hearing, but refers to any direct apprehension, including self-awareness (GRIMES 1989/1996: 246). He claims that the idea 'I experience pleasure' arises in every living being, and that the perception of such an idea generates knowledge of the self (B1.1.1). He gives a keen reply to the sceptics, who might object that such an idea of the self has no real grounds, by pointing out that such a perception is similar to the perception of colour etc. (B1.1.2).[26] One knows that something is red by seeing that it is red. Likewise, one knows that there is a self by the apprehension of an idea that involves an 'I'.

To complete this argument, Guṇaratna has to show that this awareness of the self refers to the soul. In the *pūrvapakṣa*, the Cārvākas state that the word 'I' only refers to the body and not to the soul (A1.2.1). Guṇaratna refutes this idea on several grounds (B1.1.3, B1.2). One of his arguments is that the idea of a self must refer to a conscious entity, capable of self-awareness. He points out that the body is not a valid candidate since it is unconscious (B1.2.2). However, the Cārvākas claim that the body is not unconscious due to its connection with consciousness (A1.3.1).[27] Guṇaratna refutes this idea in the following way:

> [E]ven when the body possesses consciousness, the emergence of the idea of the self is only appropriate for that which is conscious itself, and not for that which is unconscious. For instance, the quality of being illuminating is not seen in a jar, which is not shining itself by its own nature, even when possessing the light of more than a thousand lamps, but it (i.e. the quality of being illuminating) only belongs to the lamp. Likewise, even when possessing consciousness the quality of being a knower does not belong to the body, which is insentient itself; therefore it belongs indeed to the soul and the emergence of the idea of the self is to be attributed to this soul.[28]

In short, Guṇaratna claims that unlike the soul, which is essentially conscious, there is no way in which the body can *be* conscious and can have knowledge of itself in the form of self-awareness. Even when consciousness emerges from the body, one

26 'Colour etc.' (*rūpādi-*) refers to the list of qualities as defined in the *Vaiśeṣika Sūtra* 1.1.6. It includes, among other things, colour, taste and smell (GOUGH 1873: 8).

27 At first sight, this seems a trivial claim. However, this claim makes sense in comparison with the Jaina perspective. For the Jainas, who are radical dualists, consciousness is only connected to the soul, and the body itself has no connection with consciousness.

28 B1.2.1, [49.107]. {143.12} *cetanāyoge 'pi svayaṃ cetanasyaivāhampratyayotpādo yuktaḥ, na tv acetanasya* | {143.14} *yathā parahsahasrapradīpaprabhāyoge 'pi svayam aprakāśasvarūpasya ghaṭasya prakāśakatvaṃ na dṛṣṭaṃ, kiṃ tu pradīpasyaiva, evaṃ cetanāyoge 'pi na svayam acetanasya dehasya jñātṛtvam, kiṃ tv ātmana eveti tasyaiva cāhaṃpratyayotpādaḥ.*

might say that the body *has* consciousness, but this does not imply that the quality of being conscious can be applied to the body. Hence, self-awareness reveals a self that is different from the body, and this is precisely the soul. Therefore, the soul can be proven by direct perception in the form of self-awareness.

In fact, Guṇaratna could end his argumentation at this point, since he has already reached the conclusion that the soul can be proven by one of the sources of cognition, and this is enough to oppose the general claim of the Cārvākas. However, argumentatively this would be a meagre strategy, since the audience might hesitate to accept Guṇaratna's argument about self-awareness. If one disagrees with the idea that the body cannot be conscious itself, one can still maintain that self-awareness is an awareness of one's body and not of the soul.

Therefore, Guṇaratna proceeds with a double strategy. First, he shows that the Cārvākas cannot provide a consistent account of their positive claim that consciousness emerges from the elements in the shape of a body (B1.3–6).[29] Second, he also discusses other sources of cognition in a further attempt to overthrow the negative claim that there are no valid sources of cognition that can prove the existence of the soul (B2–6).

Thus, after dealing with direct perception, Guṇaratna addresses inference, in accordance with the order of arguments in the *pūrvapakṣa*. As stated above, according to the Cārvākas, proving the existence of the soul via inferences is impossible since the soul is never perceived together with any invariable mark. The fundamental problem is of course that the soul itself is never seen (A2.3). However, since Guṇaratna claims that the soul is perceptible via self-awareness, he can lay this claim aside. In fact, Guṇaratna does not explicitly address this problem but simply proceeds with a series of inferences that prove the existence of the soul.

First, Guṇaratna describes several inferences in which agency is the central notion. For example:

I. The living body is directed by something which possesses efforts,
II. due to the quality of being the locus (*āśraya-*) of activity that is compliant to one's wishes,
III. like a chariot.[30]

In other words, from the fact that the body acts intentionally, one can infer that there is a director of the body, and this is the soul (B2.1).

After a list of somewhat similar arguments (B2.1–8), Guṇaratna argues that we can also know the existence of other souls on the basis of inference based on general observations, for which he gives the following argument (B2.10):

29 This argument will be analysed in the next paragraph.
30 B2.1, [49.123], {147.15[ii]}.

I. There is a soul also in the body of another,
II. on account of the observation of activity and inactivity towards respectively that which is desirable and that which is undesirable,
III. just as in one's own body.
IV. And activity and inactivity towards that which is desirable and that which is undesirable is observed in the body of another.
V. Therefore, the body of another is something that has a soul, due to the absence of these two (i.e. activity and inactivity) in the case of absence of the soul, like in the case of a jar.[31]

Since Guṇaratna's proof on the basis of direct perception involves self-awareness, he has to provide an additional argument if he wants to show that other bodies are endowed with a soul too. On the basis of the intentionality of the actions of other people, which corresponds with one's own intentional behaviour, he concludes that there are souls in other bodies as well.

Next, Guṇaratna claims that one can infer the existence of the soul from expressions that negate the existence of the soul (B2.9, B2.11). This argument presupposes a strong correspondence between language and reality. In short, his argument states that the qualification 'not-soul' (*ajīva-*) implies the existence of a soul (*jīva-*) somewhere (B2.9). He substantiates this theory by claiming that negations never entail the absolute non-existence of things, but only negate a relation between two entities (B2.11). For example, the negation that Jack is not in the house does not imply the non-existence of Jack, but only negates the conjunction (*saṃyoga-*) of the house with Jack (B2.11.3a).

Such an argument is dependent on a specific perspective on negations, which excludes universal negations and limits negation to a denial of relational aspects. From this perspective, although one can say that there is no pot in this place, it is impossible to state that there are no pots at all (B2.11.7). To avoid obvious problems, Guṇaratna explains that only simple words[32] with a clear etymology refer to real entities. Hence, one cannot object that the word 'non-horn-of-a-donkey', which is in Sanskrit one compound (*akharaviṣāṇa-*) proves the existence of a 'horn-of-a-donkey' (*kharaviṣāṇa-*) (B2.11.3).

After showing that the existence of the soul can be proven on the basis of several inferences, Guṇaratna states that the remaining sources of cognition, i.e. verbal testimony, analogy and postulation, are included in inference (B3–5).[33]

31 B2.10.1, [49.126]. {149.4[ii]} *paraśarīre 'py asty ātmā, iṣṭāniṣṭayoḥ pravṛttinivṛttidarśanāt, yathā svaśarīre* | {149.5} *dṛśyate ca paraśarīre iṣṭāniṣṭayoḥ pravṛttinivṛttī* | {149.6} *tasmāt sātmakaṃ, ātmābhāve tayor abhāvāt, yathā ghaṭa iti.*

32 I.e. words that are not compounds.

33 At first sight, this is a strange move. However, the inclusion of these sources seems to be derived from the Buddhist idea that the other sources of cognition are actually involved in a full inference (Phyllis Granoff, personal communication, 2 May 2015).

Finally, Guṇaratna attacks the Cārvāka claim by explaining that one cannot establish the non-existence of something via negation (B6). As explained, this source of cognition provides knowledge about the non-existence of things that are not within the range of any other source of cognition. His argument in this matter is hardly convincing from a contemporary point of view. He states that even though there is no source of cognition that enables us to measure the size of the Himalayas, the hell or demons, it is evident that these things exist. Therefore, he concludes that negation is an ambiguous (*anaikāntika-*) source of cognition. Although Guṇaratna's argument is problematic, especially since the existence of the hell and demons is far from evident for a Cārvāka opponent, one can agree with Guṇaratna on the logical grounds that not being able to know *x*, does not entail the non-existence of *x*.

In short, Guṇaratna counters the Cārvāka argument by showing that the soul can be known by direct and indirect sources of cognition. Even if not all of his arguments are irrefutable, the fact remains that Guṇaratna's refutation points to several complex philosophical problems for a fully materialistic or sceptical opponent, such as the experience of a phenomenal centre (B1), the justification of perceptual claims (B1.1.2), the relation between material bodies and consciousness (B1.3–6) and the problem of universal negations (B2.11).

Refutation of the Positive Cārvāka Claim

The previous paragraph has shown how Guṇaratna refutes the negative claim that there is no source of cognition for the existence of the soul. To strengthen his own position, he not only invalidates this claim but also shows the inadequacy of the alternative account of consciousness that the Cārvākas propound (B1.3–6). This is perhaps the most challenging part of Guṇaratna's whole refutation. In this paragraph, I will comment on the main steps in this part.

In the arguments discussed so far, the Cārvākas have mainly played the role of sceptics. However, they begin their argumentation as materialists, by claiming that consciousness is an effect of the elements that are transformed into the shape of a body (A0.1). To substantiate this claim, the Cārvākas point to the positive and negative concomitance of the body and consciousness, discussed above (A1.3.3).

To overthrow the Cārvāka position, Guṇaratna inserts a comprehensive discussion of their materialistic claims. His refutation consists of four elements. First, he denies that consciousness is an effect of the body (B1.3). Next, he shows that no source of cognition can prove that consciousness is an effect of the elements (B1.4). Further, Guṇaratna explains why consciousness cannot be produced from the elements only (B1.5). Finally, he points to the fact that the Cārvākas cannot consistently explain how the elements can transform into the shape of a body (B1.6).

To invalidate the statement that consciousness is an effect of the body, Guṇaratna points to the fact that a body in deep sleep is not accompanied by consciousness (B1.3.2). This counterexample is enough to deny the positive and negative concomitance of the body and consciousness, on which the Cārvāka argument is based.

The second part shows that it is impossible for the Cārvākas to acquire knowledge about the causal link between the elements and consciousness via direct perception or inference (B1.4). Guṇaratna states that consciousness cannot be perceived via direct perception, due to its lack of a form that can be recognised by one of the senses (B1.4.1a).

Moreover, the causal link between the elements and consciousness cannot be known via an internal perception (B1.4.1b). According to Guṇaratna, one can only ascertain a causal relation between two entities on the basis of the observation of their positive and negative concomitance. However, to establish the positive and negative concomitance of one's own body and consciousness, there needs to be a separate knower who can perceive this relation. However, in the framework of the Cārvākas, a human being is nothing more than the body and the consciousness that emerges from it. Hence, there is nothing in a human being that can perceive its own consciousness together with the body (B1.4.1c). Therefore, it is impossible for a Cārvāka to claim that the causal relation between a body and consciousness can be known via an internal perception.

Likewise, inference cannot prove that consciousness is an effect of the elements (B1.4.2). This argument resembles argument B1.3.2. Nevertheless, Guṇaratna changes his example by pointing to the fact that dead bodies have no consciousness (B1.4.2b). However, the Cārvākas could object that this counterexample is not convincing, given the fact that some elements, such as air, are missing in a corpse (B1.4.2bi). Guṇaratna replies to this in the following way:

> When the body is perforated, air is actually to be expected in a high degree there. Moreover, if there is an absence of consciousness due to an insufficiency of air in the body, then consciousness should be found there if air was supplied through the pelvis etc. But even when air is supplied there through the pelvis etc., consciousness is not found. [...] Further, if one objects: 'There is no consciousness in a dead body due to the absence of fire', then we may ask, why is consciousness not found when fire is added to the dead body?[34]

34 B1.4.2b^{i}, [49.113]. {145.1^{ii}} *sati śuṣire tatra vātaḥ sutarāṃ saṃbhāvyata eva* | {145.1^{iii}} *kiṃ ca* | *yadi tatra vāyuvaikalyāc caitanyasyābhāvaḥ, tato bastyādibhiḥ saṃpādite vāyau tatra caitanyam upalabhyeta* | {145.3} *na ca tatra tatsaṃpādite 'pi vāyau caitanyam upalabhyate.*

B1.4.2b^{iii}, [49.115]. {145.10} *atha tejaso 'bhāvān na mṛthāvasthāyāṃ caitanyam iti cet, tarhi tatra tejasy upanīte sati kathaṃ na cetanopalabhyate.*

This reply is a typical example of the humorous tone that characterises several parts of the debate. However, Guṇaratna continues his argumentation with a more fundamental critique on the causal relation between the elements and the body. If consciousness results merely from the elements, consciousness should not only emerge in living being but also in pots etc. (B1.5). The materialist opponent might think that this objection can be easily countered in the following way:

> What is said before does not allow for the mistake of such an over-implication (*atiprasaṅgadoṣa-*), because of our statement: 'Consciousness is apprehended on account of the elements that have inhalation and exhalation and that are transformed into the shape of a body.'[35]

This objection tries to avoid unwanted consequences by adding extra criteria to the elements that are responsible for the emergence of consciousness: they must be transformed into the shape of a breathing body.

But this move does not solve the problems for the Cārvākas, since Guṇaratna states that the Cārvākas cannot explain the transformation of the elements into a body (B1.6). In a clever analysis, Guṇaratna explains that there are only three logical options:

I. That transformation into the shape of a body is only dependent on the elements, beginning with earth etc.;
II. it is caused by another entity; or
III. it is without a cause.[36]

Guṇaratna refutes the first option by pointing out that if the elements are the cause of their own transformation into the shape of a body, this transformation should take place everywhere (B1.6.1). The Cārvāka might say at this point that the mere presence of elements is not enough, but that there must be a cooperating cause (*sahakārikāraṇa-*), such as a specific equilibrium of elements. Guṇaratna skilfully denies this possibility by showing that there are again two options: the additional requirements, such as a specific equilibrium, are fulfilled by the elements themselves or by a non-material cause. In the case that the elements are the cause of the required equilibrium, there is no reason why this requirement would not be fulfilled, given the presence of elements everywhere. The second option is also undesirable for the Cārvākas, since they do not admit any entity apart from the elements.

35 B1.6, [49.118]. {145.18[ii]} *nanu kāyākārapariṇāmaprāṇāpānaparigrahavadbhyo bhūtebhyaś caitanyam upalabhyata iti vacanān na pūrvokto 'tiprasaṅgadoṣāvakāśa iti cet.*

36 B1.6.0, [49.118]. {145.21[ii]} *sa kāyākārapariṇāmaḥ kiṃ pṛthivyādibhūtamātranibandhana uta vastvantaranimitta utāhetuka iti trayī gatiḥ.*

Likewise, to claim that the transformation into the shape of a body is caused by something apart from the elements is undesirable for the same reason.

The third option is excluded on the basis of the rule that entities without a cause are either permanently present or absent (B1.6.3). Thus, Guṇaratna shows that none of the three options for explaining the transformation into the shape of a body is acceptable within the materialistic framework of the Cārvākas.

To sum it up, Guṇaratna's attack on the Cārvāka perspective entails that consciousness cannot emerge from the elements only, that there is no way in which the Cārvākas can explain how the elements transform into the shape of a body and that even the body cannot be the cause of consciousness. Even if one disagrees with a part of Guṇaratna's refutation, there is no way in which the Cārvākas can escape from Guṇaratna's criticism without serious modifications to their theory.

Conclusion

As shown above, Guṇaratna has a two-pronged strategy to manoeuvre the debate in favour of the Jaina position. On the one hand, he opposes the Cārvāka claim—i.e., that there are no sources of cognition that can prove the existence of the soul—by claiming that the soul can be proven by both direct perception and inference. A crucial element in this part is his statement that the soul is perceptible by direct perception in the form of self-cognition. He reinforces this position by pointing to the undesirable epistemic consequences of denying the validity of perceptual judgements.[37] On the other hand, he attacks the materialist position of the Cārvākas by showing that they cannot prove that consciousness emerges from the material elements, given their rigid epistemological framework. Thus, by giving positive arguments for his own position and by eliminating an attractive rival explanation for the existence of consciousness, Guṇaratna gives a solid reply to opponents who deny the existence of the soul.

From a conceptual perspective, one can conclude that the Cārvākas play an important role in both the defence and the development of Guṇaratna's own account. Addressing the Cārvāka account is not only a means for Guṇaratna to reinforce his own theory, but actually leads to the philosophical exploration of topics that are only tangentially related to the initial subject matter. Thus, one can say that the Cārvāka position is an ideal sparring partner for a writer with a genuine philosophical inquisitiveness.

Nevertheless, I am fully aware that there remain some questions that cannot be answered from a conceptual perspective alone. For example, the fact that there are good argumentative reasons to discuss the Cārvāka voice in a philosophical exposition does not imply that these reasons were the only motive for Guṇaratna

37 B1.1.2.

to do so. Fully answering the question why Guṇaratna discussed the Cārvākas requires an investigation of Guṇaratna's historical circumstances and the textual tradition in which he wrote. Relevant questions in this respect are how his debate with the Cārvākas relates to the *TRD* as a whole, who his audience was and how the Cārvāka arguments in the *TRD* relate to the Cārvāka arguments in other texts. Although a definite answer as to what actually motivated Guṇaratna to enter into a debate with the Cārvākas requires research into these aspects, this article has made it clear that Guṇaratna was driven by argumentative reasons as well.

Appendix: Argumentative Summary of the Debate

This appendix contains a summary of the arguments in Guṇaratna's debate with the Cārvāka perspective on the soul, as given in *TRD* 49.98–134. The paraphrase of the arguments provides the reader with an overview of the content of the debate and forms the basis of the argumentative analysis in the second section of this paper.

To clarify the structure of the argumentation, I have added titles to the main sections of the arguments, shown in bold. Further, I have provided all argumentative steps with a number. The first part of the argumentation contains the *pūrvapakṣa*, i.e. the Cārvāka arguments. The numbers of these arguments are preceded by the letter 'A'. The numbers of the arguments in Guṇaratna's refutation of the *pūrvapakṣa*, commence with 'B'. The numbers of the Cārvāka arguments that are rendered in bold correspond to the bold numbers of Guṇaratna's counterarguments. For example, the arguments under **A1** are refuted by the arguments under **B1**. The numbers between square brackets refer to the paragraph numbers of Jain's edition of the *TRD*.

A. Exposition of the Cārvāka arguments against the existence of the soul

A0 **Introduction [49.98]**

A0.1 Consciousness is only caused by material elements (*bhūtāni-*) in the shape of a body.

A0.2 There is no soul since there is no source of cognition (*pramāṇa-*) for its existence.

A1 **Direct perception (*pratyakṣa-*) cannot prove the existence of the soul.**

A1.1 The soul is not in the range of the senses.

A1.2 The idea of the self does not prove the soul.

- **A1.2.1** The word 'I' relates merely to the body, as in 'I am fat'.
- **A1.2.2** The assumption of non-perceived causes leads to a complexity of conceptual construction (*kalpanāgaurava-*) and goes against the order of elements.

A1.3 The idea of the self relates to the body, which is the cause of consciousness.

- **A1.3.1** The idea of the self relates to the body, which is sentient due to its connection with consciousness.
- **A1.3.2** One cannot state that the soul is the cause of consciousness, since the soul is unknown.
- **A1.3.3** The body is the cause of consciousness, since it has positive and negative concomitance with consciousness.

A1.3.4 Dead bodies are no counterexamples, given the absence of fire and air therein.

A1.3.5 Consciousness does not emerge from the shape of a body.

A1.4 The soul is absolutely imperceptible (*atyantāpratyakṣa-*), unlike atoms, which acquire visibility when assembled.

A2 Inference (*anumāna-*) cannot prove the existence of the soul. [49.99]

A2.1 Inference is not a source of cognition.

A2.2 The invariable mark (*hetu-*) of the inference is invalid (*kālātyayāpadiṣṭa-*).

A2.3 The soul is never perceived together with an invariable mark. [49.100]

A2.3.1 The required prior perception of the invariable mark together with the probandum makes inference a superfluous source of cognition.

A2.4 Inference based on general observations (*sāmānyatodṛṣṭa-*) cannot prove the existence of the soul since nothing qualifies as an invariable mark for the soul. [49.101]

A3 Verbal testimony (*āgama-*) cannot prove the existence of the soul. [49.102]

A3.1 There are no credible persons who claim that they have seen the soul.

A3.2 Verbal testimonies are mutually contradictory (*parasparaviruddha-*).

A4 Analogy (*upamāna-*) cannot prove the existence of the soul. [49.103]

A4.1 There is no analogue for the soul.

A4.1.1 Time, ether, space etc. are invalid analogues, since their existence is also disputable.

A5 Postulation (*arthāpatti-*) cannot prove the existence of the soul. [49.104]

A5.1 All phenomena can be explained without the assumption of a soul.

A6 Negation (*abhāva-*) proves the non-existence of the soul. [49.105]

A6.1 Since none of the sources of cognition that give affirmative knowledge can prove the soul, the non-existence of the soul can be established by negation.

Conclusion A1–6: The soul is non-existent.

B. Guṇaratna's refutation of the Cārvāka arguments

B0 Introduction

B0.1 The above is untrue since there is a source of cognition for the existence of the soul. [49.106]

B1 Direct perception can prove the existence of the soul

B1.1 Direct perception can prove the soul by self-cognition (*svasaṃvedanapratyakṣa-*).

B1.1.1 The self is perceptible when one has the idea 'I experience pleasure', which involves an 'I'.

B1.1.2 If one says that the idea 'I experience pleasure' has no grounds, then the cognition of colour etc. is unsupported too.

B1.1.3 The soul is the foundation of the idea 'I experience pleasure'. The body cannot be the underlying object since this idea emerges from the internal organ (*antaḥkaraṇa-*) while the body is an object of the external senses (*bahiḥkaraṇa-*).

B1.2 The idea of the self (*ahaṃpratyaya-*) cannot relate to the body. [49.107]

B1.2.1 The idea of the self is only appropriate for a sentient entity and not for the body, which is unconscious.

B1.2.1a One cannot object that the body is sentient by its connection with consciousness. A jar that contains the light of a lamp is not itself illuminating; only the lamp is illuminating.

B1.2.2 Hence, the body cannot be a knower but the soul is the knower.

B1.2.3 The 'I' in 'I am fat' etc. is only metaphorically related to the body. In the case of a devoted servant one can think 'this servant is actually me'. Likewise, the body is like a servant for the soul. [49.108]

B1.3 Consciousness is not an effect of the body. [49.109]

B1.3.1 Consciousness has no positive and negative concomitance (*anvayavyatireka-*) with the body.

B1.3.2 Bodies in deep sleep etc. have no consciousness.

B1.3.3 Excellent consciousness is found in thin people and inferior consciousness in people with fat bodies.

B1.4 There is no source of cognition that can prove that consciousness is the effect of the elements. [49.110]

B1.4.1 Direct perception cannot prove that consciousness is the effect of the elements.

B1.4.1a Since consciousness is formless, it is impossible to perceive that consciousness is an effect of elements by direct perception.

B1.4.1b It also cannot be known by the cognition 'I am an effect of elements' since cause and effect can only be known by positive and negative concomitance, and this would require a separate knower apart from consciousness and the elements.

B1.4.1c The acceptance of a separate knower would allow for a proof for the existence of the soul.

B1.4.2 Inference cannot prove that consciousness is an effect of the elements. [49.111]

B1.4.2a Inference is not accepted as a source of cognition by the Cārvākas.

B1.4.2b One cannot infer that consciousness is an effect of the elements from the fact that there is only consciousness when there are elements; the elements are an ambiguous (*anaikāntika-*) invariable mark since there are cases where there are elements but no consciousness, such as in a dead body. [49.112]

B1.4.2bi One cannot object that a corpse is an invalid counterexample, by claiming that consciousness is only produced when there is a combination of the four elements and that a corpse lacks the element of air. For, even when air is added to the corpse, there arises no consciousness. [49.113]

B1.4.2bii One cannot object that air must be inhaled and exhaled, since even when inhalation and exhalation are brought about in a corpse, there arises no consciousness. Moreover, a yogin in meditation who has stopped his respiration has excellent consciousness. [49.114]

B1.4.2biii One cannot object that a corpse lacks the element of fire, since even when fire is added to the corpse, there arises no consciousness. [49.115]

B1.4.2biv If fire and air are necessary for the production of consciousness, one cannot explain that conscious worms are produced in a corpse. [49.116]

B1.5 Consciousness cannot be produced from the elements only. [49.117]

B1.5.1 Consciousness would emerge everywhere.

B1.5.2 There would be no difference between pots and human beings.

B1.6 The Cārvākas can also not claim that consciousness is produced from elements that are transformed into the shape of a breathing body, since such a transformation is impossible for the Cārvākas. [49.118]

B1.6.0 There are three possibilities: this transformation is caused by the elements, by something else or by nothing.

B1.6.1 If this transformation in the shape of the body is only dependent on the elements, this transformation must take place everywhere.

B1.6.1a One cannot object that an additional cause, such as a specific equilibrium (*sāmya-*) of the elements, is needed. Such an equilibrium must either be caused by the elements or by something else. In the first case, the transformation must still take place everywhere. In the second case, there must be another principle (*tattva-*), which is unacceptable for the Cārvākas. [49.119]

B1.6.2 If this transformation is caused by something different from the elements, there would be a possible proof for the soul.

B1.6.3 If this transformation takes place without a cause, there must be a continuous transformation of elements into bodies.

Conclusion B1.3–1.6: Consciousness is not an effect of the elements but is a quality of the soul.

B1.7 The soul is perceptible since its qualities are perceptible. [49.120]

B1.7.1 By self-cognition one can perceive the several types of cognition (remembrance etc.). These are qualities of the soul.

B1.7.2 One cannot claim that ether is a counterexample to the rule that something is perceptible when its qualities are perceptible, by pointing out that ether is imperceptible although sound, as its quality, is perceptible. Sound is a quality of matter and not of ether.

B1.7.3 One cannot object that the qualities, such as knowledge, belong to the body. The body cannot be the quality-possessor since it is perceptible and has form, unlike knowledge etc. [49.121]

B1.8 Denying that the soul can be perceived by the idea of the self is fallacious. [49.122]

B1.8.1 Such a denial is opposed by direct perception (*pratyakṣaviruddha-*).

B1.8.2 It is opposed by inference (*anumānaviruddha-*), which will be shown in B2.

B1.8.3 It is opposed to the people's opinion (*lokavirodha-*).

B1.8.4 Saying 'I am not I' is a contradiction between one's own words (*svavacanavirodha-*).

Conclusion B1.1–1.8: The soul can be proved by direct perception. It is not absolutely imperceptible (A1.4), since it is perceptible by self-cognition.

B2 Inference can prove the existence of the soul. [49.123]

B2.0 The soul can be proved by the following inferences (B2.1–2.8):

B2.1 The body has a director, since it acts according to one's wishes, like a chariot.

B2.2 The senses are used by an agent, since they are instruments (*karaṇatva-*), like an axe.

B2.3 Unlike clouds, the body has a fixed form and a beginning. Therefore, it has a creator, which is the soul.

B2.3.1 Mount Meru is not a counterexample, since it has no beginning.

B2.4 There is a director of the senses, since they are instruments, like a potter's wheel.

B2.5 There is an enjoyer of the body, since it is enjoyed, like a meal.

B2.6 Although the potter etc. in the previous inferences have a fixed form and are not eternal, these inferences are not opposed to our thesis. Since the soul, when it is in the world, has a certain shape by being covered with karmic matter (*karmapudgala-*). [49.124]

B2.7 Knowledge of colour must belong to something, since it is a quality, like colour etc. [49.125]

B2.8 Knowledge, pleasure, etc. require a proximate cause, since they are an effect.

B2.8.1 One cannot object that this is proving what has already been proved (*siddhasādhana-*) since it is rejected that the body is the proximate cause of knowledge etc.

B2.9 The word 'not-soul' (*ajīva-*) implies the existence of the soul (*jīva-*), since it is the negation of a simple word (*śuddhapada-*) which has a clear etymological explanation (*vyutpatti-*), just as 'non-jar' (*aghaṭa-*) implies the existence of a jar (*ghaṭa-*). However, this does not work for 'non-horn-of-a-donkey' (*akharaviṣāṇa-*) or 'non-*Ḍittha*'[38] (*aḍittha-*) since '*kharaviṣāṇa-*' is not a simple word but a compound and '*ḍittha-*' has no clear etymological explanation.

B2.10 The existence of other souls can be proved by inference based on general observation (*sāmānyatodṛṣṭānumāna-*). [49.126]

B2.10.1 There is a soul in other bodies, since the activity of these bodies aims at that which is desirable and avoids that which is undesirable, just as one's own body, unlike a jar.

B2.11 The negation 'There is no soul' implies the existence of the soul somewhere. [49.127]

B2.11.1 Something that is negated with regard to a certain place, implies the existence of that thing in another place, just as 'there is no jar here' implies the existence of a jar elsewhere.

B2.11.2 There are no negations of absolutely non-existent entities, such as a sixth element, distinct from the five elements (*pañcabhūta-*).

B2.11.3 The negation of a horn of a donkey (*kharaviṣāṇa-*) is not a counterexample, since negations do not establish the absolute non-existence of things, but negate only one of the following four aspects: conjunction (*saṃyoga-*), inherence (*samavāya-*), universality (*sāmānya-*) and particularity (*viśeṣa-*).

B2.11.3a 'Devadatta is not in the house' negates only the conjunction (*saṃyoga-*) of the house and Devadatta.

B2.11.3b 'There is no horn of a donkey' only negates the inherence (*samavāya-*) of the donkey and the horn.

B2.11.3c 'There is no other moon' only negates the universality (*sāmānya-*) of the moon.[39]

B2.11.3d 'There are no pearls whose size is like a jar' only negates a particularity (*viśeṣa-*) of the pearls, namely the size.

B2.11.4 'There is no soul' negates only the conjunction of the soul with something at a particular place, as in 'there is no soul in this body'. The absolute existence of the soul cannot be denied.

B2.11.5 One cannot object that since whatever is negated exists, someone consequently has mastery over the three worlds when this is negated. In that case, one negates only a particularity of a person. [49.128–129]

38 *Ḍittha* is the name of a man.

39 A universal needs more than one instantiation.

B2.11.6 Likewise, one cannot object that there must necessarily exist a fifth class of negation, when it is negated that there are five classes of negation. In that case, only 'being characterised by the number five' is negated. [49.128–129]

B2.11.7 To omit fallacies, the theory concerning negations claims that 'whatever is negated, that exists in general' but not 'whatever is negated somewhere, that exists in that place.' [49.130–131]

B2.11.7a The conjunctions of Devadatta and the house etc. are non-existent but exist in other things.

B2.11.7b The qualities 'my mastery over the three worlds' and 'being characterised by five' exist respectively in Tīrthaṅkaras and the chief Vaimānika gods.

B2.11.7c One can negate the existence of the soul somewhere but not everywhere.

B2.12 From the recollection (*anusmaraṇa-*) of things when the senses are not functioning, one can infer the existence of the soul. [49.132]

Conclusion B2.1–2.12: The soul can be proved by inference.

B3–5 The existence of the soul can be proved by verbal testimony (*āgama-*), analogy (*upamāna-*) and postulation (*arthāpatti-*). [49.133]

B3.1 The foregoing shows that the existence of the soul can be established by inference. Since verbal testimony, analogy and postulation are forms of inference, these sources of cognition can prove the existence of the soul too.

B6 Negation (*abhāva-*) is an invalid means of cognition. [49.134]

The non-existence of things cannot be established on account of the inapplicability of the five sources of cognition that give affirmative knowledge, since there is no source of cognition for the measure of the Himalaya, the hell and demons. However, these entities do exist. Hence, to conclude that something is non-existent when the five sources of cognition are inapplicable is ambiguous (*anaikāntika-*).

Conclusion B1–6: The soul can be proved by the sources of cognition.

References

Abbreviations

- *ṢDS* = *Ṣaḍdarśanasamuccaya* by Haribhadra Sūri
- *TRD* = *Tarkarahasyadīpikā* by Guṇaratna Sūri
- *DCH* = D. Chattopadhyaya & M. K. Gangopadhyaya's (1990/2006) *Cārvāka/Lokāyata*
- *MKJ* = Mahendra Kumar JAIN's (1970) *Ṣaḍ-darsana-samuccaya of Ācārya Haribhadra Sūri With the Commentary Tarka-rahasya-dīpikā* ...

- *LS* = Luigi Suali's (1905–1914) *Shaḍdarśana-samuchchaya by Haribhadra with Guṇaratna's Commentary Tarkarahasya-dīpikā*

Punctuation and symbols

- Numbers between braces refer to *LS*, e.g., {138.6^{i}} corresponds with Suali's text at page 138, line 6, first sentence.
- Numbers between square brackets, e.g. [49.98], refer to the section numbers in *MKJ*. The numbers before the full stop refer to the stanzas of the *ṢDS*.
- Square brackets '[ ]' in the translation indicate my additions to the text.
- Parentheses '( )' in the translation contain my clarifications.

Athalye, Y. (1974). *Tarka-Saṃgraha of Annambhaṭṭa* (2nd ed.). Pune: Bhandarkar Oriental Institute. (Original work published 1897.)

Balcerowicz, P. (2014). Jayarāśi. In Edward N. Zalta (Ed.), *The Stanford Encyclopedia of Philosophy* (Fall 2014 Edition). Retrieved from <http://plato.stanford.edu/archives/fall2014/entries/jayaraasi/>.

Bhattacharya, R. (2012a). Cārvāka Fragments: A New Collection. In R. Bhattacharya, *Studies on the Cārvāka/Lokāyata* (pp. 69–104). London: Anthem Press.

—. (2012b). *Studies on the Cārvāka/Lokāyata.* London: Anthem Press.

Bronkhorst, J. (2012). Free Will and Indian Philosophy. *Antiquorum Philosophia, 6*, 19–29.

Chattopadhyaya, D., & Gangopadhyaya, M. K. (2006). *Cārvāka/Lokāyata: An Anthology of Source Materials and Some Recent Studies.* New Delhi: Indian Council of Philosophical Research. (Original work published 1990.)

Dasgupta, S. (1922). *A History of Indian Philosophy* (vol. 1). Cambridge: Cambridge University.

Del Toso, K. (2011). Is Cognition an Attribute of the Self or it Rather Belongs to the Body? Some Dialectical Considerations on Udbhaṭabhaṭṭa's Position against Nyāya and Vaiśeṣika. *Open Journal of Philosophy, 1*(2), 48–46.

Franco, E. (1994). *Perception, Knowledge and Disbelief. A Study of Jayarāśi's Scepticism.* Delhi: Motilal Banarsidass.

—. (2011). Cārvāka/Lokāyata. In K. A. Jacobsen, *Brill's Encyclopedia of Hinduism III* (pp. 629–642). Leiden: Brill.

Frauwallner, E. (2006). Materialism. In D. &. Chattopadhyaya, *Cārvāka/Lokāyata: An Anthology of Source Materials and Some Recent Studies* (pp. 474–486). New Delhi: Indian Council of Philosophical Research.

Gough, A. E. (1873). *The Vaiśeshika Aphorisms of Kaṇ*āda. Benares: E.J. Lazarus.

Grimes, J. (1996). *A Concise Dictionary of Indian Philosophy* (revised reprint). Albany: State University of New York. (Original work published 1989.)

Jain, M. K. (2009). *Ṣaḍ-darsana-samuccaya of Ācārya Haribhadra Sūri With the Commentary Tarka-rahasya-dīpikā of Guṇaratna Sūri and Laghuvṛtti of Somatilaka Sūri and an Avacūrṇi* (7th ed.). New Delhi: Bhāratīya Jñānapīṭha. (Original work published 1970.)

MATILAL, B. (1976). *Śaśadhara's Nyāyasiddhāntadīpa with Ṭippana by Guṇaratna Sūri (L.D. Series 56).* Ahmedabad: L. D. Institute of Indology.

NICHOLSON, A. J. (2010). *Unifying Hinduism: Philosophy and Identity in Indian Intellectual History.* New York: Columbia University Press.

OBERHAMMER, G. (1991). *Terminologie der Frühen Philosophischen Scholastik in Indien* (vol. 1). Vienna: Verlag der Österreichischen Akademie der Wissenschaften.

OBERHAMMER, G., PRETS, E., & PRANDSTETER, J. (1996). *Terminologie der Frühen Philosophischen Scholastik in Indien* (vol. 2). Vienna: Verlag der Österreichischen Akademie der Wissenschaften.

—. (2006). *Terminologie der Frühen Philosophischen Scholastik in Indien* (vol. 3). Vienna: Verlag der Österreichischen Akademie der Wissenschaften.

PATIL, P. G. (2010). History, Philology, and the Philosophical Study of Sanskrit Texts. *Journal of Indian Philosophy*, 163–202.

QVARNSTRÖM, O. (1999). Haribhadra and the Beginnings of Doxography in India. In A. Sushil Kumar, N. K. Wagle, O. Qvarnström & N. Balbir, *Approaches to Jaina Studies: Philosophy, Logic, Rituals and Symbols* (pp. 169–210). Toronto: University of Toronto, Centre for South Asian Studies.

RHYS DAVIDS, T. (2006). On Lokāyata. In D. Chattopadhyaya & M. K. Gangopadhyaya, *Cārvāka/Lokāyata: An Anthology of Source Materials and Some Recent Studies* (pp. 369–376). New Delhi: Indian Council of Philosophical Research.

RORTY, R. (1984). The Historiography of Philosophy: Four Genres. In R. Rorty, J. Schneewind & Q. Skinner (Eds.), *Philosophy in History* (pp. 49–75). Cambridge: Cambridge University Press.

SAṀGHAVĪ, S., & PĀRĪKH, R. C. (1940). Introduction. *Tattvopaplavasimha of Shri Jayarasi Bhatta (Gaekwad Oriental Series 87)* (pp. i–xiv). Baroda: Oriental Institute.

SHASTRI, I. C. (1990). *Jaina Epistemology.* Varanasi: P. V. Research Institute.

STCHERBATSKY, T. (2006). History of Materialism in India. In D. Chattopadhyaya & M. K. Gangopadhyaya, *Cārvāka/Lokāyata: An Anthology of Source Materials and Some Recent Studies* (pp. 432–440). New Delhi: Indian Council of Philosophical Research.

STEINKELLNER, E. (2013). *Dharmakīrtis frühe Logik: Annotierte Übersetzung der logischen Teile von Pramāṇavārttika 1 mit der Vṛtti* (vol. 1). Tokyo: The International Institute for Buddhist Studies.

SUALI, L. (1905–1914). *Shaḍdarśana-Samuchchaya by Haribhadra with Guṇaratna's Commentary Tarkarahasya-Dīpikā.* Calcutta: Asiatic Society of Bengal.

—. (1908). Matériaux pour servir à l'histoire du matérialisme indien. *Le Muséon, 9*(1), 277–298.

TATIA, N. (2011). *That Which Is = Tattvārtha Sūtra.* New Haven: Yale University.

TUCCI, G. (2006). A Sketch of Indian Materialism. In D. Chattopadhyaya & M. K. Gangopadhyaya, *Cārvāka/Lokāyata: An Anthology of Source Materials and Some Recent Studies* (pp. 384–393). New Delhi: Indian Council of Philosophical Research.

VAN DEN BOSSCHE, F. (1998). Jain Arguments Against Nyāya Theism: A Translation of the Īśvarotthāpaka Section of Guṇaratna's Tarka-Rahasya-Dīpikā. *Journal of Indian Philosophy, 26*(1), 1–26.

The Benign Overlord and the Restorer of Dharma

Two Cases of Viṣṇu as Political Expression in Ancient Khmer Inscriptions and Images

J. M. A. Eijsermans

Stories about Viṣṇu were a popular theme for ancient Khmer patrons and artists during the Angkorean period (ca. 802–1431 CE) of mainland Southeast Asia. In many of these stories, the (Vedic) gods ask him to aid in a specific situation. In order to help the gods, Viṣṇu takes on a specific form (an *avatāra*) that fits the situation. It often, but not always, entails fighting against beings that oppose the (Vedic) gods: *daitya*s, *asura*s and the like, bent on upsetting the *dharma* and denying the gods their proper worship.[1] Viṣṇu himself says the following about this: he manifests himself (as an *avatāra*) whenever *dharma* is on the decline and *adharma* is on the rise—to protect what is right, to destroy the wicked and to establish *dharma* (Bhagavad-Gīta 4.7–8). This reveals that the *avatāra* paradigm relies on the trope of restoring or establishing *dharma*. Viṣṇu thus performs functions not unlike the duties of a king: maintaining order and balance, protecting the righteous and fighting off enemies. It is therefore no surprise that ancient Khmer inscriptions that praise the king frequently compare him to Viṣṇu. Furthermore, the temples of the Angkorean kingdom, most of them under royal patronage, feature many depictions of stories about Viṣṇu.

The narrative temple art depicting stories of Viṣṇu—or other stories, for that matter—lacks a coherent narrative sequence.[2] There is also no apparent

1 Archaeologist Giovanni Verardi draws the conclusion that, in Śaivite and Vaiṣṇavite stories, the gods' enemies that upset the *dharma* represent (early) Buddhist and Jain communities (Verardi 2003). However, as fitting as it may seem within the Indian geographic and temporal boundaries of Verardi's discussion, this might not be applicable to the Angkorean Kingdom, certainly not in the later period, when an openly Buddhist king, Jayavarman VII, had no qualms about depicting many of Viṣṇu's deeds.

2 This is best evidenced by the discussion about the bas-reliefs on the walls of the galleries around Angkor Wat, which, for the sake of brevity, I will not reproduce here. Suffice it to say that the initial assumption—that the bas-reliefs have a narrative sequence in line with circumambulation, either clockwise or counterclockwise—has been dismissed by most scholars by now.

iconographic programme connecting the various storytelling elements of this visual art, consisting mostly of bas-reliefs on large wall panels and on lintels and pediments over doorways. I propose to interpret the stories of Viṣṇu in Angkorean temple art as visual counterparts of their occurrence in the inscriptional discourse of *praśastis*:[3] these praises present the king as equal to Viṣṇu, or even surpassing him, placing thematic emphasis on specific royal virtues, such as military prowess, righteousness or benevolence. The depictions of the stories support such an emphasis in a visual way.

In this paper, I will highlight two examples that not only demonstrate the use of stories about Viṣṇu as a (visual) eulogy, but which also move beyond mere praise and contain a deeper political meaning.[4] First, I will discuss the story of the churning of the milk ocean (*samudramanthana*) in the inscriptions and art praising king Jayavarman VII (r. 1181/2–ca. 1218/9 CE). I will outline how this particular story became the most popular royal encomium in the Angkorean period in the first place (thus it will also serve as a general model for these comparisons), and then highlight how it received a specific emphasis for Jayavarman VII, relating to his mode of rulership. I will also demonstrate the same emphasis in another example: Jayavarman VII being compared to Krisṇa lifting Mount Govardhana. Second, I will discuss the story of Viṣṇu in his Varāha *avātara*, a giant boar, rescuing the earth goddess. Although this story is an excellent example of the 're-establishing *dharma*' trope, it does not occur often in Khmer inscriptions and art. However, I will show that, when it does occur—in a specific eulogy of king Sūryavarman II (r. 1113–1150 CE)—it serves as an unequivocal political statement beyond superficial royal praise.

The *samudramanthana* in Khmer inscriptions and art

The *samudramanthana* story found its way into the *praśastis* and art of many Khmer rulers, Vaiṣṇava or not, with the same general elements.[5] The story tells how the *devas* and *asuras* cooperated to obtain *amṛta*. They churned the ocean of milk, using Mount Maṇḍara as a churning stick and the giant *nāga* Vāsuki as a rope. Viṣṇu supported the mountain in the form of a giant turtle, his Kūrma *avatāra*. At the same time, in his own form, he physically contributed to the churning, and oversaw the process. The churning produced a number of treasures (*ratnas*), such as the heavenly nymphs (*apsarases*), the elephant Airāvata, the Kaustubha jewel and Lakṣmī. Finally, the desired *amṛta* arose.

3 The inscriptions are the only other category of evidence from the Angkorean period, aside from the narrative reliefs, in which we find Viṣṇu stories. All other writing from the time was presumably done on perishable material, and is now lost due to the tropical climate.

4 In doing so, I draw inspiration from Indologist Heinrich von Stietencron, who proposes a political layer of meaning for the depiction of certain *avatāras* in Indian religious art (Von Stietencron 2005).

5 A more detailed overview of its occurrences can be found in Madeleine Giteau (1951).

The *praśasti* comparisons to the story generally follow this formula: the king in battle is like Viṣṇu presiding over the churning; the battle is the ocean; the defeat of the king's enemies is the churning; and the king, like Viṣṇu, begets the *ratna*s that result from the churning. An early example, a *praśasti* of King Indravarman I (r. 877/8–889/90 CE), illustrates this perfectly (Preah Ko stele, K.713, stanza 13, in Cœdès 1937: 1–20)[6]:

> *kṣīrodasāramathanād āharantaṃ śriyaṃ harim*
> *jahāseva prabhūtaśrīr*
> *yyo bhūbhṛnmathanena tu*[7]
>
> [Indravarman I] whose *śrī* was verily arisen from the churning of kings, made Hari a laughing stock indeed, [Hari] who obtained *śrī* [merely] from the churning of the essence of the milk ocean.

Another example is found in the praise of King Rājendravarman (r. 944–968 CE) on the Pre Rup stele (K.806, stanza 32, in Cœdès 1937: 1–81):

> *raṇārṇṇavād yasya jayāmṛtena*
> *jātaṃ yaśaḥ kosthubaratnam ārdram*
> *trailokyam āhlādayati tridhaikaṃ*
> *mūrttaṃ murārer hṛdayaṃ mudeva*
>
> The fresh glory of [Rājendravarman], the Kaustubha jewel arisen from the ocean of a battle, gladdens the three worlds with the *amṛta* of [his] victory as joy gladdens the single heart of Mura's enemy [Viṣṇu] thrice.

---

6 It is worth noting that Giteau (1951: 142) thinks that stanza 22 of the Preah Ko stele (K.713, stanza 22, in Cœdès 1937: 1–21) also alludes to the churning of the milk ocean:

> *dustare yena yuddhābdhau*
> *chinnadṛptārimastakaiḥ*
> *svapakṣatāraṇāyeva*
> *vidadhe setuvandhanam*
>
> [Indravarman I] arranged the construction of a bridge [or: 'dam'], in the difficult-to-traverse ocean that is battle, using the severed heads of [his] proud enemies, as if for the traverse of [his] own troops.

The crucial element is taking the compound *yuddhābdhau* as specifically likening battle to the ocean of milk. The construction of the bridge or dam (using his enemies' heads), however, could indicate any body of water and has little to do specifically with the ocean of milk. Therefore, in my opinion, this verse is not an allusion to the churning story.

7 This and the following transcriptions are reproduced *verbatim*, with the exception that, where applicable, an apostrophe is inserted to indicate an *avagraha*, and that the palatal sibilant ç (as it's denoted in French editions) is replaced with *ś*.

Figure 1: Highlight of Uccaiḥśravas and Lakṣmī on a lintel depicting the churning of the ocean of milk at the Phimai National Museum. Photo by author.

When depicting this story, Khmer artists usually show Viṣṇu overseeing (and sometimes lending the strength of his arms in aiding) the *deva*s and *asura*s pulling Vāsuki around Mount Maṇḍara. The mountain is usually depicted as an actual churning stick. Where its base rests on Kūrma's back—where the churning takes place—we see Lakṣmī and the horse Uccaiḥśravas arising, but not (yet) the *amṛta*. Figure 1 shows a clear example of this.

The *samudramanthana* in the inscriptions and art of Jayavarman VII

Although he was a Buddhist king, the formulaic use of the *samudramanthana* (among other Viṣṇu stories) also made its way into the art of Jayavarman VII. During his rule (1181/2–ca.1218/9 CE), however, a specific addition was made to the formula as described above. In every case, the *amṛta* and other *ratna*s (most notably Lakṣmī) serve to illustrate victory. Another, subtler use of *amṛta* is that, once obtained, Viṣṇu distributes it among the gods, granting them immortality. In the same fashion, it is easy to imagine the king distributing *amṛta* among his subjects, granting them welfare. The inscriptional stele set up to commemorate the inauguration of the Ta Prohm temple, the temple Jayavarman VII commissioned to honour his mother, uses this element. It is composed by Jayavarman VII's son, Sūryakumāra.[8] First, there is the stock comparison of the victorious king as Viṣṇu

8 A similar inscription was composed by another son, Vīrakumāra, to commemorate the inauguration of Preah Khan, the temple in honour of Jayavarman VII's father.

in the story of the churning of the milk ocean (Ta Prohm stele, K.273, stanza 21, in Cœdès 1906: 52):

āsphālitabhramitavairikarīndraśaila-
rājo bhujor ativalena raāmvudhau yah
lakṣmīsitadviradarājaturaṅgaratna-
prāpto harer jaladhīmanthanam anvakārṣit

By striking and stirring around, by the strength of his arms, the king of the mountains that was the war elephant of the enemy, in the ocean of a battle, [Jayavarman VII]—by obtaining Lakṣmī, the white elephant, the royal horse and the jewel [or: 'the jewels that are Lakṣmī, the white elephant and the royal horse']—imitated Hari's churning of the ocean.

Then, another verse of the same inscription talks about the distribution of *amṛta* (Ta Prohm stele, K.273, stanza 28, in Cœdès 1906, 53; emphasis mine):

campāgatasya yudhi yasya gṛhītamukta-
tadbhūdharasya caritāmṛtam anyabhūpaiḥ
śrutvā natair hṛtam ivāñjalibhir varāṅge
siktam mahohutavahoditatāpaśāntyai

Upon hearing of the *amṛta* of the deed of [Jayavarman VII], who had gone to Champa [and] captured and [subsequently] released the king of that country in battle, the other kings bowed to him with *añjāli*s and, as it were, took [this *amṛta*] and sprinkled it on the head to pacify the heat that was born from the flame of his glory.

The emphasized *gṛhītamuktatadbhūdhara(sya)* in this quote appears to be an allusion to a verse from Kālidāsa's *Raghuvaṃśa* (4.43; emphasis mine):[9]

gṛhītapratimuktasya sa dharmavijayī nṛpaḥ
śriyaṃ mahendranāthasya jahāra na tu medinīm

That ruler [Raghu] who conquers by *dharma*, took the *śrī* but not the land of the king [of] Mahendra, whom he captured and subsequently released.

Both verses convey a clear message: the conquered kings are captured. but (instead of being killed) are released because their conquerors, Jayavarman VII

9 Another example, quoted below, is stanza 27 from the Ban That inscription, borrowing the term *jagadekanāthaḥ* from *Raghuvaṃśa* 5.23. For more on the influence of Kālidāsa's poetry and other Indian literary works on Khmer inscriptions, see for example Goodall (2013).

and Raghu, are benevolent and true to *dharma*. Although verse 28 does not mention the churning—and, indeed, might not be related to verse 21—it does use *amṛta*. The emphasis is not on Jayavarman VII obtaining *śrī* (as with Raghu), but on the distribution of this *amṛta* among yet 'other' kings (vassals are no doubt meant here).

The verse in the inscription is about a historical fact: Cham inscriptions and Chinese historiographies corroborate the capture of a Cham king (Aymonier 1891: 48; Pelliot 1902: 130; Maspéro 2002: 97–98; Schweyer 2007: 67). The use of factual information is a rare feature in the discourse of Khmer *praśasti*s, where 'the expressive and performative functions of the inscriptions must be seen to be as important as the informational and constantive' (Pollock 2006: 147).[10] This lends some more weight to the argument that *amṛta* has some significance here.

The depiction of *amṛta* in a *samudramanthana* bas-relief situated on Jayavarman VII's state temple, the Bayon, provides even more supporting evidence for the symbolic significance of *amṛta*. The pot of *amṛta* rests on Vāsuki's back, on the side of the *asura*s (figure 2). This is one of the rare instances, possibly the only one, when the *amṛta* is depicted. Giteau has observed this as well: '... l'objet de barattage, *l'*amrita *n'apparaît, semble-t-il, qu'au Bayon* ou un grand flacon entouré d'une sorte de guirlande est posé sur le naga entre les Asuras et le pivot' (Giteau 1951: 151; emphasis mine).[11] I have noticed two other instances that feature a pot: one is a pediment at Preah Vihear (seen in person), the other a lintel at Ta Mau (in Ang Chouleаn's chapter in *Bayon: New Perspectives*).[12] However, these pots are located at the very base of the churning stick, between Uccaiḥśravas and Lakṣmī. This could mean they are mere churning pots, put in place as a visual emphasis of the act of churning. The Bayon pot is unique in that it is the only one ornamented with a garland and placed in this position, on Vāsuki's back, between a four-armed Viṣṇu and the *asura*s. Giteau (1951: 151) interprets this placement as depicting the moment when the *asura*s try to take the *amṛta* for themselves (at which they do not succeed: Viṣṇu thwarts their attempt, and it goes to the *deva*s instead). If we accept this interpretation, is the underlying message then that only those who are subservient to Viṣṇu, viz. the king, can obtain *amṛta*?

---

10 This, Sheldon Pollock says, was not recognised by the 'skilled French philologists' who 'never ceased to complain of the sheer inanity of *praśasti* texts' (Pollock 2006: 147). Indeed, George Cœdès laments that the *praśasti* in the Ta Prohm inscription 'ressemble à tous les morceaux du même genre' save for 'un seul fait positif' (Cœdès 1906: 46), i.e. the mention of this factual information.

11 However, immediately after, Giteau mentions other occurrences of *amṛta*: the lintel at Kutiśvara shows 'un personnage masculin ... debout à côté de Vishnu, tenant dans ses mains des objets indistincts' which she thinks to be 'Dhanvantari ... tenant sans doute l'amrita' (Giteau 1951: 151–52); the lintel of Prasat Lobok has a figure flying downwards towards Viṣṇu, who could also be Dhanvantari—although 'l'état du linteau ne permet pas de distinguer s'il tient quelque chose dans ses mains' (Giteau 1951: 152). Technically, however, this is not a contradiction, because these instances depict the bearer of the *amṛta*, not the *amṛta* itself.

12 Both images can be found in Chouléan (Chouléan 2007: 374, fig. 9 and 11).

Figure 2: Highlight of the pot of amṛta in the Bayon bas-relief depicting the churning of the ocean of milk. Photo by author.

Kṛṣṇa lifting Mount Govardhana in the inscriptions and art of Jayavarman VII

Modern historians describe the polity of Angkor—and other prominent Southeast Asian polities—as a mandala, or a sphere of influence around a centre of domination.

Figure 3: Pediment at Preah Khan, depicting Kṛṣṇa lifting Mount Govardhana. Photo by author.

These spheres covered various subsidiary states that we can think of as tributary kingdoms. A virtue of falling under the sphere of Jayavarman VII's influence is alluded to in the use of another Viṣṇu story: as Kṛṣṇa lifts Mount Govardhana to protect a group of cowherds from Indra's torrential rainstorm, Jayavarman VII offers his protection (in war) to the kings that come to him. The following verse from one of Jayavarman VII's other panegyrics (Prasat Crung stele, K.288, stanza 99, in Cœdès 1952: 4–218) articulates this:

> *vikrāntasiṃhākulayuddhakaṣṭe*
> *sāndreṣuvṛṣṭivyacitaś śrito yam*
> *kṛṣṇaṃ yathonmūlitabhūdharendraṃ*
> *chāyāṃ yayau gopagaṇo gatādhiḥ*

> In the hardship of battle that was crowded with lion-like warriors, the troop of kings, covered in a dense rain of arrows, turned to him [Jayavarman VII] and went into [his] shelter, as the troop of shepherds [went to] Kṛṣṇa, who uprooted the king of mountains [to offer them shelter].

This story is frequently depicted as follows in the art of the temples under Jayavarman VII's patronage:[13] Kṛṣṇa is lifting the mountain with one hand, with ease, while around him the cowherds and animals gather. Figure 3 is an example of a pediment with these features.

Varāha in an inscription about Sūryavarman II

An inscriptional stele at a temple in the village of Ban That in Laos, some 30 kilometres southwest of the town of 'Bassac' (now called Champassak) (HARMAND 1879: 1), contains information about the succession of the first kings in the Mahidharapura dynasty: Jayavarman VI (r. 1080–1107 CE), Dharaṇīndravarman (r. 1107–1113 CE) and Sūryavarman II (r. 1113–1150 CE). The closing line mentions that the temple's donor, Subhadra/Mūrdhaśiva, composed the inscription. The stele is partly damaged. The legible parts reveal that the inscription has the form of a poetic account (*ākhyāna*) in three (or perhaps four) chapters (*sarga*s), inscribed on the stele's four sides. The west side, where the third *sarga* begins, is almost intact. It details Subhadra's career as the noble *paṇḍit* of the king of kings (*śrībhūpendrapaṇḍita*) for the first three kings in the Mahidharapura dynasty. Lines 1 to 26 detail Subhadra's matrilineage (*mātṛvaṃśa*), his path towards becoming *śrībhūpendrapaṇḍita* and what honours Jayavarman [VI] bestowed upon him. Lines 27 to 29 recount how Subhadra stayed on serving Jayavarman VI's successor, his older brother Dharaṇīndravarman. Lines 30 to 35, then, are the last on this side, before the text becomes mostly illegible on the following (south) side. They form the eulogy of Sūryavarman II.

The eulogy fits into the paradigm of Viṣṇu as the establisher of *dharma*: it alludes to the importance of *dharma* for kingship and compares Sūryavarman II to Varāha, Viṣṇu's giant boar *avatāra,* who rescues the earth goddess from the *daitya* Hiraṇyākṣa's captivity. Essentially, this story is about Viṣṇu's restoring *dharma* in the world (VON STIETENCRON 2005: 13). Sūryavarman II's comparison to Varāha takes the following form in the Ban That inscription (K.364, *sarga* 3, stanza 34, in FINOT 1912: 18):

dhātrīṃ dviṣaddhvaṃsanasindhumagnāṃ
dordaṅ[ṣ]ṭrayoddhṛtya dhṛtākṣatāṅgīm
pūrvvāṃ vyavasthām ucitāṃ yathāvat
pratyarppayām āsa yathā varāhaḥ

13 For a detailed discussion of the occurrence of Kṛṣṇa lifting Mount Govardhana in Khmer art, see NARAYANAN (2015).

After taking out the earth, plunged into the sea that was the destruction caused by enemies [or: 'the destruction of [his] enemies'], in his tusk-like arms, her seized body uninjured [or: 'her whole body seized'], he rightly restored her to her proper, previous state, in the manner [that] Varāha [rescued/restored the earth].

The focus in this stanza seems to be on Sūryavarman II's formidable prowess, and indeed the preceding stanzas build up to this. The tone of these passages is best illustrated by the recounting of Sūryavarman II's coming to power (which, as we will see, forms a sharp contrast with the succession between the other two kings) (Ban That stele, K.364, *sarga* 3, stanza 30, in Finot 1912: 17):

tato 'vanīndro nṛpayos tayoś śrī-
narendralakṣmyā nijabhāgineyyāḥ
sūnur bhavānyā iva kārttikeyo
durvvāravidviḍḍviradendrasiṅhaḥ

Then, a lord of the earth [came], the son of *śrī* Narendralaksmī, the daughter of those two kings' own sister, like Kārtikeya [was the son] of Bhavānī, a lion among the war elephants that were his irrepressible enemies.

Aside from some general praise (kings bow their heads to the feet of Sūryavarman II, who is a shining moon to his people), the inscription shines some light on how Sūryavarman II came to be this rescuer of the earth, comparable to Varāha. It tells of the desire arising in him for the 'glory of kingship' (*kularājalakṣmī*) that pertains to his family. That glory, however, now resides under the subjection of *two* rulers (*dvipatyadhīnatvam*) (Finot 1912: 18). The inscription does not make clear who these two rulers are, but it stands to reason that one of them is Sūryavarman II's great-uncle Dharaṇīndravarman, his direct predecessor in the Mahidharapura line of kings, perhaps even the very 'enemy king' that the inscription says he kills in battle (Finot 1912: 18). Sūryavarman II is, at any rate, successful in overthrowing them both.

The verses that praise Dharaṇīndravarman directly precede the ones that, ultimately, render Sūryavarman II the restorer of proper *dharma*. They form a poignant contrast when they describe how Dharaṇīndravarman, unlike Sūryavarman II, does not desire the throne (but accepts it anyway) and how the inscription's stated author, the royal *paṇḍit* Subhadra, finds an apt pupil in Dharaṇīndravarman when teaching him *dharma*:

(1) Ban That stele, K.364, *sarga* 3, stanza 27, in Finot 1912: 17.
rājyāya nissprhayitāpi tato 'nukampān
nākam vrajaty avaraje jagadekanāthe

abhyarthitas tanubhṛtām nikarair anāthaiś
śāsan nayena dharaṇīn dharaṇīndravarmma

Then, out of compassion, Dharaṇīndravarman, who not even desired kingship, when his younger brother, the sole king of the world, had gone to heaven, requested by the flocks of people in want of a protector, ruled the earth in a prudent manner.

(2) Ban That stele, K.364, *sarga* 3, stanza 29, in Finot 1912: 17.
dharmmapriyaś cākhilavāṅmayajñaṃ
dharmmapravaktāram amānayad yam
yatrānurāgo (NomSgMasc?) *manaso* (GenSgMasc) *hi tasya* (GenSgMasc/Neut)
prāyeṇa saṅkīrttanam eva ratyai

And [Dharaṇīndravarman,] who holds *dharma* dear, honoured [Subhadra,] who is knowledgeable in all of the rhetoric, [his] teacher in *dharma*; for when, in general, the passion of one's mind is expounded, [this leads] to pleasure.

From these verses, we learn that Subhadra held his royal patron Dharaṇīndravarman in high regard and was in good standing with him. We learn virtually nothing about the relationship between Subhadra and his new patron, Sūryavarman II—who may very well have disposed of his predecessor Dharaṇīndravarman in a violent way—except that Subhadra praises him as if Sūryavarman II was no less a champion of *dharma*, equal to Viṣṇu in his Varāha *avatāra*. This specific *avatāra* stands out all the more since—unlike in India, where there are depictions of the story alluding to political events (Von Stietencron 2005: 13–22)—there is not a single depiction of Varāha in Cambodia.

Conclusion

Viṣṇu stories gained a politically expressive power when the ancient Khmer adapted them into *praśasti*s and narrative art. It may sometimes appear difficult to arrive at such interpretations amid the heaps of seemingly commonplace praise that Jayavarman VII's panegyrist sons bestow upon him. However, the case of the *samudramanthana*'s occurrence in the Ta Prohm inscription, reinforced by the Bayon relief, clearly shows a political expression in its sophisticated play on details. The obvious meaning, like with some of his predecessors, is that Jayavarman VII is as powerful in battle as Viṣṇu is in aiding the *deva*s and *asura*s in the churning of the milk ocean. The mention of the *amṛta* of his noble deed, releasing a captured enemy king, reveals a deeper meaning: Jayavarman benefits those who bend the knee to him as Viṣṇu benefits the *devas*. The prominent depiction of *amṛta* in the *samudramanthana* relief on the Bayon reinforces this symbolical meaning of benevolence. Both the *praśasti* comparison to Kṛṣṇa sheltering the cowherds under Mount Govardhana and the depiction of that story in his temples augment the role of Jayavarman VII as benevolent protector of his vassal kings.

In the Ban That inscription, the political meaning is wrapped up in a paradox. First, there are the kind and heartfelt words for Subhadra's pupil in the teaching of *dharma*, Dharaṇīndravarman, whom Sūryavarman II violently overthrew. Then, Subhadra praises that very Sūryavarman II as the establisher of *dharma*. It is unclear where Subhadra's sympathies really lie. Perhaps his praise is a case of ironic exaggeration, a concealed critique of Sūryavarman II's disposing of Dharaṇīndravarman. Perhaps using the trope of the *dharma*-restorer, equal to the heroic Varāha, is Subhadra's way of justifying Sūryavarman II's actions. Either way, the comparison remains a strong political statement.

References

Aymonier, É. (1891). Première étude sur les inscriptions Tchames. *Journal Asiatique, 1*, 5–86.

Chouléan, A. (2007). In the beginning Was the Bayon. In Clark, J. & Chouléan, A. (Eds.), *Bayon: New perspectives* (pp. 362–77). Bangkok: River Books.

Cœdès, G. (1906). La stèle de Ta-Prohm. *Bulletin de l'Ecole Française d'Extrême-Orient, 6*(1), 44–86.

—. (Ed.). (1937). *Inscriptions du Cambodge (vol. 1).* Hanoi: Imprimerie d'Extrême-Orient.

—. (Ed.). (1952). *Inscriptions du Cambodge (vol. 4).* Hanoi: Imprimerie d'Extrême-Orient.

Finot, L. (1912). Notes d'épigraphie: XIII. L'inscription de Ban That. *Bulletin de l'Ecole Française d'Extrême-Orient, 12*(1), 1–28.

Giteau, M. (1951). Le barattage de l'océan au Cambodge. *Bulletin de la Société des Études Indochinoises, 26*(2), 141–59.

Goodall, D. (2013). Les influences littéraires indiennes dans les inscriptions du Cambodge: L'exemple d'un chef-d'œuvre inédit du VIIIe siècle (K. 1236). *Comptes Rendus des Séances de l'Année 2012 (Janvier–Mars) de l'Académie des Inscriptions et Belles-Lettres, 157*(1), 345–357.

Harmand, J. (1879). Notes de voyage en Indo-Chine, les Kouys. Ponthey Kakeh. Considération sur les monuments dits Khmer. Communication faite à la Société Académique Indo-Chinoise le 29 avril 1879. *Annales de l'Extrême-Orient, 1*, 329–337.

Maspéro, G. (2002). *The Champa Kingdom: The history of an extinct Vietnamese culture* (W. E. J. Tips, Trans.). Bangkok: White Lotus Press.

Narayanan, V. (2015). The hero at play: Depictions of the Govardhana-Līlā story in Khmer art. *Journal of Vaishnava Studies, 23*(2), 131–47.

Pelliot, P. (1902). Mémoires sur les coutumes du Cambodge. *Bulletin de l'École Française d'Extrême-Orient, 2*(2), 123–77.

Pollock, S. I. (2006). *The language of the gods in the world of men: Sanskrit, culture, and power in premodern India.* Berkeley: University of California Press.

Schweyer, A.-V. (2007). The confrontation of the Khmers and Chams in the Bayon period. In Clark, J. & Chouléan, A. (Eds.), *Bayon: New perspectives* (pp. 50–71). Bangkok: River Books.

Verardi, G. (2003). Images of destruction, An enquiry into Hindu icons in their relations to Buddhism. *Buddhist Asia, 1,* 1–36.

Von Stietencron, H. (2005). *Hindu myth, Hindu history: Religion, art, and politics.* Delhi: Permanent Black.

Power and Piety in 'Emplaced Polities'

Temple Patronage and Donative Practice Under the North Konkan Śilāhāras (Ninth to Twelfth Century CE)

Elizabeth A. Cecil

1 Introduction*

Temples and kings: much like the old word association game, the mention of the former brings the latter immediately to mind. In studies of early medieval India, in particular, kings are typically invoked as the primary architects of the religious landscape, and the attribution of temples and religious institutions to 'royal patronage' is nearly axiomatic. In recalling this scholarly narrative, my intent is not to deny its veracity; rather, I aim to test the limits of its explanatory power by questioning some of the basic assumptions that support it. Far more than self-aggrandizing monuments to imperial power and persona, this paper presents temples as the products of collaborative acts of piety designed to cement relationships and nurture social sodalities. The various motivations that occasioned such pious acts reflect the social function of these monuments as civic spaces through which a wide range of relationships and senses of 'belonging' were expressed and affirmed (i.e. kinship groups, local identities, political alliances, economic bonds and so on). Further, evidence from inscriptions suggests that, in the early medieval period, endowing and giving to temples was not yet a definitive feature of the imperial rulers' repertoire. The Pratīhāra and Rāṣṭrakūṭa kings who controlled much of early medieval northwest India have left a rich epigraphic archive detailing donations to Brahmans, but relatively little evidence of direct investment in monumental architecture.[1] To understand the convergence of piety, politics and temple-based

* This work was supported by the Social Science Research Council under the Mellon International Dissertation Research Fellowship and the Council on Library and Information Resources under the Mellon Fellowship for Dissertation Research in Original Sources. I am also grateful to the anonymous reviewers for their suggestions and comments. All images are mine unless otherwise noted.

1 The only clear epigraphic evidence for Pratīhāra building practices comes from the inscription at Sāgar Tāl, a tank just outside of Gwalior. This record refers to the building of a palace complex or

religion requires that we take a closer look at the smaller-scale, localized polities in which religious monuments functioned as the central loci of community building.[2]

In order to illustrate these activities in practice and 'on the ground,' this study focuses on the patronage of religious institutions recorded in some inscriptions of the North Konkan Śilāhāras—a ruling family that, from approximately the ninth through the twelfth century CE, controlled the area of coastal Maharashtra that is now occupied by the modern city of Mumbai and its suburbs. Since the Śilāhāras are typically cast as political subordinates of more powerful and expansive regimes—the 'imperial' Rāṣṭrakūṭa and Cālukya dynasties—their history is usually glossed in a few lines in the historiography of this period. But despite their geographically circumscribed power, the Śilāhāras made enduring and innovative contributions to the Konkan's religious landscape. Their inscriptions memorialized their donations to Śaiva religious specialists, their pilgrimages to Śaiva *tīrtha*s and the construction of monumental temples, most notably the mid-eleventh-century Śiva temple of Ambaranātha. But these rulers did not act alone. Epigraphic and material evidence shows that the flourishing of religious institutions in the North Konkan was supported by complex patronage networks involving local residents, village headsmen, merchants, guilds, potters, gardeners and priests, among others.

2 Coming to Terms: 'Emplaced Polity'

Before moving on to discuss the Śilāhāras and their inscriptions in more detail, the following paragraphs outline very briefly the historical intervention that this paper aims to make. The first task is to explicate the term 'emplaced polity' that is introduced in the paper title.[3] My motivation for proposing this new term, and deliberately avoiding the established nomenclature,[4] is to describe a particular mode

seraglio (*antaḥpurapuraṃ*); cf. MAJUMDAR 1925–6: 99–114 and SIRCAR 1983/1942: 242–46. This record is also discussed in WILLIS 1997. On the *Rāṣṭrakūṭas*, see SCHMIEDCHEN 2014: 191–201.

2 While my presentation here is necessarily brief, the concept of 'emplaced polities' is discussed in great detail and from a cross-regional perspective in my PhD dissertation (CECIL 2016) and in the forthcoming monograph that is based upon this work (CECIL 2017).

3 The idea of emplacement is articulated in CASEY 2009, chapter 1 ('Implacement').

4 Descriptions of Indian polities often rely on terms that reflect the influence of 'western' historiography and the assumption that political and social formations in early India can be described using the same models that have been developed in studies of medieval Europe and the Classical world. The concepts and binaries that have evolved from these models—local vs. imperial empires, feudatories, vassal kings, minor vs. major dynasties etc. are not always productively applied in an Indian context. For further discussion of these issues, see TALBOT 2001: 3–10 and CHATTOPADHYAYA 1994: 1–37. But not all the vagaries can be attributed to misappropriated concepts. The use of terms such as 'the state' to refer to early complex polities is equally problematic as a kind of anachronism that reads a contemporary, decentralized apparatus of power back on the premodern. On the concept of the state in archaic societies, see SMITH 2003: 79–81.

of political formation that privileges early medieval India's unique geopolitics. In particular, the ways in which political power was coterminous with important places—i.e. sites of production, commercial centers and prestigious cultural and religious locales. Attention to the geographic situatedness or emplacement of politics and polities is revelatory insofar as it helps to address a fundamental historical quandary and this study's overarching question: namely, why would a so-called 'minor' dynasty such as the Śilāhāras invest considerably more energy and capital in the built religious landscape than their imperial contemporaries?

One possible explanation rests on the close affinity between such regimes and the regions they controlled. For example, the particular Śilāhāra clan discussed in this paper was qualified with a specific geographic moniker—i.e., the Śilāhāras of the North Konkan.[5] The term used for North Konkan in epigraphic sources is *purīkoṅkaṇa* or *purīprabhṛtikoṅkaṇa* (i.e., the Konkan headed by Purī, which was the regional capital in previous times).[6] The Śilāhāras were connected even more specifically with their capital city Sthānaka (also called Ṭhāṇeya, and which is the modern city of Thāṇā).[7] It seems that the Śilāhāras were satisfied with the limits of their territory—there is no indication from the inscriptions that they sought to expand their political reach much beyond the North Konkan, even after Rāṣṭrakūṭa power declined. This is illustrated by the map of their epigraphic find spots, which shows their donative energies were concentrated in the area surrounding their capital (figure 1). Interpreting this historical pattern as evidence of a strategic investment in the region, I propose the term 'emplaced polity' as an analytical category that best characterizes this imbrication of political authority and place.

In addition to a more specific political geography, an emphasis on emplacement also encourages us to rethink the distribution of power within the polity. In this effort, I have been influenced by recent studies of Latin American antiquity[8] that build upon the early, but important, work of Michael MANN (1986), and specifically his formulation of two types of power strategies: the *exclusionary* and the *corporate*. Discussions of political power in early India too often emphasize *exclusionary* strategies; that is, authority is viewed as concentrated in networks of personal dominance.[9] This is evident in the historiography's preoccupation with

5 Geographic designations serve as a way to distinguish between the different clans subsumed under the broader heading of 'Śilāhāra'. On the Śilāhāras of the South Konkan and Kolhapur see *CII VI*: xxi–xxxvi.

6 For example, *CII VI*, no. 14, line 152. The South Konkan, which was a distinct political entity, was called *saptakoṅkaṇa*. The exact location of Purī remains unknown. Elephanta (aka Gharapurī) has been proposed, as has Mārol village on the island of Sāṣṭī. See *CII VI*: 2.

7 *CII VI*, no. 6, line 59; no. 7, line 55. There is also a reference to the region as Kavaḍīdvīpa after the lineage progenitor Kapardin I (*EI 13*: 300).

8 Cf. BLANTON, FEINMAN, KOWALEWSKI & PEREGRINE 1996: 1–14; BEEKMAN 2008: 414–434.

9 Of course, this is not only the case for premodern India; archaic political formations are often cast in such terms. Commenting on Latin American antiquity, BLANTON et al. comment, 'It is generally assumed, in fact, that exclusionary power strategies predominate in archaic states. For example, it is

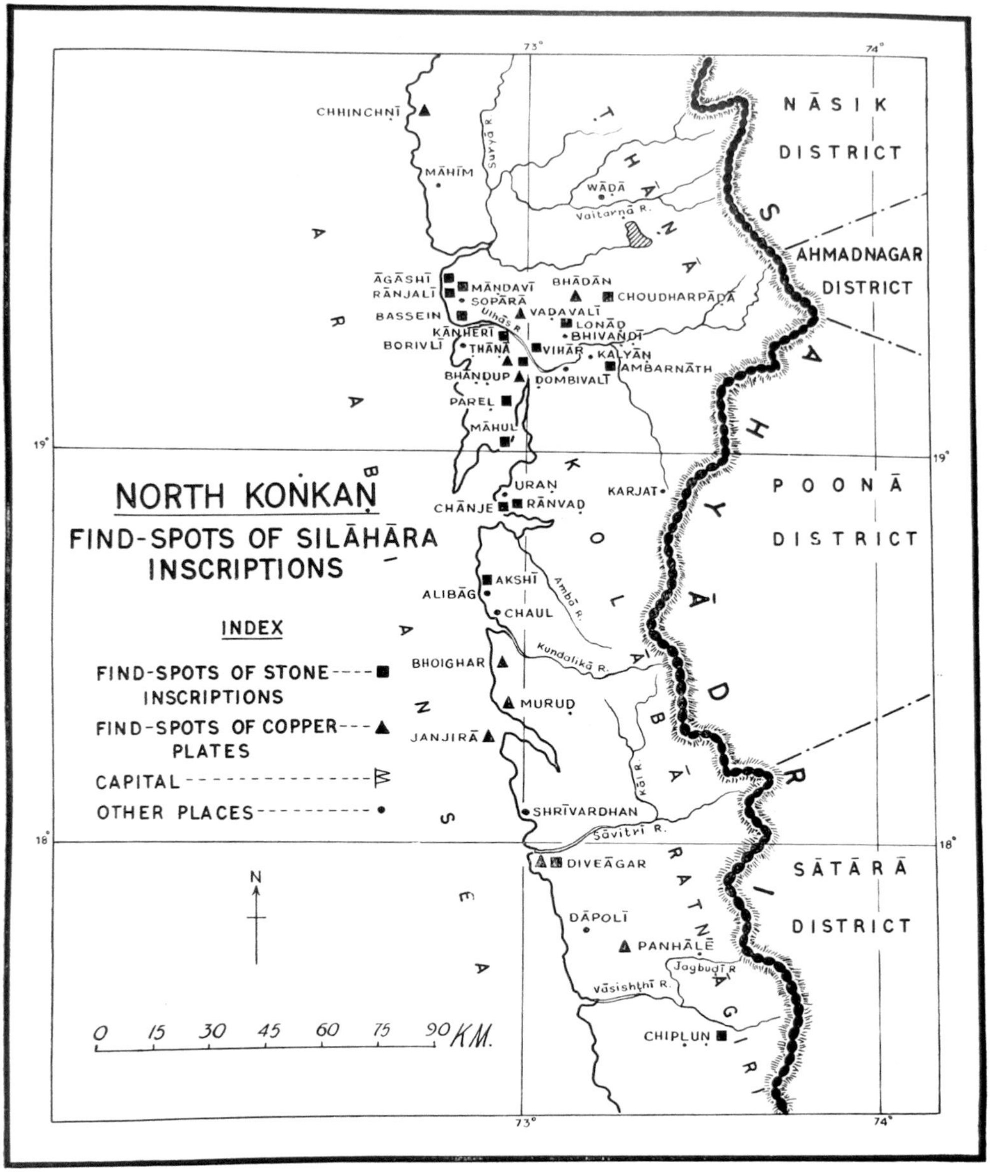

Figure 1: Śilāhāras of North Konkan: epigraphic findspots (after MIRASHI *1977; cf Map 1.).*

royal personality and genealogy, as in the description of cultural activities as a means of 'legitimizing' a ruler's exclusive claims to sovereignty.[10] One effect of this

almost always accepted that the cognitive code of an archaic state simply serves to mystify a system of power monopoly and inequality' (1996: 2).

10 On the explanatory limits of 'legitimation' theory, see POLLOCK 2006: 514–524.

preference for *exclusionary* strategies is a legacy of inexact terminology to describe political formations—feudatory, political subordinate, vassal king, minor dynasty etc. While these terms are common scholarly parlance, they are imprecise insofar as they suggest a stable and coherent political landscape rather than reflecting the reality of a highly contested political space in which multiple levels of authority were operating. If we read beyond the genealogical sections of inscriptions—and the hyperbole used to glorify particular rulers—it becomes evident that early Indian political relationships were shaped equally, if not primarily, by corporate tactics. Through a corporate strategy, power is shared across different groups and sectors of society. This corporate concept does not deny hierarchy or imply that a regime was egalitarian; rather, it encourages us to see power as claimed, materialized and contested through collectives, institutions and individuals engaged in evolving affiliations.

While a revised vocabulary of power is important for the study of political history, it is also relevant for understanding religious life. Evidence gleaned from epigraphic sources suggests that temple-based donative practices and the quotidian activities of temple care and management did not typically fall under the purview of rulers of imperial dynasties. This pattern evinces a historical phenomenon[11] that, no doubt, has multiple explanations and contingencies. With that caveat, it is important to note that the act of endowing a temple or enshrining a deity created a tangible, and often enduring, link between donor, place and community. Such practices may not have served the interests of imperial rulers, whose self-styling as universal sovereign hinged on displays of military might and control of economic surplus, but would have been critical for rulers of an emplaced polity whose authority was dependent, in a more immediate way, upon control over particular places. Taking the religious institutions of the North Konkan as a test case, the following examples show some of the ways in which residents of this emplaced polity collaborated and employed *corporate* strategies to inscribe themselves upon the regional landscape.

3 Historical Frame: Śilāhāras and Śaivism in North Konkan

Aside from three mid-ninth-century donative records found in the Kanheri caves, which date themselves to the period of Śilāhāra rule,[12] it is not until the late tenth

11 This pattern is not restricted to North India, but is observed in South India as well. The third workshop of the *Archeology of Bhakti* series, held at the EFEO in Pondicherry in August 2015, emphasized the contributions of the so-called 'minor dynasties' of medieval Tamil Nadu to the built religious landscape.

12 Kānherī Cave Inscriptions of Pullaśakti (ŚS 765/843–44 CE); Kapardin II (ŚS 775/854 CE); Kapardin II (ŚS 799/877–78). These are not donations made by the rulers themselves, but donations by various individuals for the benefit of the Buddhist community at Kṛṣṇagiri (Kānherī) (*CII VI*, nos. 1–3).

century that we have records issued from the kings themselves, and with them, the earliest articulations of a Śilāhāra political persona—beginning with Aparājita, who declares himself the *paścimasamudrādhipati* ('Lord of the Western Sea') in a set of copper plates from 993 CE found at Janjīra in the Kolābā District.[13] Verse 31 of this inscription makes two claims regarding this political ascendance. One claim is territorial—the verse's references to the specific locales that Aparājita conquered suggest a campaign aimed at gaining control of the port cities along the western coastline. The second claim is ideological and attributes this geographic expansion to the power of the God Śiva:

> Possessing the power of Hara (Śiva), he by his prowess rules impartially by his commands over the Saṁyāna country, which he has conquered, the large Puṇaka (country) which is submissive to him, the Sahya territory, which has lovely surroundings, Saṅgameśvara won by his soldiers, and the Chipulaṇa territory, which submitted to him the moment his name was mentioned. (MIRASHI 1977) [14]

The fact that Aparājita is described as accomplishing these things by means of an authority that was supported by the power of Śiva is significant because it shows the rulers as aligned with the region's dominant religious culture. The following paragraphs address in more detail why these claims are integral to understanding the formation of Śilāhāra polity.

The North Konkan was a thriving coastal center of trade and commerce. Control over this narrow strip of land—roughly 50 km wide—meant authority over one of the most lucrative port polities in the medieval subcontinent. Prior to the efforts of colonial land reclamation, the modern city of Mumbai and its suburbs were a cluster of seven islands dotted with numerous littoral ports and estuaries, the most famous of which were Sopara, Kalyan, Chaul and Elephanta Island. The coast and its ports were connected to the hinterlands by three important passes in the mountains—the Thalghat, Nannaghat and Bhorghat. Through these passes, the North Konkan maintained active ties with the agrarian regions in the Deccan and commercial centers like Ujjain and Mathurā north of the Narmadā River.

By the tenth century, long-distance trade networks between the North Konkan and the Arab world via the Persian Gulf were flourishing.[15] These

13 Janjīra Plates of Aparājita: Śaka Samvat (915/993 CE) (*CII VI*, no. 5).

14 *siddhāṃ saṃyānabhūmiṃ pṛthutarapuṇakaṃ deśam ājñāvidheyaṃ sahyaṃ pratyantakāntaṃ nijabhaṭakalitaṃ saṃgamādīśvarākhyam* /
nāmākhyānaprasādhyaṃ cipulaṇaviṣayaṃ naṣṭavaiṣamyabhāvaṃ kṛtvā tejonubhāvād hara-vibhavavibhṛt svājñayā yaḥ praśāsti // 31 //
(*Sragdharā*)

15 Recent work by archeologists and historians shows that the theory regarding the decline of trade in the early medieval period has been largely overstated. Overseas trade with the Roman Empire and

economic contacts brought new people and communities to the cosmopolitan coast. Some of these Arab traders established permanent settlements in the region as trading diasporas, a process that may have begun as early as the seventh or eighth century.[16] While the term 'trading diaspora' may typically evoke mercantile communities that occupy a disadvantaged position vis-à-vis the dominant regional culture, this does not seem to have been the case in the tenth-century Konkan.[17] By contrast, evidence from inscriptions indicates that members of these trade diasporas had established themselves in positions of power and importance within the Konkan where the Rāṣṭrakūṭas granted them control of some of the important port cities.[18]

A good example of this process of social integration is recorded in a set of copper plates from 926 CE that mention one Madhumati who controlled Saṁyāna (modern Sanjan, a port city in the Thāṇā district) as an agent of the Rāṣṭrakūṭa rulers Kṛṣṇa II and Indra III (SIRCAR 1957). This Saṁyāna is one of the same locales that Aparājita claimed to have conquered in his Janjīra grant some 67 years later. Since Madhumati is further qualified as *tājikānvaya* ('of Arab descent')[19] in verse 17, Sircar is no doubt correct in understanding this name as a Sanskritized version of Muhammad. The purpose of the grant proper is to record Madhumati's donation of

---

the Mediterranean declined, yet studies of Arab and Persian sources show that international trade continued and that new networks were established, particularly from the eighth and early ninth century. Andre WINK rejects even the hypothesis that Roman trade declined during this period and cites the continued activity of Greek and Byzantine traders in Indian Ocean commerce (1990: 45–64). In his work on Indian Ocean trade, K. N. CHAUDARI has characterized maritime trade voyages in the early medieval period as following two main patterns: one between commercial cities of the Red Sea area and Persian Gulf, and the other a trans-regional voyage that included India as well as ports in Southeast Asia and China (1985: 15). Patterns in early medieval trade in the North Konkan specifically have been discussed by CHAKRAVARTI (1986: 207–215).

16 Summarizing the descriptions of Arab geographers, Wink describes Muslim settlements as 'flourishing' in the tenth century (1990: 68). Some of these communities, he comments, may have been active as early as the seventh century. See also VON KREMER 1877: ii.

17 The term 'trade diaspora' was introduced by Philip CURTIN to describe the trade settlement in which 'commercial specialists would remove themselves physically from their home community and go and live as aliens in another town ... They could then serve as cross-cultural brokers, helping and encouraging trade between the host society and the people of their own origin who moved along the trade routes' (1984: 2).

18 Andre Wink cites the historian Mas'ūdī, who wrote in glowing terms of the respect and freedom the Ballaharā (i.e. Rāṣṭrakūṭa) rulers afforded the Muslims of the North Konkan. Also significant is the mention that some members of these communities as 'wearing the same dresses and having their beards grown in the same way as the infidels' (WINK 1990). On the use of Ballaharā/Balharā to refer to the Rāṣṭrakūṭas, see SCHMIEDCHEN 2014: 25.

19 *kṛṣṇarājadayāvāptakṛtsnasaṁyānamaṇḍalaḥ* /
āsīn madhumati[ḥ] śrīmā[n] nṛpatis tājikānvaye // 17 //
(*Anuṣṭubh*)
There was an eminent sovereign Madhumati of the Tājika community
who obtained the entire Saṁyāna territory as given by Kṛṣṇarāja.

a village to the local *maṭhikā* of a goddess called Bhagavatī.[20] But this is not the end of the Saṁyāna story. In 1034, Cāmuṇḍarāja, an officer of Śilāhāra Chittarāja, made a subsequent endowment of an oil-mill (*ghāṇaka*) to support the lighting of lamps at the same Bhagavatī *maṭha* in Saṁyāna (*CII VI*, no. 12, lines 15–20). A number of local guild masters, artisans and other notable residents are addressed directly in the grant and called upon to recognize the donation. Appearing in this list of names are the merchants Mahumata and Alliya—again, a Sanskritized version of the name Muhammad, and perhaps Ali as well (ibid., line 11). This is certainly not the same Muhammad mentioned in the grant of 926 CE, but we may assume that he and Ali were members of the same trading community whose members had formerly controlled the area, and which continued to occupy a place of prominence even after the Śilāhāras took control of Saṁyāna. Given this, and the names of the other merchants, artisans and local administrators addressed in the grant,[21] we may interpret this donative act as an instance of a *corporate* power strategy in action. In order to control the surplus generated by the prosperous port of Saṁyāna, the Śilāhāras recognized the established communities of merchants and artisans, as well as the local administration. The ritualized act of giving to the prominent Devī *maṭha* served as a tool to commemorate an act of community building and to formalize the alliance between these diverse groups.

In addition to the territorial claim, the ideological implications of Aparājita's record—namely, that he acted with the power of Śiva—are also important. It is worth drawing attention to this point because Śaivism, and particularly the Pāśupata tradition, had a highly visible presence in the North Konkan. The earliest Śaiva monuments of the region date to a period as early as the sixth or seventh century. The famous cave temples located on Elephanta Island and the Jogeśvarī caves are two notable examples. While no donative inscriptions have survived from these monuments, the iconography attests to the popularity of the Śaiva tradition (figures 2 to 5). The regional dominance of Śaivism continued in the subsequent centuries, and Śaiva institutions and religious preceptors from lineages with connections to the Śaiva Siddhānta tradition were the recipients of the majority of the Śilāhāra grants While it is not possible to explore these sources in detail here, I think the brief survey below indicates that the patronage of these institutions and teachers served as an important tool for community building under the Śilāhāra regime.

20 Perhaps the goddess Durgā Mahiṣāsuramardinī who is called upon for protection in Verse 2:
śūlabhinnasya vinyasto mahiṣasya balād gale /
durggāyāḥ pātu vaḥ pādas tadraktālaktakāṁkitaḥ // 2 //
(*Anuṣṭubh*)

21 Lines 10–11. Those individuals and groups mentioned included: *haṁyamanīya* (artisan guild); *pauramukhya* (city administrator); *saṃvyavahārika* (merchants, including Mahumata and Alliya); *śreṣṭhin* (guild leader); and *suvarṇṇaka* (goldsmith).

Figure 2: Śiva Naṭeśa panel, Elephanta Caves, ca. sixth to seventh century.

Figure 3: Lakulīśa with four attendants, Jogeśvarī Caves, ca. sixth to seventh century.

Figure 4: Śiva from Parel, Maharashtra, ca. sixth century. CSMVS Mumbai.

Figure 5: Parel stele, Mumbai, ca. sixth century.

4 Patronage in Practice

The early eleventh-century Khārepāṭan Plates of Śilāhāra Raṭṭrāja are an important example of the donative pattern mentioned above.[22] In this instance, three villages were donated to a temple dedicated to Śiva as Avveśvara, most likely a *liṅga* shrine in honor of Raṭṭarāja's father, Avasara III—evidence of the popular practice of naming a *liṅga* after a family member or superior.[23] The seaside villages donated in honor of the god were given to support not only temple rituals and repair, but to provide funding for the Śaiva religious specialists in residence and for visiting devotees. More specifically, these resources are designated in honor of Raṭṭarāja's guru Ātreya, the student of Ambhojaśambhu, both of the Karkaroṇī branch of the Mattamayūra lineage (lines 51–56). Discussions of this important school have figured in previous studies of Richard H. Davis and, most recently, Tamara Sears;

22 Khārepāṭaṇ Plates of Raṭṭarāja: ŚS 930/1008–9 CE (*CII IV*, no. 41).

23 The details of the donation of the villages and provisions for repair of the temple are given in lines 42–50.

suffice it to say here this lineage was quite expansive, with links to important centers in central Madhya Pradesh and northern Rajasthan.[24] Raṭṭarāja also succeeded in ensuring that the temple would benefit from the local maritime trade: he allotted one *gaiyāṇa* of gold as a tax for foreign ships, and a *dharaṇa* for boats from regional ports (with the exception of Cemūlya and Candrapura).[25]

But rulers and gurus do not alone a temple make. Raṭṭarāja also provided for his chosen deity a variety of families whose unique trades and skills would provide the necessary provisions for a functioning religious center: included were households of temple-women (*dārikākuṭumba*), oil-pressers (*tailikakuṭumba*), gardeners (*mālākārakuṭumba*), potters (*kumbhakārakuṭumba*) and washermen (*rajakakuṭumba*), as well as land for a courtyard and a flower garden (lines 58–59). This picture of the temple complex as a micro-society is similarly reflected in a twelfth-century record from the Jogeśvarī temple complex.[26] Work on the expansive cave temple at Jogeśvarī was likely initiated as early as the sixth century, and this inscription suggests that the complex was still an important institution centuries later. This record grants numerous families connected with the temple exemption from a 'house tax'.[27] Included are the houses of the head of the *maṭha*, the *liṅga* priest, gardener and potter, among others. That these individuals were given specific mention suggests that they were integral to the functioning of the institution and therefore worthy of a royal boon.

In addition to those temples sponsored by members of the ruling family, Śilāhāra piety also extended to those sponsored by local people. For example, early eleventh-century copper plates issued by Chittarāja record his donation of a field in honor of the temple of Bhaiyapeśvara, commissioned by a village headsman named Bhaiyapa.[28] This donation provided for ritual practice and repair of the shrine as well as food and clothing for the resident ascetics, led by one Jñānaśiva. Such donations no doubt fostered relationships between these rulers and their constituents.

5 Ambaranātha & Lonāḍ

The monumental temple of Ambaranātha serves as the final example of patronage in practice. A dedicatory record from 1060 CE carved on a stone beam within the

24 On the Mattamayūras, see Sears 2014: 37–41 and Davis 2000: 131–145.

25 *dvīpāntarāyātavahitrās svarṇṇagadiyāṇaṃ cemūlyacandrapuravarjjakandalamūliyāyāt pravahaṇāt svarṇṇadharaṇaṃ* (lines 56–57). The inscription also mentions that Cemūlya (Chaul) and Balipaṭṭana (Khārepātan) are exempted from this temple tax. The reason for this specific designation is unclear to me. Perhaps these important trade centers were considered to be too far north, so therefore not considered as within this temple's sphere of influence.

26 Cintra Stone Inscription of Aparāditya 1: Śaka Samvat 1059/1137 ce (*CII VI*, no. 21, lines 10–18).

27 *bhūmideṇaka* [*deyaka*?], line 14.

28 Berlin Museum Plates of Chittarāja: Śaka Samvat 956/1034 CE (CII VI, no. 11).

temple sanctum records the names of a group of political officials with ties to the Śilāhāra family who completed the work on the temple during the time of Māṁvāṇirāja.[29] This ruler's elder brothers and predecessors, Chittarājadeva and Nāgārjuna, had initially commissioned this temple, but apparently it had not been finished during their respective reigns. Although a very brief documentary record, it is still a significant one insofar as it reinforces the multiplicity of modes and motivations for patronage within the polity. In completing this temple initiated by their superiors, the ministers made a powerful statement of allegiance to the rulers and recorded in stone their close ties to the court. In this way, the temple in honor of Śiva also served to memorialize enduring relationships and social hierarchies between the Śilāhāra family and those in their service.

The Ambaranātha Temple is quite well preserved, having been the subject of ASI supervision and repair from the early 1900s. While the *structure* itself was reportedly commenced by Chittarāja, it is likely that this ruler was not promoting a new religious center, but rather augmenting an important feature of the local religious landscape. I suggest this because the monumental temple is built up around a *liṅga* set in a recess nearly eight feet in the ground. Devotees reach the *liṅga* through a short flight of stairs, as can be seen from the temple plan (figure 6).[30] The iconography at Ambaranātha is also well preserved and attests to the development of Śaiva mythology in the region (figures 8 and 9).

Remarkable in its state of preservation, this temple is remarkable for other reasons as well. If Chittarāja sought to use a place of local prestige in order to promote his own rule, he did so in an innovative way, adopting a structural form previously unknown in the region. The Ambaranātha Temple is the earliest example of a monumental structural temple in the North Konkan or the Deccan. Prior to this, the cave-temple had been the favored style. Ambaranātha is also heralded as the forerunner of a particular style of temple architecture called Bhūmijā, which was the inspiration for structurally comparable temples built in the Deccan—like the Goṇḍeśvara Śiva temple built by the Yādavas at Sinnar (figure 10).

Remains of a very similar, but slightly later, temple are preserved nearby in the village of Lonāḍ in the Thāṇā District (figure 11). Unlike Ambaranātha, however, the structure is largely in ruins and very little remains of the iconography (figure 13). The *liṅga* at Lonāḍ is also set deep in a recessed *garbhagṛha*, perhaps an indication that it, too, was considered *svyambhū* (figure 12). Unfortunately, no inscriptions have been found at the temple, making the sources of its patronage uncertain. With that caveat, I conclude this discussion with a rather speculative suggestion. A stone inscription was discovered just outside of the village in 1882—the Lonāḍ Inscription

29 Ambarnāth Temple Inscription of Māṁvāṇirāja: ŚS 982/1060 CE (*CII VI*, no. 17).

30 This unique structure led Mirashi to suggest that this was a *svayambhū liṅga* (*CII VI*: lxxxii).

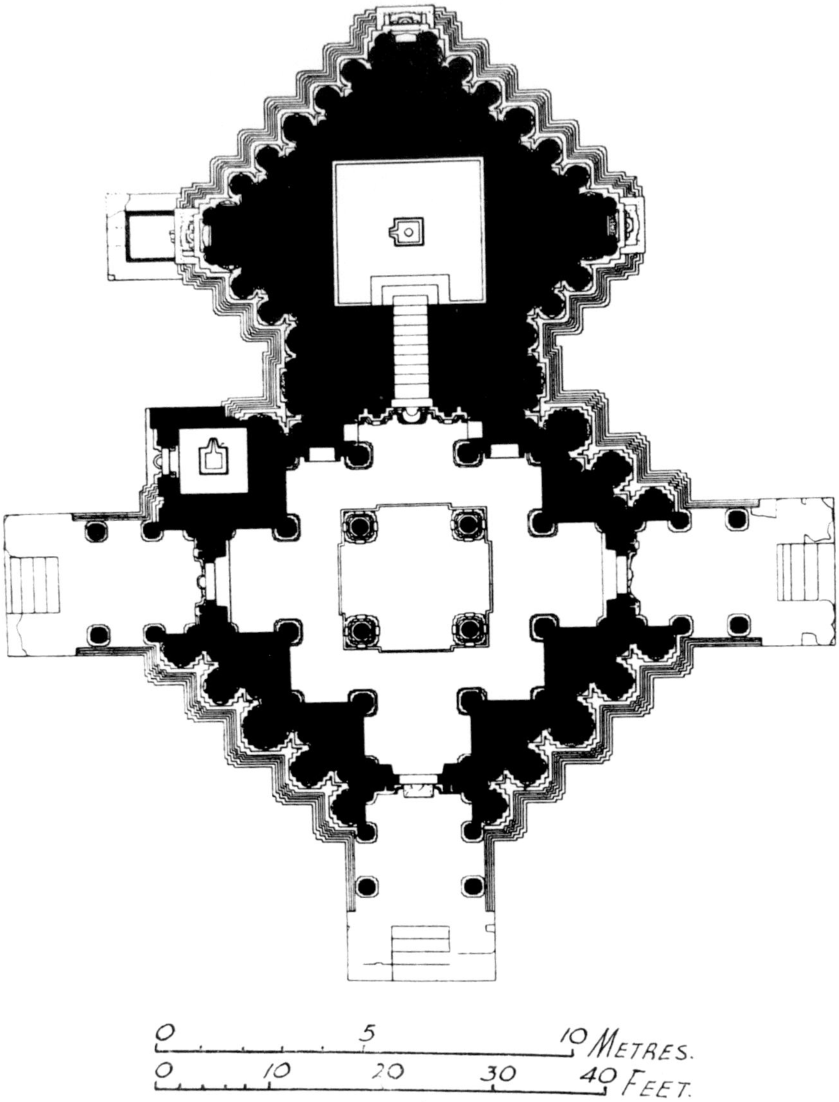

Figure 6: Ambaranātha Temple, ground-plan (after MIRASHI *1977, fig. 29).*

of Aparāditya II.[31] This record commemorates the donation of a field to the temple of Vyomeśvara by a *bhopaka* (minister?) named Vyomaśambhu. This donation was made with the permission of Śilāhāra ruler, Aparāditya II. Perhaps the temple to which the inscription refers is the Lonāḍ Śiva temple. Questions of its provenance

31 Lonāḍ Inscription of Aparāditya II: Śaka Samvat 1106/1184 CE (*CII VI*, no. 30).

Figure 7: Ambaranātha Temple, ca. tenth century.

Figure 8: Śiva Naṭeśa, exterior niche of Ambaranātha Temple.

Figure 9: Liṅgodbhavamūrti, exterior niche of Ambaranātha Temple.

Figure 10: Sinnar Goṇḍeśvara Temple, ca. twelfth century.

Figure 11: Lonāḍ Śiva Temple, ca. twelfth century.

Figure 12: Liṅga *in a recessed* garbhagṛha, *Lonāḍ Śiva Temple.*

Figure 13: Śiva Naṭeśa, exterior niche of Lonāḍ Śiva Temple.

aside, this inscription provides further evidence of a pattern of collaborative acts of piety characteristic of donations in emplaced polities.

6 Conclusions

The description of early medieval temples as acts of 'royal patronage' often obscures the collaborative or *corporate* nature of pious giving. Albeit very brief, this survey of some Śilāhāra donative practices reveals an historical pattern whereby religious institutions functioned as tangible and enduring monuments that materialized the relationships that connected ruler, deity, community and place. Inscriptions show that the acts of piety converging around Śaivism in the North Konkan succeeded in catalyzing remarkable social synergies between individuals and communities from a wide variety of social strata. While such technologies of community-building are not unprecedented or particularly innovative, the evidence from the North

Konkan is unique in that it enables a relatively nuanced reconstruction of the social history of Śaivism and religious life in practice; a reconstruction with implications for trans-historical and cross-regional studies of piety and patronage in emplaced polities.

References

Beekman, C. (2008). Corporate power strategies in the late formative to early classic Tequila valleys of Central Jalisco'. *Latin American Antiquity, 19*(4), 414–434.

Blanton, R. E., Feinman, G. M., Kowalewski, S. A. & Peregrine, P. N. (1996). Dual-processual theory for the evolution of Mesoamerican civilization. *Current Anthropology, 37*(1), 1–14.

Casey, E. (2009). *Getting back into place: Toward a renewed understanding of the place world.* Bloomington: Indiana University.

Cecil, E. A. (2016). *Mapping the Pāśupata landscape: The Skandapurāṇa, Lakulīśa and the Śaiva imaginary in early medieval North India (6th–10th century* ce*)* (Unpublished doctoral dissertation). Brown University, Providence, RI.

—. (2017). Mapping the Pāśupata landscape: Polity, Piety, and the Śaiva imaginary in early medieval North India. Manuscript submitted for publication.

Chakravarti, R. (1986). Merchants of Konkan. *Indian Economic and Social History Review, 23*, 207–215.

Chattopadhyaya, B. D. (1994). *The making of early medieval India.* Oxford: Oxford University Press.

Chaudari, K. N. (1985). *Trade and civilisation in the Indian Ocean: An economic history from the rise of Islam to 1750.* Cambridge: Cambridge University Press.

Curtin, P. (1984). *Cross-cultural trade in world history.* Cambridge: Cambridge University Press.

Davis, R. (2000). Praises of the drunken peacocks. In White, D. (Ed.), *Tantra in practice* (pp. 131–145). Princeton: Princeton University Press.

EI 13 = Konow, S. (Ed.). (1915–16). *Epigraphia Indica* (vol. 13). New Delhi: ASI.

Majumdar, R. C. (1925–6). The Gwalior Prasasti of the Gujara-Pratihara King Bhoja. *Epigraphia Indica, 18*, 99–114.

Mann, M. (1986). *The sources of social power: Vol. 1. A history of power from the beginning to AD 1760.* Cambridge: Cambridge University Press.

CII VI = Mirashi, V. V. (1977). *Corpus inscriptionum Indicarum: Vol. VI. The inscriptions of the Śilāhāras.* New Delhi: ASI.

Pollock, S. *The language of the gods in the world of men: Sanskrit, culture, and power in premodern India.* Berkeley: University of California Press.

Schmiedchen, A. (2014). *Herrschergenealogie und Religiöses Patronat: Die Inschriftenkultur der Rāṣṭrakūṭas, Śilāhāras und Yādavas (8. bis 13. Jahrhundert).* Leiden: Brill.

Sears, T. (2014). *Worldly gurus and spiritual kings: Architecture and asceticism in medieval India.* New Haven: Yale University Press.

Sircar, D. C. (1957). Rashtrakuta charters from Chinchani: Grant of the time of Indra III, Śaka 848. *Epigraphia Indica, 32*, 45–55.

—. (1983). *Select inscriptions bearing on Indian history and civilization* (vol. 2). Delhi: Motilal Banarsidass. (Original work published 1942.)

Smith, A. T. (2003). *The political landscape: Constellations of authority in early complex polities.* Berkeley: University of California Press.

Talbot, C. (2001). *Precolonial India in practice: Society, region, and identity in medieval Andhra.* Oxford: Oxford University Press.

von Kremer, A. (1877). *Culturgeschichte des Orients unter den Chalifen* (vol. 2). Vienna: Braumüller.

Willis, M. (1997). Religious and royal patronage in North India. In Desai, V. & Mason, D. (Eds.), *Gods, guardians, and lovers: Temple sculptures from North India A.D. 700–1200* (pp. 49–65). New York, NY: Asia Society Galleries.

Wink, Andre. (1990). *Al-Hind: The making of an Indo-Islamic world.* New Delhi: Oxford.